AF361419

Doing Democracy

SUNY series, Praxis: Theory in Action

Nancy A. Naples, editor

Doing Democracy

Activist Art and Cultural Politics

Edited by

Nancy S. Love

and

Mark Mattern

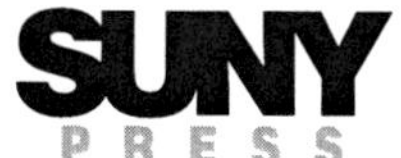

Cover art © Julie Dermansky.

Published by State University of New York Press, Albany

For information, contact State University of New York Press, Albany, NY
www.sunypress.edu

Production by Cathleen Collins
Marketing by Kate McDonnell

Library of Congress Cataloging-in-Publication Data

Doing democracy : activist art and cultural politics / edited by Nancy S. Love
  and Mark Mattern.
       pages cm. — (Praxis: theory in action)
  Includes bibliographical references and index.
  Summary: "Demonstrates how activists and others use art and popular culture to
strive for a more democratic future"—Provided by publisher.
  ISBN 978-1-4384-4911-1 (hardcover : alk. paper)
  1. Arts—Political aspects. 2. Popular culture—Political aspects. 3. Politics in art.
4. Democracy and the arts. 5. Artists—Political activity. I. Love, Nancy Sue, 1954–
editor of compilation. II. Mattern, Mark, 1954– editor of compilation.

  NX650.P6D65 2013
  700.1'03—dc23   2013002470

Contents

PART IV. LITERATURE AND POETRY

PART V. MUSIC

PART VI. THEATER

PART VII. FESTIVAL AND SPECTACLE

Acknowledgments

We would like to thank our editor at SUNY Press, Beth Bouloukos, and her assistant, Rafael Chaiken, for their assistance in bringing this project to fruition. We would also like to thank the progressive scholars and activists of the Caucus for a New Political Science for demonstrating that activism and scholarly rigor are compatible.

The following chapters are revised from original articles in a special issue on "Art After Empire: Creating the Political Economy of a New Democracy," *New Political Science: A Journal of Politics and Culture* 32, no. 4 (2010), copyright © Caucus for a New Political Science, by permission of Taylor & Francis Ltd., www.tandfonline.com on behalf of Caucus for a New Political Science.

Chapter 1. "Introduction: Art, Culture, Democracy," Nancy S. Love and Mark Mattern, revised from "Introduction," 463–69.

Chapter 2. "Photo-Activism in the Digital Age: Visions from Rio de Janeiro," Frank Möller, revised from "Photography after Empire: Citizen-Photographers or Snappers on Autopilot?," 501–13.

Chapter 5. "The National D-Day Memorial: An American Military Monument as 'Doing Democracy,'" Timothy W. Luke, revised from "The National D-Day Memorial: Art, Empire, and Nationalism at an American Military Monument," 547–59.

Chapter 7. "Tragedy and Democracy: The Fate of Liberal Democratic Values in a Violent World," Wairimu Njoya, revised from "'Mindful of the Sacrifices Borne by Our Ancestors': Terror, Historical Consciousness, and the Slave Sublime," 575–91.

Chapter 8. "'You're an American rapper, so what do you know?' The Political Uses of British and U.S. Popular Culture by First-Time Voters in the United Kingdom," Sanna Inthorn and John Street, revised from "'You're an American rapper, so what do you know?' The Political

Uses of British and US Popular Culture by First-Time Voters in the UK," 471–84.

Chapter 10. "Betrayed by Democracy: Verbatim Theater as Prefigurative Politics," Mark Chou and Roland Bleiker, revised from "Dramatizing War: George Packer and the Democratic Potential of Verbatim Theater," 561–74.

Chapter 13. "Democracy despite Government: African American Parading and Democratic Theory," Peter G. Stillman and Adelaide H. Villmoare, revised from "Democracy Despite Government: African American Parading and Democratic Theory," 485–99.

"Strange Fruit" (U.S. copyright permission): Words and Music by Lewis Allan. Copyright © 1939 (Renewed) by Music Sales Corporation (ASCAP). All Rights for the United States controlled by Music Sales Corporation (ASCAP). International Copyright Secured. All Rights Reserved. Used by Permission.

"Strange Fruit" (International copyright permission): Written by Lewis Allan. Used by Permission of Edward B. Marks Music Company.

Part I

Introduction

Chapter 1

Introduction

Art, Culture, Democracy

NANCY S. LOVE AND MARK MATTERN

Along with the political speeches and the oath of office, the historic inauguration of Barack Obama as the first African American president of the United States featured music, poetry, and prayer. We believe that this signaled a propitious moment to inquire whether these alternative and aesthetic modes of public discourse prefigure a more democratic future. In various ways, contributors to this volume ask: What arts and cultural forms present in the world today provide grounds for optimism about moving toward a more democratic society? What is the promise of the arts and popular culture as partial bases for political activism to move us toward a new political economy and a more democratic politics? How does this promise engage with existing economic and political realities? In what concrete ways are contemporary arts and popular culture forms used to increase the capacities of individuals and groups to act effectively in the world? In particular, how do historically marginalized groups employ the arts and popular culture to advance their political claims and exemplify democratic practices? In sum, how might the arts and popular culture help us do democracy?

These questions arise in a context of rapidly expanding global communications networks. Access to the arts and popular culture has increased commensurately with access to smart phones and the internet experienced across the globe. Musicians, photographers, graffiti artists, painters, dancers, performance artists, filmmakers, writers, and many others now take advantage of internet platforms such as Facebook, Twitter, and YouTube to disseminate their work. Many do so with explicit political intent. One result is a rapidly changing and expanding terrain for political thought and action using arts and culture. The internet has blurred borders between local and global communities as well as traditional and modern cultures. However, the result has not been a world without borders. The digital divide between rich and poor, north and south, persists. Internet technology has also supported the creation of new borders, such as virtual diasporic communities, global hybrid movements, and even internet-based cybernations.[1]

Another important element of this changing context is the rise of so-called culture wars that link the traditional politics of nation-states with globalization and multiculturalism. At stake is control of the hearts and minds of citizens around the world. Various forms of expression, including and especially those related to the arts and popular culture, carry profound significance for this challenge of engaging reflectively and critically with diverse citizens. While much of popular culture undermines the development of critical consciousness and globalization often homogenizes or even Americanizes, the arts and popular culture also have been used extensively and successfully to nurture critical consciousness and diverse perspectives. The central questions remain: To what degree will political and economic elites continue to fashion the world, both materially and symbolically, in their own interests, and to what degree can activists harness the arts and popular culture to shatter this hegemony and challenge elite power? Although most contributors here focus on how activist art supports progressive causes, some consider how the arts and popular culture are used to resist democratic change and restore traditional hierarchies of class, gender, and race, though perhaps in new forms. These different emphases work together to show how the creation of a democratic society is an ongoing process and that democracy can also unfortunately be undone by some of the popular forces often thought to foster it.

The Arts and Popular Culture

What do we mean by the arts and popular culture? Many have found it tempting to define a separation between so-called high art and low art.[2] Art hanging on museum walls and performed in magnificent concert halls is deemed high art, while art sprayed-painted on railroad underpasses and performed in anarchists' squat houses qualifies as low art or, presumably, popular culture. We intend to avoid this temptation, because it is ultimately an untenable distinction. Institutional definitions such as these focus on artworks as beautiful objects created for an art world, especially art critics. The effect of this approach is to perpetuate established artistic traditions, including the concept of autonomous art, and to exclude innovative and nonwestern art forms.[3] According to Marshall McLuhan, new art forms are routinely regarded as corrupting or degrading the standards of high art. However, these new art forms often simultaneously serve to legitimate the elevated status of the "great" artworks that preceded them and many new forms are eventually granted the status of high art.[4] At the very least, these interrelationships suggest that historical context shapes our definitions of what constitutes high and low art. However, more than historical context is at stake here. The arts associated with popular culture are also often dismissed as mere entertainment, as commercialized art produced for mass markets.[5] Yet the arts and popular culture also serve a variety of important functions in everyday life. These functions involve more than the artistic beauty that is often found in the ordinary objects that enhance our daily lives. They also include the role of the arts in catalyzing the imagination, expressing creativity, integrating aspects of the self, providing meaningful symbols, sustaining a sense of beauty and harmony, and, most important here, resisting conformity and even subverting the status quo.[6] In these ways, especially the last one, the popular quality of the art forms included here potentially increases their importance for democratic and undemocratic politics.

Although all of our contributors demonstrate the significance of the arts and popular culture for "doing democracy," they differ in their approaches to defining and analyzing the art forms they discuss. For this reason, we have chosen not to focus on the aforementioned debates over how to define art in general, or even on how to define the individual art forms included in this volume.[7] We would instead emphasize the aesthetic experience of the arts and popular culture, a theme the authors here share. The term "aesthetics" comes from the Greek *aesthesis*, and refers to "the whole region of human perception and sensation" or "the whole of our sensate life together."[8] Aesthetic experience extends beyond the arts proper to include everyday life, the natural world, and the spiritual realm. Although aesthetic experience is conceptually distinct from artistic experience, it is often closely related in practice. John Dewey, who laments the lack of a single term that unites artistic and aesthetic experience, famously joins them. He writes: "the conception of conscious experience as a perceived relation between doing and undergoing enables us to understand the connection that art as production and [aesthetic] perception and appreciation as enjoyment sustain to each other."[9] Dewey's concept of aesthetic experience expands our experience of "the arts." It can recognize innovations in content, form, or both as "art"; it also includes the artistic expressions of popular and nonwestern cultures. For Dewey, the arts and popular culture draw on non- and extra-rational dimensions of human identity and experience, while also potentially stimulating critical reflection and shaping political interactions. Like the arts and popular culture, these affective and corporeal dimensions of human experience, which some claim may even constitute an alternative and aesthetic rationality, have arguably received too little attention.[10]

The distinction between high art and popular culture overlaps with another distinction between formal (or technical) and performative aesthetics.[11] A formal aesthetic focuses primarily on the abstract systems, structures, and techniques of artworks. For example, a formal analysis of a classical music composition would emphasize its harmonic development, melodic lines, and rhythmic meter. Abstract forms can and sometimes do provide models and metaphors for sociopolitical arrangements. The musical counterpoint of a fugue may mirror the distinct voices in a political dialogue; likewise, perspective lines in an artist's portrait may reveal complex social hierarchies.[12] As we have seen, more popular art forms often fail to qualify as "art" when measured by the standards of formal aesthetics. We would expand the notion of artistic form beyond the requirements of high art to a variety of popular forms including, for example, military monuments, political cartoons, popular festivals, and public parades. Contributors to this volume also offer more dynamic and democratic understandings of what have traditionally been regarded as forms of high art, including literature, music, poetry, and theater. The capacity of musical form—classical and popular—to "speak" without words plays a role in multiple chapters. Digital forms that incorporate multiple earlier media—television, radio, and newspaper—also increase the power of art for politics. In these and many other cases, to use Marshall McLuhan's famous phrase, "the medium is the message," and the various art forms can carry democratic or undemocratic content.[13]

A performative aesthetic better incorporates this more dynamic and inclusive concept of aesthetic form(s). It also places greater emphasis on the affective, corporeal effects of art, especially its capacity to shape the identities and express the needs of groups excluded and marginalized by mainstream politics. Rap music, for example, involves much more than a musical style. It is part of a wider hip hop scene that includes break dancing, dee-jaying, and remixing, as well as "authentic" dress, parapher-nalia, fanzines, and websites, all part of the larger Do-It-Yourself (DIY) movement.[14] Most important, a performative aesthetic construes audiences as participants in artistic experiences and stresses the artist's engagement with a wider community. Unlike formal aesthetics that elevate art, in part, by making it an object of detached observation in designated spaces, a performative aesthetic explores how people enter into artistic experiences. In doing so, it challenges the assumption that art is somehow autono-mous and embraces its role in processes of socioeconomic and political change. Although the arts and popular culture carry and convey content in written form, such as cartoon captions, song lyrics, and theater scripts, they often seek to erode the very distinction between form and content. Many contributors here show how the arts and popular culture ultimately present "form *as* content" by modeling new ways of doing and sometimes undoing democracy.[15]

This understanding of the arts and popular culture as integral to political and, more specifically, democratic processes calls into question the liberal-democratic idea that society has distinct public and private spheres, and that art belongs in the latter realm of personal experience. According to John Locke, liberal individuals demonstrate their capacity to bear the full rights and responsibilities of citizenship through their rationality, industry, and property.[16] For the rational citizens of a liberal democracy, aesthetic sensibilities are largely private matters of personal taste and individual choice. The liberal state tolerates differences in artistic preferences, as well as a variety of political views and religious beliefs, as long as those differ-ences do not violate the rights of other citizens.[17] Of course, one way a rising middle class can display its excellent and quasi-aristocratic taste is by enjoying and acquiring critically acclaimed or high art and emphasizing high art's superiority over all lower art forms. Wider access to high art through concerts, museums, and theaters open to the public only became possible in Europe very gradually over a period of several centuries. The liberal tendency to locate the arts in the private sphere contributed to perceptions of the artist as an individual, even solitary, creative genius, rather than part of a community. This also reinforced the concept of art as autonomous, as somehow transcending the pressures of economic and political reality.[18] Locating art in the private sphere also served to reinforce the "rationality" of liberal democratic politics. The affective, corporeal ex-periences associated with the arts became personal matters that were most appropriately confined to the inner worlds of liberal subjects.[19] Members of marginalized groups, such as women and children, laborers, and other races, were also thought to be more vulnerable to these less-than-rational forms of experience. This greater vulnerability served to further justify their exclusion from full political rights.[20] Although some aesthetic sensibilities, like imagination and sympathy, remained important factors that informed the political judgment of liberal subjects, these qualities needed to be carefully cultivated and controlled. An aesthetic concept of the sublime might indirectly guide political judgments, but it was not an adequate or appropriate foundation for political institutions and processes.[21] From this larger perspective, the liberal privatizing of the aesthetic can itself be seen as a cultural-political project with significant implications for how citizens understand and practice democracy.[22]

There is no question that aesthetic experiences often prompt visceral responses that can prove dangerous to political orders, including purportedly democratic ones.[23] The arts and popular culture are often romanticized as sites of popular resistance, as inherently democratic terrains of struggle against hopeless odds, as authentic expressions of the people, and as naturally effective counterweights to power exercised in the interests of domination. Aesthetic experience sometimes does counter hegemonic powers, and the popular expressions of the arts considered here serve a variety of functions for progressive social movements. These include: "survival/identity, resistance/opposition, consciousness-raising/education, agitation/mobilization."[24] Yet a balanced look at the arts and popular culture will quickly reveal that they are also sites of domination and oppression where citizens are misled and their interests distorted; where various undemocratic ends are pursued, often successfully; where the possibility of resistance is systematically erased; and where the notion of authenticity is hopelessly obfuscated. Antonio Gramsci uses the term "hegemony" to describe how a ruling class can establish political control by shaping the dominant cultural institutions of civil society. For Gramsci, cultural projects are a primary field of political struggle, a site where counterhegemonic artists and intellectuals can also prefigure a new society and join with others to create it.[25] The liberal depoliticization of the aesthetic potentially decreases the capacity of citizens to evaluate critically such cultural-political projects, whether they are democratic or undemocratic in character.

"Doing (and Undoing) Democracy" with the Arts

The arts and popular culture offer an array of resources for people, especially those in marginalized groups, to use politically. They can contribute to political equality by increasing political capacity, especially for those who need it the most. As Rousseau and others have argued, political equality is a precondition for political freedom.[26] Freedom requires that each of us is able to participate in the determination of the rules and laws that govern us, and this requires that each of us has a meaningful say in decisions affecting those laws and rules. This presumes a semblance of political equality, where each person has a voice through which they can exercise political influence. Popular sovereignty means that the people rule. Common people need access to decision-making arenas, and for some, the arts and popular culture afford them this access. Iris Young argues that even citizens who have voting rights may experience "internal exclusions" due to their unfamiliarity with the formal procedures of politics such as voter registration requirements or rules of evidence in courts of law. She calls for an expanded understanding of communication that includes the arts and popular culture, specifically greeting and ceremony, various forms of rhetoric, and storytelling, as part of the political vernacular.[27] By pluralizing forms of political communication, the arts and popular culture can enable many citizens to exercise their share of popular sovereignty.

The sites of political participation are also expanded by the arts and popular culture, especially for those who enjoy little, if any, access to institutionalized politics. The arts and popular culture represent a terrain in which new spaces can be opened for political action. As our contributors illustrate, these spaces can include the streets, public monuments, theaters and concert halls, private homes, local bars and clubs, and wherever citizen-photographers engage in countersurveillance of public figures, as well as more traditional spaces such as public assemblies and voting booths. The new spaces opened up in the terrain of the arts and popular culture are often more accessible for relatively marginalized people. Power is potentially rendered accountable through arts and cultural practices in the same way it is rendered accountable through more traditional political avenues; that is, through the political engagement of citizens. Younger citizens in particular often get their information about politics and gain a sense of political efficacy through the arts and popular culture. Participating in these alternative political spaces is one means of drawing ordinary citizens into political engagement and, for some, one that engages them deeply and passionately.

Finally, the arts and popular culture deeply influence character and can foster or undermine civic virtue. Rousseau feared that increased access to the arts would corrupt public morals by creating a desire for wealth and luxury and increasing the distance between rich and poor. For this reason, he ultimately opposed the introduction of a public theater in Geneva.[28] However, by cultivating the imagination, citizens also can increase their capacity to understand that they share the world with others who are different from them. In *Not for Profit: Why Democracy Needs the Humanities*, Martha Nussbaum argues that the arts and literature develop our ability to empathize, a crucial component of ethical decision-making. Drawing on John Dewey, Nussbaum argues that exposure to culturally diverse art forms and reflection on our responses to them enhances a sense of world citizenship.[29] Dewey sees art as a powerful way of sharing experience; it introduces us to the lives and worlds of other people.[30] This sharing of experience occurs partly through the affective dimension of arts and popular culture. Without dismissing or even qualifying the importance of understanding others' lives through our rational and analytical faculties, this volume builds on the presumption that a whole person engages with the world affectively as well as rationally. Often, and perhaps typically, the two faculties are deeply intertwined, and they rely on each other. The arts and popular culture represent the diverse experiences and identities of individuals and the cultures in which they exist. As such, they are also a window into those experiences and identities. They are unique in intentionally drawing upon the whole person, affectively and physically as well as rationally and analytically. As a means of understanding others' lives and experiences, they thus represent a valuable resource for character development and moral decision-making.

At the deepest level, artistic experiences can invoke a shared sense of our all-too-human vulnerability to pain, suffering, and death. In *The Ethos of a Late-Modern Citizen*, Stephen K. White explores the contours of a new ethos of global citizenship that is at once cognitive, moral, and aesthetic-affective. Moving beyond the association of western reason with the domination and the exclusion of difference, White focuses on the limited capacity of human reason to control external reality. He urges us to bring a spirit of generosity to our encounters with different individuals and cultures. Instead of a politics of resentment, he would infuse our political interactions with a sense of reasonableness that springs from an understanding of our shared human limits.[31] Artistic experiences are especially conducive to positive encounters with difference because they can balance anxiety over identity, even mortality, with the pleasure of creativity. As we have seen, the arts and popular culture can represent a terrain of human experience where creativity and experimentation are expected and valued. In creating new artistic and popular cultural forms, artists and popular culture workers are simultaneously shaping new possibilities for human experience including, for the purposes of this edited volume, new possibilities for political thought and action.

The Arts and Prefigurative Politics

The arts and popular culture have a prefigurative capacity that rivals or exceeds other areas of human experience. According to the *Oxford English Dictionary*, to "prefigure" means to provide "an early indication or version of, to represent beforehand by a figure or type."[32] Prefigurative politics is often associated with New Left movements of the 1960s, whose political activism also employed the arts and popular culture to challenge "the system" in innovative ways. Their continuing influence can be seen in several contributions to this volume. Drawing on the experience of the New Left, Wini Breines writes that prefigurative politics:

> may be recognized in counter institutions, demonstrations and the attempt to embody personal and anti-hierarchical values in politics. Participatory democracy was central to prefigurative politics. "Anti-organization" should not be construed as disorganized. Movements are organized in numerous obvious and often hidden ways. . . . The crux of prefigurative politics imposed substantial tasks, the central one being to create and sustain within the lived practice of the movement, relationships and political forms that "prefigured" and embodied the desired society.[33]

In addition to participatory democracy, prefigurative politics has a long history in anarchist direct action and is frequently described as a call to "build a new world in the shell of the old."[34] In the process of exemplifying this new world, prefigurative politics usually creates further disruptions in the old order. Sometimes, though, the prefigurative politics of artists simply involves bearing witness to the possibility of a more democratic politics. For example, Herbert Marcuse argued that the arts invoked another dimension of experience, a third dimension beyond the two-dimensional conformity of mass society.[35] Theodor Adorno, who was more pessimistic about the prospects for democratic change, defended the intransigence of the artist or philosopher as itself a democratic form of political practice.[36]

Doing Democracy: Activist Art and Cultural Politics attempts to take advantage of a historical opportunity presented by the central, and growing, importance in the contemporary life of the arts and popular culture. As widely noted in academic and popular media, younger generations spend countless hours on electronic forms of media exploring various forms of the arts and popular culture.[37] Many older people are rapidly catching up. Through YouTube, Facebook, Bit Torrent, cell phones (with cameras), Blackberries, and iPods, contemporary citizens consume and create various forms of the arts and popular culture, including especially music, film, videos, and photography. For many of them, these worlds of the arts and popular culture define the main parameters of their everyday lives. While most (especially young) people find traditional politics dreary and alienating, they are quickly and readily drawn into political life through the arts and popular culture. Today this means they are also drawn into an increasingly global reality.

The arts and popular culture have traditionally been located in place, defined geographically as the cultural products of a particular nation, people, or region. The new spaces of the twenty-first century—the internet, multinational corporations, transnational movements—bring diverse populations together in ways that flow across these borders and create an increasingly global environment for the arts and popular culture. Although some citizens of modern as well as traditional societies have responded to these rapid changes with attempts to fortify their borders, others have reached out to share cultural resources in a spirit of mutual understanding. Many Indigenous peoples, in particular, are currently sharing their cultural traditions. For example, Native Americans have long embraced what Gregory Cajete calls a "geopsyche" that integrates mind, body, and spirit with the land. Their understanding of place is not only deeply rooted, but also radically open to changing contexts, a survival necessity for groups who were forcibly relocated.[38] The increasing fluidity and hybridity of the arts and popular culture today again prompt the realization that "where we come from" in our interactions with other peoples transcends geographic location along with other standard markers of identity. The arts and popular culture have long played a major role in shaping such a creative, expansive, and democratic understanding of the relationships between peoples and can do so today in new ways.[39]

The contributions to this volume engage these new global realities from a variety of perspectives. The contributors come from Austria, Canada, England, India, and Finland, as well as the United States. More important, they study how the arts and popular culture are used politically in a variety of local, regional, and national contexts, including Afghanistan, Brazil, Canada, Great Britain, Iraq, Mexico, South Africa, and the United States. While some contributors emphasize the impact of global interactions on more traditional understandings of place and space, others explicitly focus on how the arts and popular culture, including new digital media and the internet, facilitate aesthetic experiences across cultural and political traditions. They also consider how the arts and popular culture can either diversify or homogenize aesthetic experiences and thereby contribute to a more or less democratic world.

Since Plato's famous discussion of the tensions between poetry and philosophy, many in the west have recognized the political importance of the arts and popular culture.[40] Although the relationship between aesthetics and politics is not new, it is changing today in significant ways that political scientists cannot afford to ignore.[41] With relatively few exceptions, including the coeditors and contributors to this volume, political science as a discipline has been strangely silent on the political importance of the arts and popular culture.[42] Instead, we have made scientific attempts to represent the "real" world of politics our top priority. The prefigurative quality of art and popular culture redirects our attention instead to the gap between actually existing democracy and democratic possibilities.[43] Researchers in many disciplines, such as sociology, anthropology, musicology, communications, American studies, and others, have extensively explored the political significance of aesthetic experiences. While our contributors acknowledge research from these other disciplines that has contributed much to our understanding of the arts and culture, the general absence of contributions from political scientists and political theorists suggests that their unique concerns and insights are either underrepresented or absent entirely. These unique concerns and insights include, for example, power and its many faces; the various forms of political action including, for example, deliberation, problem-solving, and resistance; extra- or nonrational dimensions of human experience; democracy in its strongest forms; freedom and equality; and the many issues related to the theory and practice of citizenship. The following chapters provide important insights on these and other issues crucial for the ongoing creative and collective process of "doing democracy."

Contributions to This Volume

The contributors to this volume consider how a variety of artistic media contribute to processes of doing (and undoing) democracy. We begin with two chapters that discuss the visual arts, specifically photo-activism and political cartoons, and engage questions of visibility and agency, including how images construct democratic (and undemocratic) spaces. In "Photo-Activism in the Digital Age: Visions from Rio de Janeiro," Frank Möller examines how the relationship between knowing and seeing changes when we move beyond the written word to photographic images, especially digital photography. Möller notes that photographic images potentially challenge power in several ways: they tend to be user-driven; they often reveal otherwise unseen phenomena, such as war zones; and they can strengthen political awareness. In the digital age, the emergence of the citizen-photographer creates new possibilities by expanding the possible relationships between the subjects, agents, and spectators of photography. Möller discusses three examples of photo-activism from popular communities in Rio de Janeiro. In the Morro da Providência area, the French visual artist JR's project, Women Are Heroes, displayed women's photos on the walls of prominent buildings. In Jacarezinho, residents and citizens used security cameras to observe and record the activities of police and drug dealers in their neighborhood. Both examples reveal complex relationships between surveillance, including self-surveillance, and what Möller calls "sousveillance," a kind of countersurveillance that involves ordinary citizens creating images of political authorities. A third example, Vik Muniz' images of the *catadores* (garbage pickers) of Jardim Gramacho, reveals how trash becomes art and art becomes cash. Drawing on Arendt's work, Möller concludes that photo-activism in the digital age multiplies the ways individuals can appear in public. However, he concludes with a cautionary note: seeing and being seen do not necessarily involve active participation, and much remains to be studied regarding the roles images play in "doing democracy."

In "Framing the Obama Political Cartoons: Injury or Democracy?," Sushmita Chatterjee asks when and how the process of visual image-making that she calls "cartooning democracy" is also "doing democracy." Beginning with the violence in 2005 that followed the Mohammed cartoons published in a Danish newspaper, Chatterjee notes the ambivalent quality of cartoon frames. Are the caricatures and stereotypes of political cartoons inherently subversive or do they simply add insult to injury? In an argument informed by Judith Butler, Art Spiegelman, and critical race theorists, Chatterjee reveals the complex associations of injury and democracy found in the aforementioned cartoons and the more recent Obama cartoons. In the process, she presents a method for reading political cartoons that recognizes their porous frames, the play of image and text, and the "drawing out" of the "ridiculous under the real and recognizable." For Chatterjee, ongoing power relations ultimately contextualize and thereby influence how the mix of injury and democracy works in political cartoons. In other words, responsibility for redeeming democracy, if not beauty, is in the eye and intention of the beholder of political cartoons.

The next two chapters move beyond visual imagery to explore the uses of memorials and monuments in cultural rituals that honor the dead. Regina Marchi's "The Moral Economy: 'Doing Democracy' via Public Day of the Dead Rituals" examines how Mexico's Dia de los Muertos celebrations were recreated among Latino communities in Los Angeles and San Francisco as, what Eric Hobsbawn calls, an "invented tradition." Since the 1970s U.S. Day of the Dead celebrations have been held on November 1 and 2 (Roman Catholics' All Saints Day and All Souls Day) and combined Indigenous, Catholic, and Mexican-U.S. cultural traditions in syncretistic personal and public rituals. The celebrations include altar installations with harvest offerings and ancestral photos, art exhibits of sugar skulls (*Calaveras*), street processions, as well as decorated gravesites and family picnics. Marchi argues that Day of the Dead rituals simultaneously reinforce communal identities, protest political injustices, and uphold moral obligations to the deceased. They exemplify what E. P. Thompson called "a moral economy of social protest." Day of the Dead rituals protest the farm workers poisoned by pesticides, the illegal immigrants killed crossing the United States/Mexico border, and the innocent victims of U.S.-sponsored wars, including drug-related gang violence. These injustices highlight the harsh realities of U.S. imperialism and the living presence of Hispanic communities within U.S. borders, while employing multiple media that allow participants simultaneously to engage in cultural celebration and political protest.

Timothy W. Luke's "The National D-Day Memorial: An American Military Monument as 'Doing Democracy'" provides an important comparison with Marchi's analysis of Day of the Dead rituals. It tells the convoluted history of the National D-Day Memorial in Bedford, Virginia. Constructed as a national memorial and regional economic stimulus, the memorial immortalizes soldiers from the small Virginia town that suffered the most casualties per capita in the D-Day invasion. The memorial serves many ideological functions: it enshrines the United States as a superpower fighting for democracy across the globe; symbolizes national unity in a region still haunted by the legacy of the civil war; exemplifies a collaborative corporate, public, and private initiative; immortalizes the horrors and sacrifices of war; and celebrates freedom and hope, values highlighted and compromised by the ongoing War on Terror. Most important, it presents the United States as, what Luke calls, "a doing democracy," a nation with imperial aspirations, some of whose effects appear very differently in the Day of the Dead rituals Marchi discusses. Drawing on Benedict Anderson's concept of "imagined communities," Luke presents war memorials as public sites where ordinary citizens and political elites can meet and share their stories of national heroes and values. Read together, Marchi's and Luke's chapters highlight the variability and vulnerability of these stories, and the need to continually revisit and recreate them.

Poetry and literature have long immortalized heroic conquests and exploits for future generations, and they are the media on which the next two chapters focus. In "The Message in the Medium: Poetry Slam as Democratic Practice," Mark Mattern presents changing forms of poetry as examples of the tensions between high art and popular culture. He notes that even as some pundits lamented the decline of poetry (more precisely, its shift from public fora to academic institutions), a more democratic form of performance poetry—poetry slams—was emerging. As Mattern notes, public poetry has a longer history in oral traditions that include "Homeric epics, African griots, Zuni priests, Japanese kojiki poets, and Greek bards." Mattern locates the politics of poetry in its form, and he argues that poetry slams embrace many democratic features: broad access, active participation, critical judgment, egalitarian community, individual freedom, and communal responsibility. Poetry slams reconnect audiences with poetry and mirror a more participatory politics in the process. The message is: "anybody can write and perform poetry and everyone is encouraged to do so." What began as a local phenomenon—Marc Smith invented poetry slams in Chicago, Illinois—has now become an organized network of national and international competitions. Mattern argues that the participatory politics at work here revitalizes poetry; challenges hegemonic power in its many guises, ranging from high art to commercial entertainment; and resurrects deeply rooted democratic traditions.

In "Tragedy and Democracy: The Fate of Liberal Democratic Values in a Violent World," Wairimu Njoya writes of literary and musical traditions that have survived the racial terrors of slavery and now offer renewed hope to a deeply compromised American democracy. With Schiller and Kant as philosophical foundations, Njoya turns to Angela Davis, Toni Morrison, and Cornel West to reveal how black political culture has given meaning to "ineffable suffering" by rehumanizing, memorializing, and thereby atoning for it. The "slave sublime," Njoya argues, models a political alternative to the strategic violence and security politics of America's ongoing War on Terror. It steadfastly refuses to reproduce the violence. Instead, the "blues people" sustain the understanding that some things matter more than mere life, especially the values Americans share as a democratic people, values they have long held in trust. Njoya turns to Billie Holiday's hauntingly beautiful rendition of "Strange Fruit" to illustrate this deeply democratic ethos of the blues people. Njoya suggests that Barack Obama's call for Americans today to "choose our better history" reinvokes this tragic legacy.

The next two selections more directly engage the relationships between music and democracy. In "'You're an American rapper, so what do you know?': The Political Uses of British and U.S. Popular Culture by First-Time Voters in the United Kingdom," Sanna Inthorn and John Street present their empirical research on how popular culture affects the political capacities of first-time voters in the United Kingdom. This chapter makes a unique contribution to the volume with its focus on "what popular culture in its commercial, everyday form contributes to 'doing democracy,'" specifically, mainstream electoral politics. Street and Inthorn argue that popular culture plays three roles in politics: representing the wider world, forming collective identities, and mobilizing action. Their focus here is on the second contribution, and they emphasize how television and music industry celebrities—for example, Britney Spears, Kanye West, and Eminem—shape young voters' sense of collective identity. Drawing on questionnaires, focus groups, and interviews, they find that celebrities have impact on young voters' sense of national identity. That impact varies, though, depending on their perceptions of the artist's integrity, especially whether the artist has an "authentic" voice or speaks for the music industry. Perhaps most important, Street and Inthorn find that popular culture has a positive effect on political engagement by contributing to the creation of collective identities that give young voters a basis for action.

In "Playing with Hate: White Power Music and the Undoing of Democracy," Nancy S. Love examines another example of how music and popular culture influence the political identity of teenage youth. Variously described as the "soundtrack to the white revolution," "a common language and a unifying ideology," and, in the case of Skrewdriver, "'the musical wing' of the National Front," White Noise or White Rock has created a music scene that is fueling and funding white supremacist groups across the globe. Love situates these right-wing extremist movements in a longer history of cultural-political projects of racial hegemony in western liberal democracies. Through an analysis of song lyrics and musical performances, she shows how Skrewdriver's music globalizes and inverts a traditional fascist aesthetic. Her title phrase, "playing with hate," refers not only to Skrewdriver's identity-based aversion to nonwhites, but also to what Wendy Brown has called liberal "tolerance talk." By positioning white supremacists as disturbed, even pathological, individuals, liberal toleration minimizes the deep complicity of hegemonic liberalism with white supremacy and denies that racist skinheads may be an external manifestation of liberalism's internal demons. Love argues that the future of democracy depends on citizens' capacity to recognize and redeem this history of racialized liberalism, and she reminds readers that such an "undoing" offers an opportunity to begin "doing democracy" anew.

The next two pieces examine the role of theater in "doing democracy." In "Betrayed by Democracy: Verbatim Theater as Prefigurative Politics," Mark Chou and Roland Bleiker compare George Packer's work as a journalist and a playwright in order to understand what his play, *Betrayed*, adds to the story of Iraqi interpreters who served U.S. forces and found themselves caught between the United States and their home country. Chou and Bleiker argue that theater can evade the censorship—legal and informal—that often marks public discourse in times of war. It offers an alternative site for representing reality and engages questions artistically that are too painful and volatile for political deliberation, including representing people who are otherwise rendered silent or invisible. Packer's play is an example of "verbatim" or "reality" theater, a genre that "uses facts to create fictional representations." In *Betrayed*, Iraqi interpreters give firsthand accounts of their experiences and engage their audience in a dialogue. This positions the audience as participants in the drama as well as its spectators and witnesses. Unlike commercialized entertainment, the play uses art to create a democratic dialogue and to reveal the ambiguous, complex, and uncertain quality of "truth." Like the Iraqi interpreters, the audience of *Betrayed* is positioned as "in between"; it confronts anew the reality of war, but only in its fictional representation. Through the dialogue of verbatim theater audiences are urged to rethink the meaning of war, including their own roles as democratic citizens.

In "Political Actors: Performance as Democratic Protest in Anti-Apartheid Theater," Emily Beausoleil also examines how theater can contest power when other channels of participation are closed. She focuses on how those who resisted apartheid in South Africa used theater against a coercive state that censored scripts, enforced codes, and restricted spaces for their productions. Beausoleil focuses on two aspects of theater—polyphony and transience—that are crucial for democratic resistance. Like Chou and Bleiker, she discusses the multiple voices theater represents, but extends polyphony beyond language to include the affective codes, embodied metaphors, and sonic texts of live theater. These aspects of theater are politically powerful precisely because their meanings are indeterminate and, hence, less vulnerable to censorship. Dramatic performances also have a transient or ephemeral quality that South African resistant theater embraced. Building on oral traditions, including improvisation and storytelling, South Africans extended their medium to guerilla theater and propertyless theater. In the process, they increased the capacity of theatrical productions to evade state control. Beausoleil ultimately argues that this very *unruliness* of theater makes it a potentially powerful site of democratic engagement. Like Chou and Bleiker, Beausoleil argues that theater blurs lines between fact and fiction, and between art and politics.

Our next two chapters examine festivals and parades as ways of using the arts and popular culture to turn city neighborhoods and streets into public spaces where historically marginalized groups can engage in political expression and democratic resistance. Bruce Baum's "Art in the House: Cultural Democracy in a Neighborhood" explores how performative art that is nondidactic, nonpartisan, or even apolitical can nonetheless prefigure forms of democratic community. The June 2011 In the House Festival in Vancouver, British Columbia, brought artworks representing many media and genres into the everyday lives of local residents by using private homes as performance venues. Drawing on Mikhail Bakhtin, Baum compares In the House to a postmodern carnival, though now the democratic-capitalist culture industry rather than a feudal hierarchy is being inverted. As an alternative to the commercialized artworks of mass culture, this festival also resembles what Theodor Adorno calls "autonomous art." For Baum, In the House creates a counterspace where diverse artists and art forms meet the everyday lives of people in local communities. If there is a politics here, it is a "politics of generosity" or, as Baum puts it, artistic "intimations of a more humane world." As Baum notes, In the House is a model other cities can use to stage similar festivals that offer popular experiences, however, brief, of democratic freedom in community.

In "Democracy despite Government: African American Parading and Democratic Theory," Peter G. Stillman and Adelaide H. Villmoare examine parading as an example of what they call "democracy despite government." This phrase describes a parallel politics of "doing democracy" that expresses citizens' needs and empowers them to act on their own behalf, regardless of the less-than-democratic features of neo-liberal political orders. In a fascinating, richly historical analysis, Stillman and Villmoare show how parades transform the public streets of New Orleans, Louisiana, from privatized, commercial spaces into expressive and communal sites of political action. The African American "second line," a parade style that originated with enslaved Africans and included Native Americans in colonial New Orleans, powerfully illustrates how parading can foster an egalitarian, participatory politics. Precisely because parading remains deinstitutionalized, Stillman and Villmoare claim it can prefigure another way of being political; parades bridge past and future by carrying forward the living democratic traditions that government institutions ignore, occlude, and silence.

These last two pieces lead directly into our concluding chapter on "Activist Arts, Community Development, and Democracy." In the introduction, we challenged the distinction between high art and low art, and we appropriately conclude by troubling another related distinction between elites-driven and community arts projects. Community arts, we argue, is a more democratic mode of arts activism that suggests how elites-driven arts projects might be moved in the direction of greater democracy. That is, these categories mark poles of a continuum on which some of the contributions to this volume might be arrayed. They also engage explicitly with arts-based approaches to public policy, a topic that earlier chapters often address only indirectly. Two concluding case studies serve to highlight the elites-driven and community arts distinction. On the elites-driven end of the continuum, the Artists' Village community development project in Santa Ana, California, tells a story of arts-based development narrowly focused on economic growth. A second community-arts-based project, the Music and Performing Arts community development program created by Trinity Cathedral in the Quadrangle neighborhood of downtown Cleveland, illustrates a broader notion of democratic community. The latter example reintegrates the arts and popular culture into the daily lives of community members and challenges liberal notions of the arts as non- or apolitical, the artist as an individual genius, and popular culture as commercialized mass entertainment. Instead, as many of our contributors' pieces so aptly convey, the arts and popular culture play a crucial role in celebrating and criticizing, creating and sustaining, the many and varied communal ties that bind citizens together in the ongoing processes of "doing democracy."

Notes

1. Marco Adria, *Technology and Nationalism* (Montreal: McGill-Queen's University Press, 2010), chap. 6.

2. For an extensive historical discussion of this distinction, see Terry Eagleton, *The Ideology of the Aesthetic* (New York: Basil Blackwell, 1990).

3. For an excellent history of attempts to define art, including the distinction between institutional and historical definitions, see Richard Shusterman, *Pragmatic Aesthetics, Living Beauty, Rethinking Art* (New York: Rowman & Littlefield, 2000), chap. 2. On the tendency of such definitions to exclude innovative and non-European art forms, see Paul Crowther, *Defining Art, Creating the Canon, Artistic Value in an Era of Doubt* (Oxford, UK: Clarendon Press, 2007), part 1.

4. Marshall McLuhan, *Understanding Media: The Extensions of Man* (New York: New American Library, 1964), viii.

5. For a popular version of this argument, see Allan Bloom, *The Closing of the American Mind* (New York: Simon and Schuster, 1988).

6. For a concise summary of functional and other definitions of art, see Thomas Adajian, "The Definition of Art," *Stanford Encyclopedia of Philosophy*, ed. Edward N. Zalta, Winter 2012 edition, http://plato.stanford.edu/archives/win2012/entries/art-definition/.

7. See Aaron Meskin, "From Defining Art to Defining the Individual Arts: The Role of Theory in the Philosophies of Arts," in *New Waves in Aesthetics*, eds. Kathleen Stock and Katherine Thomson-Jones (New York: Palgrave Macmillan, 2008), 125–49.

8. Eagleton, *Ideology of the Aesthetic*, 13.

9. John Dewey, *Art as Experience*, in *John Dewey: The Later Works, 1925–1953*, volume 10, 1934, ed. Jo Ann Boydston (Carbondale: Southern Illinois University Press, 1989 [1934]), 53.

10. Morton Schoolman, "Avoiding 'Embarrassment': Aesthetic Reason and Aporetic Critique in *Dialectic of Enlightenment*," *Polity* 37, no. 3 (2005): 335–64; Eagleton, *Ideology of the Aesthetic*, chap. 14.

11. Barbara Engh, "Loving It: Music and Criticism in Roland Barthes," in *Musicology and Difference: Gender and Sexuality in Music Scholarship*, ed. Ruth A. Solie (Berkeley: University of California Press, 1993), 73–74.

12. On musical counterpoint and democratic discourse, see John Schleuter, "The Art of Debate: Disagreement, Consensus, and Democratic Association," *Soundings: An Interdisciplinary Journal* 92, nos. 3–4 (Fall/Winter 1990): 279–302. Also see Michel Foucault's well-known discussion of Velasquez's use of perspective in his painting, *Las Meninas*, in *The Order of Things: An Archaeology of the Human Sciences* (New York: Vintage Books, 1994), 3–16.

13. McLuhan, *Understanding Media*, 7.

14. See Anthony Kwame Harrison, *Hip Hop Underground: The Integrity and Ethics of Racial Identification* (Philadelphia: Temple University Press, 2009).

15. Mark Chou, *Greek Tragedy and Contemporary Democracy* (New York: Bloomsbury, 2012).

16. John Locke, *Second Treatise of Government* in *Two Treatises of Government*, ed. Peter Laslett (New York: Cambridge University Press, 1960), chap. 5.

17. John Locke writes, "Civil interests I call life, liberty, health, and indolency of body, and the possession of outward things, such as money, lands, houses, furniture, and the like." *A Letter Concerning Toleration* (London: J. Brook Printers, 1796), 10.

18. Marc Redfield, *The Politics of Aesthetics, Nationalism, Gender, Romanticism* (Stanford, CA: Stanford University Press, 2003).

19. Marcel Henaff and Tracy B. Strong, "The Conditions of Public Space: Vision, Speech, and Theatricality," in *Public Space and Democracy*, eds. Marcel Henaff and Tracy B. Strong (Minneapolis: University of Minnesota Press, 2001), 1–40.

20. Andrew Hewitt, *Fascist Modernism: Aesthetics, Politics, and the Avant-Garde* (Stanford, CA: Stanford University Press, 1993) and Kaja Silverman, *The Acoustic Mirror: The Female Voice in Psychoanalysis and Cinema* (Bloomington: Indiana University Press, 1988).

21. Immanuel Kant, *Critique of Judgment*, ed. Nicholas Walker, trans. James Creed Meredith (Oxford, UK: Oxford University Press, 2007). Also see George Kateb, "Aestheticism and Morality: Their Cooperation and Hostility," *Political Theory* 28, no. 1 (February 2000): 5–37; and Arne Johan Vetlesen, *Perception, Empathy and Judgment: An Inquiry into the Preconditions of Moral Performance* (State College: Pennsylvania State University Press, 1994).

22. Daniel Fischlin, "Take One/Rebel Musics: Human Rights, Resistant Sounds, and the Politics of Music Making," in *Rebel Musics: Human Rights, Resistant Sounds, and the Politics of Music Making*, eds. Daniel Fischlin and Ajay Heble (Montreal: Black Rose Books, 2003), 10–43.

23. For a discussion of body/brain/culture networks and politics, see William Connolly, *Neuropolitics: Thinking, Culture, Speed* (Minneapolis: University of Minnesota Press, 2002). Recent works by neuroscientists examining these linkages include Daniel J. Levitin, *This Is Your Brain on Music: The Science of a Human Obsession* (New York: Dutton, 2007) and Oliver Sacks, *Musicophilia: Tales of Music and the Brain* (New York: Vintage Books, 2008).

24. Rebee Garofalo's succinct summary of the functions of music for social movements also applies more broadly here. Rebee Garofalo, "Introduction" to *Rockin' the Boat: Mass Music and Mass Movements* (Boston: South End Press, 1992), 2.

25. Antonio Gramsci, *Selections from the Prison Notebooks*, ed. and trans. Quintin Hoare and Geoffrey Nowell-Smith (New York: International Publishers, 1971). For a discussion of how Gramsci's views compare with more orthodox Marxist analyses of base and superstructure relations, see Martin Jay, *Marxism and Totality: The Adventures of a Concept from Lukács to Habermas* (Berkeley: University of California Press, 1984), chap. 4.

26. Jean-Jacques Rousseau, *Discourse on the Origin of Inequality* in *The Basic Political Writings*, ed. and trans. Donald A. Cress (Indianapolis: Hackett, 1987).

27. Iris Young, *Inclusion and Democracy* (New York: Oxford University Press, 2000).

28. Jean-Jacques Rousseau, *Discourse on the Sciences and the Arts* in *The Basic Political Writings*, ed. and trans. Donald A. Cress (Indianapolis: Hackett, 1987). Also see, Jean-Jacques Rousseau, *Politics and the Arts: Letter to M. D'Alembert on the Theatre*, trans. Allan Bloom (Ithaca, NY: Cornell University Press 1968).

29. Martha C. Nussbaum, *Not for Profit: Why Democracy Needs the Humanities* (Princeton, NJ: Princeton University Press, 2010).

30. Dewey, *Art as Experience*.

31. Stephen K. White, *The Ethos of a Late-Modern Citizen* (Cambridge, MA: Harvard University Press, 2009).

32. *Oxford English Dictionary Online*, s.v. "prefigure" and "prefigurative," http://www.oed.com.

33. Wini Breines, *Community and Organization in the New Left, 1962–1968: The Great Refusal* (New Brunswick, NJ: Rutgers University Press, 1989), 6.

34. This common anarchist phrase originated in the Preamble of the 1908 Constitution and Bylaws of the Industrial Workers of the World. The preamble reads: "By organizing industrially we are forming the structure of a new world in the shell of the old," http://www.iww.org/PDF/2002.pdf.

35. According to Marcuse, "Art fights reification by making the petrified world speak, sing, perhaps dance." Herbert Marcuse, *The Aesthetic Dimension: Toward a Critique of Marxist Aesthetics* (Boston: Beacon Press, 1978), 73.

36. Theodor Adorno, *Minima Moralia: Reflections from a Damaged Life* (New York: Schocken Books, 1974).

37. Elizabeth Chaves, "The Internet as Global Platform? Grounding the Magically Levitating Public Sphere," *New Political Science: A Journal of Politics and Culture* 32, no. 1 (March 2010): 23–41.

38. Gregory Cajete, *Look to the Mountain: An Ecology of Indigenous Education* (Rio Rancho, NM: Kivaki Press, 1994), chap. 4.

39. John Connell and Chris Gibson, *Sound Tracks, Popular Music, Identity, and Place* (New York: Routledge, 2003).

40. Plato, *The Republic of Plato*, trans. Allan Bloom (New York: Basic Books, 1968).

41. Crispin Sartwell, *Political Aesthetics* (Ithaca, NY: Cornell University Press, 2010).

42. See, for example, Nancy S. Love, *Musical Democracy* (Albany: State University of New York Press, 2006); Mark Mattern, *Acting in Concert: Music, Community, and Political Action* (New Brunswick, NJ: Rutgers University Press, 1998).

43. Two recent works bring aesthetic insights to international politics: Roland Bleiker, *Aesthetics and World Politics* (New York: Palgrave Macmillan, 2009) and Brent J. Steele, *Defacing Power: The Aesthetics of Insecurity in Global Politics* (Ann Arbor: University of Michigan Press, 2010).

Bibliography

Adajian, Thomas. "The Definition of Art." In *Stanford Encyclopedia of Philosophy*, edited by Edward N. Zalta. Winter 2012 edition. http://plato.stanford.edu/archives/win2012/entries/art-definition/.

Adorno, Theodor. *Minima Moralia: Reflections from a Damaged Life*. New York: Schocken Books, 1974.

Adria, Marco. *Technology and Nationalism*. Montreal: McGill-Queen's University Press, 2010.

Bleiker, Roland. *Aesthetics and World Politics*. New York: Palgrave Macmillan, 2009.

Breines, Wini. *Community and Organization in the New Left, 1962–1968: The Great Refusal*. New Brunswick, NJ: Rutgers University Press, 1989.

Cajete, Gregory. *Look to the Mountain: An Ecology of Indigenous Education*. Rio Rancho, NM: Kivaki Press, 1994.

Chaves, Elizabeth. "The Internet as Global Platform? Grounding the Magically Levitating Public Sphere." *New Political Science: A Journal of Politics and Culture* 32, no. 1 (March 2010): 23–41.

Chou, Mark. *Greek Tragedy and Contemporary Democracy*. New York: Bloomsbury, 2012.

Connell, John, and Chris Gibson. *Sound Tracks, Popular Music, Identity, and Place*. New York: Routledge, 2003.

Connolly, William. *Neuropolitics: Thinking, Culture, Speed*. Minneapolis: University of Minnesota Press, 2002.

Crowther, Paul. *Defining Art, Creating the Canon: Artistic Value in an Era of Doubt*. Oxford, UK: Clarendon Press, 2007.

Dewey, John. *Art as Experience*. In *John Dewey: The Later Works, 1925–1953*, volume 10, 1934, edited by Jo Ann Boydston. Carbondale: Southern Illinois University Press 1989 (1934).

Eagleton, Terry. *The Ideology of the Aesthetic*. New York: Basil Blackwell, 1990.

Engh, Barbara. "Loving It: Music and Criticism in Roland Barthes." In *Musicology and Difference: Gender and Sexuality in Music Scholarship*, edited by Ruth A. Solie, 66–82. Berkeley: University of California Press, 1993.

Fischlin, Daniel. "Take One/Rebel Musics: Human Rights, Resistant Sounds, and the Politics of Music Making." In *Rebel Musics: Human Rights, Resistant Sounds, and the Politics of Music Making*, edited by Daniel Fischlin and Ajay Heble, 10–43. Montreal: Black Rose Books, 2003.

Foucault, Michel. *The Order of Things: An Archaeology of the Human Sciences*. New York: Vintage Books, 1994.

Garofalo, Rebee. Introduction to *Rockin' the Boat: Mass Music and Mass Movements*, 1–14. Boston: South End Press, 1992.

Gramsci, Antonio. *Selections from the Prison Notebooks*. Translated and edited by Quintin Hoare and Geoffrey Nowell-Smith. New York: International, 1971.

Harrison, Anthony Kwame. *Hip Hop Underground: The Integrity and Ethics of Racial Identification.* Philadelphia: Temple University Press, 2009.

Henaff, Marcel, and Tracy B. Strong. "The Conditions of Public Space: Vision, Speech, and Theatricality." In *Public Space and Democracy*, edited by Marcel Henaff and Tracy B. Strong, 1–32. Minneapolis: University of Minnesota Press, 2001.

Hewitt, Andrew. *Fascist Modernism: Aesthetics, Politics, and the Avant-Garde.* Stanford, CA: Stanford University Press, 1993.

Jay, Martin. *Marxism and Totality: The Adventures of a Concept from Lukács to Habermas.* Berkeley: University of California Press, 1984.

Kant, Immanuel. *Critique of Judgment*, edited by Nicholas Walker, translated by James Creed Meredith. Oxford, UK: Oxford University Press, 2007.

Kateb, George. "Aestheticism and Morality: Their Cooperation and Hostility." *Political Theory* 28, no. 1 (February 2000): 5–37.

Levitin, Daniel J. *This Is Your Brain on Music: The Science of a Human Obsession.* New York: Dutton, 2007.

Locke, John. *A Letter Concerning Toleration.* London: J. Brook Printers, 1796.

———. *Second Treatise of Government.* In *Two Treatises of Government*, edited by Peter Laslett. New York: Cambridge University Press, 1960.

Love, Nancy S. *Musical Democracy.* Albany: State University of New York Press, 2006.

Marcuse, Herbert. *The Aesthetic Dimension: Toward a Critique of Marxist Aesthetics.* Boston: Beacon Press, 1978.

Mattern, Mark. *Acting in Concert: Music, Community, and Political Action.* New Brunswick, NJ: Rutgers University Press, 1998.

McLuhan, Marshall. *Understanding Media: The Extensions of Man.* New York: New American Library, 1964.

Meskin, Alan. "From Defining Art to Defining the Individual Arts: The Role of Theory in the Philosophies of Arts." In *New Waves in Aesthetics*, edited by Kathleen Stock and Katherine Thomson-Jones, 125–49. New York: Palgrave Macmillan, 2008.

Nussbaum, Martha C. *Not for Profit: Why Democracy Needs the Humanities.* Princeton, NJ: Princeton University Press, 2010.

Oxford English Dictionary Online, s.vv. "prefigure" and "prefigurative," http://www.oed.com.

Plato. *The Republic of Plato*, translated and edited by Allan Bloom. New York: Basic Books, 1968.

Preamble of the 1908 Constitution and Bylaws of the Industrial Workers of the World. http://www.iww.org/PDF/2002.pdf.

Redfield, Marc. *The Politics of Aesthetics: Nationalism, Gender, Romanticism.* Stanford, CA: Stanford University Press, 2003.

Rousseau, Jean-Jacques. *Politics and the Arts: Letter to M. D'Alembert on the Theatre*, translated by Allan Bloom. Ithaca, NY: Cornell University Press, 1968.

———. *Discourse on the Origin of Inequality.* In *The Basic Political Writings*, translated by Donald A. Cress. Indianapolis: Hackett, 1987.

———. *Discourse on the Sciences and the Arts.* In *The Basic Political Writings*, translated by Donald A. Cress. Indianapolis: Hackett, 1987.

Sacks, Oliver. *Musicophilia: Tales of Music and the Brain.* New York: Vintage Books, 2008.

Sartwell, Crispin. *Political Aesthetics.* Ithaca, NY: Cornell University Press, 2010.

Schleuter, John. "The Art of Debate: Disagreement, Consensus, and Democratic Association." *Soundings: An Interdisciplinary Journal* 92, nos. 3–4 (Fall/Winter 1990): 279–302.

Schoolman, Morton. "Avoiding 'Embarrassment': Aesthetic Reason and Aporetic Critique in *Dialectic of Enlightenment.*" *Polity* 37, no. 3 (2005): 335–64.

Shusterman, Richard. *Pragmatic Aesthetics: Living Beauty, Rethinking Art.* New York: Rowman & Littlefield, 2000.

Silverman, Kaja. *The Acoustic Mirror: The Female Voice in Psychoanalysis and Cinema.* Bloomington: Indiana University Press, 1988.

Steele, Brent J. *Defacing Power: The Aesthetics of Insecurity in Global Politics.* Ann Arbor: University of Michigan Press, 2010.

Vetlesen, Arne Johansen. *Perception, Empathy and Judgment: An Inquiry into the Preconditions of Moral Performance.* State College: Pennsylvania State University Press, 1994.

White, Stephen K. *The Ethos of a Late-Modern Citizen.* Cambridge, MA: Harvard University Press, 2009.

Young, Iris. *Inclusion and Democracy.* New York: Oxford University Press, 2000.

Part II

Photography and Cartoons

Chapter 2

Photo-Activism in the Digital Age

Visions from Rio de Janeiro

FRANK MÖLLER

The first thing my father taught me was that I was invisible. And the second was that I was worthless.

—Patrícia Melo, *Lost World*

In 1927, Siegfried Kracauer argued that in the illustrated magazines flourishing at the time, "people see the very world that the illustrated magazines prevent them from perceiving." Kracauer separated visual information from knowledge production: "Never before has an age been so informed about itself. . . . Never before has a period known so little about itself."[1] Thus, we see the world but we do not know it. The photographer Mário Macilau disagrees: he argues that it "is through photography that people learn something about realities that they had never even imagined."[2] Photography, however, does not only help us learn something about realities. It also constructs realities, and it constructs realities other than those constructed by means of language or other forms of representation. Photographs help us envision "a new landscape of the possible" expanding the range of "what can be seen, what can be said and what can be thought" and consequently what can be done.[3] Photographs help diversify our perspectives on the world and move center-stage configurations that are normally invisible or marginalized. They help us envision new ways of "doing democracy."

If, as the editors of this volume suggest in the introduction, the arts and popular culture are increasingly important, and if this increase in importance offers opportunities for a stronger democracy, then technological developments in connection with digitization cannot be ignored. In this chapter it is argued that the various activities in connection with photo-activism in the digital age offer many possibilities for people, including marginalized people, to engage with and expand the limits of democratic representation and participation. These activities include, but are not limited to, activist art, self-surveillance, and various forms of participatory photography turning former subjects of the photography of others into agents of their own image. Rather than establishing a hierarchy of approaches to photography—that *this* approach is better than *that* one with regard to "doing democracy"—it is suggested here that different approaches have advantages and disadvantages in any given situation. In any case, they are not normally mutually exclusive. The aim of the chapter, then, is to direct attention to photography's contribution to the construction of more democratic societies by increasing the visibility of those groups of people that are normally excluded from representation. As "there is no absolute 'marginality,'" attention has to be paid both to "the unequal processes through which some (more or less successfully) marginalize others" and to strategies by means of which these processes can be reversed.[4] The chapter tries to avoid the pitfall of idealizing or romanticizing photography as a site of resistance; neither uncritical celebration nor exaggerated concern with regard to photography and its potentialities in the digital age would be appropriate.

Photo-Activism in the Digital Age

It is almost a truism to say that political space is nowadays to a large extent constructed by means of images and meaning discursively assigned to images.[5] The visual construction of political space influences political participation by, for example, increasing visibility, obscuring the distinction between the private and the public, and offering many ways with which to strengthen or even trigger political consciousness. These ingredients of the visual construction of political space are important in connection with the cases discussed later in this chapter and shall therefore briefly be sketched here. Indeed, digitization has increased people's visibility as subjects of others' photography or as producers of their own images. The traditional distinction in liberal societies between the private and the public becomes blurred in an age of surveillance and self-surveillance, virtual networks, visual exhibitionism, and blogs. Visibility may exploit and violate the feelings of the people depicted, especially the feelings of people living in unfavorable conditions, and it may demand of spectators to make very difficult decisions indeed.[6] Even if politically useful in that it may help raise political awareness among spectators—the old impetus underlying socially concerned photography—strategies of making visible are not always appreciated by those made visible. Thus, there is a need to rethink, in the light of current trends in image production and dissemination, traditional assumptions regarding the relationship between images and political participation without, however, losing sight of the history of photography, especially participatory photography.

Assuming that photographs are capable of challenging established power relations and empowering those normally excluded from representation, *Arbeiter Illustrierte Zeitung* (*AIZ; Workers Illustrated Journal*) called upon their readers, mostly workers, to submit their own photographs as early as the mid-1920s—calls for user-generated images, ubiquitous nowadays, are no invention of the digital age. At the time, photography was seen as a vehicle for workers' self-realization and empowerment by documenting the everyday lives of the working class unromantically and in ways absent from bourgeois publications.[7] In 1926, *AIZ* even launched *Der Arbeiter-Fotograf* (*The Worker Photographer*),[8] a journal dedicated entirely to photographs taken by workers. Participatory photography projects, currently thriving, are no invention of the digital age, either. Historically, such projects reflected the conviction of the Communist Party that workers should generate their own culture rather than appropriating and, by so doing, confirming the culture of others. They have to be seen within the context of utopian approaches to photography after the Russian Revolution, which regarded photography as "the primary visual vocabulary" of the working class in its struggle for self-realization.[9] Rather than depicting "how the other half lives"[10]—one of the classical tasks of social documentary photography—this photography was interested in enabling "the other half" to represent themselves and to become agents of their own image—a clear precursor of many current participatory photography projects.

I would certainly not be the first to argue that there is a connection between visibility and political agency, between visual representation and democratic participation. Hannah Arendt, for example, argued as early as 1959 that in "the public realm, where nothing counts that cannot make itself seen and heard, visibility and audibility are of prime importance."[11] While criticizing the reduction of politics to image-making, Arendt emphasized the connection between visibility, public appearance, and politics. Recent engagements with her work argue that in the civil rights struggle, which inspired Arendt's reflections, photography "afforded ordinary citizens the means to realize their role in effecting political change, by letting them become visible agents in the public sphere."[12] In the academic discourse on images and participation, the active role of the spectator has also been noted. It is argued that people become involved in politics qua spectator and that they exert political influence by viewing and responding to images: the act of viewing constitutes the political public only as a part of which the individual might have power by acting together with others in response to the conditions depicted in images.[13]

However, hopes pinned to photography since its inception—articulated by both photographers and critics—seem to have been exaggerated; solemnity and pathos to be found in classical texts on photography are slightly irritating. Photography is often alleged to be not simply one of many different forms of visual representation but a privileged one, superior to others by realistically documenting the world. It is also frequently seen as a democratizing and emancipatory form of visual representation, capable of raising awareness and helping to fight social, economic, and political injustice. Seen in light of these hopes, the history of photography would seem to be a history of failure. On the other hand, the fact that photographs are capable of *strengthening* an already existing political awareness could be observed perhaps most obviously during the Vietnam War. The revolutions in northern Africa in early 2011, have also been facilitated by digital means of communication and image dissemination, which, however, hardly caused the popular uprisings. Thus, whether or not photography is also capable of *triggering* political consciousness is a different question entirely.

Those citizens who use a camera, either as professional or as nonprofessional photographers, to inform and educate others politically (rather than taking pictures primarily for the purpose of personal gratification or aiming to gratify others aesthetically) certainly possess a "relevant political consciousness" that is seen as a condition for "being morally affected by photographs" and that they want to communicate visually to others.[14] They can be defined as citizen-photographers or photo-activists and the digital age offers them a huge palette of possibilities.[15] As photography is a medium by means of which all sorts of stories can be told, it is often far from clear, however, whether or not photographers succeed in motivating others to become politically active and in communicating their political message to the audience: they might succeed in communicating a message, but it is not automatically the message they want to communicate; they might succeed in triggering a political response, but it is not necessarily the response they are looking for. Those citizens who become politically active may do so in response to images and the conditions depicted therein, but images are hardly the only influence people are exposed to in the current multimedia world. Those citizens who do not engage in political activism may do so because they have seen too many images or because they have not seen enough images. Images are tricky vehicles for theory-building, and people's readings of and responses to images are notoriously difficult to predict. The one thing that can perhaps be said with some degree of certainty is that resistance can be a part of image reception—albeit hardly the most common one—and, as for example the public response to some Vietnam War photographs shows, sometimes it is a part of it.

In what follows I will focus on selected issues pertaining to photo-activism in the digital age: the relationship between photography, agency, and activism; the connection between visual surveillance and self-surveillance; and collaborations between artists and their subjects. I am not going to engage with images from an art historical or art theoretical perspective. Rather, the issue is one of investigating—in accordance with the overall mission of the book—the ways selected images operate within communities so as to increase the degree of political participation of the people living in these communities. Recent developments in popular communities in Rio de Janeiro are discussed here so as to respond to the necessity of engaging with images in light of concrete cases. If photography succeeds in shaping the ways democracy is being done in a given community then it will arguably serve as a model according to which residents of other communities will want democracy to operate in their own community as well.

Three Visions from Rio de Janiero

Artivism in Morro da Providência, Rio de Janeiro

Morro da Providência (Providence Hill) is a popular community in the center of Rio de Janeiro.[16] It is the location chosen by the French visual artist JR for a part of his project Women Are Heroes.[17] JR is a photographer who, connecting art with activism, considers himself an *artivist*. He is well known for portrait photographs that he exhibits, enlarged, in public spaces. By so doing he circumvents the galleries and museums that normally ensure that photographic work is seen only by a tiny portion of the population and anchors his work in the communities from which it emerged, to which it is connected, and without which it would not be possible. The depiction of women living in Morro da Providência in large-scale photographs that are then mounted on walls and stairs is an important deviation from the ways women living in Rio de Janeiro's poorer communities are normally visually represented.

In films located in popular communities, for example, women, if represented at all, are often depicted as, and thus reduced to, girlfriends of drug traffickers or powerless victims devoid of their own agency. Many representations of girls and young women follow the scheme of (would-be)-young-bride-of-drug-trafficker-soon-to-become-mother-soon-to-become-widow.[18] Such mainstream films as *Cidade de Deus* (*City of God*) and *Tropa de Elite* (*Elite Squad*), focusing on Rio's drug wars, are not particularly interested in the role of women in the communities. Likewise, documentaries such as Jeff Zimbalist and Matt Mochary's film about the cultural movement AfroReggae, *Favela Rising: a Musica é uma Arma* (*Favela Rising: Music Is a Weapon*) and Jon Blair's *Dancing with the Devil* focus on male individuals—the former on Anderson Sá, one of AfroReggae's protagonists, and the latter on a drug boss, a priest, and a policeman.[19] Patrick Neate and Damian Platt's book on AfroReggae documents the evolution of the movement and its impact on the communities, but girls and women appear—rather clichéd—as participants in dance classes and funk parties, as representatives of international organizations cooperating with AfroReggae, or as domestic help in the wealthier parts of the city.[20] The authors' heroes clearly are men. As parts of the book are about the reintegration into society of former drug traffickers, the story is necessarily to some extent a story about men. However, women are increasingly playing roles in both the drug gangs and the police, and they are playing important roles outside the drug gangs and the police as well.[21] To make these roles visible is an important part of JR's visual approach.

Living in a popular community is often said to be the single most important and almost insurmountable obstacle to individual and collective upward social mobility and political participation.[22] To make the residents of popular communities and their unfavorable living conditions visible is as important today as it was at the end of the nineteenth century when Jacob Riis did his work in New York.[23] Life in Rio de Janeiro has historically been based, and continues to be based, on pernicious forms of structural violence including the systematic exclusion of many people living in popular communities from visibility, representation, and political participation. For a long time, the popular communities were not even included in official city maps; they were represented as nonplaces, apart from, rather than a part of, the city proper. Indeed, strategies of making *in*visible, including the demolition of centrally located communities and the dislocation of their residents to remote areas, belong to the repertoire of policies aiming to maintain essentially unjust and unequal living conditions in the city, copied in recent photographic work claiming to depict the whole city while focusing only on selected, decidedly nonfavela aspects of it.[24] What is needed, then, is an approach that makes visible, people normally excluded from representation, an approach that recognizes the difficult living conditions of the people depicted without, however, reducing the people depicted to people living in difficult conditions, devoid of their own agency and in need of help. The struggle in Rio's popular communities is to "'become *gente*'—literally to become a person, to move from invisible to visible or from a nonentity to a respected human being"[25] (remember the epigraph that opened this chapter). Is visibility a necessary or a sufficient condition for becoming a respected human being? And does JR's photography help people become *gente*?

JR reportedly wanted to take pictures of women in a popular community in Rio de Janeiro, enlarge them, and stick them to the sides of houses, thus creating "a wall of faces and eyes on the side of a hill overlooking the city."[26] (It is tempting but beyond the scope of this chapter to compare the operation on the viewer of JR's wall of faces with the physical wall built around the centrally located popular community of Santa Marta in anticipation of the forthcoming major sports events in the city, allegedly to protect the environment and to control the drug traffic. This wall obviously contributes to the invisibility of the residents of the community. It is not surprising that they "feel imprisoned and demeaned by the walls."[27]) Morro da Providência seemed to be an ideal location for JR's project owing to the area's central location, its topographical features, and its historical importance to both the violent military expeditions in connection with the consolidation of the Brazilian Republic at the end of the nineteenth century and the beginning of squatter settlements in Rio de Janeiro. Thus, Morro da Providência is a very specific hill, symbolically laden. For a long time, it has also been one of the most dangerous places in the city and even nowadays it is regarded as "a chilling reminder of the status quo: a forgotten community, subject to countless police invasions, political meddling, and now army occupation."[28]

An important ingredient of JR's work is the absence of explanations, thus (according to his website) "leav[ing] the space empty for an encounter between the subject/protagonist and the passer-by/interpreter."[29] Meaning-making in connection with JR's work is not seen as a hegemonic act of designation—reflecting the politics of naming inevitably connected with such speech acts—performed by the photographer or another person with sufficient authority. Instead, it is seen as an ongoing and open-ended process of democratic negotiation between the spectator and (the image of) the subject. This approach acknowledges that different viewers may quite legitimately have different ways of substantializing their encounter with JR's photographs, not all of them in accordance with the photographer's intentions. This can hardly be otherwise given the heterogeneity and ambiguity of the city's social, cultural, and economic texture.

It also has to be noted that establishing by means of language what an image shows has become more difficult in the digital age in parallel with the tightening of the triangular relationship between photographer, subject, and spectator. In any case, designations of meaning are never universally accepted because images always carry with them "*excess* meaning."[30] Such designations always invite objections—especially nowadays as more people than ever before engage in photographic discourse and image producers have less control than ever before over the use of their images given numerous ways of digital dissemination, appropriation, and alteration of images. Thus, the photographic discourse has become more democratic with many more people than ever before participating in it. From the democratization of the photographic discourse, however, it does not follow that all participants speak from the same power position. Only by asking "Says who?" in connection with designations of meaning is it possible to identify the interests underlying a given speech act and to reveal the power relations on the basis of which reality is defined and legitimacy assigned to a given definition of reality.[31] Ideally, the negotiation between the spectator and the subject renders possible "forms of questions about power and authority which are closed or silenced within the most frequently circulated and authoritative discursive practices,"[32] thus both helping photography to fulfill a political role and people to become *gente*.

Questions about power and authority include questions about the degree to which politico-economic conditions in Rio's popular communities differ from living conditions in the wealthier parts of the city and the political mechanisms for maintaining such essentially unjust conditions. There is a close relationship between economic status and access to space: "to be confined to a small place is to be poor, while to have access to abundant light and room is to be rich."[33] This condition can certainly be observed in Rio de Janeiro, characterized by huge differences in living conditions, access to space, and exposure to light. JR's images, however, are exposed to abundant light and room. They and, with them, the people they depict, claim and reclaim urban space—space that, prior to recent pacification campaigns, was abandoned by the city authorities and captured by the drug gangs—while simultaneously refusing their confinement to a small place. JR's images operate within the space of both landscapes, owing to the quality of the images and their spectacular setting in Rio's cityscape, and architecture, owing to their organization as a wall of faces. Both spaces are effective tools for engaging vision, the one—landscape—by "seducing you or inviting you," the other—architecture—by raising such obstacles as walls: "obstacles encourage the desire to conquer them, to do something when it is forbidden, to try something when it is impossible, to intrude on a space that is not yours and has to be respected as secret or somebody else's."[34] In Morro da Providência, the space of landscape and the space of architecture appear to be mutually supportive.

Obviously, however, the "encounter" between subject and passer-by JR envisions on his website does not take place in a political or discursive vacuum. Looking is not a neutral act either because the one who watches engages in an act of interpretation and meaning-making vis-à-vis the one who is watched, who cannot normally reciprocate—especially if the one who is watched is reduced to a two-dimensional representation.[35] The "space," within which passers-by watch and assign meaning to the images, is not empty but filled with a set of clichés, stigmata, stereotypes, and prejudices that characterize the relationship between the city's popular communities and the wealthier parts. The passers-by may interpret JR's images within the existing discursive patterns rather than seeing them as an invitation to interrupt these patterns. Applying to images what has been said with regard to the mass media in general, it can then be said that images "are massively potentializing, but the potential is inhibited," among other things, by the established discursive structures within which they are regarded.[36] Success of *artivist* strategies thus is never guaranteed. Moving from invisible to visible does not automatically imply moving from a nonentity to a respected human being. Visibility, then, would seem to be a necessary but not a sufficient condition for becoming *gente*.

Surveillance and Self-Surveillance in Jacarezinho, Rio de Janeiro

In 2001, the Residents' Association of Jacarezinho, a large popular community in Rio de Janeiro's Zona Norte, had an unusual idea: given that the condominiums of the middle and upper classes in other parts of the city were protected by diverse surveillance devices, "why not adopt the same strategies in an attempt to curb police abuse and drug dealing?"[37] Why not install surveillance and self-surveillance devices operated by the Residents' Association of Jacarezinho so as to convert the popular community into a popular condominium? This idea challenged the prevalent understanding according to which such devices were reserved for the rich and the police. It challenged space controlled by the police by means of CCTV systems ("state space"[38]), but it also challenged what can be called drug space, that is to say, space controlled by the drug gangs who normally control access to and exit from many popular communities (which is not to say that state space and drug space are necessarily mutually exclusive). The initiative also challenged media space and the media's particular ways of representing popular communities. The media assumed that the initiative had at least the tacit approval of the drug gangs and that the devices, rather than deterring these gangs, would actually facilitate their operations in the community, thus undermining police efforts to curb these operations.

The criticism also reflected the disruption of "hegemonic understandings of racialized urban spaces defined by illicit activities and persons devoid of legitimate political agency" that seem to have been linked to equally hegemonic understandings of visibility, surveillance, and security.[39] For example, the surveillance cameras monitoring the condominiums of the rich are not normally criticized for facilitating the operations of the drug gangs in the rich quarters, although it is here that a considerable part of the drug consumption in the city takes place. Furthermore, by focusing on the drug trade, the media effectively downplayed the second—and from the residents' perspective, equally important—dimension motivating the Jacarezinho initiative: police violence and misconduct in the community, their "routine treatment of the poor as criminals," and the "use of excessive force" in the popular communities.[40] While Vargas discusses the newspaper discourse revolving around the aforementioned story in light of the politics of race and space in the city, I want to engage with it in terms of surveillance, sousveillance, and self-surveillance. As the initiative failed, it is not suited for empirical analysis, for example, of the question of whether or not self-surveillance images are capable in fact of altering the social relations between residents and nonresidents. It is suitable, however, for analysis of the basic lines of thought with regard to images underlying the initiative. This requires terminological clarification.

Surveillance is an umbrella term for various forms of practices linked to law enforcement agencies by means of which authorities—or private agents commissioned by the authorities—systematically monitor selected aspects of the behavior of the citizens (for example, by means of microphones and cameras). "Surveillance cameras threaten autonomy" even if they are operated in a lawful, democratically controlled and accountable way.[41] Self-surveillance describes various activities by means of which individuals and groups of individuals monitor their own behavior. It does not normally have links to law enforcement agencies on which surveillance relies. Sousveillance is a neologism derived from the French words *sous* (below) and *veiller* (to watch), describing various practices in connection with countersurveillance by means of which individuals monitor the activities of the authorities, including activities pertaining to surveillance. Sousveillance devices offer individuals technologies to monitor the activities of the authorities.[42] The public performative display and use of sousveillance devices as well as various forms of self-surveillance contest the authorities' monopoly over the production of pictures and aims to turn state space into public space, to return state space to the public.

Photo-activists may perform a control function in a political environment where increased and occasionally exaggerated surveillance generates and, arguably, necessitates some form of visual opposition, which may include civil disobedience in circumstances where private photography is not permitted, for example, in the vicinity of security installations but also, increasingly, in commercial environments such as shopping centers. While surveillance infringes on autonomy, sousveillance challenges authority. However, inasmuch as sousveillance confronts individuals with organizations backed by law enforcement agencies, it describes a fundamentally asymmetrical relationship; it is not an encounter among equals. Sousveillance reduces neither the degree to which individuals are exposed to the controlling view of the authorities nor the number of surveillance cameras operating in metropolitan areas. And sousveillance can easily become peer-to-peer monitoring "understood as the use of surveillance tools by individuals . . . to keep track of one another," establishing new hierarchies within the sousveilling community.[43] By explicitly targeting the police as representative of the prevailing social order, the Jacarezinho initiative represented a specific approach to monitoring: it combined self-surveillance with sousveillance.[44] What, then, can be said about the Jacarezinho initiative in terms of the visual construction of political space?

The first thing that can be said is that conceptually the initiative operated firmly within the logic of the surveillance society; it was not a critique of surveillance but its confirmation. While strengthening the *idea* of surveillance, it criticized the monopoly claimed by the authorities over the production, use, and interpretation of images taken in critical areas of the public space. However, practices aiming to criticize surveillance by copying its modes of operation "may support the power structures by fostering broad accessibility of monitoring and ubiquitous data collection."[45] Although aiming to monitor the police and the drug gangs, the Jacarezinho initiative also included monitoring patterns of mobility among ordinary residents, thus infringing upon their lives. It may have been internalized by individuals to such a degree that the mere refusal to participate in monitoring activities (by means of camera phones, blogs, or webcams documenting one's activities) or to use the streets monitored by cameras would have been regarded by others as suspicious (that is to say, as a sign that this person has something to hide). The sousveillance part of the initiative (vis-à-vis the police) necessarily coincided with surveillance vis-à-vis the residents. It would have strengthened the residents' association's power within the community unless the association had planned to involve ordinary residents in the evaluation of the images in a participatory and equal manner.

The second thing that can be said is that the Jacarezinho initiative did not necessarily reflect the *free* decision of individuals and groups of individuals to engage in monitoring practices. Rather than being a "willing step," countersurveillance may be "forced upon the individual as an enactment of resistance to hierarchical forms of monitoring and surveillance."[46] Thirdly, while following the logic of visually constructed political space underlying contemporary societies, the Jacarezinho initiative also interrupted its normal operating procedure: the association, by insisting on the production of and control over its own surveillance images, challenged the monopoly usually claimed by the state authorities over the production of such images in public space. From the point of view of democracy and visual agency, this aspect seems to be the most important one: just as we are still "liv[ing] in societies and cultures where individuals are spoken *for*, much more than they speak in their own name," we are also living in societies and cultures where people are visually represented by others more than they represent themselves.[47]

In a world dominated by images it is indeed critical for people at the margins to produce their own images. Representing others is a powerful contributor to cultural hegemony, which can be interrupted when marginalized groups of people represent themselves. The residents of Jacarezinho, for example, regarded surveillance images in both state space and media space as vehicles serving the interests of the people outside the community. These images were seen to represent the residents mainly as criminals and drug dealers, thus seemingly justifying police operations in the community. Indeed, one of the main reasons for the strong opposition to the initiative from outside the community seems to have been that a poor and predominantly Afro-Brazilian community dared to reject the taken-for-granted right of the rich and predominantly white part of the population (and their media outlets) to engage in acts of representation that furthered their own interests rather than the interests of the people depicted. In Jacarezinho, then, surveillance threatened the autonomy of the residents while supporting the overall structures of authority prevailing in Rio de Janeiro; the Jacarezinho initiative aimed to strengthen the autonomy of the residents while undermining the overall structure of authority in the city. The initiative, thus, was seen as a way of establishing political autonomy and reclaiming political space by symbolically refashioning the status of the community within the wider city.

Control over the interpretation of these images, however, would have been difficult. As noted earlier, the legitimacy of designations of meaning reflects power relations and established politico-discursive structures. The residents' association is compelled to operate in urban space shared with the drug gangs.[48] While the association's legitimacy in the local community may nevertheless be high, its designations of meaning in connection with self-surveillance images may appear discredited to people from outside the community: the power of speech acts depends on the social position of the speaker vis-à-vis his or her audiences; thus, different audiences may assign different degrees of legitimacy to a given speech act. The extent to which visual self-representation may have helped people hitherto excluded from political participation to gain political autonomy and to empower them—in other words, the degree to which self-surveillance images may have helped the residents of Jacarezinho to become *gente*—cannot be explored here conclusively as the initiative failed. However, if political space is visually constructed, then forms of participation in this construction have to be explored conceptually even if their translation into politics may face strong resistance. What seems to be clear is that the Jacarezinho initiative can be conceptualized in terms of photo-activism as previously defined: its aim was to inform and educate others politically, to diversify their perspectives on the popular community, to show them something about the residents that they did not know (or did not want to know), and to pave the way to more equal and just forms of social interaction between the rich and the poor parts of the city. Self-surveillance aimed to establish a more representative and participatory form of democracy in the city; for precisely this reason, it had to be suppressed.

Vik Muniz and the Catadores of Jardim Gramacho, Rio de Janeiro

If the arts and popular culture can serve as vehicles with which to increase the political engagement of marginalized groups of people, then Vik Muniz' work with *catadores* (garbage pickers) in Rio de Janeiro's major garbage dump, Jardim Gramacho, would seem to be especially important in the present context: a more marginalized group of people is hardly conceivable. The *catadores*, approximately three thousand people, represent a way of life that does not exist in the sophisticated urban imagination of the city. Like many residents of popular communities, they are indispensable for the functioning of the city given the absence of a regular system of recycling. If we agree with the editors that a performative aesthetic is based on the engagement of an artist with a given group of people and the transformation of this very group of people into artists, then, too, Muniz' work deserves special attention. According to Muniz, the *catadores* are people who, living "in the bleakest condition I have ever encountered in my entire life," survive by recycling the objects they find in Jardim Gramacho; Muniz, in turn, used the material they recycled to create, with their assistance, allegorical portraits of them.[49]

Transforming trash into art was a natural step for an artist who has for a long time used in his work such everyday objects as paper, wire, thread, dust, soil, puzzle pieces, sugar, lumps of cotton, and chocolate sauce. The production process of the series *Pictures of Garbage* (2008) is well documented in the film *Lixo Extraordinário* (Waste Land).[50] After choosing Jardim Gramacho as the location for his work with garbage, Muniz took photographs of selected *catadores*—the most charismatic and most photogenic ones—tailored after examples from art history and chose the strongest photographs or recreated in the studio some of the photographs taken on location.[51] He then projected the portraits on the floor of the studio, recreated together with the *catadores* the original scene by means of garbage, and photographed the whole installation from above with a large-format camera, thus creating large photographic portraits. Some of the artworks were subsequently sold at auctions generating substantial sums of money that flowed back into the community to the benefit of the *catadores*, including those who were not involved in the project.

"What I really want to do," Muniz explains in the film at the beginning of both the project and the film, "is to be able to change the lives of a group of people with the same material that they deal with every day" (6'15"). According to Muniz, mixing art with social projects is about "taking people away—even if it is [only] for a few minutes—from where they are and showing them another world, another place" (7'46"). Such earlier projects as portraits of children Muniz met on the island of St. Kitts—drawn with sugar and then photographed—were produced after his return to New York; rather than working "with" the children (5'35") this project was *about* them and their subject positions within an environment dominated by sugar cane plantations. His series *Pictures of Garbage*, on the other hand, represents a performative aesthetics by involving the *catadores* immediately and directly, thus introducing them into artistic experience and sharing with them artistic space. "We have to go there [to Jardim Gramacho] to see what they really need," Muniz says in the film (9'12"). The iconography of his project was to be developed both from his interaction with the *catadores* and from "what is important to them" (9'18"); what is important to them was to be found out through dialogue with them. The ideal product, according to Muniz, would be artworks with which the *catadores* could identify completely and of which they would not say, "Vik did it" but "We did it" (56'05"). At the end of the film Muniz, acknowledging initial arrogance, self-critically asks, "how am I to help anybody?" (1:25'30"). However, a certain degree of naivety, idealism, and, perhaps, arrogance would seem to have been essential for undertaking this project. In any case, they are preferable to the cynicism, fatalism, indifference, and pity often observed in attitudes toward people living in unfavorable conditions.

Is *Pictures of Garbage* what Peter Bradshaw calls "exploitative"? Bradshaw answers this question in the affirmative: "Very possibly, yes." He also ponders if "these people [are] being treated as human rubbish to be recycled into collectable art for rich people" and refers to the artist's patronizing statement that the life of the *catadores* after *Pictures of Garbage* cannot possibly be worse than it used to be before the project. However,

Bradshaw also suspects that Muniz "has an artist's ruthlessness."[52] But then the question is, to what end does he use his ruthlessness? After all, some *catadores* have been helped (although Muniz suspects that actually they have helped him more than he managed to help them). The visibility of one of the most marginalized groups of people in Rio de Janeiro has increased. For a limited period of time, the *catadores* have entered the world of fine art, which, according to Muniz, normally is "a very exclusive, a very restrictive place" (6'00"), and they have entered this world not as objects of someone else's work but as coartists, as coagents of their own image. Furthermore, the optimism radiated by Muniz—his belief in the power of art to transform people, to help them both "see another reality" and "change their way of thinking" (1:09'01")—is contagious, and the *catadores'* "appetite for life [is] inspiring" (1:25'03"). At the end of the project, some *catadores* have managed to escape from Jardim Gramacho while at least one person, missing her colleagues, returned. Jardim Gramacho stopped operating in May 2012.

It is tempting, but ultimately misleading, to discuss *Pictures of Garbage* in terms suggested by the literature on visual representations of people in pain, assuming suffering and emphasizing exploitation.[53] It is equally misleading to reduce the discussion of Muniz' work to accusations of aestheticization, focusing on depoliticization. And it is also misleading to encounter Muniz' work primarily or even exclusively through Lucy Walker's film with its penchant for social romanticism. To be sure, all these elements—exploitation, aestheticization, and social romanticism—can be found in Muniz' *Pictures of Garbage*, but his work cannot be limited to them. It can better be understood as performative and participatory photo-activism: it engages with a group of people beyond the narrow confines of the art world, it shares artistic space and experience with these people, and it does so not as an abstract artistic project but as one aiming to improve the living conditions of the people involved. Furthermore, the process of the production of *Pictures of Garbage* is as important as are the resulting photographs because it was during this process that people entered into artistic experiences by performing photography—not as objects of somebody else's art but as coartists. A certain degree of uneasiness surely remains in light of the tension between the quality of the composition of the pictures and the virtuosity of the artists, on the one hand, and the dreadful living conditions of the *catadores*, on the other hand. However, to "be compelling, there must be tension in the work; if everything has been decided beforehand, there will be no tension and no compulsion to the work."[54]

Conclusion

In this chapter I have argued that digitization offers people many possibilities to engage with the visual construction of political space and to become photo-activists. Digitization also offers diverse possibilities to turn invisibility into visibility, which is seen here as a prerequisite for political participation. Finally it is suggested that by means of digital image production, people—including marginalized people—can become agents of their own image rather than being objects of the representations of others. Representation is never neutral; it is never unpolitical. Based on the assumption that visibility is a precondition for political representation and participation, I sketched three different photographic projects located in popular communities in Rio de Janeiro: JR's artivist work in Morro da Providência, forms of self-surveillance in Jacarezinho, and Vik Muniz' performative collaboration with garbage pickers in Jardim Gramacho. There are obvious limits to a conceptual analysis such as the one suggested here. Empirical issues have to be analyzed on location: Do the women represented by JR feel accurately represented? What meaning did passers-by assign to JR's images? Did the residents of Jacarezinho share the association's enthusiasm for self-surveillance?[55] Does *Pictures of Garbage*, when exhibited in museums, make spectators think about the social realities of the city, or are the photographs just perceived as beautiful images? Whatever else the photography discussed in this chapter is and does, it is a powerful reminder that the popular communities "are not the shadow side of the city; rather, the city is the shadow side of the favelas."[56]

Notes

1. Siegfried Kracauer, "Photography," trans. Thomas Y. Levin, *Critical Inquiry* 19, no. 3 (1993): 432.

2. Silvia Vieira, "Fragments of Reality: Interview with Mário Macilau," in *BES PHOTO 2011: Mário Macilau*, eds. Clara Távora Vilar and Nuno Ferreira de Carvalho, trans. Per Christopher Foster (Lisbon: Museu Colecção Berardo/ Banco Espirito Santo, 2011), 18.

3. Jacques Rancière, *The Emancipated Spectator*, trans. Gregory Elliott (London: Verso, 2009), 103.

4. Nick Couldry, *Inside Culture: Re-imagining the Method of Cultural Studies* (London: Sage, 2000), 106.

5. See W. J. T. Mitchell, *Picture Theory: Essays on Verbal and Visual Representation* (Chicago: University of Chicago Press, 1994); Robert Hariman and John

Louis Lucaites, *No Caption Needed: Iconic Photographs, Public Culture, and Liberal Democracy* (Chicago: University of Chicago Press, 2007); Ariella Azoulay, *The Civil Contract of Photography* (New York: Zone Books, 2008); Susie Linfield, *The Cruel Radiance: Photography and Political Violence* (Chicago: University of Chicago Press, 2010); Fred Ritchin, *After Photography* (New York: W.W. Norton, 2009).

6. Frank Möller, "Associates in Crime and Guilt," in *Ethics and Images of Pain*, eds. Asbjørn Grønstad and Henrik Gustafsson (New York: Routledge, 2012), 15–32.

7. Matthew S. Witkovsky, *Foto: Modernity in Central Europe, 1918–1945* (London: Thames & Hudson, 2007), 143.

8. Ibid., 143.

9. Robin Kelsey and Blake Stimson, "Introduction: Photography's Double Index (A Short History in Three Parts)," in *The Meaning of Photography*, eds. Robin Kelsey and Blake Stimson (Williamstown, MA: Sterling and Francine Clark Art Institute/New Haven: Yale University Press, 2008), xviii.

10. Jacob Riis, *How the Other Half Lives: Studies among the Tenements of New York* (New York: Charles Scribner's Sons, 1890).

11. Hannah Arendt, *Responsibility and Judgment*, edited and with an introduction by Jerome Kohn (New York: Schocken Books, 2003), 199.

12. Ulrich Baer, "The Less-Settled Space: Civil Rights, Hannah Arendt, and Garry Winogrand," *Aperture*, no. 202 (Spring 2011): 64.

13. Hariman and Lucaites, *No Caption Needed*.

14. Susan Sontag, *On Photography* (London: Penguin, 2008), 19.

15. See Ritchin, *After Photography*, and Frank Möller, "Celebration and Concern: Digitization, Camera Phones and the Citizen-Photographer," in *Images in Mobile Communication: New Content, New Uses, New Perspectives*, eds. Corinne Martin and Thilo von Pape (Wiesbaden, Germany: VS Verlag für Sozialwissenschaften, 2012), 57–78.

16. I use the term "popular community" because the more widely used term "favela" has contributed to the stigmatization, marginalization, and criminalization of the residents of these communities. The term is increasingly being rejected by the residents. See Janice Perlman, *Favela: Four Decades of Living on the Edge in Rio de Janeiro*, Foreword by Fernando Henrique Cardoso (New York: Oxford University Press, 2010).

17. JR, *Women Are Heroes: A Global Project by JR* (New York: Abrams, 2012), 144–221. For the background of JR's project in Rio de Janeiro, see Patrick Neate and Damian Platt, *Culture Is Our Weapon: Making Music and Changing Lives in Rio de Janeiro*, Foreword by Caetano Veloso (London: Penguin, 2010), 193–95.

18. "Young-bride-soon-to-become-poor-mother" is the condition many young women in both Rio de Janeiro's and Salvador's black communities want to escape from. See Livio Sansone, "The Localization of Global Funk in Bahia and in Rio," in *Brazilian Popular Music and Globalization*, eds. Charles A. Perrone and Christopher Dunn (New York: Routledge, 2002), 149.

19. *Cidade de Deus*, directed by Fernando Meirelles (2002); *Tropa de Elite*, directed by José Padilha (2007); *Dancing with the Devil*, directed by Jon Blair (2009); *Favela Rising: a Musica é uma Arma*, directed by Jeff Zimbalist and Matt Mochary (2005). For an exception, see *Complexo: Universo Paralelo* (Complexo: Parallel Universe), directed by Mario Patrocínio (2011); see also Ricardo Martins Pereira, *Complexo: Universo Paralelo—a História de Mário e Pedro Patrocínio* (Lisbon: Editorial Presença, 2011).

20. Neate and Platt, *Culture*, 71, 55, 24–25, 1–3, respectively.

21. See, respectively, Enrique Desmond Arias, *Drugs and Democracy in Rio de Janeiro: Trafficking, Social Networks, and Public Security* (Chapel Hill: University of North Carolina Press, 2006), 32, and Tom Phillips, "Feminism and M-16s: Transforming Macho Policing in Rio," *Guardian*, July 28, 2009, http://www.guardian.co.uk/world/2009/jul/28/rio-female-drugs-policing-brazil.

22. See Perlman, *Favela*; Teresa A. Meade, *"Civilizing" Rio: Reform and Resistance in a Brazilian City, 1889–1930* (University Park: Pennsylvania State University Press, 1997), and Donna M. Goldstein, *Laughter Out of Place: Race, Class, Violence, and Sexuality in a Rio Shantytown* (Berkeley: University of California Press, 2003).

23. It should be noted that what to the outside observer seem to be unfavorable living conditions may actually be seen in a more positive light by the people actually living in these conditions. Thus, judging living conditions as unfavorable often reveals more about the values of the observer than about the perceptions of the residents. For example, the residents of popular communities often do not evaluate their living conditions in comparison with the wealthy Zona Sul (as most observers do) but with the conditions of absolute rural poverty in the Sertão—the hinterlands of Bahia and Pernambuco—from which many of them escaped; see Perlman, *Favela*, 161. On Riis, see note 10.

24. See Mario Testino, *Mario de Janeiro Testino* (Cologne, Germany: Taschen, 2009).

25. Perlman, *Favela*, 7.

26. Neate and Platt, *Culture*, 193.

27. Perlman, *Favela*, 28. Physical walls regularly attract artistic engagement; see, for example, William Parry, *Against the Wall: The Art of Resistance in Palestine* (London: Pluto Press, 2010) and Marlene Dumas, *Contra o Muro* (Porto, Portugal: Fundação de Serralves, 2010).

28. Neate and Platt, *Culture*, 195. Recent "pacification projects" in selected popular communities aim to liberate these communities from the dominance of the drug gangs and to reestablish police presence in the communities. Morro da Providência was "pacified" in the spring of 2010. See Tom Phillips, "Rio de Janeiro Police Occupy Slums as City Fights Back against Drug Gangs," *Guardian*, April 12, 2010, http://www.guardian.co.uk/world/2010/apr/12/rio-de-janeiro-police-occupy-slums.

29. See http://jr-art.net.

30. David MacDougall, *Transcultural Cinema*, edited and with an introduction by Lucien Taylor (Princeton, NJ: Princeton University Press, 1998), 68.

31. Peter Berger and Thomas Luckmann, *The Social Construction of Reality: A Treatise in the Sociology of Knowledge* (London: Penguin, 1967), 134.

32. Michael J. Shapiro, *The Politics of Representation: Writing Practices in Biography, Photography, and Policy Analysis* (Madison: University of Wisconsin Press, 1988), 130.

33. Stephen F. Eisenman, *The Abu Ghraib Effect* (London: Reaktion Books, 2007), 99.

34. Ernst van Alphen, *Art in Mind: How Contemporary Images Shape Thought* (Chicago: University of Chicago Press, 2005), 92.

35. Eisenman, *Abu Ghraib*, 99.

36. Brian Massumi, *Parables for the Virtual: Movement, Affect, Sensation* (Durham, NC: Duke University Press, 2002), 43.

37. João H. Costa Vargas, "When a Favela Dared to Become a Gated Community: The Politics of Race and Urban Space in Rio de Janeiro," *Latin American Perspectives* 33, no. 4 (2006): 50. These strategies included the installation of cameras at strategic points, the distribution of hand-held cameras, and the erection of sheet-metal gates. The following description of the Jacarezinho initiative is derived from Vargas' article.

38. Henry Porter, "Protecting the Media from the Police," *Guardian*, January 7, 2010, http://www.guardian.co.uk/commentisfree/henryporter/2010/jan/07/police-photography-public-space.

39. Vargas, "Gated Community," 51.

40. Goldstein, *Laughter*, 180.

41. Steve Mann, Jason Nolan, and Barry Wellman, "Sousveillance: Inventing and Using Wearable Computing Devices for Data Collection in Surveillance Environments," *Surveillance & Society* 1, no. 3 (2003): 347.

42. Mann, Nolan, and Wellman, "Sousveillance," 332.

43. Mark Andrejevic, "The Work of Watching One Another: Lateral Surveillance, Risk, and Governance," *Surveillance & Society* 2, no. 4 (2005): 488.

44. Strictly speaking, sousveillance refers to individuals observing organizations; in Jacarezinho, however, one organization, the residents' association, aimed to monitor another organization, the police. Owing to the power discrepancy between the residents' association and the police, such terms as coveillance or peer monitoring would seem to be inappropriate in this case; see Mann, Nolan, and Wellman, "Sousveillance," 347; Andrejevic, "Watching One Another," 479.

45. Mann, Nolan, and Wellman, "Sousveillance," 347.

46. Kingsley Dennis, "Viewpoint: *Keeping a Close Watch*—The Rise of Self-Surveillance and the Threat of Digital Exposure," *The Sociological Review* 56, no. 3 (2008): 355.

47. Couldry, *Inside Culture*, 58.

48. Perlman, *Favela*, 193, reports that many residents' associations have lost their independence and are controlled by either drug gangs or militias.

49. Leonel Kaz and Nigge Loddi, eds., *Vik* (Rio de Janeiro: Aprazível Edições, 2009), 26.

50. *Lixo Extraordinário*, directed by Lucy Walker; codirected by João Jardim and Karen Harley (2010).

51. See http://www.wastelandmovie.com/catadores.html.

52. Peter Bradshaw, "Waste Land—Review," *Guardian*, February 24, 2011, http://www.guardian.co.uk/film/2011/feb/24/waste-land-review.

53. See the essays in Mark Reinhardt, Holly Edwards, and Erina Duganne, eds., *Beautiful Suffering: Photography and the Traffic in Pain* (Williamstown, MA/ Chicago: Williams College Museum of Art/University of Chicago Press, 2007). See also Asbjørn Grønstad and Henrik Gustafsson, eds., *Ethics and Images of Pain* (New York: Routledge, 2012).

54. David Levi Strauss, *Between the Eyes: Essays on Photography and Politics*, with an introduction by John Berger (New York: Aperture, 2003), 10.

55. Vargas notes that the activists did not consult the residents before introducing the cameras. See Vargas, "Gated Community," 50.

56. Perlman, *Favela*, xxiii.

Bibliography

Andrejevic, Mark. "The Work of Watching One Another: Lateral Surveillance, Risk, and Governance." *Surveillance & Society* 2, no. 4 (2005): 479–97.

Arendt, Hannah. *Responsibility and Judgment*. Edited and with an introduction by Jerome Kohn. New York: Schocken Books, 2003.

Arias, Enrique Desmond. *Drugs and Democracy in Rio de Janeiro: Trafficking, Social Networks, and Public Security*. Chapel Hill: University of North Carolina Press, 2006.

Azoulay, Ariella. *The Civil Contract of Photography*. New York: Zone Books, 2008.

Baer, Ulrich. "The Less-Settled Space: Civil Rights, Hannah Arendt, and Garry Winogrand." *Aperture*, no. 202 (Spring 2011): 62–65.

Berger, Peter, and Thomas Luckmann. *The Social Construction of Reality: A Treatise in the Sociology of Knowledge*. London: Penguin, 1967.

Bradshaw, Peter. "Waste Land—Review." *Guardian*, February 24, 2011. http://www.guardian.co.uk/film/2011/feb/24/waste-land-review.

Couldry, Nick. *Inside Culture: Re-imagining the Method of Cultural Studies*. London/ Thousand Oaks/New Delhi: Sage, 2000.

Dennis, Kingsley. "Viewpoint: *Keeping a Close Watch*—The Rise of Self-Surveillance and the Threat of Digital Exposure." *The Sociological Review* 56, no. 3 (2008): 347–57.

Dumas, Marlene. *Contra o Muro*. Porto, Portugal: Fundação de Serralves, 2010.

Eisenman, Stephen F. *The Abu Ghraib Effect*. London: Reaktion Books, 2007.

Goldstein, Donna M. *Laughter Out of Place: Race, Class, Violence, and Sexuality in a Rio Shantytown*. Berkeley: University of California Press, 2003.

Grønstad, Asbjørn, and Henrik Gustafsson, eds. *Ethics and Images of Pain*. New York: Routledge, 2012.

Hariman, Robert, and John Louis Lucaites. *No Caption Needed: Iconic Photographs, Public Culture, and Liberal Democracy*. Chicago: University of Chicago Press, 2007.

JR. *Women Are Heroes: A Global Project by JR*. New York: Abrams, 2012.

Kaz, Leonel, and Nigge Loddi, eds. *Vik*. Rio de Janeiro: Aprazível Edições, 2009.

Kelsey, Robin, and Blake Stimson. "Introduction: Photography's Double Index (A Short History in Three Parts)." In *The Meaning of Photography*, edited by Robin Kelsey and Blake Stimson, vii–xxxi. Williamstown, MA: Sterling and Francine Clark Art Institute/New Haven: Yale University Press, 2008.

Kracauer, Siegfried. "Photography." Translated by Thomas Y. Levin. *Critical Inquiry* 19, no. 3 (1993): 421–36.

Linfield, Susie. *The Cruel Radiance: Photography and Political Violence*. Chicago: University of Chicago Press, 2010.

MacDougall, David. *Transcultural Cinema*. Edited and with an introduction by Lucien Taylor. Princeton, NJ: Princeton University Press, 1998.

Mann, Steve, Jason Nolan, and Barry Wellman. "Sousveillance: Inventing and Using Wearable Computing Devices for Data Collection in Surveillance Environments." *Surveillance & Society* 1, no. 3 (2003): 331–55.

Martins Pereira, Ricardo. *Complexo: Universo Paralelo—a História de Mário e Pedro Patrocínio*. Lisbon: Editorial Presença, 2011.

Massumi, Brian. *Parables for the Virtual: Movement, Affect, Sensation*. Durham, NC: Duke University Press, 2002.

Meade, Teresa A. *"Civilizing" Rio: Reform and Resistance in a Brazilian City, 1889–1930*. University Park: Pennsylvania State University Press, 1997.

Melo, Patrícia. *Lost World*. London: Bloomsbury, 2010.

Mitchell, W. J. T. *Picture Theory: Essays on Verbal and Visual Representation*. Chicago: University of Chicago Press, 1994.

Möller, Frank. "Associates in Crime and Guilt." In *Ethics and Images of Pain*, edited by Asbjørn Grønstad and Henrik Gustafsson, 15–32. New York: Routledge, 2012.

———. "Celebration and Concern: Digitization, Camera Phones and the Citizen-Photographer." In *Images in Mobile Communication: New Content, New Uses, New Perspectives*, edited by Corinne Martin and Thilo von Pape, 57–78. Wiesbaden, Germany: VS Verlag für Sozialwissenschaften, 2012.

Neate, Patrick, and Damian Platt. *Culture Is Our Weapon: Making Music and Changing Lives in Rio de Janeiro*. Foreword by Caetano Veloso. London: Penguin, 2010.

Parry, William. *Against the Wall: The Art of Resistance in Palestine*. London: Pluto Press, 2010.

Perlman, Janice. *Favela: Four Decades of Living on the Edge in Rio de Janeiro.* Foreword by Fernando Henrique Cardoso. New York: Oxford University Press, 2010.

Phillips, Tom. "Feminism and M-16s: Transforming Macho Policing in Rio." *Guardian,* July 28, 2009, http://www.guardian.co.uk/world/2009/jul/28/rio-female-drugs-policing-brazil.

———. "Rio de Janeiro Police Occupy Slums as City Fights Back against Drug Gangs." *Guardian,* April 12, 2010, http://www.guardian.co.uk/world/2010/apr/12/rio-de-janeiro-police-occupy-slums.

Porter, Henry. "Protecting the Media from the Police." *Guardian,* January 7, 2010, http://www.guardian.co.uk/commentisfree/henryporter/2010/jan/07/police-photography-public-space.

Rancière, Jacques. *The Emancipated Spectator.* Translated by Gregory Elliott. London: Verso, 2009.

Reinhardt, Mark, Holly Edwards, and Erina Duganne, eds. *Beautiful Suffering: Photography and the Traffic in Pain.* Williamstown, MA/Chicago: Williams College Museum of Art/University of Chicago Press, 2007.

Riis, Jacob. *How the Other Half Lives: Studies among the Tenements of New York.* New York: Charles Scribner's Sons, 1890.

Ritchin, Fred. *After Photography.* New York: W.W. Norton, 2009.

Sansone, Livio. "The Localization of Global Funk in Bahia and in Rio." In *Brazilian Popular Music and Globalization,* edited by Charles A. Perrone and Christopher Dunn, 136–60. New York: Routledge, 2002.

Shapiro, Michael J. *The Politics of Representation: Writing Practices in Biography, Photography, and Policy Analysis.* Madison: University of Wisconsin Press, 1988.

Sontag, Susan. *On Photography.* London: Penguin, 2008.

Strauss, David Levi. *Between the Eyes: Essays on Photography and Politics.* Introduction by John Berger. New York: Aperture, 2003.

Testino, Mario. *Mario de Janeiro Testino.* Cologne, Germany: Taschen, 2009.

van Alphen, Ernst. *Art in Mind: How Contemporary Images Shape Thought.* Chicago: University of Chicago Press, 2005.

Vargas, João H. Costa. "When a Favela Dared to Become a Gated Community: The Politics of Race and Urban Space in Rio de Janeiro." *Latin American Perspectives* 33, no. 4 (2006): 49–81.

Vieira, Silvia. "Fragments of Reality: Interview with Mário Macilau." In *BES PHOTO 2011: Mário Macilau,* edited by Clara Távora Vilar and Nuno Ferreira de Carvalho, translated by Per Christopher Foster, 14–21. Lisbon: Museu Colecção Berardo/Banco Espirito Santo, 2011.

Wasteland movie, http://www.wastelandmovie.com/catadores.html.

Witkovsky, Matthew S. *Foto: Modernity in Central Europe, 1918–1945.* London: Thames & Hudson, 2007.

Chapter 3

Framing the Obama Political Cartoons

Injury or Democracy?

Sushmita Chatterjee

Often denigrated as non-serious art, cartoons have a complex relation with democracy and violence. Recent years have seen the controversy with the Muhammad cartoons published in a Danish newspaper (September 2005) that led to heated debate, worldwide protests, and resulted in one hundred deaths. Seen as tacky and racist by its critics, the cartoons were also defended as an exemplification of the right to free speech and liberty of communication. The cartoon clash has waged on in the recent controversial cartoons of President Obama. The *New York Post* was accused of racism for publishing a political cartoon that, according to many, compared President Obama to a chimpanzee. In the cartoon, two police officers are shown killing a chimpanzee. One officer says, "They'll have to find someone else to write the next stimulus bill." A year before, in July 2008, cartoonist Barry Blitt had designed a magazine cover for *The New Yorker* that portrayed the Obamas as Al Qaeda followers. Some other cartoons of Obama portrayed him as a clown or in a Mexican sombrero. Described as outrageous, offensive, tacky, and racist, these cartoons have generated a whirlpool of controversy.[1]

In my essay, I study cartoons of President Obama and analyze the politics of cartoons that necessitate questioning because of their deep

---

I would like to thank Nancy S. Love and Mark Mattern for their insightful and thought-provoking comments and suggestions.

involvement with democracy and violence. Art is a dynamic weapon, and antiestablishment, antistatus quo art has been used by dissenters to critique and frame alternate perspectives. Art as politics has acted as a fiery catalyst in political mobilizations. Oftentimes seen as an inherently subversive art form in its bending of genres, and use of words and pictures, political cartoonists' insolent portrayal of power politics has marked historical precedents. From marking historical landmarks to everyday life, cartoons are present in different spaces of people's lives. Oftentimes, in everyday life, people encounter national news and see their representatives at work through editorial cartoons. Notwithstanding its democratic salience, the use of cartoons for racist propaganda is insidiously dangerous through the sleight of hand that justifies violence as humor. How do the frames of injury and democracy collide in a cartoon? Can we delineate violence from democracy and the right of free speech without cartooning democracy itself? In other words, in "Doing Democracy," how should we generate an effective response to violent pictures without cartooning democracy? My essay works through these questions via a study of two controversial political cartoons of Obama and theorizes on the multifaceted nature of cartooning democracy where the frames of injury and democracy have a sinister overlap and urge us to rethink the politics of "Doing Democracy."

This essay weaves its way through the following trajectory. I first analyze frames and framing mechanisms before studying the politics of framing in political cartoons. I use theoretical insights from social theorists Judith Butler, Mari J. Matsuda and other critical race theorists, cartoonist Art Spiegelman, and *The Daily Show* host Jon Stewart to talk about the ambivalence in framing political cartoons. Next, I specifically study two cartoons of President Obama that have received wide publicity and criticism to understand the problematic relationship between cartoons and democracy. In conclusion, my essay theorizes on the nature of cartooning democracy and its conspiracy with injury and democracy. Through this essay I grapple with multiple questions, often without providing an answer, that demand attention in the context of "cartooning democracy." The frames of analysis are often ambiguous, and a univocal answer seldom represents the complexity at hand. Thus, I ask the reader to think of incessant overlaps, blurred boundaries, and shifting terrains in order to visualize the polychromatic landscape of cartooning democracy.

Cartooning democracy refers not only to drawing a political cartoon that comments on the functioning of democracy, it also caricatures democracy and thus showcases the complexity involved in "doing democracy." Democracy as a term or practice is often conceptualized through models in order to delineate types of democracy. Political scientist Iris Marion Young draws our attention to the "aggregative" and the "deliberative" models of democracy that occupy pivotal positions in conceptualizing democracy. While the aggregative model "interprets democracy as a process of aggregating the preferences of citizens in choosing public officials and policies," the deliberative model emphasizes discussion and dialogue as democratic process.[2] Young argues that the deliberative model better serves our commitment to democratic values than the aggregative model. However, working toward an "agonistic" model of democracy, Young seeks to broaden the scope of deliberative democracy in order to make it more inclusive.[3] She thus urges us to recognize greetings, rhetoric, and narratives in an attempt to make political communication inclusive and more democratic. Young's emphasis on understanding rhetoric engages with stylistic aspects of communication such as the use of play, humor, and irony in discourse.[4] Young maintains that rhetoric has an important place in any theory of democracy. Rhetoric, or the "ways something can be said," influences the substantive content of communication considered integral to a functioning democracy.[5] Thus doing democracy necessarily involves itself with formal and informal methods of recognition and inclusion. However, can doing democracy undo itself when the way something is said provides a shelter for the content that could be antidemocratic or exclusionary? Answering this question requires an understanding of frames and framing mechanisms that determine the meaning of political messages. "Doing Democracy," if seen as an agonistic process-oriented democratization, urges us to "see" modes of inclusion and exclusion that can play with each other and slide mischievously from one to the other.

Framing Cartoons

Judith Butler writes about the complexities associated with frames, framers, framing, and being framed in her 2009 book titled *Frames of War*. She writes that frames "contain, convey, and determine what is seen."[6] Frames help to delimit the intelligibility of an image and articulate its readability. In being framed, one's terms of appearance or intelligibility are both established and manipulated, and it is generally difficult to break out of the frame. To "be framed" means to be conned, deceived, or falsely constructed.[7] However, framing is a complex process, and it is often very difficult to delineate the frames and the framing process. In a way, as social beings, we are framed through social intelligibility-making processes in gender, class, age, and other social markers. Moreover frames are reproduced and move from place to place with different meanings. Butler cites examples from digital images of Abu Ghraib and the poetry in Guantanamo circulated throughout the world as manifestations of the shifting temporal dimensions of the frame.[8] The shifting temporal dimension in frames may radically subvert a meaning play or further cement the orchestrated effect. Frames work in an insidious manner to govern social relations and determine the possibility of their rupture. Multiple frames pervade our social, political, and economic lives, and govern the construction of socialized beings. Poetry, prose, photography, films, and cartoons all have their own framing mechanisms intrinsic to their working.

Different from photographs, cartoons frame issues or characters in a number of ways. As Myra Marx Ferree, William Anthony Gamson, Jürgen Gerhards, and Dieter Rucht point out, frames delineate an object from its surroundings, and thus frames showcase the significance of an object under consideration.[9] Cartoons frame people and issues through exaggerated caricature and thus center an issue and (or) a personality. Moreover, as the aforementioned authors write, frames provide a basic foundation or shape that even when invisible can be keenly felt in the structure of the ensuing product.[10] Using this analysis to see how cartoons work as framing devices can be useful because even when cartoons are rimmed with a visible border, the frames can be explicitly hidden from sight. Cartoonists use a variety of styles in their drawing, varying from realistic drawings to more abstract figures caricatured to pull out the pith of a character or issue as considered appropriate by the particular cartoonist. As Art Spiegelman writes, "The cartoon is a drawing that gets to essences."[11] Because of the use of image and text, a cartoon has a unique framing process, specifically flexible due to the deployment of humorous meaning play.[12] While a cartoon is appreciated for its drawing and technical finesse, the use of humor to draw out ridiculous reality is particularly appreciated. An issue or character in a cartoon is framed: that is, subject to a con that amplifies humor. In a way, cartoons are all the more effective through the artistry that maintains its relation to the real and recognizable and shows the ridiculous underpinnings to the real and recognizable. A cartoon is a drawing "out," a condensed storytelling through a projected frame, and the art of image construction is used by the cartoonist to deliver messages that may be variously interpreted by the audience. Thus cartoons are framed through an artistic impulse that uses caricature mischievously to maintain its identification with the real, along with maintaining a porous frame that allows for the play with reality. I must reiterate that not all cartoons are drawn in the same way or with a similarly intended framework. However, most cartoons maintain their relation to the real (and are anthropomorphic) in order to draw out dimensions of the real in a humorous manner.[13]

If a good laugh is the only aspiration of a cartoon, why do cartoons evoke vitriolic responses? Why did cartoons evoke worldwide protests in September 2005? And, more recently, why were cartoons the center of media controversy and criticized for being racist in the context of U.S. presidential politics? In response to the Danish cartoon controversy of 2005, Pulitzer Prize-winning cartoonist Art Spiegelman wrote:

> The tragedy of the Danish "cartoon war" that erupted in February is that it really wasn't about cartoons at all. Cartoons, even hateful ones, are symptoms of a disease, not the cause. . . . The cartoon insults were used as an excuse to add more very real injury to an already badly injured world, and in this at least they succeeded. They polarized the West into viewing Muslims as the unassimilable Other; for True Believers, the insults were irrefutable proof of Muslim victimization, and served as recruiting posters for the Holy War.[14]

The "tragedy" that Spiegelman refers to killed one hundred and left eight hundred injured as millions mobilized worldwide in response to cartoon images of Muhammad drawn in the Danish newspaper *Jyllands-Posten*. Spiegelman emphasizes that the cartoons were certainly not "the" causal factor in the ensuing violence that killed many and further polarized and stereotyped the Muslims and the west. The cartoons were used to add insult to injury, and in a "badly injured world" they certainly exacerbated the situation at hand. In this article Spiegelman studies the controversial cartoons with the hope that "open discourse ultimately serves understanding and that repressing images gives them too much power."[15] Spiegelman notes the subversive valiance in cartoons and refers to historical precedents in Honoré Daumier, Art Young, and George Grosz as "masters of insult."[16] Spiegelman does not equate the controversial Danish cartoons with the work of these cartoonists, but does emphasize that the right to see and draw images that provoke and insult as mastery of the art of insult is the discerning mark of a cartoonist. Going back to my question about why cartoons evoke vitriolic responses, this might very well be the efficacy of a cartoon in drawing out that which is politically salient but unrecognized and ignored. This is not to suggest that cartoons are meant to be violent. As Spiegelman noted, the violence is oftentimes a domino effect beyond a cartoonist's control. Thus the framer can also be framed when the effects of a cartoon resonate beyond the cartoonist's orbit of control. Not being able to control the effect of a cartoon or the different meanings that are read into its frame, however, does not situate the cartoonist as "innocent" because the play with characters and issues precipitates the effect.

The act of framing and being framed involves multidimensional power politics that involve reckoning with privilege and hierarchy in social and political relations. The "act" of framing is agential and involves a position of privilege. Some people are incessantly framed and the representation formulates their identity and life possibilities. I would like to make a distinction between positive and negative framing. Positive framing enhances the life possibilities of an individual or group, like an election campaign for an individual and party. Negative framing, on the other hand, undermines and encases an individual or group, and it is very difficult to climb out of the erected frame. However, a strict demarcation between the positive and the negative is oftentimes very difficult. Cartoons can be notoriously ambivalent in the use of frames and suggested interpretations therein. By using stereotypical representations, do cartoons further cement identity formulation along those lines or, by reiterating caricatured stereotypes, can cartoons make these representations less powerful and thus subvert their negative associations?

Next, I study two widely publicized cartoons of President Obama in order to think through the aforementioned questions. The cartoons chosen for analysis in this essay are two among many cartoons of Obama. Obama has been caricatured prolifically, along with other public figures, in various forms and guises. Here, I want us to specifically think about two chosen cartoons because of the controversy that the cartoons generated and the difference of opinion exhibited by people who question different aspects of their meaning play. The two cartoons used in this essay enable us to study ambivalent frames and their (ir)resonance with democracy. The two cartoons frame this essay and beseech an exploration of injury and democracy. As we will soon see, the two cartoons work with a distinctive mode of "Other-ing" as "animal" or as "terrorist" and bring to the forefront critical issues dealing with racism, insider-outsider dynamics, and the need to keep borders secure from the Other. Interestingly, the medium used to emphasize the need for secured borders is one that plays with borders (for example, caricatured frames) and may therefore enable either a subversion of stereotypes or a further cementing of injury and harm.

Controversial Cartoons and Contending Opinions

It is important to remember that cartoons are framed by contemporary politics. The two cartoons selected for this analysis operate within a specific sociopolitical milieu and comment on events in contemporary politics and economics. The first cartoon that I want us to think about created vociferous controversy. Drawn by cartoonist Sean Delonas for the *New York Post* (February 18, 2009), the cartoon frames two policemen killing a chimpanzee, and one of the policemen says, "They'll have to find someone else to write the next stimulus bill." The cartoon works with two stories (and multiple associations) at the same time. It refers to the killing of a chimpanzee in Connecticut after it attacked a person. Also, the cartoon comments on ineffective efforts to revive the economy through the stimulus bill drafted as it is by an animal without economic acumen. In response to criticisms about the racist image that likened President Obama to a chimpanzee and thus redrew the association of African Americans with monkeys, the *New York Post* defended the cartoon as a "parody" or mockery of contemporary news and Washington's incentives to revive the economy.[17]

The New Yorker cartoon, drawn a year earlier (July 21, 2008) by Barry Blitt, shows the Obamas bumping fists dressed as Muslims and terrorists. Michelle Obama is shown carrying a gun and Osama bin Laden's picture looks on from the wall in the oval office portrayed in the cartoon. The American flag burns in the fireplace.[18]

The two cartoons generated a swirl of controversy. *The Daily Show*'s Jon Stewart commented on the official reaction of the Obama campaign to the cartoon of 2008. The Obama campaign said that the cartoons were "tasteless and offensive."[19] Stewart pointed out that the reaction should have been otherwise. To Stewart, the official reaction should have read "Barack Obama should in no way be upset about the cartoon that depicts him as a Muslim extremist, because you know who gets upset about cartoons? Muslim extremists."[20]

Stewart's "should have" is not a declarative suggestive policy statement, as he is commenting on cartoons from within the frame of a comedy show. By attempting to showcase the supposedly "should be" divide between the Obama camp and Muslim extremists, Stewart satirizes the workings of a democracy where very different viewpoints often overlap with one another. And, according to Stewart, a progressive Obama camp should maintain their difference from Muslim extremists by celebrating the freedom of expression.

Both Art Spiegelman and Jon Stewart emphasize the need to move away from censorship and let images and words do their work. As Spiegelman wrote, "repressing images gives them too much power."[21] While I do certainly believe that Spiegelman and Stewart are not advocating the irresponsible use of racist images, I worry about freedom leading to violence and democratic free speech leading to racist injury. Critical race theorists Charles R. Lawrence III, Mari J. Matsuda, Richard Delgado, and Kimberle Williams Crenshaw emphasize that free speech does not lead to "freedom" for everyone when words have the critical capacity to wound under the protection of the First Amendment. They write and

> fight for a vision of society where the substance of freedom is freedom from degradation, humiliation, battering, starvation, homelessness, hopelessness, and other forms of violence to the person that deny one's full humanity. It is a fight for a constitutional community where "freedom" does not implicate a right to degrade and humiliate another human being any more than it implicates a right to do physical violence to another or a right to enslave another or a right to economically exploit another in a sweatshop, in a coal mine, or in the fields.[22]

The critical race theorists point out that "[t]he first amendment arms conscious and unconscious racists—Nazis and liberals alike—with a constitutional right to be racist."[23] The critical race theorists emphasize and articulate one of the central dilemmas of democratic theory: How much democracy is democratic? Or, in other words, we need to rethink the relationship between democratic procedures and the actual playing out of democracy as oftentimes the two do not necessarily correlate.

The situation gets further complicated in the context of jokes, humor, and laughter. For instance, Henry Louis Gates, Jr. points out that the use of racist stereotypes by 2 Live Crew could in fact be subversive. When one listens to 2 Live Crew, the ridiculous rhetoric makes the listener "burst out laughing."[24] Kimberle Williams Crenshaw does not agree with Gates' assessment that the Crew was engaged "in a postmodern guerilla war against racist stereotypes."[25] Crenshaw writes that "[t]rading in racial stereotypes and sexual hyperbole are well-rehearsed strategies for achieving laughter; the most extreme representations often do more to reinforce and entrench the image than to explode it."[26] Crenshaw points out how racist humor has often been defended as antiracist and with the potential to overturn the stereotypes that it portrays. She substantiates her argument with reference to the "racism and sexism of Andrew Dice Clay," which could be seen as destroying stereotypes or as "simple humor not meant to be taken seriously."[27] Crenshaw's arguments make us discern the power play in ambivalent situations by studying "one's positioning vis-à-vis a targeted group."[28] For instance, do black comedians have a broader license to play with stereotypes?[29] And, in the context of the two cartoons described earlier, would knowing the race of the cartoonist enable a different reading or provide us with an image that does not wound?

Judith Butler in *Excitable Speech* eloquently summarizes Matsuda's argument: "As the linguistic rearticulation of social domination, hate speech becomes, for Matsuda, the site for the mechanical and predictable reproduction of power."[30] Butler studies the power in speech that constitutes subjects through a study of words and their power to injure. What is it that constitutes the force of an utterance? When and why do words wound? In her chapter titled "On Linguistic Vulnerability" in *Excitable Speech*, Butler refers to Toni Morrison's 1993 Nobel Lecture in Literature in which the novelist told the story of children who play a "joke" asking a blind woman to guess whether the bird they are holding is living or dead.[31] The blind woman responds by saying: "I don't know . . . but what I do know is that it is in your hands. It is in your hands."[32] Morrison thinks of the bird as embodying language and language as living. Language is thus figured as life, agency, and performance.[33] Morrison's parable offers a poignant insight into the politics of language and power that guides the enactment of agency through language. As Butler writes, "the blind woman, according to Morrison, 'shifts attention away from the assertions of power to the instrument through which that power is exercised.'"[34] The instrument through which power is exercised is an extremely important consideration when attempting to fathom both the agency of language and actual power configurations that limit or propel that agency.

Though Butler's analysis of excitable speech and its workings differs from Matsuda, Crenshaw, and others on words that wound, all the theorists draw out the potency of language to injure. The critical race theorists emphasize that "[t]he first amendment goal of maximizing public discourse is not attained in a marketplace of ideas distorted by coercion and privilege."[35] In a similar tone, Butler notes that language is a place for injury. However, the intended effects can exceed the intentions and language can "subordinate" and "enable."[36] Butler notes:

> The word that wounds becomes an instrument of resistance in the redeployment that destroys the prior territory of its operation. Such a redeployment means speaking words without prior authorization and putting into risk the security of linguistic life, the sense of one's place in language, that one's words do as one says. That risk, however, has already arrived with injurious language as it calls into question the linguistic survival of the one addressed. Insurrectionary speech becomes the necessary response to injurious language, a risk taken in response to being put at risk, a repetition in language that forces change.[37]

As Butler notes in the previous quote, language has potency to change and may unsecure the scripting of linguistic life when redeployed in a specific way. "Words that wound" may become instruments of resistance when the redeployment questions its earlier associations and works toward negating the association. Insurrectionary speech acts as an antidote to injurious language through reiterated risk-taking that forces the birth of change. Inspired by Butler's analysis, I am led to question the mechanisms through which political cartoons become instruments of resistance. Why is it important to extend an analysis of "words" that wound to the imagery of political cartoons where imaged humor has to be insulting to be effective and wherein insurrection and injury are oftentimes placed within a single frame? Does the confluence of image and text put cartoons in a different ambit of operation that is particularly amenable to meaning play and the desanctification of established stereotypes? Moreover, Butler's theorization leads me to understand that certain wounds can be democratic and inspire change. How do we demarcate between a democratic injury and an injury that spreads hate and victimizes people?

In the confluence of image and text, cartoons constitute a unique communicative media, different from film or photograph. Cartoons have played a role in varied social and political movements ranging from the Reformation, the civil rights movement, and the women's suffrage movement. The neo-Nazi movement also uses cartoons to spread its agenda.

Cartoons can be democratic or nondemocratic.[38] Parallel to the hybrid nature of cartoons, the distinction between democracy and its antithesis cannot be distinctively separated through all times and contexts. Demarcations of democratic/antidemocratic have their own interpretive ideological frames. While the chimpanzee cartoon can be seen to be an image of hate speech, others view the image through a different interpretive frame. Seeing Obama as Osama bin Laden is offensive to many in a post-9/11 world. The image can also be seen as ridiculing the stereotype that associates African Americans as Others and "outsiders" or "un-American."

The Obama cartoons urge us to delve further and question: What is the "right" interpretation? And who has the "right" to interpret? These questions are not easily or immediately answerable and have implications far beyond the scope of this essay. The easy sway of democracy into antidemocracy makes us question the nature of democratic functioning when establishing freedom does not guarantee freedom for everyone. In a way, cartoons cartoon democracy. Cartooning democracy moves beyond imaging political personalities or issues. Cartooning democracy entails a parody of the limit(ations) of a democracy.

In my essay so far, I have studied framing mechanisms in cartoons that through the use of humor maintain ambivalence and work toward cartooning democracy. Next, I look at the relation between the state and political cartoons. This relation needs to be studied in order to further uncover dimensions of cartooning democracy and the vacillation between injury and democracy.

Cartooning Democracy

Cartoons have commented on the role of the state, and personalities configuring and deconfiguring the state through periods of peace and war. Art Spiegelman rightly emphasized that the democratic role of cartoons is emphasized through their ability to speak "truth to power."[39] Political cartoons have a special relationship to the state when they provide a sparkling commentary and critique on state actions. They remain dependent on the state for stories and characters that provide food for humor, and thus, in a way, the state provides inspiration for its own nemesis. In other words, the object of critique becomes the source of creative sustenance.

Thinking about the relation between political cartoons and the state, we need to address an important question about the need for state surveillance of violent pictures and texts. Critical race theorists like Matsuda comment on the failure of the state to protect people from words that wound. To Matsuda, the state permits certain wounds, and she writes that the "victim [of hate speech] becomes a stateless person."[40] The state, according to Matsuda, needs to intervene and address these wounds. On the other hand, Butler urges us to rethink the expansion of the power of the state through the following questions: "What happens when we seek recourse to the state to regulate such speech? In particular, how is the regulatory power of the state enhanced through such an appeal?"[41]

The borders are certainly murky with regard to cartoons that are characteristically elusive and often difficult to categorize as "hate" speech. Moreover, cartoons can act as catalysts in political change. Subjecting them to state surveillance would inhibit change and frustrate political activism. Notwithstanding the democratic salience of cartoons, we do need to reckon with power politics that provide the context for activism and frame its meaning and efficacy. Oftentimes violent representations are camouflaged under humor, and even without ostensibly pinpointing specific intentions, humor can lead to violent effects in augmenting or cementing stereotypes. How do we separate a space for democracy free of violence and maintain the right of free speech without cartooning democracy itself? And, is cartooning democracy, democratic? Were the two cartoons of Obama representative of democratic politics with the right to provoke? Or, were they a cartooning of democracy under the protection of free speech?

These questions are difficult to answer in a declarative manner because of the many issues that embroil an answer. While cartooning democracy can certainly be a democratic enterprise in spreading information and helping people see the pith of an issue or character, it also showcases the frames of democratic functioning that seek to inhibit change. Political art oftentimes legitimizes and makes "right" the present through aesthetic representations. However, when writing about the ambivalent nature of political art we need to reckon with the amorphous nature of the state. The boundaries of the state are porous in terms of the movement of goods and people. And, we live in an increasingly interdependent world described by the rhetoric of globalization, neoliberalism, Empire, or Multitude.[42] Terrorism or economics is not bounded by a static framework for the state in terms of geographic cartography. The Obama cartoons drew on the economy and terrorism (the stimulus bill and Osama bin Laden) and portrayed pictures of the leader (and a campaigning candidate) of the United States. These images were certainly not restricted within the frame of a single state due to its subject matter, but also traveled in keeping with the supra-mobile nature of our contemporary world. How do we interpret these images in the context of a post-9/11 world seeking to move toward a more equitable and just relationship between people, communities, and nations?

Here I ask us to revisit the two cartoons of President Obama under introspection keeping in mind the broader picture that analyzes representations knowing full well that images present the past and draw out a future imagining. This analysis will work keeping in mind multiple frames that influence the reading and (w)riting of a cartoon. The cartoon by Sean Delonas narrates the incident that led to the killing of a chimpanzee after it mauled a woman in Connecticut. It also refers directly to the stimulus bill and ineffective efforts to promote economic growth. The frame also showcases some people hunting and others being hunted. We see two white policemen killing a black animal. The frame of racism is explicit. The cartoon makes visible the rhetoric of domination where keeping order means curbing the animality of Others who are certainly not to be trusted with important decisions or even a space for life. Social theorists like bell hooks and Harriet Ritvo have written about representations of black people as animals and the imagery of hunting that maintains power hierarchy.[43] What a dangerous image after the celebratory election of President Obama when many felt that racism in American life was gradually receding! Other presidents have oftentimes been portrayed as different animals and specifically as chimpanzees. However, history and memory demand that we separate the frames of the two kinds of representation—white people as animals and black people as animals.

The New Yorker cartoon portrays the Obamas as terrorists. Drawn before the elections, the image clearly parodies debates about Obama's patriotism and loyalty to the United States. In a post-9/11 world, the image of the burning American flag in the background shows the distrust and antipathy toward those seen as Others. The drawing of humor from portrayals of a black candidate as terrorist emphasizes the continuous distrust toward those seen as "outsiders." This cartoon contains no text except the title of the publication and the date of issue. Is Obama, drawn as an Osama bin Laden follower, "The New Yorker"?

The two cartoons represent power hierarchy and make visible a world divided between the hunters and the hunted, "us" and "them." Drawn within the frame of a cartoon, it is difficult to single out the intention and the effect of the images. Cartooning democracy is indeed a complex affair, keeping in mind Butler's note that insurrectionary language can provide an antidote to injurious speech. The two cartoons could be seen as insurrectionary if we read them as visibly representing the status quo of a divided world, and the provocation to laugh may itself lead to an introspective revelation of pervasive racism. However, the two cartoons are injurious, and the overlapping frames of insurrection and injury illuminate the complexity of cartooning democracy.

My essay has grappled with the blended trajectory of injury and democracy in its study of cartooning democracy though an analysis of two political cartoons. I have consistently emphasized the politics of framing as displayed in the two cartoons. The politics of framing is seen stylistically in the intrinsic nature of a cartoon to humorously caricature issues and characters, and in the "subject" matter of the cartoons. Broader in scope, the frame of the present world has been taken into account through a brief analysis on the role of the state in our contemporary world. Reckoning with the state becomes necessary to understand cartooning democracy stylistically and in subject matter. Stylistically and in "subject" matter, the contemporary state is as ambivalent as the frame of a cartoon in drawing borders and wanting to cross out borders of race and territory. President Obama as part of the state can also be rendered stateless. Cartooning democracy is fertile in possibilities when it yanks out the kernel of a supposedly democratic society. And, it can be dangerously violent in framing stereotypes and Others.

I hope to have demonstrated in this essay that "doing democracy" also carries with it the potential for "undoing democracy" if we work without an awareness of power configurations that situate meaning and carry specific implications for different groups of people. The use of humor and play to showcase political issues is often democratic in permitting alternative conceptualizations and permitting a space for critique. However, methods of inclusion may turn into exclusionary tactics. This ambivalence with regard to inclusion and exclusion takes us back to the discussion in the beginning of my essay on broadening the scope of deliberative democracy through agonistic contestation. Iris Marion Young had asked us to consider styles of communication in a democracy where what is said influences how it is said and vice versa. Attentive to inclusionary modes of political practice, Young asked for recognition of play, humor, and irony as political rhetoric that would considerably broaden the orbit of democratic practices. Working with Young's insights about various styles of communication and Butler's emphasis on framing and the role of *Excitable Speech*, I analyzed two political cartoons and their tricky waltz with democracy and injury, inclusion and exclusion. Through the conception of "cartooning democracy," I seek to understand this ambivalence in the functioning of everyday democracy where creative modes of communication may not necessarily inspire freedom for everyone. Cartooning democracy as agonistic play straddles injury with democracy, and ambiguity with the potential to reframe.

Recognizing the potential and problems pertaining to cartooning democracy, I remain enthused by Judith Butler's inspiration for change through an understanding of frames and being framed. As Butler piquantly writes, "To learn to see the frame that blinds us to what we see is no easy matter."[44] Thus, I urge us to "see," and "see" with democratic yearning, multiple frames that restrict and exclude. Perhaps, we can endeavor to "see" like Toni Morrison's blind woman who cannot see images and says, "I don't know . . . but what I do know is that it is in your hands. It is in your hands."[45]

Notes

1. For additional discussion, see Dylan and Ethan Ris, "The Five Most Racist Obama Cartoons?" *Politics Daily*, http://www.politicsdaily.com/2009/02/19/the-five-most-racist-obama-cartoons/.

2. Iris Marion Young, *Inclusion and Democracy* (New York: Oxford University Press, 2000), 19. As Young writes, "In the deliberative model democracy is a form of practical reason. Participants in the democratic process offer proposals for how best to solve problems or meet legitimate needs, and so on, and they present arguments through which they aim to persuade others to accept their proposals" (22).

3. Young refers to Chantal Mouffe and her emphasis on "agonistic pluralism," which is more attentive to diverse political expressions and takes note of "antagonism and contestation as endemic to the process of democratic politics." Ibid., 49.

4. Ibid., 65.

5. Ibid., 64–65.

6. Judith Butler, *Frames of War: When Is Life Grievable?* (London: Verso, 2009), 10. Myra Marx Ferree, William Anthony Gamson, Jürgen Gerhards, and Dieter Rucht note the different meanings of frames and framing, and call a frame a "thought organizer." They note three meanings of frame. The first meaning refers to a frame as "rim for encasing." Here, "A Frame in this sense specifies what is relevant and what should be ignored." Second, a frame gives "shape or support." And the third meaning is to "rig evidence." The authors use the first

two meanings in their work and write that "[f]raming deals with the *gestalt* or pattern-organizing aspect of meaning." See their *Shaping Abortion Discourse: Democracy and the Public Sphere in Germany and the United States* (New York: Cambridge University Press, 2002), 13, 14.

7. Butler, *Frames of War*, 11.

8. Butler writes, "This happened when the photos of Guantanamo prisoners kneeling and shackled were released to the public and outrage ensued; it happened again when the digital images from Abu Ghraib were circulated globally across the internet, facilitating a widespread visceral turn against the war. What happens at such moments? And are they merely transient moments or are they, in fact, occasions when the frame as a forcible and plausible con is exposed, resulting in a critical and exuberant release from the force of illegitimate authority?" Ibid., 11.

9. Ferree et al., *Shaping Abortion Discourse*, 14.

10. Ibid., 14.

11. Art Spiegelman, *MetaMaus: A Look Inside a Modern Classic, Maus* (New York: Pantheon, 2011), 168.

12. I base my understanding of cartoons on the works of Scott McCloud, Will Eisner, and Art Spiegelman. McCloud examines cartooning as a form of "amplification through simplification" as a cartoon focuses on specific details and amplifies meaning. He writes, "When we abstract an image through cartooning, we're not so much eliminating details as we are focusing on specific details. By stripping down an image to its essential 'meaning,' an artist can amplify that meaning in a way that realistic art can't." See Scott McCloud, *Understanding Comics: The Invisible Art* (New York: HarperPerennial, 1994), 30. Spiegelman notes that cartoons sit on the "hyphen between words and pictures" and have a "predisposition toward insult." Art Spiegelman in "Drawing Blood: Outrageous Cartoons and the Art of Outrage," *Harper's Magazine* (June 2006): 45.

13. Anthropomorphized drawings are used effectively in animal cartoons that poke fun at humans and have very little to do with the animals through which they speak. This is often called the "Talking Animal" genre of cartooning.

14. Spiegelman, "Drawing Blood," 43.

15. Ibid., 43.

16. Ibid., 45.

17. See Ashley Fantz, "Racism Row over Chimp Cartoon Sparks Debate" (CNN, February 19, 2009) http://www.cnn.com/2009/US/02/19/chimp.cartoon.react/index.html. See also http://www.nypost.com/opinion/cartoons/delonas.htm.

18. See http://www.newyorker.com/online/covers/slideshow_blittcovers#slide=1.

19. In http://www.thedailyshow.com/watch/tue-july-15-2008/obama-cartoon.

20. Ibid.

21. Spiegelman, "Drawing Blood," 43.

22. Mari J. Matsuda, Charles R. Lawrence III, Richard Delgado, and Kimberle Williams Crenshaw, eds., *Words That Wound: Critical Race Theory, Assaultive Speech, and the First Amendment* (Boulder, CO: Westview Press, 1993), 15.

23. Ibid., 15.

24. See Kimberle Williams Crenshaw, "Beyond Racism and Misogyny: Black Feminism and 2 Live Crew," in Matsuda et al., *Words That Wound*, 128.

25. Ibid.

26. Ibid.

27. Ibid., 129.

28. Ibid.

29. Ibid.

30. Judith Butler, *Excitable Speech: A Politics of the Performative* (New York: Routledge, 1997), 19.

31. Ibid., 6.

32. Toni Morrison, quoted in Butler, *Excitable Speech*, 6.

33. Toni Morrison reads the blind woman as a writer who "thinks of language partly as a system, partly as a living thing over which one has control, but mostly as agency—as an act with consequences. So the question that the children put to her, 'Is it living or dead?,' is not unreal, because she thinks of language as susceptible to death, erasure . . ." Toni Morrison, quoted in Butler, *Excitable Speech*, 6–7.

34. Ibid., 7.

35. Mari J. Matsuda and Charles R. Lawrence III, "Epilogue: Burning Crosses and the R. A. V. Case," in Matsuda et al., *Words That Wound*, 136.

36. Butler, *Excitable Speech*, 163.

37. Ibid.

38. I work with a notion of democracy that is characterized by the urge to spread rights and inclusivity, rather than to limit the rights of others and spread violence and hate. Democratic theory is a rich area of study, and different schools of thought have their own interpretation of democracy. While Liberals emphasize rights and equality, Marxists urge us to move beyond the liberal conception of democracy that is essentially the freedom of capital. Borrowing from different schools of thought, I understand democracy to be a process-oriented growth of just and equitable representation. I will discuss "democracy" in more detail in the concluding portion of this essay.

39. Spiegelman, "Drawing Blood," 46.

40. Quoted in Butler, *Excitable Speech*, 73.

41. Ibid., 77.

42. Michael Hardt and Antonio Negri in their seminal book *Empire* write about the dominance of a "new global form of sovereignty," Empire. Different from imperialism characterized by an "extension of the sovereignty of the Eu-

ropean nation-states beyond their own boundaries," Empire does not establish a territorial center of power and does not have fixed borders. Hardt and Negri maintain that the United States does not compose Empire, though it "does indeed occupy a privileged position in Empire." See Michael Hardt and Antonio Negri, *Empire* (Cambridge, MA: Harvard University Press, 2000), xii, xiv. The distinction between Empire and imperialism is extremely interesting and needs to be further refined as cultural imperialism may not end with economic globalization and economic globalization does not guarantee a borderless world for everyone living in a "global" society. More recently, Hardt and Negri have emphasized the politics of the "Multitude." The Multitude is "the living alternative that grows within Empire." A Multitude is an "open and expansive network" that enables us to "work and live in common." See Michael Hardt and Antonio Negri, *Multitude: War and Democracy in the Age of Empire* (New York: Penguin Books, 2004), xiii–xiv.

43. bell hooks in *Black Looks* writes about animalistic representations of black people, the equation of black people with "primitive" culture, and the commodification of "primitive" culture through representation of black people in popular culture. Hooks writes, "There is a direct and abiding connection between the maintenance of white supremacist patriarchy in this society and the institutionalization via mass media of specific images, representations of race, of blackness that support and maintain the oppression, exploitation, and overall domination of all black people." See bell hooks, *Black Looks: Race and Representation* (Cambridge, MA: South End Press, 1992), 2. Harriet Ritvo writes about how the bodies of dead animals were used to showcase British power, and remnants of animals' bodies "clearly alluded to the violent, heroic underside of imperialism." See Harriet Ritvo, *The Animal Estate: The English and Other Creatures in the Victorian Age* (Cambridge, MA: Harvard University Press, 1987), 248.

44. Butler, *Frames of War*, 100.

45. Quoted in Butler, *Excitable Speech*, 6.

Bibliography

Blitt, Barry. Cover Illustration. *The New Yorker*. July 21, 2008. http://www.newyorker.com/online/covers/slideshow_blittcovers#slide=1.

Butler, Judith. *Excitable Speech: A Politics of the Performative*. New York: Routledge, 1997.

———. *Frames of War: When Is Life Grievable?* London: Verso, 2009.

Crenshaw, Kimberle Williams. "Beyond Racism and Misogyny: Black Feminism and 2 Live Crew." In Matsuda et al., *Words That Wound*, 111–32.

Delonas, Sean. Illustration. *New York Post*. February 18, 2009. See http://www.nypost.com/opinion/cartoons/delonas.htm.

Eisner, Will. *Comics and Sequential Art: Principles and Practices from the Legendary Cartoonist.* Tamarac, FL: Poorhouse Press, 1985.

Fantz, Ashley. "Racism Row over Chimp Cartoon Sparks Debate," CNN. February 19, 2009. http://www.cnn.com/2009/US/02/19/chimp.cartoon.react/index.html.

Ferree, Myra Marx, William Anthony Gamson, Jürgen Gerhards, and Dieter Rucht. *Shaping Abortion Discourse: Democracy and the Public Sphere in Germany and the United States.* New York: Cambridge University Press, 2002.

Hardt, Michael, and Antonio Negri. *Empire.* Cambridge, MA: Harvard University Press, 2000.

———. *Multitude: War and Democracy in the Age of Empire.* New York: Penguin Books, 2004.

hooks, bell. *Black Looks: Race and Representation.* Cambridge, MA: South End Press, 1992.

Matsuda, Mari J., and Charles R. Lawrence III. "Epilogue: Burning Crosses and the R. A. V. Case." In Matsuda et al., *Words That Wound,* 133–36.

Matsuda, Mari J., Charles R. Lawrence III, Richard Delgado, and Kimberle Williams Crenshaw, eds. *Words That Wound: Critical Race Theory, Assaultive Speech, and the First Amendment.* Boulder, CO: Westview Press, 1993.

McCloud, Scott. *Understanding Comics: The Invisible Art.* New York: HarperPerennial, 1994.

Ris, Dylan, and Ethan Ris. "The Five Most Racist Obama Cartoons?" *Politics Daily.* http://www.politicsdaily.com/2009/02/19/the-five-most-racist-obama-cartoons/.

Ritvo, Harriet. *The Animal Estate: The English and Other Creatures in the Victorian Age.* Cambridge, MA: Harvard University Press, 1987.

Spiegelman, Art. "Drawing Blood: Outrageous Cartoons and the Art of Outrage." *Harper's Magazine* (June 2006): 43–52.

———. *MetaMaus: A Look Inside a Modern Classic, Maus.* New York: Pantheon, 2011.

Stewart, Jon. *The Daily Show,* July 15, 2008. http://www.thedailyshow.com/watch/tue-july-15-2008/obama-cartoon.

Young, Iris Marion. *Inclusion and Democracy.* New York: Oxford University Press, 2000.

Part III

Monuments and Memorials

Chapter 4

The Moral Economy

"Doing Democracy" via Public Day of the Dead Rituals

REGINA MARCHI

Introduction

The 1960s and 1970s marked a pivotal period in U.S. history, when Latinos and other people of color were collectively engaged in struggles to gain civil rights, public recognition, and respect within mainstream Anglo society. Blossoming in the 1970s (with roots going back to the 1930s), the Chicano[1] Movement began in California and the American Southwest as a political and cultural movement that worked on a broad cross-section of issues affecting the Mexican American community. These included farm workers' rights; Native American land rights; efforts to improve educational opportunities; voting and political rights; and the public celebration of cultural traditions. Emerging at a time of widespread activism by disenfranchised populations, the Chicano Movement was influenced by black civil rights struggles, the American Indian Movement, the women's liberation movement, and the anti–Vietnam War Movement.[2] Chicano activists identified strongly with anticolonial struggles around the world (for example, in Puerto Rico, Cuba, Vietnam, and Africa) and proclaimed solidarity with these movements for self-determination. They supported the struggles of elderly Filipinos in San Francisco trying to avoid eviction from affordable

---

Some material from this essay originally appeared in Regina Marchi, *Day of the Dead in the USA: The Migration and Transformation of a Cultural Phenomenon* (New Brunswick, NJ: Rutgers University Press, 2009).

housing; striking coal miners in Kentucky; and the boycott of Nestlés because of that company's aggressive promotion of infant formula to nursing mothers in Africa.[3] At home in the United States, Chicanos were waging multipronged political battles to improve the segregated and substandard schooling provided to Latino children (who were typically tracked into vocational rather than university paths). They also worked to increase Latino voter registration and representation in the U.S. political system and combated the labor abuses, substandard housing, and environmental contamination facing Latino and other minority neighborhoods.

In discussing how cultural traditions can provide the moral force and infrastructure needed to critique the dominant society, cultural critic E. P. Thompson argued that the popular food riots of eighteenth-century England were not merely compulsive responses to economic stimuli. Rather, they were a "moral economy" form of social protest—"self-conscious behavior modified by custom, culture and reason" in which people used moral indignation to defend community rights and challenge official descriptions of reality.[4] The grievances expressed by the common people, he explained, were grounded in traditional views of norms and obligations that "operated within a popular consensus as to what were legitimate and what were illegitimate practices" among various sectors of society, such as workers, consumers, business, and government.[5] This was a community or class response to crisis that expressed resistance to exploitation and challenged the authorities, on moral grounds, to attend to the common good. Tracing the origins of the highly organized eighteenth-century English working class to long-standing social traditions of mutual aid, he argued that the widespread participation of common folk in communal rituals and ceremonies sustained collectivist values that, in turn, allowed the working class to maintain solidarity under difficult political conditions. Chicano Day of the Dead celebrations frequently operate along a moral economy model of protest, encouraging moral reflection on issues of political importance and revealing dimensions of repression too often overlooked by the dominant culture. As we shall see, they illustrate Thompson's view that cultural ritual is not merely an extraneous variable but a political necessity in struggles for justice.

Political Art as Alternative Media

In order to combat the long-standing injustices facing Latinos in the United States, Chicanos felt it was crucial to communicate with the public—both Latino and non-Latino—to increase consciousness and encourage political organizing. But how could this be accomplished when so few Latinos occupied positions in the mass media, and both the news and popular media routinely portrayed Latinos via negative stereotypes? Historically, U.S. news coverage depicted Mexicans and other Latinos as lazier, less intelligent, less moral, and more prone to crime than Anglo-Americans.[6] The same patterns of representation existed in magazine and television advertising.[7] In Hollywood films, Latinos were stereotyped as bandits, gang bangers, over-sexed Latin lovers, dangerous and flirty temptresses, or doltish buffoons.[8] Mainstream U.S. news portrayed Latinos primarily within "problem" and "social disadvantage" frames, as people who lived in crime-infested neighborhoods, lacked basic educational and job skills, and were not legitimate U.S. citizens.

In addition to legal and advocacy efforts toward diversifying the mainstream media and improving representations of minorities, Chicanos engaged in political and cultural media work that included the creation of literature, theater, music, and visual art meant to transmit Chicano histories and political struggles. They created *arte contestatario*—protest art designed to challenge mainstream racist tropes, in which they integrated culture, art, and politics for the goal of building community and progressive political change.[9] For a minority community unaccustomed to seeing positive images of itself in the mass media, the significance of publicly honoring collective experiences and cultural traditions cannot be overstated.

Neglected and abandoned buildings in Mexican American neighborhoods became canvases for giant public murals that educated onlookers about Aztec legends, Mexican revolutionary heroes and heroines, and Mexican American labor struggles such as the grape boycott of the United Farm Workers' Union.[10] Chicano performance artists and theater troupes traveled to urban neighborhoods and rural farming towns producing *teatro popular*—a street theater tradition common in Mexico—to educate immigrant laborers about their legal rights in the United States. The most prominent example of this was the itinerant bilingual theater troupe El Teatro Campesino, which performed free public theater particularly aimed at Mexican American farm workers. Performances portrayed the daily realities of Mexican Americans, while educating people about the collective political organizing efforts taking place to combat racial injustices.[11] Chicano poets, novelists, musicians, and painters expressed both the beauty and pain of the Mexican American experience, communicating alternative and oppositional messages that represented the first time that Mexican American culture was so visibly celebrated in the U.S. public sphere.[12]

In the 1970s, rejecting the Eurocentrism that had dominated the United States for generations, many racial minorities began to consciously study and reclaim their cultural roots—languages, clothing, art, music, spiritual practices, and other ancestral traditions that had been lost via slavery, colonization, reservation systems, or forced assimilation. Since there were no Latino studies programs in U.S. universities at the time, many Chicanos (most of whom were born and/or raised in the United States) undertook independent historical research and traveled to Mexico to learn about the country's history and cultural traditions.[13] In particular, they went to southern Mexico to study the Indigenous cultures they associated with their ancestral roots.[14] Then as now, southern Mexico was renowned for having the country's largest concentration of Indigenous peoples. Then as now, it was the poorest, most "underdeveloped" region of Mexico, and its inhabitants were considered by those in the north to be the custodians of Mexico's most authentic cultural traditions. Many Chicanos dedicated themselves to learning Indigenous languages, Mayan weaving, Aztec *danza*,[15] or other Indigenous arts. Known as neo-Indigenism (a movement to reaffirm and celebrate the contributions and achievements of ancient Indigenous civilizations), the collective espousal of Mexico's Indigenous past became a dominant theme of Chicano artistic expression. A particularly strong influence on Chicano art was the pageantry of Mesoamerican sacred rituals, religious symbols, and spiritual beliefs.[16] With its stunningly colorful rituals, the celebration of El Día de los Muertos, or "The Day of the Dead," would become one of the most widely observed and cherished annual traditions of the Mexican American community.

Folk Rituals and Politics

Associated with a preindustrial past that is seemingly unrelated to the modern world, ethnic folk rituals practiced in the United States are often considered to be apolitical activities that serve only to entertain. As a result, rituals as alternative media for critiquing dominant systems of power have been relatively neglected by social scientists. Yet, critical cultural scholars have argued that folk rituals are *not* merely substitutes for politics, but communicate important messages about identity and social struggle that help shape individual and collective practice.[17] Much current thinking about the political importance of folk rituals is influenced by the work of Antonio Gramsci and E. P. Thompson. Gramsci discouraged the conceptual separation between "modern" and "folk" culture, believing that folk practices had the potential to challenge hegemonic beliefs and "bring about the birth of a new culture." Thompson felt that folk practices were contexts in which working-class people could define and express their own values, which could be "antagonistic to the overarching system of domination and control."[18] Similar to the protests of the Mothers of the Disappeared in Chile and Argentina, politicized Day of the Dead rituals in the United States have allowed what anthropologist Michael Taussig calls "the tremendous moral and magical power of the unquiet dead to flow into the public sphere, empower individuals and challenge the would-be guardians of the Nation-State."[19]

Before discussing politicized Day of the Dead activities in the United States, it is worth observing the historical connection between Day of the Dead and popular resistance in Latin America. Much to the chagrin of Spanish missionaries in Latin America, Indigenous peoples forced to convert to Catholicism resolutely retained "pagan" customs of honoring their ancestors.[20] Finding it impossible to eradicate them, Catholic missionaries eventually "tolerated" these rituals, as long as they were observed on the Catholic holy days of All Saints' Day and All Souls' Day.[21] While remembrance rituals were not overtly political activities, honoring the departed invited contemplation about the myriad inequities faced by Indigenous peoples living under colonialism. To remember the dead, after all, was also to remember how and why they died. In colonial times, death among the Indigenous majority was, more often than not, the result of preventable phenomena such as malnutrition, poverty, or abuse by colonial authorities. Thus, the period set aside each year to remember the dead, known colloquially as "The Day(s) of the Dead," was simultaneously a space in which the poor could publicly express frustration toward the injustices of the existing social order responsible for so many untimely deaths. With normal inhibitions lowered during "festival time," pent-up emotions were manifested through riotous festivities and drunkenness in Mexico's cemeteries during the Days of the Dead.[22]

Max Gluckman, Peter Burke, and Mikhail Bakhtin have all famously described the place of festival in traditional societies as a time of social inversion—a privileged time when what was often thought privately could finally be expressed publicly with relative impunity.[23] The unregulated "carnivalesque" atmosphere that historically accompanied public festivals provided a space in which the world was temporarily turned upside down, social hierarchies were disrupted, and "truths" were contested. Day of the Dead in colonial America was such a time, when special foods and alcoholic beverages were prepared in honor of the dead, and boisterous music, ritual dancing, and street processions occurred. Historical evidence suggests that the special closeness people felt with departed loved ones during this holiday stimulated communal reflections about the conditions under which they lived and died. Writing on the resistance of Andean peasants to Spanish colonial rule, Steve J. Stern contends that a certain interplay existed between the heightened moral consciousness experienced while ritually remembering the dead and an increased collective consciousness of material exploitation.[24] Similarly, William B. Taylor notes that by connecting communities to their past, cemeteries in colonial Latin America were frequently sites for rebellions.[25] So threatening to the ruling elites were the social tensions expressed during the Days of the Dead in Mexico that the Spanish Royal Office of Crime passed decrees in 1766 prohibiting gatherings in cemeteries and banning the sale of alcohol after 9:00 p.m. during the Days of the Dead.[26]

A Brief Description of Day of the Dead in Mexico

The Days of the Dead (observed officially on November 1 and 2) are a fusion of Roman Catholic All Saints' Day and All Souls' Day activities and pre-Columbian Indigenous rituals for remembering ancestors. Like many other Latin Americans, Mexicans routinely visit cemeteries between October 30 and November 2 to clean and decorate family graves.[27] In predominantly Indigenous areas of the country, picnics and vigils are held in the cemeteries to await the souls traditionally believed to visit the living at this time of the year, and elaborate home shrines are constructed to honor the dead. These altars have pre-Columbian roots as harvest offerings for the deceased and are referred to in Spanish as *ofrendas* ("offerings"). The southern regions of Oaxaca, Michoacán, Puebla, Chiapas, Vera Cruz, and Yucatán (home to Mexico's highest concentration of Indigenous peoples), are known for their elaborate Day of the Dead altars. Reflecting religious and cultural syncretism, they are laden with Indigenous foods such as maize, squash, grains, fruits, legumes, tortillas, and fermented corn or grain beverages that were offered to the dead in pre-Columbian times, along with Catholic iconography such as images of Jesus, the Virgin Mary, or various saints, along with crucifixes, rosary beads, statuettes of angels, and votive candles emblazoned with Catholic images. Tables, shelves, or crates are used to create multitiered altars, which may be crowned with large arches or square frameworks overlaid with marigolds and/or hanging fruits, (said to be gateways to symbolically welcome the traveling spirits home).[28] Photos of the deceased may also be placed on altars.

A Chicano Tradition Is Born

Prior to the 1970s, public praise of Latino cultures was rare in U.S. art and educational institutions as well as in the mainstream media. When Latino heritage was noted at all, it was exclusively Spanish rather than Indigenous ancestry that was lauded. In both Latin America and the United States, Eurocentrism had relegated "Indian" heritage to a shameful status so that Indigenous people and even mixed-blood Mestizos[29]—the majority of the Mexican population—were consigned to inferior socioeconomic status vis-à-vis Europeans or Anglos. Rejecting this mentality, Day of the Dead celebrations and other actions emerging from the Chicano Movement emphatically commemorated the customs and beliefs of working-class Mestizo and Indigenous Mexicans.

Prior to the 1970s, most Mexican Americans did not identify with Indigenous Mexican customs and observed November 1 and 2 as did other U.S. Catholics: by attending Mass, visiting family gravesites, and preparing a special family meal. In Spanish and English, they typically referred to this holiday by the Catholic nomenclature of All Saints' Day and All Souls' Day, rather than the term El Día de los Muertos (commonly used today in the United States to refer to these dates). At the time, sugar skulls, *pan de muerto* (bread of the dead), and the elaborate Indigenous altar-making styles of southern Mexico were unknown to most Mexican Americans.[30] However, as Chicanos traveled to Mexico's Indigenous communities and learned about these traditions, they brought them back to the United States, where Día de los Muertos art installations and educational programming were showcased in galleries, community centers, schools, and, later, in major museums such as the National Smithsonian Institute and New York City's Metropolitan Museum of Art.

These altar-making rituals were "invented traditions"—hybridizations of Indigenous and Catholic spiritual practices mixed with U.S. popular culture and politics to reflect and celebrate varied components of Mexican American identity.[31] Mexican Day of the Dead sugar skull imagery quickly became popular as Chicano iconography because of the perceived connection of the skull treats to ancient Aztec skull motifs. Chicana educator Yolanda Garfias Woo, one of the first to introduce Day of the Dead curricula in U.S. schools, noted the "attention-grabbing" appeal of the sugar skulls as a motif for the Chicano Movement. Compared with other holidays observed in the United States, she argued, Day of the Dead "was *so far out!* It was a shocking kind of thing to be doing. It literally *shocked* the non-Latino community. And that's exactly the emphasis that Chicanos were looking for. They wanted to make a statement and make it *big*."[32]

Chicanos exercised syncretism by combining the personal and the political. Besides honoring departed family and friends via public altar installations, they transformed the holiday into a commemoration of the collective "ancestors" of all Latinos, creating altars for beloved Latino singers, actors, writers, activists, and artists (for example, Frida Kahlo, Diego Rivera, Che Guevara) as a way to educate the public about the many contributions of Latinos to U.S. and world culture. In addition, they utilized the holiday's focus on remembrance to criticize dominant U.S. power structures by creating altars that raised public awareness of socio-political causes of death disproportionately affecting people of color.[33] In so doing, they enlarged a tradition originally reserved for family members into one that also honored groups of people not personally known to the altar makers. Chicano altar installations have commemorated Mexican American farm workers poisoned by pesticides; Latino migrants who died in attempts to cross the U.S./Mexican border in search of better jobs; factory workers killed in alarming numbers in industrial accidents; victims of U.S.-funded wars in Chile, Argentina, El Salvador, Guatemala, Vietnam, Iraq, and Afghanistan; and other political issues.

Early Beginnings

The first documented Day of the Dead activities in U.S. art gallery spaces occurred in 1972, organized separately by artists at Self-Help Graphics, in Los Angeles, and La Galería de la Raza, in San Francisco. Self-Help, a community-based visual arts center in the predominantly Latino neighborhood of East Los Angeles, hosted its inaugural Day of the Dead street procession in which people dressed up as skeletons and walked to a local cemetery. Latino Studies professor Sybil Venegas notes that none of the Chicanos who helped organize this initial celebration were personally familiar with Day of the Dead, but learned about it from Mexican-born and -raised artists Antonio Ibañez and Carlos Bueno, who were among the founders of Self-Help Graphics. She notes: "While these artists were initially unfamiliar with El Día de los Muertos, they were undoubtedly attracted to its potential to generate cultural awareness, ethnic pride, and collective self-fulfillment for the East Los Angeles community."[34] Through Ibañez and Bueno, the Self-Help Graphics community of artists and supporters were introduced to Mexican skull imagery and Indigenous-style altar making. In subsequent years, performances by the political theater troupe El Teatro Campesino became part of the festivities. Over time, Self-Help's Day of the Dead procession expanded to include Aztec dancing, mariachi music, giant skeleton puppets and stilt walkers, stylized Chicano "low rider" cars, decorated floats, and more. Self-Help artists worked with local schools to educate students and teachers about Day of the Dead, so each year hundreds of children attended the annual processions, displaying their Day of the Dead art projects. Workshops teaching the public how to make sugar skulls, skeleton masks, and altars became an important part of the organization's annual Day of the Dead festivities.

In the same year, Chicano art gallery La Galería de la Raza, located in the heart of San Francisco's predominantly Latino "Mission" district, held the city's first Day of the Dead altar exhibition, which, along with related educational activities, also evolved into an annual city tradition. In 1981, La Galería organized its first Day of the Dead street procession with about twenty-five participants who walked around the block holding candles and photos of departed loved ones. Within just a few years, the procession burgeoned into an annual manifestation of thousands, with Aztec dance groups, curbside altar installations, sidewalk chalk art, giant puppets, portable sculptures, Cuban Santería practitioners, flame throwers, and an itinerant Jamaican steel drum band. Individuals there to honor deceased family members walked alongside contingents of activists seeking to draw public attention to sociopolitical causes of death, such as U.S. military interventions abroad, gun violence, and AIDS. The procession today attracts an estimated twenty thousand participants[35] of diverse ages, races, and ethnicities, and is considered the largest Day of the Dead procession in the United States. Inspired by the activities of these two Chicano art galleries, myriad community centers, schools, libraries, museums, folk art stores, city parks, and commercial districts throughout California, and later, throughout the rest of the United States, developed annual Day of the Dead programming.

Activist Art

Because Chicano Day of the Dead celebrations in the United States were a cultural reclamation project that was part of larger social justice organizing work, the altars on exhibit often expressed political themes. The celebration's geographical migration and change of status from private and family-centered to secular and public liberated it from traditional Latin American religious frameworks, enabling it to become a performative expression of U.S. Latino identity, designed to communicate messages to the living, as well as the dead. Advertised via TV, radio, print media, and the internet, U.S. exhibits and celebrations are today seen by hundreds of thousands of spectators each year, as they communicate about "life and death" issues that go unreported or underreported in the mainstream news. Through public altar exhibitions, vigils, poetry slams, and street processions, many Latinos who are marginalized from formal channels of U.S. political participation (such as running for public office, voting, or writing to elected officials) due to barriers related to their educational, economic, or immigration status can put their issues "on the altar." The public spaces in which these events occur—streets, parks, schools, libraries, community centers, and art galleries—are freely accessible to people of all walks of life.

An important part of expressing U.S. Latino identity has involved acknowledging the exploitation and discrimination faced by Latinos as racial and cultural minorities in the United States.[36] During U.S. Day of the Dead celebrations, the deaths of local people are often used to invoke political discourses around issues of national and global importance. Illustrating E. P. Thompson's concept of the moral economy, they "elevate the defense of the interests of the working community above those of the profits of a few."[37] Moral arguments are made with the use of colorful aesthetics and rituals to attract the attention of the general public and the media in ways that ordinary political work usually does not. Whether implicitly or explicitly, U.S. Day of the Dead exhibits and events often draw attention to the classism and racism in U.S. society that cause low-income and minority people to be disproportionately the victims of violence, drugs, environmental injustice, and the least desirable and most dangerous occupations. Consider, for example, Day of the Dead altars erected at a local community center in San Ysidro, California, a town on the U.S./Mexican border where many residents have worked in the fields. To commemorate farm workers and their struggle for fair working conditions, the altars displayed photos of deceased farm workers and union activists, along with wooden fruit crates, grapes, citrus tree cuttings, lettuce, strawberries, potatoes, and other fruits and vegetables grown in the region, farming tools and empty pesticide cans. On the wall behind the altar were posters, flyers, and newspaper articles regarding the United

Farm Workers' Union (UFW) strikes and boycotts. In the U.S. context, the ancient tradition of placing harvest offerings on altars has become a way to make political claims about the rights of workers. Seen throughout California and the Southwest since the 1970s, farm workers' altars, often featuring a photo of deceased UFW cofounder, Cesar Chavez, highlight U.S. society's dependence on immigrant farm workers for its food supply, while simultaneously revealing the exploitation and abuse these workers face at the hands of industrial farms and food-processing corporations.

Thompson argued that the moral economy exposed "confrontations in the market place over access (or entitlement) to necessities."[38] Some of the most poignant Day of the Dead rituals to stir moral reflection over social inequalities have been organized by families of teens lost to violence, alcohol, drugs, and other ills besetting low-income, urban neighborhoods. A Day of the Dead candlelight vigil attended by over one thousand people in Santa Monica, California, protested the rising number of gang-related deaths in Los Angeles. The vigil included photos and shrines honoring youth slain in gang violence. It was followed by a weekend of negotiations that resulted in the signing of a truce between warring Culver City and Santa Monica gangs.[39] With calls to "create jobs, increase educational opportunities and end a pattern of social neglect that feeds a violent gang lifestyle," local residents utilized traditional rituals of honoring the dead to support moral claims about the government's disinvestment in inner city neighborhoods.[40] For the many community members who attended, this was an opportunity to consider the problems they faced in collective rather than individual terms, reflecting together on the root causes of gang violence and the need for collective rather than individual responses. Similarly, a Day of the Dead altar dedicated to teens lost to drugs and suicide was erected in November 2009, at the Sherman Heights Community Center in San Diego. This altar displayed photos of the teens; some of their personal clothing, jewelry, and stuffed animals; their favorite foods and candies; and handwritten notes from friends and family telling the youth how much they were missed and loved. The pungent aroma of thousands of fresh marigolds on the altar, combined with the smells of melting candle wax and Indigenous "copal"[41] incense, evoked the attention, sympathy, and moral indignation of passersby, reminding them of the educational, social, and economic inequalities faced by too many minority youth living in the wealthiest country on earth.[42]

On November 1, 2005, some three hundred residents of Vista, California, created a giant outdoor altar in a popular community park adjacent to the town's baseball field. The altar, which spanned the length of three cars, was dedicated to several unarmed Latino young men who had been shot and killed that year by Vista police. The town's Latino residents claimed that dozens of Latino youth were victims of racially motivated police brutality each year. Photos of victims were arranged on the altar, along with traditional flowers, candles, and foods. In an unlikely juxtaposition of two very different cultural pastimes, the Latino community held an evening vigil—singing, praying, and crying—directly across from a well-attended town baseball game, while Vista sports fans cheered for their teams and a baseball announcer's voice echoed in the background. The public altar and vigil for the dead youth evoked intellectual reflection on an emotional and corporal level that went beyond the experiences of merely hearing about such shootings in the news media. The affective effects of this collective remembrance created a sense of solidarity among Latinos and other concerned community residents who were present. It communicated the vulnerabilities, realities, and needs of Vista's Latino immigrants—exploited for their labor yet largely excluded from mainstream media and politics because of their "outsider" status. At the same time, this colorful and "exotic" public ritual attracted media attention for the families of the victims and for the entire Latino community, as local news crews that had initially been sent to cover the game were drawn to the adjacent altar and vigil, approaching participants to interview and photograph them.[43] In conjunction with ongoing community organizing work, this Day of the Dead event was one strategy used by Vista's Coalition for Peace, Justice, and Dignity to raise public consciousness about racial profiling and police brutality.

A recurrent theme of U.S. Day of the Dead celebrations in the late twentieth and early twenty-first century is the issue of migration across the U.S./Mexican border. In San Diego, the Interfaith Coalition for Immigrant Rights has held vigils on the U.S./Mexican border to protest the controversial U.S. government border patrol program, Operation Gatekeeper. Each November 1, an Interfaith religious service is held, and wooden crosses are placed along the border fence listing the names, ages, and places of origin of the nearly six thousand migrants who have died while attempting to cross the border since Gatekeeper's inception in 1994. Also placed along the border are Day of the Dead altars heaped with flowers, candles, and *pan de muerto* in memory of the dead migrants. Mixing the cultural and the political, these rituals compel the public to remember the economic desperation of millions of people south of the border and to reflect on the U.S. government's role in maintaining a "favorable investment climate" for transnational corporations that translates into poverty wages for a majority of Latin Americans. By honoring migrants who die attempting to cross the border in search of a living wage, these rituals emphasize contradictions between the rights of Latin Americans and North Americans to "life, liberty, and the pursuit of happiness." Each year, from California to Chicago to New York, immigrant rights activists observe Day of the Dead with processions and altars critical of U.S. border patrol and immigration policies.[44]

Sometimes, the focus of Day of the Dead events is on deadly situations rather than dead people. Throughout the United States, altars have been created for the anonymous victims of global political crises such as genocide, infanticide, the "slow death of homelessness," the "death of the arts," the "death of organized labor," and "the death of the environment." LA CAUSA (Los Angeles Communities United for a Sustainable Environment) has held Day of the Dead community forums and exhibits to draw attention to environmentally caused illnesses. Residents in El Paso, Texas, and other border towns hold annual Day of the Dead marches and public altar exhibits to draw attention to environmental contamination, labor abuses, and violence associated with the North American Free Trade Agreement. Annual Day of the Dead exhibits in memory of the Women of Juarez are now common in Los Angeles, San Francisco, Chicago, New York, and other major cities across the country. Altars are built to remember the hundreds of young Mexican women, most of whom worked in transnational factories (*maquiladoras*) on the border, who have been raped, mutilated, and murdered en route to and from their factory jobs. In local manifestations of the global problems of female exploitation and misogyny, Day of the Dead organizers transmit moral discourses about the value of human life over corporate profit.[45] Such events embody what Thompson calls "certain essential premises . . . [about] what humans owe to each other."[46] As a legacy of the Chicano Movement, politicized Day of the Dead altars are now erected throughout the United States each year.

Conclusion

Day of the Dead is observed in a variety of ways in the United States, and this essay has focused on an important subset of these rituals—those with political messages. In countries as culturally diverse as the United States, public rituals create important spaces in which minority groups can criticize, respond to, and attempt to change mainstream norms and values. By personalizing public issues and infusing traditional rites with contemporary meanings, Day of the Dead participants employ moral arguments to open public consciousness on behalf of those members of society who are commonly victimized, discarded, and forgotten. This can cultivate greater understanding and solidarity among diverse populations, creating the groundwork necessary for civic engagement, whether in the form of volunteering at a local community organization or becoming active in more overtly political work.

While this research did not track the relationship between people's participation in Day of the Dead and subsequent forms of community activism, anecdotal evidence from conversations with participants suggests that, after being profoundly moved by politicized Day of the Dead exhibits or events, some event participants were inspired to become involved in their local community centers, art councils, museums, or chambers of commerce. Others were awakened to disturbing sociopolitical issues while attending these events. For example, numerous people interviewed on both the East and West coasts stated that they had not heard of Operation Gatekeeper, *maquiladoras*, or the Women of Juarez before attending Day of the Dead exhibits. Three elderly Mexican American women, unable to hold back tears as they helped decorate the unmarked graves of dead migrants at a cemetery ritual held along the U.S./Mexican border, said that the event made them want to get more active in immigrant rights and social pastoral work on the border where they lived. A Guatemalan American reported that he had never thought about the connections between race, class, and military recruitment in U.S. high schools before seeing an antiwar altar at a Day of the Dead festival. All of these people were drawn to Day of the Dead events because of the *cultural* aspects of the celebration, but left with increased *political* awareness. Civic engagement such as voting, volunteerism, political organizing, and protest marches must be preceded by consciousness-raising processes that create a foundation for more elaborate political action. As political scientist James C. Scott notes, "material and symbolic resistance are part of the same set of mutually sustaining practices," with the latter not only supporting practical resistance, but serving as a condition for it.[47] Chicano Day of the Dead celebrations illustrate how cultural rituals are valuable resources with which populations can construct narratives of self-affirmation, solidarity, and human rights. For people who come from linguistically, racially, economically, or politically marginalized communities, as well as for many others who may find traditional politics boring, depressing, or alienating, activist art and ritual provide ways to engage with politics by creating emotional connections to fellow humans in ways that are essential in order to work toward a more democratic society.

Notes

1. "Chicano/a" is a self-identifying term for Mexican Americans dedicated to progressive political organizing work.

2. George Lipsitz, *Time Passages: Collective Memory and American Popular Culture* (Minneapolis: University of Minnesota Press, 1990); George Lipsitz, "Not Just Another Social Movement: Poster Art and the Movimiento Chicano," in *Not Just Another Poster: Chicano Graphic Arts in California*, ed. Chon Noriega (Santa Barbara: University of California Press, 2001), 71–87; Tere Romo, "Points of Convergence: The Iconography of the Chicano Poster," in *Not Just Another Poster*, 91–115.

3. A U.S. boycott against Nestlé began in 1977 and expanded in the 1980s and 1990s. As a marketing strategy, the company offered free samples of baby formula to impoverished African women who, believing it was better for their infants, used it instead of breastfeeding. When the free samples ran out and lactation ceased as a result of not nursing, women were forced to buy the expensive formula. Babies often starved to death or became malnourished, as mothers mixed the formula with too much water, attempting to make it last longer.

4. E. P. Thompson, *Customs in Common* (London: Merlin Press, 1991).

5. Ibid., 188.

6. Lester Friedman, *Unspeakable Images: Ethnicity and the American Cinema* (Chicago: University of Chicago Press, 1991); Clara Rodriguez, *Latin Looks: Images of Latinos and Latinas in the U.S. Media* (Boulder, CO: Westview, 1997); Ron Carveth and Diane Alverio, *Network Brownout: The Portrayal of Latinos in Network Television News* (Washington, DC: National Association of Hispanic Journalists/ National Council of La Raza, 1997); Otto Santa Ana, *Brown Tide Rising: Metaphors of Latinos in Contemporary American Public Discourse* (Austin: University of Texas Press, 2002).

7. "Combating the Network 'Brownout,'" *Hispanic Business* 21, no. 46 (1999): 46; Clint Wilson, Felix Gutiérrez, and Lena Chao, *Racism, Sexism and the Media: The Rise of Class Communication in Multicultural America*, 4th ed. (Thousand Oaks, CA: Sage, 2003).

8. Rosa Linda Fregoso, *The Bronze Screen: Chicana and Chicano Film Culture* (Minneapolis: University of Minnesota Press, 1993); Chon Noriega, 2001, *Chicano Studies Reader: An Anthology of Aztlán, 1970–2000* (Los Angeles: Regents of the University of California, 2001); Charles Ramirez-Berg, *Latino Images in Film* (Austin: University of Texas Press, 2002).

9. Guillermo Gomez-Peña, "A New Artistic Continent," in *Made in Aztlán*, eds. Philip Brookman and Guillermo Gomez-Peña (San Diego: Centro Cultural de la Raza, 1986), 86–97; Tomas Ybarra-Frausto, "The Chicano Movement/The Movement of Chicano Art," in *Beyond the Fantastic: Contemporary Art Criticism from Latin America*, ed. Gerardo Mosquera (Cambridge, MA: MIT Press, 1996), 196–216.

10. For a discussion of Chicano mural art, see Eva Sperling Cockcroft and Holly Barnet-Sanchez, *Signs from the Heart: California Chicano Murals* (Venice, CA: Social and Public Art Resource Center; Albuquerque: University of New Mexico Press, 1993).

11. Jorge Huerta, "El Teatro de la Esperanza: Keeping in Touch with the People," *The Drama Review* 21, no. 1 (March, 1977): 37–46; Yolanda Broyles-González, *El Teatro Campesino: Theater in the Chicano Movement* (Austin: University of Texas Press, 1994).

12. During this time, similar multimedia work was carried out by East Coast Puerto Rican artists responding to the racism and discrimination they faced as minorities in the United States. Although the Chicano Movement and Boricua Movement were distinct movements that sprung organically from each community, both utilized public art as a medium for political education and organizing.

13. Many of them had not been to Mexico or spent much time there and quite a few did not speak Spanish.

14. In this essay, Indigenous refers to the autochthonous peoples of Mexico, whose ancestors had the earliest human presence there. Today, there are more than sixty Indigenous linguistic groups in Mexico, comprising about 13 percent of the national population.

15. *Danza* is a form of dancing-in-prayer based on ancient Aztec spiritual dances.

16. Rodolfo González, "El Plan Espiritual de Aztlán," in *Atzlán: An Anthology of Mexican American Literature*, eds. Luís Valdez and Stan Steiner (New York: Vintage Books, 1972), 402–06; Davíd Carrasco, *Religions of Mesoamerica: Cosmovision and Ceremonial Centers* (San Francisco: HarperCollins, 1990); Tere Romo, ed., *Chicanos en Mictlán* (San Francisco: Mexican Museum of San Francisco, 2000).

17. José Limón, "Western Marxism and Folklore: A Critical Introduction," *Journal of American Folklore* 96, no. 379 (1983): 34–52; Americo Paredes, *Folklore and Culture on the Texas-Mexican Border* (Austin: University of Texas Press, 1993); Mark Mattern, "Cajun Music, Cultural Revival: Theorizing Political Action in Popular Music," *Popular Music and Society* 22, no. 2 (1998): 31–48; Olivia Cadavál, *Creating a Latino Identity in the Nation's Capital: The Latino Festival* (New York: Garland, 1998); Mark Mattern, "Let the Good Times Unroll: Music and Race Relations in Southwest Louisiana," *Black Music Research Journal* 17, no. 2 (1998): 159–68.

18. Limón, "Western Marxism and Folklore," 42.

19. Michael Taussig, "Violence and Resistance in the Americas: The Legacy of Conquest," in *Violence, Resistance, and Survival in the Americas: Native Americans and the Legacy of Conquest*, eds. William B. Taylor and Franklin Pease (Washington, DC: Smithsonian Institution Press, 1994), 280.

20. Robert Ricard, *The Spiritual Conquest of Mexico* (Berkeley: University of California Press, 1982), 269–87; Steve J. Stern, *Resistance, Rebellion and Consciousness in the Andean Peasant World, 18th to 20th Centuries* (Madison: University of Wisconsin Press, 1987), 161; and Stern, *Peru's Indian Peoples and the Challenge of Spanish Conquest* (Madison: University of Wisconsin Press, 1993), 117.

21. This is considered a form of cultural resistance by Chicanos today, who feel pride in the fact that Indigenous rituals dating back thousands of years still exist. Others may consider this a form of cultural accommodation or assimilation. Yet, accommodation does not necessarily equal co-optation, and has historically been an effective strategy for survival.

22. Elizabeth Carmichael and Chloe Sayer, *The Skeleton at the Feast: The Day of the Dead in Mexico* (Austin: University of Texas Press, 1991), 43.

23. Max Gluckman, *Essays on the Ritual of Social Relations* (Frome, UK: Butler and Tanner, 1962); Peter Burke, *Popular Culture in Early Modern Europe* (New York: Harper & Row, 1978); Mikhail Bakhtin, *Rabelais and His World* (Bloomington: Indiana University Press, 1984).

24. Stern, *Resistance, Rebellion and Consciousness*, 31.

25. William B. Taylor, *Drinking, Homicide and Rebellion in Colonial Mexican Villages* (Stanford, CA: Stanford University Press, 1979), 118–19.

26. Juan Pedro Viqueira, "Religion Popular e Identidad," *Cuicuilco: Revista de la Escuela Nacional de Antropologia e Historia* 14/15 (July–December 1984): 13.

27. For more information about the diverse Day of the Dead traditions throughout Latin America, see Regina Marchi, *Day of the Dead in the USA: The Migration and Transformation of a Cultural Phenomenon* (New Brunswick, NJ: Rutgers University Press, 2009).

28. From pre-Columbian times through the present, marigolds have been used to honor the dead in Mesoamerica.

29. A term used to describe peoples and/or cultures that are the product of racial mixing—usually referring to Latin Americans or U.S. Latinos of mixed European, Indigenous, Asian, and/or African ancestries.

30. James Griffith, *Respect and Continuity: The Arts of Death in a Border Community* (Tucson: The Southwest Folklore Center, University of Arizona, 1985); Lynn Gosnell and Suzanne Gott, "San Fernando Cemetery: Decorations of Love and Loss in a Mexican American Community," in *Cemeteries and Gravemarkers: Voices of American Culture*, ed. Richard Meyer (Ann Arbor, MI: UMI Research Press, 1989), 217–36; James Griffith, *A Shared Space: Folklife in the Arizona-Sonora Borderlands* (Logan: University of Utah Press, 1995); Sybil Venegas, "The Day of the Dead in

Aztlán: Chicano Variations on the Theme of Life, Death and Self-Preservation," in Romo, *Chicanos in Mictlán*, 42–43; Marchi, *Day of the Dead in the USA*.

31. Eric Hobsbawm and Terrance Ranger, *The Invention of Tradition* (Cambridge, UK: Cambridge University Press, 1983).

32. Personal interview with Yolanda Garfias Woo, San Francisco, California, June 6, 2003.

33. Marchi, *Day of the Dead in the USA*, 70–82.

34. Venegas, "The Day of the Dead in Aztlán," 47.

35. According to estimates from procession organizers and information published in newspapers.

36. George Sanchez, *Becoming Mexican American: Ethnicity, Culture and Identity in Chicano Los Angeles, 1900–1945* (New York: Oxford University Press, 1983); Juan Flores, "The Latino Imaginary: Meanings of Community and Identity," in *From Bomba to Hip Hop: Puerto Rican Culture and Latino Identity* (New York: Columbia University Press, 2000), chap. 9.

37. Thompson, *Customs in Common*, 339.

38. Ibid., 337.

39. John L. Mitchell, "1000 Hold Vigil against Violence in Santa Monica," *Los Angeles Times*, November 3, 1998, B1.

40. Ibid.

41. Incense made of pine resin, used throughout Mesoamerica since pre-Columbian times to communicate with the spirit world.

42. Personal observation, Sherman Heights Community Center, San Diego, October 31, 2009.

43. Personal observation, Townsite Park, Vista, California, November 2, 2005.

44. According to newspaper articles and websites I reviewed, as well as my personal observations, such activities have occurred since 1995 in at least twenty U.S. cities, including Phoenix, Austin, Chicago, Boston, Seattle, New York, San Francisco, Los Angeles, and Washington, DC.

45. Such altars typically have printed pamphlets with information about the Women of Juarez and phone numbers to call for action.

46. Thompson, *Customs in Common*, 350.

47. James C. Scott, *Domination and the Arts of Resistance: Hidden Transcripts* (New Haven, CT: Yale University Press, 1990), 184.

Bibliography

Bakhtin, Mikhail. *Rabelais and His World*. Bloomington: Indiana University Press, 1984.

Broyles-González, Yolanda. *El Teatro Campesino: Theater in the Chicano Movement*. Austin: University of Texas Press, 1994.

Burke, Peter. *Popular Culture in Early Modern Europe.* New York: Harper & Row, 1978.

Cadavál, Olivia. *Creating a Latino Identity in the Nation's Capital: The Latino Festival.* New York: Garland, 1998.

Carmichael, Elizabeth, and Chloe Sayer. *The Skeleton at the Feast: The Day of the Dead in Mexico.* Austin: University of Texas Press, 1991.

Carrasco, Davíd. *Religions of Mesoamerica: Cosmovision and Ceremonial Centers.* San Francisco: HarperCollins, 1990.

Carveth, R., and D. Alverio. *Network Brownout: The Portrayal of Latinos in Network Television News.* Washington, DC: National Association of Hispanic Journalists/National Council of La Raza, 1997.

Cockcroft, Eva Sperling, and Holly Barnet-Sanchez. *Signs from the Heart: California Chicano Murals.* Venice, CA: Social and Public Art Resource Center/Albuquerque: University of New Mexico Press, 1993.

"Combating the Network 'Brownout,'" *Hispanic Business* 21, no. 46 (1999).

Flores, Juan. "The Latino Imaginary: Meanings of Community and Identity." In *From Bomba to Hip Hop: Puerto Rican Culture and Latino Identity,* chap. 9. New York: Columbia University Press, 2000.

Fregoso, Rosa Linda. *The Bronze Screen: Chicana and Chicano Film Culture.* Minneapolis: University of Minnesota Press, 1993.

Friedman, Lester. *Unspeakable Images: Ethnicity and the American Cinema.* Chicago: University of Chicago Press, 1991.

Gluckman, Max. *Essays on the Ritual of Social Relations.* Frome, UK: Butler and Tanner, 1962.

Gomez-Peña, Guillermo. "A New Artistic Continent." In *Made in Aztlán,* edited by Philip Brookman and Guillermo Gomez-Peña, 86–97. San Diego: Centro Cultural de la Raza, 1986.

González, Rodolfo. "El Plan Espiritual de Aztlán." In *Atzlán: An Anthology of Mexican American Literature,* edited by Luís Valdez and Stan Steiner, 402–406. New York: Vintage Books, 1972.

Gosnell, Lynn, and Suzanne Gott. "San Fernando Cemetery: Decorations of Love and Loss in a Mexican American Community." In *Cemeteries and Gravemarkers: Voices of American Culture,* edited by Richard Meyer. Ann Arbor, MI: UMI Research Press, 1989.

Griffith, James. *Respect and Continuity: The Arts of Death in a Border Community.* Tucson: The Southwest Folklore Center, University of Arizona, 1985.

———. *A Shared Space: Folklife in the Arizona-Sonora Borderlands.* Logan: University of Utah Press, 1995.

Hobsbawm, Eric, and Terrance Ranger. *The Invention of Tradition.* Cambridge: Cambridge University Press, 1983.

Huerta, Jorge. "El Teatro de la Esperanza: Keeping in Touch with the People." *The Drama Review* 21, no. 1 (March 1977): 37–46.

Limón, José. "Western Marxism and Folklore: A Critical Introduction." *Journal of American Folklore* 96, no. 379 (1983): 34–52.

Lipsitz, George. *Time Passages: Collective Memory and American Popular Culture.* Minneapolis: University of Minnesota Press, 1990.

———. "Not Just Another Social Movement: Poster Art and the Movimiento Chicano." In *Not Just Another Poster: Chicano Graphic Arts in California,* edited by Chon Noriega, 71–87. Santa Barbara: University of California Press, 2001.

Marchi, Regina. *Day of the Dead in the USA: The Migration and Transformation of a Cultural Phenomenon.* New Brunswick, NJ: Rutgers University Press, 2009.

Mattern, Mark. "Cajun Music, Cultural Revival: Theorizing Political Action in Popular Music." *Popular Music and Society* 22, no. 2 (1998): 31–48.

———. "Let the Good Times Unroll: Music and Race Relations in Southwest Louisiana." *Black Music Research Journal* 17, no. 2 (1998): 159–68.

Mitchell, John L. "1000 Hold Vigil against Violence in Santa Monica." *Los Angeles Times,* November 3, 1998, B1.

Noriega, Chon. *Chicano Studies Reader: An Anthology of Aztlán, 1970–2000.* Los Angeles: Regents of the University of California, 2001.

Paredes, Americo. *Folklore and Culture on the Texas-Mexican Border.* Austin: University of Texas Press, 1993.

Ramirez-Berg, Charles. *Latino Images in Film.* Austin: University of Texas Press, 2002.

Ricard, Robert. *The Spiritual Conquest of Mexico.* Berkeley: University of California Press, 1982.

Rodriguez, Clara. *Latin Looks: Images of Latinos and Latinas in the U.S. Media.* Boulder, CO: Westview, 1997.

Romo, Tere. "Points of Convergence: The Iconography of the Chicano Poster." In *Not Just Another Poster: Chicano Graphic Arts in California,* edited by Chon Noriega, 91–115. Santa Barbara: University of California Press, 2001.

———, ed. *Chicanos en Mictlán.* San Francisco: Mexican Museum of San Francisco, 2000.

Sanchez, George. *Becoming Mexican American: Ethnicity, Culture and Identity in Chicano Los Angeles, 1900–1945.* New York: Oxford University Press, 1983.

Santa Ana, Otto. *Brown Tide Rising: Metaphors of Latinos in Contemporary American Public Discourse.* Austin: University of Texas Press, 2002.

Scott, James C. *Domination and the Arts of Resistance: Hidden Transcripts.* New Haven, CT: Yale University Press, 1990.

Stern, Steve J. *Resistance, Rebellion and Consciousness in the Andean Peasant World, 18th to 20th Centuries.* Madison: University of Wisconsin Press, 1987.

———. *Peru's Indian Peoples and the Challenge of Spanish Conquest.* Madison: University of Wisconsin Press, 1993.

Taussig, Michael. "Violence and Resistance in the Americas: The Legacy of Conquest." In *Violence, Resistance, and Survival in the Americas: Native Americans and the Legacy of Conquest*, edited by William B. Taylor and Franklin Pease, 269–84. Washington, DC: Smithsonian Institution Press, 1994.

Taylor, William B. *Drinking, Homicide and Rebellion in Colonial Mexican Villages.* Stanford, CA: Stanford University Press, 1979.

Thompson, E. P. *Customs in Common.* London: Merlin Press, 1991.

Venegas, Sybil. "The Day of the Dead in Aztlán: Chicano Variations on the Theme of Life, Death and Self-Preservation." In *Chicanos in Mictlán,* edited by Tere Romo, 42–54. San Francisco: Mexican Museum of San Francisco, 2000.

Viqueira, Juan Pedro, "Religion Popular e Identidad." *Cuicuilco: Revista de la Escuela Nacional de Antropologia e Historia* 14/15 (July–December 1984): 7–14.

Wilson, Clint, Felix Gutiérrez, and Lena Chao. *Racism, Sexism and the Media: The Rise of Class Communication in Multicultural America,* 4th edition. Thousand Oaks, CA: Sage, 2003.

Woo, Yolanda Garfias. Personal interview by Regina Marchi. San Francisco, California, June 6, 2003.

Ybarra-Frausto, Tomas. "The Chicano Movement/The Movement of Chicano Art." In *Beyond the Fantastic: Contemporary Art Criticism from Latin America,* edited by Gerardo Mosquera, 196–216. Cambridge, MA: MIT Press, 1996.

Chapter 5

The National D-Day Memorial

An American Military Monument as "Doing Democracy"

Timothy W. Luke

This study evaluates art as a means of "doing democracy" by reconsidering the cultural politics surrounding the creation of a World War II battle memorial in the United States of America—namely, the National D-Day Memorial in Bedford, Virginia. Both as a local civic monument to nationalist values and as a public historical artifact of American nationalism, the D-Day Memorial articulates a vision of the United States of America becoming a global superpower by tracing its origins to the D-Day invasion of June 6, 1944. Seen as a project of local and state government, which worked with a citizen-supported nonprofit organization to build and operate the D-Day Memorial, this art project also ironically aims at connecting Virginia—the Old Dominion, the seedbed of the American Revolution, and keystone of the Confederacy—to more modern cultural concerns that reposition the Commonwealth in a contemporary global context. Ultimately, this monument is a study in how deeply the collective life of powerful nations allows for local activist art to celebrate the individual deaths incurred in the democratic cause of civic continuity and renewal.

Assaying the means of memory-generation at sites like the National D-Day Memorial is important for understanding how "doing democracy" for a nation requires particular forms of remembering and forgetting to construct its heritage through works of art. Looking out into the future, "remembrance shapes our links to the past, and the ways we remember define us in the present."[1] Yet, at the same time, this monument project is necessarily ambivalent and conflicted, because its constructs also "underline the extent to which the art of memory for the modern world is both for historians as well as ordinary citizens and institutions very much something to be used, misused, and exploited, rather than something that sits inertly there for each person to possess and contain."[2]

In many ways, the National D-Day Memorial is an unusual instance of local heritage defenders, mobilized citizens, and engaged civic leaders using the arts to advance their political claims and exemplify democratic practices through their unceasing commitment to building a major work of public art. Community members took ownership of this enterprise from its start, and it has been regarded as a culturally enriching enterprise for many different audiences in addition to being a local economic development engine. Far from being "plop art," this memorial engaged members from surrounding communities—young and old, male and female, black and white, working class and well heeled, Democratic and Republican, civilian and military.

Often such memorials are located in major capital cities, but not always. The landscape of this hill is sculpted to carry a nationalistic memory whose narratives recollect significant historical events as well as distort, erase, or neglect other memories. To ask why Bedford, Virginia, rather than Washington, DC, or some other location in the United States with another symbolic significance was chosen to retell the stories of the June 6, 1944, Allied invasion of Normandy is an important opportunity to study how the American nation-state connects with particular social groups and geographical localities as political actors to invent their sense of the United States by "doing democracy." Indeed, the many twists and turns in constructing this memorial in rural Virginia are suggestive of creative tensions in the American body politic.

"Doing Democracy" with Public Art

Organizing a public artwork, like the National D-Day Memorial in Bedford, Virginia, exercises and increases the capacities of individual citizens, local civic associations, and veterans groups locally and regionally, because the arts can begin engaging citizens critically, inventively, and reflectively. Artistic enterprises like the D-Day Memorial plainly pluralize the forms and sites of communication, if ever so slightly, to enable citizens to open their vision of the nation, share their moment of political community with others, or blend their local vernacular experiences with a larger official heritage. This openness is crucial, because nations are made.

Connor argues that a nation is "a group of people who feel that they are ancestrally related," or, "are indeed characterized by a sense—a feeling—of consanguinity."[3] This naturalized vision of nationality, however, often does not work easily in large, multisectional, polyglot, and multi-cultural countries, like the United States. Smith's view of nationalism, as "a social and political movement to achieve the goals of a nation and realize its political will," gets closer to its constructed activist qualities in the United States.[4] Yet, such movements, as Ernest Renan suggested in 1882, must become "a daily plebiscite" anchored in the continuous exercise of popular and elite will through constant consent and daily dissent.[5] To do this, special places, like war memorials, use public art to mix popular and elite wills and thereby mark their joint consent. In turn, the arts of sculpture, landscape design, architecture, writing, theatrical staging, photography, historic preservation, and cinema all are mobilized as part of a local heritage effort, to create a regional, national, and even global work of public art.

While nation-building is challenging, it is plain that nationalism can be understood as "a *process*, a kind of *sentiment* or *identity*, a form of *political rhetoric*, an *ideology*, a *principle* or set of principles, and a kind of *social-political movement*."[6] Such work is conflicted, and it at times sparks ambivalence. Creating sentiments, expressing principles, and sustaining a social-political movement with artworks are decisive means for producing community, even when that community rests upon an expansionist militant nationalism. As an ideology, nationalism remains "unlike most other isms" inasmuch as the project of "nationalism has never produced its own grand thinkers: no Hobbes, Tocquevilles, Marxes, or Webers."[7] Without grand thinkers, nationalism must nest in more modest discourses. It perhaps goes too far to reduce this community-building activity only to "banal nationalism," but conflictual militant nationalist sentiments can be embedded in public cultural sites where their aggressive rhetorics can be encountered by citizens every day.[8]

Ironically, for the United States as a liberal democratic state, many of its most salient civic rituals of national unity were forged as part of wars at home—both the Revolutionary War and the Civil War. Memorializing nationalistic rhetorics for democratic publics on battlefields became more significant after President Lincoln's famous Gettysburg Address and its secular consecration of that battle's horrendous losses as sacrifices to the ideological cause of a United States of America becoming one nation "united and indivisible."[9] In fact, the principles for "doing democracy," especially in the United States, presume that the citizenry's allegiance ultimately demands occasional popular sacrifice and constant civic devotion to "the Flag." The D-Day Memorial in Bedford, Virginia, then, is a telling example of how "memory and its representations touch very significantly upon questions of identity, of nationalism, of power and authority" in such a manner that their ongoing construction and reconstruction serve "to some considerable extent a nationalist effort premised on the need to construct a desirable loyalty to an insider's understanding of one's country, tradition, and faith."[10]

In nationalist political rhetorics, wars and their battles are violent points of inflection, but they can re-energize everyday social-political practices of civic or national unity. The recognition of soldiers—as surviving, wounded, or dead bodies after battle—meets nationalism's requirements for sacrifice, or, as the *Oxford English Dictionary* defines it "a destruction or surrender of something valued or desired for the sake of something having a higher or more pressing claim," or, more directly, "the loss entailed by devotion to some other interest." Rites of nationalist remembrance as well as sites for self-interpretation become surrogates for grand thinkers about nationalism, because their public arts justify or mystify how the brutal deaths of loved ones are a devotion to some higher interest of keeping the republic for which they fell. National holidays, popular religious values, civic instruction, and civil symbolic artifacts all promote the ideological continuation of nationalism as a popular movement. Yet, war memorials are among the most salient works devoted to the ideological process of building national sentiments of citizens-living-in-peace by tying them to other citizens in their continuous reimagination of the warriors-going-to-war.

In the absence of grand thinkers, then, the cultural normalization of grandiose practices, like war-making and war-memorialization, helps sustain the cultural projects of American nationalism. The material and symbolic underpinnings of civic identity at the local, community, and national levels presume war is the enduring constant of living as a democracy amid the modern nation-state system, so sacrifices made in battle allegedly are never in vain. Instead they confer the devotion, as Weber suggests, demanded by "the autonomous dignity of the polity resting on force."[11] For republics whose citizens are, were, or can be soldiers, Weber's appreciation of warriors' deaths echoes in Lincoln's memorialization of Gettysburg's "hallowed ground."

D-Day is the American name for a great battle on June 6, 1944, in which the Operation Neptune (sea) and Operation Overlord (land) invasion forces from the United States, the United Kingdom, and Canada assaulted five beachhead sectors—code-named Utah, Omaha, Gold, Juno, and Sword—in Normandy assisted by smaller Allied units from Australia, Belgium, Czechoslovakia, France, the Netherlands, Greece, New Zealand, Norway, and Poland. For this invasion, the Allies pitched over 155,000 soldiers, 50,000 vehicles, 11,000 airplanes, and over 5,300 ships against a battlefront about six miles wide on the French coast. In taking and holding all these beaches on D-Day, the Allied invasion forces suffered 9,758 dead and wounded, which included 6,603 American casualties.[12] Historians in the United States, like Stephen Ambrose, extravagantly claim this one day was *the* decisive battle of World War II.[13] This interpretation, on the one hand, reveals the recurrent need to revitalize the citizenry's belief in American global power. That nationalist imperative becomes clearer after closing out each new American war in 1945, 1953, 1975, or 1991, as Washington has maintained the nation's global hegemony despite occasional reversals during the Cold War. On the other hand, Ambrose's claim underscores how much D-Day was a major American World War II battle, and it affords a rich cultural opportunity for fueling American nationalism across the generations.[14]

The D-Day Memorial presents itself as a national monument to "the valor, fidelity, and sacrifice" of American and Allied servicemen and women in World War II, but June 6, 1944, also marks a day of origin for all Americans to admire the spread of the United States' immense global empire of bases and businesses over the past seventy years. Even when the widely celebrated sacrifice, fidelity, and valor of those World War II years might seem to be eclipsed by newer, less radiant, more questionable, and quite problematic acts of American power, particularly since Operations Enduring Freedom and Iraqi Freedom began in 2001 and 2003, this edifice affirms the shaky faith that all American soldiers fighting anywhere always embody the sacrifice, fidelity, and valor of the entire American nation.

From Omaha Beach, Normandy to Bedford, Virginia

While the U.S. Congress authorized the establishment of the National D-Day Memorial in Bedford, Virginia, on November 11, 1994, the federal government gave very little financial support to help build the monument. Bedford residents and surviving World War II veterans in southwest Virginia pushed hard to win this distinction from Congress since 1987, and constant pressures from the region clearly moved the national government to endorse the construction of this impressive edifice during 1997. So the imperatives of creating a worthy monument to the American nation-state have had to be met mostly with the financial resources and organizational skills of local civic activists across Virginia. Launched as the United States became engaged in the chaos of failed states and wars of choice in Bosnia, Afghanistan, and Iraq, this memorial has served new nationalistic interests by lending mythic energies drawn from America's allegedly "Good War" with millions of conscripts from 1941–1945 to the military struggles fought by thousands of volunteers since 9/11.

As a nationalistic public art installation, the D-Day Memorial sits on Bedford's highest hill. The forty-four-foot, six-inch-tall arch with five rectangular insets rising in a "V" on its span—representing the five beachheads of Sword, Juno, Gold, Omaha, and Utah—is inscribed with "Overlord," and this soaring simple feature serves as the striking, but also conventional, centerpiece of the monument. Beneath and before it—where the symbolic simulation of the invasion beach is filled with bronze sculptures of G.I.s—one sees the military figures set on sand actually taken from the Normandy beaches. The Overlord Plaza, where the massive granite and marble arch sits, makes a striking sight, surrounded by the flags of all the eleven countries that invaded France on June 6, 1944.

The larger memorial complex, in turn, lies within a ring road with four large overlapping circles of different sizes. In one circle, a small U.S. Army Air Force observation plane is at the center. Opposing it is a space for the U.S. Coast Guard Bell to memorialize this service's part in the D-Day landings. The largest circle is the space representing "the Beach," with many replicas of hedgehog antilanding craft barriers, pneumatic jets to imitate bullets hitting the water, and a simulated landing craft to evoke the invasion itself. Several realistic, life-sized sculptures of G.I.s crossing the beach are staged in this area. They are shown dead, wounded, fit, and fighting in a string of struggle leading up to a huge bas-relief of the U.S. Army Ranger assault on Pointe-du-Hoc that tops out into the space where the Overlord Arch sits. On the opposite side, a stone walkway with a bullet-torn sculpture of Nike, representing a beaten but not defeated France (it is a copy of one in a Norman village near the invasion beaches) bids visitors up to the arch and the flags of the Allied nations. The edifice itself feels austere but also resplendent in its materials and design. It has only minor historical displays, because its role as a museum remains a secondary goal. Instead, the public artwork here is a solemn effort "to memorialize the valour, fidelity and sacrifices of the Allied Forces on D-Day, June 6, 1944."[15]

The memorial's sculptures of U.S. soldiers are the work of an unconventional artist, Jim Brothers, based in Lawrence, Kansas. The individual pieces have titles like "Death on the Shore," "Through the Surf," "Across the Beach," and "The Wall."[16] Born the year that Pearl Harbor was bombed, Brothers came of age during the Vietnam generation. Still, his personal 1960s counterculture qualities proved to be no obstacle to the memorial's planners. As the D-Day Foundation's chairman Bob Slaughter laconically put it: "Jim's an artist. And artists are different."[17] Brothers' antiestablishment qualities as an artist, in fact, have enabled him to glorify the ordinary citizen soldiers, who mostly were common everyday working-class men that the social movements of nationalism must enroll.

The small city of Bedford, Virginia, is a village of seven thousand that prides itself as "the best little town in the world." It was founded originally during 1839 as Liberty, Virginia. Bedford County lies on the fringes of both the Commonwealth's traditional Appalachian and new NAFTA-devastated old industrial Southside counties. Not far from Appomattox, Virginia, Bedford immediately reminds one that all Americans live in that world of death the Civil War created.[18] As a place so surrounded by the sites of America's most savage war, its patriotic residents "take for granted the obligation of the state to account for the lives it claims in its service."[19] Renamed Bedford in 1912, it had less than 3,500 residents in 1940, but thirty of its men were in the first wave of D-Day invasion forces during 1944 on Omaha Beach. Nineteen were killed hitting the beach on D-Day, and four more afterward—two during June 1944, and two more by May 1945. In fact, the first nineteen died during the first fifteen minutes of the landing.

Out of a population of just over 3,200, then, twenty-three Bedford men fell in the D-Day invasion and its immediate aftermath—the highest per capita loss of any single community across the United States in this battle.[20] It is this historical loss that deeply anchors D-Day in Bedford and Virginia, for the United States of America. Hence, the D-Day Memorial is to a very real extent an empathic engine. As John Dewey or Martha Nussbaum would have it, this edifice exposes its visitors to historically different times, culturally varied organizations, and morally diverse motivations with the hopes of shaping visitors' sense of citizenship.[21] Designed as one part historical simulation, one part national monument, one part roadside attraction, the memorial is an alternative political space for doing democracy. And, its artistic design is pitched to draw out affective, corporeal, and reflective engagements from every visitor to engage their passion and intellect in how they do democracy after experiencing its effects.

How "Local" Is the "National" D-Day Memorial?

A generation ago on June 6, 1984, in an election year that coincided with a fortieth anniversary, President Ronald Reagan said to the world on Omaha Beach: "We will always remember. We will always be proud. We will always be prepared, so we may always be free."[22] A decade later on June 6, 1994, for the fiftieth anniversary of D-Day, Stephen Ambrose published his *Citizen Soldiers*, which is an extensive sentimental exaltation of the U.S. Army and its material role in creating the Pax Americana President Reagan had extolled during his first administration.

Public art sites like these are mobilized to concretize and continue the ties of victorious nations and peoples in common projects by consecrating soldiers' deaths and injuries. June 6, 1944, implicitly has been regarded since 1945 by many as the birthday of a New World Order, which the United States now has dominated for over six decades. As President George W. Bush said in Bedford, Virginia, when he keynoted the D-Day Memorial's dedication during 2001:

> Today we give thanks for all that was gained on the beaches of Normandy. We remember what was lost, with respect, admiration, and love.
>
> The great enemies of that era have vanished. And it is one of history's remarkable turns that so many young men from the new world would cross the sea to liberate the old. Beyond the peaceful beaches and quiet cemeteries lies a Europe whole and free—a continent of democratic governments and people more free and hopeful than ever before. The freedom and these hopes are what the heroes of D-Day fought and died for. And these, in the end, are the greatest monuments of all the sacrifices made that day.
>
> When I go to Europe next week, I will reaffirm the ties that bind our nations in a common destiny. These are the ties of friendship and hard experiences. They have seen our nations through a World War and a Cold War. Our shared

values and experiences must guide us now in our continued partnership, and in leading the peaceful democratic revolution that continues to this day.

We have learned that when there is conflict in Europe, America is affected, and cannot stand by. We have learned, as well, in the years since the war that America gains when Europe is united and peaceful.

Fifty-seven years ago today, America and the nations of Europe formed a bond that has never been broken. And all of us incurred a debt that can never be repaid. Today, as America dedicates our D-Day Memorial, we pray that our country will always be worthy of the courage that delivered us from evil, and saved the free world.

God bless America. And God bless the World War II generation.[23]

Eerily, one hears in President Bush's words how much nationalism has never produced grand thinkers. Bush's thoughts are simple. Battles always require sacrificial deaths, but such losses also will supposedly deliver the nation from evil enemies and save its partners in the Free World. Many continuing partnerships in Europe have held fast, but not with all of Europe. In fact, the shared democratic values and freedom-loving experiences that have guided the United States in 1944, 1954, 1964, 1974, or 1994, seemed to unravel in 2001, after Bush's election to the White House.[24]

In 2004, during the same month that sixty years earlier the Allies started taking back Nazified France, President Bush and his "coalition of the willing" handed back power to post-Ba'athist Iraq. Most of "Old Europe" was not united with the United States, and the world has become less peaceful because of what the United States has done abroad and at home since 9/11. Certainly, many see the freedom and hope of the post-Cold War world system as one of the greatest monuments to the sacrifices of June 6, 1944, but this D-Day Memorial is an ethico-political text wrought of stone, bronze, granite, and steel that has tied June 1944, to the misadventures of America in Iraq and Afghanistan for nearly a decade. The cultural politics of its local architects clearly are those of national hope—namely, the faith that it effectively teaches hard civic values to new national audiences every day. Indeed, the nationalistic remembrance of D-Day every day in the United States since 2001, in the War on Terror is meant to be as highly charged symbolically as it was in 1984, when President Reagan fought to keep "the evil empire" at bay overseas, while campaigning to defeat Walter Mondale and the Democrats at home.

This same nationalistic animus from Bedford sustained President Obama's declaration on June 6, 2009, that "the selflessness of a few was able to change an entire century" at Normandy; and, for Americans, those who will fall or shall stand strong together, since "our history has always been the sum total of the choices made and the actions taken by each individual man and women. It is always up to us."[25] The fallen's full measure of selflessness is paid with their deaths on battlefields. And, for the survivors still in service, the returned veterans, and the citizens at home, the work of changing an entire century—whatever century it is for the republic—continuously demands their selfless service to attain all that destiny leaves open to them.

Marcuse's assessment of remembrance is significant here, as he notes, "remembrance is a mode of dissociation from the facts, a mode of 'mediation' which breaks, for short moments, the omnipresent power of the facts."[26] While posing as the most legitimate guarantor of the historical meaning of the D-Day invasion, the National D-Day Memorial does substitute a heritage-based faith in force, national power, and personal valor for a history-driven awareness of the authenticity of tactical confusion, strategic caution, and collective caution at Normandy. Remembrances of individual, municipal, and national sacrifices on "one day that changed the world" occlude the realities of a republic "doing democracy" by striding forward for decades to build a New World Order out of its empire of bases from 1945, into the present. Monumental artistic landscaping projects, like the National D-Day Memorial, as Mitchell observes, "might be seen more profitably as something like the 'dream work' of imperialism, unfolding its own movement in time and space from a central point of origin and folding back on itself to disclose both utopian fantasies of the perfected imperial prospect and fractured images of unresolved ambivalence and unsuppressed resistance."[27]

While a "local" undertaking, the National D-Day Memorial is significant "nationally" because of the ways it reveals how memorializing D-Day for the American nation concretely represents this nation to itself and the world by celebrating brutal losses. As the National World War II Memorial in Washington, DC, affirms, Pax Americana plainly begins building in the months after the Battle of Midway, the invasion of North Africa, and the landings in Salerno and Anzio on the Italian boot. However, D-Day June 6, 1944, is the nation's key foundational myth as a superpower, and this highly local, quite transnational, and intensely national representation of how one town on one day sacrificed so much for Washington's vision of order cannot be ignored. It suggests any little town or remote county could just as easily be a focal point of America imagining itself with newfound importance as an international force by paying a comparable price in a battle somewhere to defend the republic.

Of course, the hundreds of thousands of other Allied soldiers lost by the Red Army on the Russian front as Berlin slugged it out with Moscow are nearly forgotten in reimagining the fall of the Third Reich as a by-product of 6,603 Americans either giving their lives or suffering terrible wounds for truth, justice, and the American way on Utah and Omaha Beach on June 6, 1944.[28] Yet, this forgetting is an integral part of its remembering D-Day. Its annual reaffirmations by veterans, politicians, and tourists from the 1950s to the present have become a rite of global empowerment that tells Americans and the world how Washington—not London, Moscow, or Paris—turned the tide against totalitarianism and then accepted the lonely responsibilities of hegemonic primacy from the firefights in Normandy's hedgerows during 1944, to the dustups in Fallujah's side streets in 2004, to the surge around Kandahar in 2010.[29]

Public Art as Nationalism-in-Action

A nation made by memorializing D-Day in such monuments is, or, at least struggles to become, a monumental historic power worthy of the myths wrought from marble and blazed into bronze at the National D-Day Memorial. Such edifices explicitly make such ethical and political claims. Whether they are made by President Roosevelt, Kennedy, Reagan, Bush, Clinton, or Obama in going to battle, the locals from Bedford, Virginia, guarantee Washington's assertions. Any nation that remains able, ready, and willing to sacrifice this number of lives from many small towns on some given day to oppose "evil" and evince "freedom and democracy" mobilizes cultural politics to transform itself into a selfless order of civic righteousness.[30] Such sites enable citizens to imagine such actions in terms of unavoidable world historical burdens as the nation stands ready to serve as the planetary policeman against whatever threat History throws forth—fascism, communism, anticolonialism, anarchism, or fundamentalism. The National D-Day Memorial recalls one day in one war increasingly long ago and far away, but it also puts the nation on notice that its citizens must prepare for many D-Days "anytime anywhere against foe to defend," in the words of JFK and his greatest generation, "the cause of freedom." Plainly, for the United States since 1945, the community activists from southwest Virginia use this public artwork to make clear to all Americans that "we still seek to use our deaths to create meaning where we are not sure any exists."[31]

For seventy years, D-Day has served as a potent polyvalent sign of American power, if not a provocation for the merits of preemptive war. From the first reports on the beach by BBC and NBC radio to the latest repeats of *Band of Brothers* on The History Channel, D-Day continues to be this nation's most iconic cluster of nationalistic images, conveying a sense of purposeful and principled power. World War I today is mostly forgotten. The dim memories of it are terrifying. What once was imagined to be World III between the USSR and the United States as a world-ending thermonuclear cataclysm of missile strike and counterstrike never came to pass. Some cast today's battles that "the coalition of the willing" from the secular West are fighting—now in low-intensity warfare with Islamic fundamentalists—as World War IV. World War II, however, is still guarded in the mass imagination as "the Good War" fought at great cost, but for noble ends, to defeat the evils of fascism.

D-Day was a day of real carnage, but the total Allied losses of 9,758 dead and wounded were tolerable, especially given the subsequent Allied victories from June 7, 1944, through the Allied victory in Europe by May 8, 1945.[32] Bloody-minded French, British, and Italian generals would mindlessly sacrifice this many men in an afternoon against the Germans and Austrians on small sections of the Western Front from 1914 to 1918 for nothing. Yet, on June 6, 1944, such losses, as American presidents from Roosevelt to Obama have maintained, allegedly turned History's tide. Consequently, on another level, the historical explorations of actually existing democracy in the 1940s against the backdrop of existing actual governance in the 2000s, which are both tagged as being "times of war," bear witness to the possibilities of a unified public consensus seeking more democratic participation, shared sacrifice, and common purpose in the hard years ahead.

For local activists and national leaders, then, D-Day survives as an ambivalent and conflicted symbol—it reveals war's destruction, but celebrates battle survivors. The fighting on Omaha and Utah Beach is shown as a worthy contest: terrible, but necessary; wasteful, but also redemptive; hellacious, but ultimately life-giving. The D-Day Memorial circulates an elaborate system of signs to recall the deaths of young men decades ago as well as affirm the lives of aging men and women who lived on afterward through subsequent decades as citizen soldiers, home-front toilers, and grateful survivors. A society of the spectacle, filled with average consumers and producers, went to World War II, won this struggle, and then returned to produce and consume images, memories, and experiences of that war as spectacular nationalism-in-action.[33]

Midas Dekkers observes about death, "people are very good at prolonging life, like children who refuse to go to bed."[34] In his *The Way of All Flesh: The Romance of Ruins*, he considers how humans work to ignore or evade the decay of mortality. Remaining uneasy about the existential realities of being, many recognize how the longer lasting life is a very hard way of dying slowly. By arguing that beauty actually rises out of, or indeed resides with, death, decay, and deterioration, Dekkers unintentionally sheds some new light on war and its memorialization. War memorials are often romantic ruins for "the fallen," marking for a nation its victories over other nations. Yet, war memorials also belie implicitly a darker celebration of war's sacrificial necessities, namely, the admiration for easy deaths coming so quickly, too soon, and quite violently in ways that grant greater meaning for life in and for itself.

A warrior's death usually is the death of boys, young men, or, sometimes, people at their prime. All those who survive wars, then, are left, as Dekkers muses, prolonging their hours like children, but in often more elderly manners. In turn, they build war memorials to those who can never deteriorate, decay, or dissolve in age's decrepitude as only the living old know and suffer them. Commemorating the fallen gives every war's survivors a few key acts and artifacts symbolically to prolong life, celebrate evading death, and postpone decay as adults. Civil society idealizes in its nationalist movements those who always are beyond life's decay, because the fallen accepted death willingly in their youth for the sake of kin and country in a common call to the state's colors.

The D-Day Memorial then can be seen as an infernal symbolic engine for extending indefinitely the collective memories of easy brutal deaths for those who were once young adults and then died meaningfully in battle. Their sentimental celebration as forever-vigorous souls, given up to the bloody sacrifices of war for their comrades and communities, is a civic secular eternity of sorts. Indeed, the evocative power of such hidden truths in the marble and bronze edifices shaped to celebrate "the fallen" often overwhelms one as he or she contemplates the astounding horrors of "the Great War," "the War to End All Wars," or "World War I" all over the world.[35] The nine major combatant nations of the Allied Powers and the Central Powers gave 8,946,000 of their citizens up to death.[36] Plainly, the Great War did not end all war.[37]

Nonetheless, its losses gave survivors in the 1920s and 1930s pause to prolong their own decaying existences by celebrating the once-tender youth of those conscripts and volunteers butchered in the trenches, gassed in no man's land or obliterated in bombardment at "the front." A similar spirit plays out among the locals of Bedford, Virginia. It is particularly pointed during 2009 or 2010—seventy years after D-Day—as one, five, eight, or a dozen more servicemen a day in America's all-volunteer forces sacrifice themselves across Iraq and Afghanistan in "the War on Terror" while visitors drop by this monument. Someday these casualties also will be remembered with other stone and bronze edifices for their deaths. For now, others left at home, postponing their own demise, join these visitors in daily celebration of warriors' deaths as forever young souls sacrificed for the nation, even if many of today's fallen are foreign nationals signed up to get U.S. passports and better economic opportunities.

A vivid example of how individual death and collective survival interrelate for Americans is found in cinema, and the film itself tacitly scripts for its audiences the nationalist ties of sacrifice, survival, and service. In *Saving Private Ryan*, Steven Spielberg puts Tom Hanks into battle as a U.S. Army Ranger company commander, Captain John Miller, on Omaha Beach.[38] He and his men survive the first hours of battle and then are detailed to find a very young Matt Damon as Private James Ryan, the last surviving son of an American family that has had three other sons fall in battle around the world in the same week. The squad of rescuers fights their way into contested territory, finds Ryan, and holds a vital bridge against overwhelming odds against a fierce German counterattack. Captain Miller and several other G.I.s die valiantly, but they "save Private Ryan."

The movie opens and closes with James Ryan as a much older man, standing in tears before Captain Miller's grave in Normandy, and asking, "Tell me I led a good life . . . tell me I'm a good man." This scene is a singular monument to death, reeling out of the film. As he and other survivors of D-Day, World War II, and the twentieth century look back to June 6, 1944, they ask this same question of their aged lives. Their prolonged existences played out as perhaps fuller lives during peacetime. In many ways, however, this dying slowly is almost cast as ignoble unliving. Captain Miller, and his comrades-at-arms buried around him nobly accepted death as a very special way of living quickly, but Miller also told Ryan before dying in 1944, "Earn this!" Here Spielberg's cinematography, the film's plot, and actors' performance unstably, if not dangerously, capture a cultural politics bearing the tacit social contracts of American nationalism.[39] They depict the nationalist credo of liberal capitalist democracy surviving as empire by accepting readily the hard way of "earning this." For the ongoing social movement of nationalism, the greatest way of living is boldly dying in a good life cut short. Consecrating the soldier's life as a life-in-itself experienced gloriously, grandly, and even graciously is, therefore, essential for nationalism's renewal. So too are Bedford's local activists "doing democracy" in recognizing, restaging, and remembering these circuits of sacrifice.

Many American boys fell in Normandy, but too many more Americans will never be able to travel to the American military cemeteries there in France. The National D-Day Memorial serves crucial civic purposes as a nationalist cenotaph in Bedford, Virginia. There World War II veterans, octogenarian home-front citizens, and all of their progeny can ask, like Spielberg's *Saving Private Ryan*, "was (or am) I a good man, woman, citizen?" As they evade decay, deterioration, and death, they also struggle to "earn this" in "peacetime." And, they can duly recognize those who served, but did not survive, celebrating how their valiant deaths came fast when they were young. Thus, both sides of American nationalism are burnished. The dead do not need to ask if they were good men: the republic or empire affirms that they were, and the civic solemnities performed daily by citizens at memorials are meant to assure them, as well as their countrymen and women, that they still are, and will be forever. Ironically, everyone is called to affirm Captain Miller's order to "earn this."

From World War II, a great meaning of the war for American nationalism was its hard-fought defeat of the Third Reich at high human costs.[40] Indeed, for the United States, the Commonwealth of Virginia, and the city of Bedford, "the nation's value and importance were both derived from and proved by the human price paid for survival."[41] For this wartime generation, and many of their offspring, D-Day, June 6, 1944, is *the* day to remember the rigors of war, for its sacrifices led to strengths. Memorial Day comes a week earlier, but it began to memorialize the Civil War. Veteran's Day started as Armistice Day to honor the fallen of the Great War. D-Day implicitly is a day of imperial triumph to mark the victory of America over its adversaries, almost everywhere and every time, as a great superpower for the first time.

Democracy is a participatory form of government, and the D-Day Memorial has been designed in a collaborative communal manner to impart to all of its visitors that one vital form of democratic participation can be service at arms to the nation during war. Simulating the spare essence of landing under fire on a contested beach in a battle is meant to evoke an emotional, embodied, and intellectual response from every visitor. How a five-year-old kindergartener, a fifteen-year-old high schooler, a fifty-five-year-old baby boomer, or an eighty-five-year-old Normandy survivor responds will vary considerably, but they all artfully are shown how "doing democracy" requires certain sacrifices of every citizen.

Here the material practices of a republic's social contract—both tacit and explicit—are rehearsed by those living for those yet unborn by reaffirming simple pacts of silent respect in honor for the dead. Sites of ritual, rites of commemoration, and cites of national sacrifice constantly combine in the local civic displays of flag-and-rifle drill teams, benedictions to bravery, and quiet moments before the grave markers of lost sons, fallen brothers, beloved spouses, caring fathers, and unknown soldiers. In a small town deep in rural Virginia, the residents share their National D-Day Memorial with the world to make this moment a nearly 365-day-a-year opportunity in addition to serving as an education center for youngsters, not even born until the twenty-first century, to learn about the supposedly most glorious war ever waged by the United States by reliving one of its longest, and most decisive, days.

Closing

As President Obama claimed on June 6, 2009, at the sixty-fifth anniversary of D-Day, "much of the progress that would define the twentieth century, on both sides of the Atlantic, came down to a battle for a slice of beach only 6 miles long and 2 miles wide," and therefore this site of sacrifice in Normandy (as well as its national memorial in Virginia) still is a critical nationalistic pivot for a president intent upon steeling twenty-first-century citizens for action at any given moment: "As we face down the hardships and struggles of our time, and arrive at that hour for which we are born, we cannot help but draw strength from those moments in history when the best among us were somehow able to swallow their fears and secure a beachhead on an unforgiving shore."[42] Of course, this is the ambivalent and conflicted politics of the D-Day Memorial. It identifies a moment in history, names the best among us, recounts how they overcame their fears whether dying on the beach or fighting on through V-E Day, defines the twentieth century as one of American progress and pushes ahead into the future.

As a public artwork, the D-Day Memorial also is now a significant local industry. It draws 75,000 plus visitors annually to Bedford city and county, and they have invested in a new $2.4 million "welcome center" close by to publicize the area's many attractions. Yet, neither city, county, nor commonwealth "think it would make sense for us to run a national monument," so they hope Washington will take it over.[43] With its $2.2 million operating budget, and only $600,000 in annual revenues, however, the National Park Service is hesitant. Even Senator Mark Warner (D-VA) realizes the National Park Service also is strapped for funds, and "there are a number of other venues around the country that would like to be part of the National Park Service."[44] Nevertheless, Warner and Senator Jim Webb (D-VA) successfully won legislative approval for a national study by the federal government to consider assuming ownership and operation of the D-Day Memorial as "an important part of both Virginia and our nation's cultural history" while ensuring "today's military men and women—and their families—get the additional support that they need and deserve."[45] The grand civic purposes for public art, then, continuously clash with gritty private worries about low taxes, smaller government, and less debt under post-Reaganite neoliberalism.

Still, local works of public art, like the D-Day Memorial, cannot be ignored. As material manifestations of nationalist sentiments, they substitute for grand thinkers. Their biggest ideas probably are expressed most succinctly by Oliver Wendell Holmes Jr. in his "The Soldier's Faith" address on Memorial Day 1895, about the sanctity of armed service by citizens caught up in times of war. Coming "in the midst of doubt, the collapse of creeds,"[46] the fate of the Bedford Boys at Omaha Beach on June 6, 1944, affirmed the faith of the Allied nations in Operation Overlord and the eventual victory of America's "Greatest Generation" as citizens and soldiers.[47] Nevertheless, Holmes would claim each and every American visitor to the D-Day Memorial should be moved to recognize "that the faith is true and adorable which leads a soldier to throw away his life in obedience to a blindly accepted duty, in a cause he little understands, in a plan of campaign of which he has no notion, under tactics of which he does not see the use."[48] To those who were called to the colors, but who survive; and, to all the successor generations, who also are asked to recall "the fallen," Holmes asserts Americans probably will regard the call to arms for any war as "horrible and dull."[49] For him, however, "its message was divine" to the extent the combat of nations reveals how each American citizen-at-arms is "capable of miracle, able to lift himself by might of his own soul."[50] Nations rise clearly on the energetic tides of such nationalist teachings. And, as conflicted and ambivalent as such teachings are, it is clear the democratic empire known as the United States of America is no exception. The National D-Day Memorial underscores this deep, if not dark, martial republican ethic in its art, and Holmes' faith in soldiers continues to run deep and strong in the spirit of local activists all across the land.

Notes

1. Andreas Huyssen, *Twilight Memories: Marking Time in a Culture of Amnesia* (New York: Routledge, 1994), 249.

2. Edward Said, "Invention, Memory, and Place," in *Landscape and Power*, 2nd ed., ed. W. J. T. Mitchell (Chicago: University of Chicago Press, 2002), 245. Highlighting the significance of the arts and their display in politics as sites of public memory, tools for a nation-building pedagogy, or markers of unsettled political conflict has been one of my ongoing research programs. See, for example, Timothy W. Luke, *Ideology and Soviet Industrialization* (Westport, CT: Greenwood Press, 1985); Timothy W. Luke, *Shows of Force: Power, Politics, and Ideology in Art Exhibitions* (Durham, NC: Duke University Press, 1992); and Timothy W. Luke, *Museum Politics: Power Plays at the Exhibition* (Minneapolis: University of Minnesota Press, 2002).

3. Walker Connor, *Ethnonationalism: The Quest for Understanding* (Princeton, NJ: Princeton University Press, 1994), 3.

4. Anthony Smith, *National Identity* (Harmondsworth, UK: Penguin, 1991), 72.

5. Ernst Renan, *Qu'est-ce qu'une nation?* (Paris: Sorbonne, 1882), 2.

6. Wayne Norman, "Theorizing Nationalism (Normatively)," in *Theorizing Nationalism*, ed. Ronald Beiner (Albany: State University of New York Press, 1999), 51–65; emphases in original.

7. Benedict Anderson, *Imagined Communities: Reflections on the Origin and Spread of Nationalism*, rev. ed. (London: Verso, 1991), 5.

8. Michael Billig, *Banal Nationalism* (London: Sage, 1995), 1–12.

9. For more discussion, see Garry Wills, *Lincoln at Gettysburg: The Words That Remade America* (New York: Simon & Schuster, 2006).

10. Said, "Invention, Memory, and Place," 245. Also see Timothy W. Luke, "Actualized Affinities: A Nation's Memories as Accumulating Artifacts and Appropriating Aesthetics from the Times of Reconstruction," *Journal of the Royal Anthropological Institute* (2011), S56–68.

11. Max Weber, *From Max Weber: Essays in Sociology*, eds. H. H. Gerth and C. Wright Mills (New York: Oxford University Press, 1946), 335.

12. See http://www.defenselink.mil/news/june2001/N6072001_20010672.html.

13. See Stephen Ambrose, *D-Day June 6, 1944: The Climactic Battle of World War II* (New York: Simon & Schuster, 1994).

14. Stephen Ambrose, *Citizen Soldiers: The U.S. Army from the Normandy Beach to the Bulge to the Surrender of Germany, June 7, 1944 to May 7, 1945* (New York: Simon & Schuster, 1997); and Stephen Ambrose, *Band of Brothers: E Company, 506th Regiment, 101st Airborne from Normandy to Hitler's Eagle's Nest* (New York: Simon & Schuster, 2001).

15. James Morrison, "June 6, 1944, Has the Memorial It Deserves," *Roanoke Times*, June 6, 2005, V7.

16. See http://www.roanoke.com/dday/memorial.

17. See http://www.roanoke.com/dday/memorial/memorial119.html. A local veteran, Bob Slaughter, who went ashore in Normandy on Omaha Beach in the third wave with the 29th Division, began a campaign to build a D-Day memorial in Bedford, Virginia, after retiring in 1987. Age nineteen in 1944, he later became chairman of the National D-Day Memorial Foundation in the 1990s. At age seventy-six, he escorted President George W. Bush to the dedication ceremony on June 6, 2001.

18. Drew Gilpin Faust, *This Republic of Suffering: Death and the Civil War* (New York: Knopf, 2008), 271.

19. Ibid. Also see Kenneth E. Foote, *Shadowed Ground: America's Landscapes of Violence and Tragedy*, rev. ed. (Austin: University of Texas Press, 2003), 278–86.

20. See http://www.defenselink.mil/news/june2001/n06072001_2001 6072.html.

21. See John Dewey, *Art as Experience* (New York: Capricorn Books/G. P. Putnam's Sons, 1958); and Martha C. Nussbaum, *Not for Profit: Why Democracy Needs the Humanities* (Princeton, NJ: Princeton University Press, 2010).

22. See http://www.dday.org/html/calendar.html, accessed October 15, 2011.

23. See http://www.whitehouse.gov/news/2001/06/print/20010606-2.html.

24. Timothy W. Luke, "History as an Ideo-Political Commodity: The 1984 D-Day Spectacle," *New Political Science: A Journal of Politics and Culture* 5, no. 1 (1984): 49–67.

25. Scott Wilson, "Destiny . . . Has Always Been Up to Us," *Washington Post*, June 7, 2009, A1, A15.

26. Herbert Marcuse, *One-Dimensional Man* (Boston: Beacon Press, 1964), 98.

27. W. J. T. Mitchell, "Imperial Landscape," in Mitchell, *Landscape and Power*, 10.

28. Gregor Dallas, *1945: The War That Never Ended* (New Haven, CT: Yale University Press, 2005).

29. Timothy W. Luke, "Hyper-Power or Hype-Power? The USA after Kandahar, Karbala and Katrina," in *Insecure States: Geopolitical Anxiety, the War on Terror, and the Future of American Power*, eds. François Debrix and Mark J. Lacy (New York: Routledge, 2009), 18–33.

30. See Anderson, *Imagined Communities*, 3–6.

31. Faust, *Republic of Suffering*, 271.

32. For more discussion, see Ambrose, *Band of Brothers*.

33. Luke, "History as an Ideo-Political Commodity," 49–67.

34. Midas Dekkers, *The Way of All Flesh: The Romance of Ruins* (New York: Farrar, Straus and Giroux, 1997), 243.

35. Stephen Croad, *The War Memorials Handbook* (London: Imperial War Museum, 2001).

36. John Garfield, *The Fallen: A Photographic Journey through the War Cemeteries and Memorials of the Great War, 1914–1918*, 2nd ed. (Kent, UK: Spellmount, 2003), 14.

37. Lyn MacDonald, *1914–1918: Voices and Images of the Great War* (London: Penguin, 1988).

38. *Saving Private Ryan*, Steven Spielberg, Director (DreamWorks, 1998).

39. Steven Spielberg, ed., *Saving Private Ryan* (New York: New Market Press, 1998).

40. Richard J. Evans, *The Third Reich at War* (New York: Penguin, 2009).

41. Faust, *Republic of Suffering*, 268.

42. Scott Wilson, "Destiny . . . Has Always Been Up to Us," *Washington Post*, June 7, 2009, A1, A15.

43. Courtney Cutright, "D-Day Memorial at Risk of Closing," *Roanoke Times*, May 29, 2009, N1, 10.

44. Rex Bowman, "D-Day Shrine's Status Is Mulled," *Roanoke Times*, August 27, 2009, N1, 22.

45. Mason Adams, "Bill Calls for Study of Memorial," *Roanoke Times*, July 25, 2009, N8.

46. See http://www.hardvardregiment.org/memorial.htm for Oliver Wendell Holmes Jr., "The Soldier's Faith: An Address Delivered on Memorial Day, May 30, 1895, at a Meeting Called by the Graduating Class of Harvard University" (Boston: Little, Brown & Co., 1904).

47. Tom Brokaw, *The Greatest Generation Speaks: Letters and Reflections* (New York: Random House, 1999).

48. Holmes, "The Soldier's Faith."

49. Ibid.

50. Ibid.

Bibliography

Adams, Mason. "Bill Calls for Study of Memorial." *Roanoke Times*, July 25, 2009, N8.

Ambrose, Stephen. *D-Day June 6, 1944: The Climatic Battle of World War II*. New York: Simon & Schuster, 1994.

———. *Citizen Soldiers: The U.S. Army from the Normandy Beach to the Bulge to the Surrender of Germany, June 7, 1944 to May 7, 1945*. New York: Simon & Schuster, 1997.

———. *Band of Brothers: E Company, 506th Regiment, 101st Airborne from Normandy to Hitler's Eagle's Nest*. New York: Simon & Schuster, 2001.

Anderson, Benedict. *Imagined Communities: Reflections on the Origin and Spread of Nationalism*, rev. edition. London: Verso, 1991.

Andreas, Huyssen. *Twilight Memories: Marking Time in a Culture of Amnesia*. New York: Routledge, 1994.

Billig, Michael. *Banal Nationalism*. London: Sage, 1995.

Bowman, Rex. "D-Day Shrine's Status Is Mulled." *Roanoke Times*, August 27, 2009, N1, 22.

Brokaw, Tom. *The Greatest Generation Speaks: Letters and Reflections*. New York: Random House, 1999.

Connor, Walker. *Ethnonationalism: The Quest for Understanding*. Princeton, NJ: Princeton University Press, 1994.

Croad, Stephen. *The War Memorials Handbook*. London: Imperial War Museum. 2001.

Cutright, Courtney. "D-Day Memorial at Risk of Closing." *Roanoke Times*, May 29, 2009, N1, 10.

Dallas, Gregor. *1945: The War That Never Ended*. New Haven, CT: Yale University Press, 2005.

Dekkers, Midas. *The Way of All Flesh: The Romance of Ruins*. New York: Farrar, Straus and Giroux, 1997.

Dewey, John. *Art as Experience*. New York: Capricorn Books/G. P. Putnam's Sons, 1958.

Evans, Richard J. *The Third Reich at War*. New York: Penguin Press, 2009.

Faust, Drew Gilpin. *This Republic of Suffering: Death and the Civil War*. New York: Knopf, 2008.

Foote, Kenneth E. *Shadowed Ground: America's Landscapes of Violence and Tragedy*, rev. edition. Austin: University of Texas Press, 2003.

Garfield, John. *The Fallen: A Photographic Journey through the War Cemeteries and Memorials of the Great War, 1914–1918*, 2nd edition. Kent, UK: Spellmount, 2003.

Holmes, Oliver Wendell, Jr. "The Soldier's Faith: An Address Delivered on Memorial Day, May 30, 1895, at a Meeting Called by the Graduating Class of Harvard University." Boston: Little, Brown & Co., 1904 [1895]. http://www.hardvardregiment.org/memorial.htm.

Luke, Timothy W. "History as an Ideo-Political Commodity: The 1984 D-Day Spectacle." *New Political Science* 5, no. 1 (1984): 49–67.

———. *Ideology and Soviet Industrialization*. Westport, CT: Greenwood Press, 1985.

———. *Shows of Force: Power, Politics, and Ideology in Art Exhibitions*. Durham. NC: Duke University Press, 1992.

———. *Museum Politics: Power Plays at the Exhibition*. Minneapolis: University of Minnesota Press, 2002.

———. "Hyper-Power or Hype-Power? The USA after Kandahar, Karbala and Katrina." In *Insecure States: Geopolitical Anxiety, the War on Terror, and the*

Future of American Power, edited by François Debrix and Mark J. Lacy, 18–33. New York: Routledge, 2009.

———. "Actualized Affinities: A Nation's Memories as Accumulating Artifacts and Appropriating Aesthetics from the Times of Reconstruction." *Journal of the Royal Anthropological Institute* (2011): S56–68.

MacDonald, Lyn. *1914–1918: Voices and Images of the Great War.* London: Penguin, 1988.

Marcuse, Herbert. *One-Dimensional Man.* Boston: Beacon Press, 1964.

Mitchell, W. J. T. "Imperial Landscape." *Landscape and Power*, edited by W. J. T. Mitchell, 5–34. Chicago: University of Chicago Press, 2004.

Morrison, James. "June 6, 1944, Has the Memorial It Deserves." *Roanoke Times*, June 6, 2005, V7.

Norman, Wayne. "Theorizing Nationalism Normatively." In *Theorizing Nationalism*, edited by Ronald Beiner, 51–65. Albany: State University of New York Press, 1999.

Nussbaum, Martha C. *Not for Profit: Why Democracy Needs the Humanities.* Princeton, NJ: Princeton University Press, 2010.

Renan, Ernst. *Qu'est-ce qu'une nation?* Paris: Sorbonne, 1882.

Said, Edward. "Invention, Memory, and Place." In *Landscape and Power*, 2nd edition, edited by W. J. T. Mitchell, 241–260. Chicago: University of Chicago Press, 2002.

Smith, Anthony. *National Identity.* Harmondsworth: Penguin, 1991.

Spielberg, Steven, ed. *Saving Private Ryan.* New York: New Market Press, 1998.

———, director. *Saving Private Ryan.* DreamWorks, 1998.

Weber, Max. *From Max Weber: Essays in Sociology*, edited by H. H. Gerth and C. Wright Mills. New York: Oxford University Press, 1946.

Wills, Garry. *Lincoln at Gettysburg: The Words That Remade America.* New York: Simon & Schuster, 2006.

Wilson, Scott. "Destiny . . . Has Always Been Up to Us." *Washington Post*, June 7, 2009, A1, A15.

Part IV

Literature and Poetry

Chapter 6

The Message in the Medium

Poetry Slam as Democratic Practice

MARK MATTERN

To have great poets, there must be great audiences, too.

—Walt Whitman, "Notes Left Over: Ventures, on an Old Theme"[1]

It is debatable whether or not American poets have ever been able to count on the "great audiences" identified by Whitman as essential for good poetry. But one thing is certain: The twentieth century saw a slow, steady decline of interest among most Americans in poetry. While earlier generations saw poets as important literary and public voices, with their work printed routinely in mass-circulation newspapers and magazines, during the twentieth century the prominence and relevance of poets steadily declined. For the most part, poetry was increasingly consigned to pockets of aficionados, academics, and subscribers to obscure literary magazines. Given the relative isolation of poetry from a mass market, and from the lives of ordinary people, it is no surprise that by the end of the twentieth century, poetry was viewed as "staid, divorced from the world."[1]

Joseph Epstein, in a 1988 article entitled "Who Killed Poetry?," argued that poetry's decline was the result of the increasing migration of poets into academic writing programs.[2] Three years later in an *Atlantic* magazine article (May 1991) entitled "Can Poetry Matter?," poet and critic Dana Gioia affirmed Epstein's argument, while ruing the loss

121

of a nonacademic audience that "cut across lines of race, class, age, and occupation" and was "poetry's bridge to the general culture." Individual poets, he wrote, "are almost invisible."[3]

Similarly, John Barr, while president of the Poetry Foundation, observed in 2006 that "poetry is missing and unmissed," and that "a general, interested public is poetry's foremost need." He identified a "fatigue, something stagnant about the poetry being written today." Contemporary poets, he argued, have lost touch with ordinary lives. Poets who had learned to write for select audiences no longer captured "the way things are, how things have changed." Reality outgrew the art form; consequently "the art form is no longer equal to the reality around it." Poets still wrote, but they wrote for each other. Because few people bought their books, poets took jobs in academia, where they were even more insulated and isolated from ordinary people's lives. One result "is a poetry that is neither robust, resonant, nor—and I stress this quality—entertaining."[4]

Barr concluded that "American poetry is ready for something new." However, he was uncertain what that "something" would look like. He plaintively wished that he could "offer a distinct picture of what . . . the next poetry will look like," but asserted that it would emerge "not from further innovations of form, but from an evolution of the sensibility based on lived experience." This new poetry must "meet a standard of pleasure as well as profundity" if it was to recover its importance and stature in the public world. Poetry "needs to find its public again, and address it."[5]

What is especially interesting about the laments of Gioia and Barr is not only their often insightful diagnosis, but also that they appeared precisely during a renaissance of poetry. Both were well aware of this renaissance but, anchored as both were in the prejudices of so-called high art, apparently rejected its significance. Limited by this high art, or what I will call a Brahmin conception of what quality poetry should look and sound like, they were unable to recognize or acknowledge the political and cultural significance of the renaissance of popular poetry. This renaissance in poetry slam and other forms of performance poetry (such as rap) saw poets once again seizing a critical public role; writing for "great audiences"; generating new, engaged publics; capturing the "way things are" in diverse communities; and reaching deeply into the lives of ordinary people for inspiration and sustenance.

This chapter explores these themes by examining poetry slam in terms of "doing democracy." Most major institutions of U.S. culture, like its political economy writ large, are organized according to undemocratic principles of centralized power, inequality, hierarchy, and control by an elite few with predictable undemocratic results: a "public" unaware of, or indifferent to, domination; lack of critical consciousness; and wholesale distraction from pressing problems and issues. Yet, some cultural forms break partly or wholly from this undemocratic model. Poetry slam is one such form.

Sometimes the politics of an art form can be found in its content: an explicitly political song, for example, or a drama with a political agenda, or a painting celebrating workers' revolutionary fervor. Sometimes, though, the politics of an art form can be found in its form. Poetry slams are one good example. Although many slam poets integrate explicitly political messages into their performances, in this chapter I concentrate primarily on the politics of slam as found in its form.[6] I argue that slam poetry represents a democratic art form because of the way it is typically organized and practiced. As such, slam is a public space in which direct widespread participation is invited and expected and barriers to participation eliminated; where critical consciousness is systematically encouraged; where power is challenged and leveled, and elitism routinely confronted; where norms of equality and freedom are deeply embedded; and where participants model a type of freedom that is more realistic, sustainable, and democratic than dominant liberal understandings.

Slam Poetry: Description and History

Stripped to its bare essentials, slam poetry is poetry that is performed in a competitive environment before a live audience. Judges, usually five, are chosen randomly from the audience with no attempt to first ascertain their ability to judge good from bad poetry. They rate the poets on a scale of 0 to 10, with high and low scores tossed and the remaining three averaged. Generally, poems must be three minutes or less, with points deducted for going over the time limit, though this can vary significantly across local slams. Poets are judged on the poem itself and its performance. A slam master emcees the show and also does much of the organizing and preparation.

The roots of slam are traced back several millennia to ancient oral traditions found, for example, in the Homeric epic, African griots, Zuni priests, Japanese Kojiki poets, and Greek bards who related communal stories via song, poetry, and narrative.[7] According to one source, slam as a competition goes back at least to the first century BC, when the Greek lyric poet Pindar was bested five times by lesser-known poet Korinna and Pindar went on to ridicule her as a sow.[8] Others note that the ancient Olympics included poetry competitions, with winners receiving laurel crowns. Other competitive roots include Japanese haiku contests and African "signifying," or word battles.

Twentieth-century roots and influences include early twentieth-century Dadaism, emphasizing childlike spontaneity, intellectual nihilism, and moving art outside the museum and concert hall. The 1950s and 1960s beat poets, who sought to transform poetry from a sedate, genteel diversion enjoyed by elites into something more immediate and accessible, are also cited as influences on slam poetry. Beat poets read in coffeehouses, bars, lofts, and cellars. They broke other rules of academic poetry by inviting audience participation, using music, and injecting elements that sometimes made the readings appear like drunken chaos. Beat poets also began hosting open mic readings. Many of the same dynamics occurred in the Black Arts movement of the mid-1960s and early 1970s. Affiliated with Black Nationalism, this movement primarily sought to address black audiences, celebrate black culture, and increase cultural autonomy. Black Arts poets anticipated slam in treating the poem as a performance script rather than simply a written text. They drew from various African and African American cultural elements, including street vocabulary and cadence, West African vocabulary, percussion and other musical elements, call-and-response, African spirituality, and the speech cadences of black preachers. Their use of live performance, nontraditional performance venues, an attitude of political resistance, democratic ideals, and a conscious stance of marginality from dominant and official verse cultures would eventually be found as well in slam poetry. Performance art and hip hop culture of the 1970s and 1980s also laid the foundations for slam.

The genesis of slam can also be found in a reaction against the mid-twentieth-century literary world's New Criticism focusing on structure and content of literary texts. New Critics focused on literary texts in isolation from both audience response and social context. Some also insisted that the author's intention was irrevelant.[9] What mattered was meaning derived from texts through a close reading of the text qua text, separated from its historical and cultural coordinates. Finally, slam poets would react against the poverty of the traditional poetry scene of the 1970s and 1980s, and against the elitism of traditional poetry and literary worlds.

By the early 1980s, these various influences were congealing into new forms of poetry performance. In 1980, Stone Wind poet Al Simmons began hosting poetry bouts. He formed the World Poetry Association

(WPA) modeled after pro wrestling and boxing. These poetic boxing matches introduced entertainment and show into the world of poetry.

Marc Smith, a construction worker and poet in Chicago, is widely cited as the person who created the poetry slam in its modern form.[10] In the late 1970s and early 1980s, various Chicago venues hosted poetry readings either routinely or occasionally. One early venue was the Get Me High Lounge, on Chicago's north side, in a blue-collar neighborhood. Smith secured Monday nights for poets, and this became the Monday Night Poetry Readings and open mic at the Get Me High Lounge, starting in 1984. In 1986, he started a poetry cabaret on Sundays at the Green Mill Cocktail Lounge, known mostly as a jazz club, on Chicago's north side. The first slam was held there on July 20, 1986. No official competition occurred at that one. Instead, Smith came up with the competition idea out of creative desperation: he ran out of material to finish an ensemble show. He turned it over to the audience to judge via boos and applause. Smith was also creatively responding to some of the perceived problems associated with poetry readings, especially poets who read too long at open mics, and the lack of surprises and variety in many readings.

The new format quickly took off, and the idea began spreading to other cities. The first National Poetry Slam occurred in 1991, in San Francisco. Since then, the National Poetry Slam has been held annually in a different city each year, often with upward of one hundred cities competing. Slam continued its rise to attention and prominence in 1994, with its inclusion in that year's Lollapalooza tour through over thirty cities. At each stop, a poetry slam was hosted in a "revival tent." To help promote the event, local slams were also held in host cities in advance of the arrival of the tour. This tour led to the proliferation of local slams in places like Austin, Dallas, and Pittsburgh.

One of the defining features of slam poetry in the last decade has been its reach into communities of youth. Various groups have formed to introduce slam to younger populations. These include: Urban Word, which sponsors an annual teen poetry slam in New York City aimed at increasing youth literacy; the University of Iowa's Arts Share program, which sponsors a summer youth camp; America Scores, found in various U.S. cities, which combines poetry performance with soccer, songwriting, and community service for eight- to twelve-year-olds; Youth Speaks, based in San Francisco, which sponsors performance poetry across the West Coast; Writers Corp, which introduces poetry to inner-city children to develop reading and writing skills; and many more. Youth now participate in their own national and regional (as well as local) slam competitions through such organizations as the College Unions Poetry Slam Invitational (CUPSI) and the Brave New Voices National Youth Poetry Slam Festival.

Slam has also gone international, with slam competitions now occurring routinely in Germany, Switzerland, Israel, England, Sweden, Canada, France, Poland, Norway, and elsewhere. At various levels of organization and among many different populations, slam poetry is now an established feature of culture production and consumption.[11]

Participation and Critical Judgment

Slam poets embrace an ethos of accessibility and widespread participation. The dominant sensibility in slam is that anybody can write and perform poetry, and everyone is encouraged to do so. Most slams begin with an open mic in which participants sign up on a first-come-first-served basis and perform in that order. Although some slams feature invited poets who are guaranteed a slot later in the evening, most poets must earn their later performance slot by surviving early rounds and advancing to the later rounds. This breaks from the Brahmin approach in which poets with credentials are featured, and where a sharp distinction is made between poet and audience. The governing sensibility in Brahmin poetry emphasizes the degree to which the credentialed poet has the necessary skills and artistic sensibility to write and read poetry, while audience members are relegated to the role of passive listeners. The competitive framework of slam ensures that every poet gets a chance to perform in the opening round and, if good enough, later rounds. Of course, this competitive framework also ensures that some poets—those who garner the favor of audiences and judges—will be more likely to advance to later rounds and thus get more performance time.

Many slam variations occur. These include, for example, cover slams where the poets perform work of famous poets, erotica slams featuring sexual themes, haiku slams in which each poem lasts seventeen syllables, hip hop slams, prop slams where performers are invited and sometimes required to use props, speak-out slams where political advocacy is required, heckler slams where audience members are encouraged to heckle, bad poem slams where the worst wins, music slams where poems are performed to musical accompaniment, improv slams featuring improvised poems, group poem slams in which all performance is in groups, specific theme slams such as Slam to Get Mumia Off Death Row and Slam for Peace, and many more. Anything goes at the local level, where variations are limited only by the slam masters' and other participants' imagination. Across all these variations, the central defining elements of slam remain: it is performed in a competitive environment before a live audience.[12]

One of the features of slam poetry that offends many Brahmins is its deliberate attempt to entertain, because it requires a certain level of accessibility to audiences. Slammers ask, "Why couldn't poetry entertain as well as enlighten? Why couldn't poetry be accessible as well as intelligent?"[13] Slam poets remind us that Shakespeare, too, had deep roots in entertainment and in the everyday lives of common people. He wrote to entertain common people, and his plays were widely accessible.

Slam venues accentuate the accessibility of slam. These are typically places where average people congregate anyway: bars, restaurants, coffee shops, community centers, and sometimes performance halls. During the 1980s in Cleveland, slams were held notoriously at Pearl Road Auto Wrecking, on the back of a flatbed semi truck. Slam poets still sometimes compete not only with each other but also with the television and rowdy patrons watching a ball game on television; and audience members are not expected to stay glued to their seats through a slam performance.[14]

Audience members are encouraged and expected to participate actively as critical judges of poets' performances. This is true most obviously of those audience members who are selected to serve as judges for the slam. But it also holds true for all audience members. There is "no such thing as passive listening at a slam."[15] Audience members react to the poet's performance with boos, cheers, jeers, finger-snapping (indicating the poem is boring), hissing (generally at sexist poems), stomping, groaning, and guessing-the-rhyme (shouting out the word in predictable poetry).[16] Some venues offer a more structured role for audience members including discussion after a reading, or having an entire audience involved in scoring. Slammers hone the same poem during its shelf life, and deliver it in repeated slams. Audiences come to expect certain poems and recite or shout certain lines along with the poet. Rather than being frowned upon, as it would be in a Brahmin poetry reading, audience participation signifies positively that the poet is connecting with the audience (unless it is done sarcastically, as sometimes happens).

What is the basis for audience members' judgment and critique? Partly in response to the perception of rigid codes and standards of quality imposed in Brahmin poetry circles, codes and standards that inevitably exclude average people, slammers have intentionally attempted to subvert rigid expectations. This does not mean that there are no codes and stan-dards. It just means that those codes and standards, which are derived in part from the audience and what its members want and expect, emphasize different things, especially the connection and resonance between poet and audience. For slam poetry, a good poem communicates deeply with audience members. It engages them as whole persons, both cognitively and affectively. This requires both a good poem and a good performance. A slam poem is good if it touches the lives of ordinary people in mean-ingful ways; if it captures recognizable experiences and shared meanings, and uses these to broaden experience and shared understandings while establishing connections between poet and audience member.

All this is sometimes true of Brahmin poetry too. However, Brah-min poetry in general emphasizes the text and structure of a poem, divorced from social circumstances, more so than slam poetry. For many Brahmin poets, the questions change from "what does it mean to be human now?" and "how can we cope with our current reality and solve current problems?" to "what is a well-crafted poem?"[17] The point is not that slam poets and audiences do not admire a "well-crafted poem"; the point is that that goal is complemented and sometimes superseded by the priority of meaningful connections to people and their everyday lives. As described by Jeff Kass, "At base, we humans want to connect with each other. . . . Performance poetry . . . is a way to clear the swirling debris of false language and connect. That is its power."[18]

These elements of slam echo the democratic and aesthetic com-mitments of John Dewey, the philosopher, pragmatist, and participatory democrat who wrote extensively on aesthetics. Dewey rejected distinc-tions between so-called high and low art and instead proposed to dis-tinguish between good and bad art according to how well it captures human experience and communicates it to others in a way that draws them into a shared experience. These shared experiences help us bridge our differences; they help us overcome the "uncivility of civilization" when it is "divided into non-communicating sects, races, nations, classes and cliques."[19] The art experience becomes "a manifestation, a record and celebration of the life of a civilization" and the "ultimate judgment upon the quality of the civilization."[20] The "civilization" created by slam poetry integrates deep democratic commitments to access and participa-tion by average people.

Assuming that human character is at least partly a result of inter-action with a social environment, participation in the slam experience encourages the development and exercise of a capacity for critical judgment. As noted by democratic pedagogists, subjecting people to cultural forms in which average people play passive, uncritical roles teaches them to be passive and uncritical.[21] It instills character traits that are not conducive to the critical thinking and engaged activism needed for democracy. Exposing people to slam poetry offers an alternative experience in which passivity is institutionally and structurally rejected in favor of active, critical participation. This contributes to habits of critical thinking and engaged citizenship.

A critic might respond that, if the slam poet must win the sympathy of audience members in order to succeed competitively, does this encourage pandering and the expression of cheap, sentimental, and distorted ideas and sentiments? In other words, does slam imitate the distortions and manipulations of public opinion in liberal democracies dominated by private power and self-interest? Does slam give audience members basically what they want rather than what a democratic citizen needs to engage in critical debate? Do slammers educate and challenge members of their audience? In short, are slam poets demagogues or modern-day Socrates?

A definitive answer to any of these questions is impossible. Much depends on the venue, the poet, and the makeup of the audience. Undoubtedly, some slammers pander to the audience by using clichés and cheap sentimentality in order to succeed competitively. But slam is also replete with poets whose performance challenges the audience in myriad ways to examine and rethink the basic assumptions, beliefs, and practices that characterize everyday life in the United States. Slam offers no magic pill that can fully overcome the cumulative and collective weight of a political economy and culture oriented toward mass propaganda and delusion. At a minimum, however, slam cuts against the grain of these dominant forces by demanding that poet and audience alike constantly read each other, exercise judgment, and think critically.

Challenging and Leveling Power

For the most part, slam poetry is organized along a horizontal, decentralized model. Power is leveled and decision-making dispersed within this model of organization. With partial exception, there is no individual or entity with the authority to impose rules and guidelines. The many local slams are autonomous, organized by local promoters, poets, and enthusiasts. Rules and guidelines are frequently adapted, rather than adopted uncritically.[22]

The partial exceptions are Poetry Slam, Inc. (PSI) and National Poetry Slam (NPS). Slammers found it necessary to impose some structure in order to maintain a level competitive field and attempt to ensure that the open, democratic spirit of slam remain intact. PSI, a nonprofit organization representing slammers and slam venues, incorporated in 1997, to oversee competition, seize control of the increasing attempts to profit from slams, and create and enforce rules. Its bylaws were adopted after public deliberation among leading participants at the time. PSI now hosts two major annual events: National Poetry Slam (NPS) and Individual World Poetry Slam (IWPS).[23] Poets must join PSI if they wish to compete at the nationals. All members can share in governance by voting on general principles and proposals for changes in slam. An executive council oversees the routine management of PSI. This executive council meets at least twice each year to determine host sites, conduct elections to the council, propose and approve new projects, and organize and conduct work through subcommittees. The seven members of this elective body serve two-year terms.[24]

While local slams can, and often do, depart from scripts and rules, NPS is highly structured as a four-day tournament, with preliminary, semi-final, and final competition nights. As in all other slams, however, five judges are selected from the audience. The NPS adheres to rigid rules. The three-minute time limit is strictly enforced, with a half point deducted for every ten seconds over the three minutes. No props or costumes are allowed, though debate often occurs over what constitutes a costume and who pushes the boundaries too far. For example, is a naked chest a costume?[25] Additionally, while many local slams allow "cover" poems, at NPS all poems must be original. Most of these rules were instituted to ensure a level playing field. For example, someone who brought along several musicians to a slam performance would have a better chance of impressing members of the audience. The three-minute rule was instituted initially as well to fend off "stage hogs" and increase the number of participants. All of these rules are subject to challenge through the governing structure of PSI. Only certified slam teams can compete at NPS. To become certified, you must provide evidence of ties to a local community, and each local slam must conduct an open competition to form a team. To do the work of preparing for each year's NPS, slammers formed an organizing committee called SlamMasters Council, representing registered venues around the country. SlamMasters meet in the upcoming host city to evaluate preparations and conduct other NPS business.

Organizing a national slam competition requires many hours of work by the host city's participants to prepare the host city for NPS.[26] Many volunteers are needed to make contacts, arrange funding, work with the media and other promotional outlets, secure and prepare venues for the competition, and staff the actual slam and associated events. Volunteers are needed during the slam itself as emcees, ticket-takers, lighting and sound technicians, doorkeepers, scorekeepers, timers, judges, and merchandise sellers. This grassroots approach to preparing and hosting a slam helps ensure the sharing and dispersion of control. It also helps broaden ownership of the event and slam poetry more generally.

In addition to the PSI and NPS network, the slam community is connected via an infrastructure of local slams geared in part toward touring slammers. As slam developed, poets increasingly booked tours in slam venues exclusively. Touring allows for "cross-pollination" across different slam scenes and venues, and makes the notion of a "national community" concrete.[27] Slammers are also networked electronically via listserv and email lists. Many informal connections are developed and sustained through touring and through networking at national and regional slams. These can be translated into support during touring. For example, slam poets often end up staying with host slammers while touring, and reciprocity is expected.[28]

These aspects of slam reflect democratic principles of decentralization, power leveling, and grassroots organizing through a network of local slam venues and resources. Though outsize personalities and key administrative positions (which generally rotate) collect some power and control, in general, power remains dispersed.

Equality

Slam's commitment to equality is evident from the previous discussion: in its insistence that anyone can write and perform poetry; that common people are capable of appreciating and judging poetry; that barriers to participation should be eliminated; that power should be leveled and decentralized; and that control should be dispersed among countless individuals and local slams. Slam poetry's commitment to equality can also be understood in contrast to Brahmin poetry (and Brahmin art in general). Earlier, I noted the ruminations of Brahmin poets and critics who regretted the decline and disappearance of poetry from popular scenes. These poets and critics for the most part have simply ignored slam poetry. Sometimes, however, defenders of Brahmin poetry have openly expressed their disdain for slam. Harold Bloom's elitist screed against slam is illustrative:

> Of course, now it's all gone to hell. I can't bear these accounts I read in the *Times* and elsewhere of these poetry slams, in which various young men and women in various late-spots are declaiming rant and nonsense at each other. The whole thing is judged by an applause meter which is actually not there, but might as well be. This isn't even silly; it is the death of art.[29]

For the most part, slammers respond in kind: they either ignore their Brahmin critics or lob the insults back at them. Brahmin critics and poets, especially those found in academia, are charged with elitism, snobbery, and disconnection from the real world. Slammers' response reveals a deep anti-authoritarianism, and a desire to flatten hierarchies. Both contribute to the egalitarian ethos that pervades slam poetry.

A central goal of slam poets from the outset has been an attempt to reconnect poetry to a vital audience, and part of this mission has involved encouraging art from the masses and taking it straight to the masses. As Smith argues, slam poets are "not scholarly snobs, not preachers or saints more perfect than the masses they stood before. Slammers were, and are, just part of the crowd."[30] This embrace of common people, their everyday experiences, and their capacity for art helps explain the venues often chosen for slams—bars, nightclubs, and community centers, for example, as well as theaters and auditoriums. Slammers have been on a mission to rekindle popular poetry among a large and diverse audience, something that Brahmin poets have largely failed to do in several generations at least. They have sought to overcome the notion that art occurs in a rarified atmosphere in which participation requires credentials and the stamp of approval from elite critics. They have emphasized instead that average people can create, perform, and appreciate poetry.

Does the competitive element of slam undermine this commitment to equality? After all, any competitive system produces and reproduces winners and losers, where winners gradually acquire status and power over others. As a general answer, it should be acknowledged that a tension exists between the competitive aspect of slam and its commitment to equality, given that some slam poets inevitably garner more attention, acquire prestige, and claim more stage time accordingly. Some specific evidence can also be cited of competition undermining the egalitarian ethos of slam. For example, to gain a competitive advantage, in 1997, slammaster Bob Holman offended many by securing corporate sponsorship for his NPS team from Mouth Almighty Records/Mercury. Similarly, the NYC-Urbana team, based in the Bowery Poetry Club, was sponsored by the board game manufacturer Scrabble. Many saw these as opening the floodgates of corporate sponsorship.[31] That same offending Mouth Almighty team of 1997, was handpicked by Holman to better ensure competitive success. Prior to that, all national teams were composed of poets who had earned their way onto the team via an open competition at a local venue. Naturally, Holman's handpicking a team offended many as contradicting the open, populist spirit of slams. The following year, in response, NPS banned handpicking.

That said, most slammers respond that the competition is not driven by money or by corporate sponsorship, but by a commitment to the art form. The competition, they insist, is "tongue-in-cheek . . . , a method of enticing people to gather on a Monday night and watch poetry instead of *Ally McBeal*."[32] Competition is "window dressing . . . , a theatrical device intended to stoke the competitive fires of the performing poets, encourage audience participation and pump some fuel into an entertaining evening of poetry, friendship, and camaraderie." It is "a way to get the audience involved." It "fires up the audience and encourages them to interact with the poets and emcees. And it provides a structure for the poetry slam that holds the whole crazy show together, energizing all those involved, including the audience."[33] Poets who care too much about winning are referred to as "Score Creeps"[34] whose pandering is "disgusting."[35] Defenders of slam competitions also note that if the competition were meant to separate good from bad poetry according to Brahmin standards, judges would not be selected randomly from the audience; they would be chosen based on their experience and expected ability to recognize quality when they see and hear it. The competitive dimension of slam helps maintain its nonhierarchical, grassroots element by forcing slam poets to heed their public, to listen to the "voices of the people" who judge their work, and to head off Brahmin impositions of taste and elitism.

Freedom in Community

People are free if they have a meaningful voice in the creation of the rules and laws that determine the character of everyday life. The alternative is to live by rules and laws set by others. Meaningful participation in the creation of rules and laws requires, in turn, some level of equality so that each person's voice can be heard in the decision-making process, and each person's contribution is weighed equally. Slam's deep egalitarianism thus provides a foundation for a type of freedom, an older and relatively submerged strain of freedom in which freedom is understood partly in terms of participation in public life.

Slam poets, and those who write about slam poetry, emphasize its "communal nature."[36] Slam poetry is "a resurrection of community storytelling."[37] It creates and sustains a "deep sense of community" among slammers.[38] Poetry slam "brings us together."[39] Slam poets "master the power of the word to bring us together to listen to each other and celebrate what we have in common, learn what we don't, hear what we need to, and grow together."[40] The communal nature of slam is most pronounced and apparent in group poems, which are created and performed collaboratively by two or more poets who weave multiple voices and sounds imitating a particular social environment. In a group poem, "four poets become one voice."[41] A good group poem exceeds the sum of its parts as individual poets' separate voices amplify each other, and the separate poets feed off each other's creativity and energy. In a sense, all slam poems are group poems since they *never* come to life in isolation. Slam poems attain their fullness in performance, which presumes an audience whose members are expected and urged to participate actively as judges and sounding boards.

In addition to these structural elements, community is also developed affectively. Slam poetry, like many other art forms, draws deliberately on both rational and affective faculties in order to engage others fully. The structure of slam poetry, which presumes and ensures that poets and audience members must communicate with each other, combined with the affective dimensions of poetry, sometimes results in a "deep connection" among poets and audience members.[42] Barriers that Brahmin poets erect deliberately or unintentionally break down in slam.

Slam's deep roots in community could be viewed as an impediment to human freedom. The dominant liberal ideology poses freedom in terms of the absence of restrictions on human choice and action.[43] Major impediments to human freedom include government and, inevitably, other people who thwart the individual's will. This appears in a popular conception of artists as solitary figures, often tortured, standing outside society and perhaps even independent of its influences. As John Barr, once president of the Poetry Foundation, put it, "The creation of art is not a matter of fellowship. Writing a poem is a fiercely independent act."[44] This conception of the artist as a solitary figure has much in common with the dominant liberal understanding of freedom as freedom from undue influences from others. Freedom is maximized through separation from the limiting influences of others and undermined to the degree that the individual is subjected to social influences and pressures.[45]

There are at least two problems with this portrayal of an artist and the conception of freedom it models. First, while this picture of the solitary artist-as-genius no doubt accurately portrays some artists and their lives, in important ways it is a romanticized caricature. No artist lives completely apart from human society and influence. Every human is at least partly a creation of human society through the myriad social influences that mold human personality and character. Secondly, underlying this high-art portrayal of artists is the presumption that good art *can*, and perhaps *should*, be created in separation from social influence. It portrays a person divorced precisely from the human intercourse that generates art that can speak meaningfully to diverse audiences.

Whatever the merits of this version of art and its creation, poetry slam presents a sharp contrast. Although most slam poets actually write their poems alone, they cannot afford to do so in isolation from their audiences. They must write with their audience in mind, if they want to be competitive. They have to write poetry that they think will connect in performance with their audience. This means that slam poets must write for others, not in spite of, or while ignoring, others. In the liberal sense of freedom, this of course limits their choices and thus their freedom. However, it also makes necessary a more sociable conception of art than the high art caricature noted earlier.

Slam models a relationship in which the community and individual freedom are both inextricably tied and mutually supportive, and where sociability is viewed not as an impediment to human autonomy but as a requirement for it. Slam poetry is a world of free expression, inspiration, and creation. Slam poets experience their freedom because of social connections and the community ties in which they are embedded. Their freedom, in short, is made possible by community, not threatened by it. This is a more democratic conception because, to do democracy, citizens must find or create common ground where shared issues and problems can be recognized, acknowledged, and addressed. Precisely part of the problem today in the contemporary United States is the failure to find or create this common ground, which can be attributed in part to the radical individualism and related liberal freedom that dominates.

Closing: Slam as Prefiguration

The arts, based as they are on a foundation of imagination and creativity, offer fertile terrain for developing and identifying new possibilities for thought and action. Artists attempt to reach beyond convention to create and express new meaning. They help us "articulate the unspoken," and this "brings about interesting futures."[46]

I have argued that slam's structure—the way it is organized and practiced—reflects and sustains an ethos of democracy where norms of equality and freedom pervade, and in which active, widespread participation is expected and encouraged, barriers to participation removed, critical consciousness systematically encouraged, and power leveled. It gives participants a direct experience of "doing democracy" that is deeper and more tangible than the thin version most take for granted in a liberal democracy. In all of these ways, slam suggests future, more democratic, possibilities. It opens new horizons of thought and action.

Of course, slam is not immune from undemocratic influences and pressures. The generally progressive and liberal leanings of slam poets and audiences do not ensure the absence of occasional racist, sexist, hetero-sexist, homophobic, and other undemocratic messages in the content of slam poetry. Similarly, can slam as a democratic art form survive against the pressures of a profoundly undemocratic political economy and mass culture? Despite the overt opposition to commercialization of slam, in recent years some slammers have expressed concern that slam is never-theless slipping increasingly toward commercialism in the same way as occurred with rap, that "there is a developing shift within slam from art to commerce."[47] According to Marc Smith, despite having "resisted the commercial exploitation of the slam . . . the door to commercialization is now wide open."[48]

This remains a dilemma within the slam community. As expressed by one observer, "there is an anti-commercial, anti-capitalistic strain within the slam community, but also slam poets realize that's really the way they're going to make it, by 'selling out.'"[49] Some continue to reject commercialism of any sort, while others seek commercial opportunities via touring, recording albums, and appearing in mainstream media. This leaves at least some slammers wondering how to maintain some level of integrity uncorrupted by market institutions and ethos, while also earn-ing a living. This dilemma is hardly unique to slammers. Many people across many different occupations face it every day. To the degree that slammers commercialize, for whatever reason, it threatens to undermine the grassroots, community-oriented, democratic commitments preferred by many. Finally, it should be remembered that the vast majority of slammers do their art at local, relatively informal levels where commercial considerations rarely, if ever, apply.

Notes

1. Daniel Nester, Foreword to Cristin O'Keefe Aptowicz, *Words in Your Face: A Guided Tour through Twenty Years of the New York City Poetry Slam* (New York: Soft Skull, 2008), xiii.

2. Joseph Epstein, "Who Killed Poetry?" *Commentary* 86, no. 2 (1988): 14–15.

3. "Can Poetry Matter?" reprinted in Dana Gioia, *Can Poetry Matter? Essays on Poetry and American Culture*, 10th anniversary edition (St. Paul, MN: Graywolf Press, 2002 [1992]), 10, 19, 1.

4. John Barr, "American Poetry in the New Century," *Poetry* 188, no. 5 (2006): 1–2, http://www.poetryfoundation.org/archive/print.html?id=178560.

5. Ibid., 1, 2, 5.

6. Explicitly political messages found in slam poetry tend to be liberal and left. Slam audiences also tend toward the left end of the political spectrum. See, especially, Susan Somers-Willett, *The Cultural Politics of Slam Poetry: Race, Identity, and the Performance of Popular Verse in America* (Ann Arbor: University of Michigan Press, 2009), 68, 78.

7. On the roots of slam poetry, see, for example, Gary Mex Glazner, "Poetry Slam: An Introduction," in *Poetry Slam: The Competitive Art of Performance Poetry*, ed. Gary Mex Glazner (San Francisco: Manic D Press, 2000), 11; Cecily von Ziegesar, ed., *Slam* (New York: Alloy Books, 2000), 3; Mark Eleveld, ed., *The Spoken Word Revolution: Slam, Hip Hop and the Poetry of a New Generation* (Naperville, IL: Sourcebooks MediaFusion, 2003), 80; Gregory Harms, "Performance Art: Blood, Ice Skates, and Coyotes in the 20th Century," in Eleveld, *The Spoken Word Revolution*, 76–78; Terry Jacobus, "Poetic Pugilism," in Eleveld, *The Spoken Word Revolution*, 85–88; Anne MacNaughton, "The Taos Poetry Circus," in Eleveld, *The Spoken Word Revolution*, 101–02; Richard Prince, "Once a 'virgin, virgin' at the Green Mill," in Eleveld, *The Spoken Word Revolution*, 141; Marc Kelly Smith with Joe Kraynak, *The Complete Idiot's Guide to Slam Poetry* (Indianapolis: Alpha Books, 2004), 4–7, 22; Aptowicz, *Words in Your Face*, 4; Nester, "Foreword," xiv; and Somers-Willett, *The Cultural Politics of Slam Poetry*, 16, 52–67.

8. Nester, Foreword, xiv.

9. On New Criticism see, for example, Mark Jancovich, *The Cultural Politics of the New Criticism* (Cambridge, MA: Cambridge University Press, 1993); and Vincent B. Leitch, ed., *The Norton Anthology of Theory and Criticism* (New York: W. W. Norton & Company, 2001).

10. On the genesis of poetry slam in its modern form, see, for example, Glazner, *Poetry Slam*, 11–12; Jean Howard, "Performance Art, Performance Poetry—The Two Sisters," in Eleveld, *The Spoken Word Revolution*, 65; Marc Smith, "About Slam Poetry," in Eleveld, *The Spoken Word Revolution*, 117–18; Smith and Kraynak, *The Complete Idiot's Guide*, 17, 31, 297, 304–13; Guy Le Charles Gonzalez, "The Revolution Will Be," in *The Spoken Word Revolution, Redux*, ed. Mark Eleveld (Naperville: Sourcebooks MediaFusion, 2007), 23; Jeff Kass, "The 'Youuuuths': 'At base, we humans want to connect with each other . . .'" in Eleveld, *The Spoken Word Revolution, Redux*, 198; Susan Somers-Willett, "Can Slam Poetry Matter?," *Rattle* 13, no. 1 (2007): 85; and Aptowicz, *Words in Your Face*, 94–96.

11. For a very partial list of slam venues, see www.poetryslam.com, which also hosts a listserv.

12. On slam variations, see especially Bob Holman, "The Room," in Glazner, *Poetry Slam*, 15–21; and Smith and Kraynak, *The Complete Idiot's Guide*, 290.

13. Jacobus, "Poetic Pugilism," 83.

14. See Ray McNiece, "Cleveland Slam Team Championship Season and Other Reminiscences," in *Cleveland Poetry Scenes: A Panorama and Anthology*, eds. Nina Freedlander Gibans, Mary E. Weems, and Larry Smith (Huron, OH: Bottom Dog Press, 2008), 117.

15. Susan McAllister, "Slam Poetry Demystified," in *A Bigger Boat: The Unlikely Success of the Albuquerque Poetry Slam Scene*, eds. Susan McAllister, Don McIver, Mikaela Renz, and Daniel S. Solis (Albuquerque: University of New Mexico Press, 2008), 29.

16. See, for example, Smith and Kraynak, *The Complete Idiot's Guide*, 23.

17. On this point, see especially Mark Eleveld, "Beat Remnants: Introduction," in Eleveld, *The Spoken Word Revolution*, 11–12.

18. Kass, "The 'Youuuuths,'" 200.

19. John Dewey, *Art as Experience*, in *John Dewey: The Later Works, 1925–1953*, volume 10: 1934, ed. Jo Ann Boydston (Carbondale: Southern Illinois University Press, 1989 [1934]), 339.

20. Dewey, *Art as Experience*, 329.

21. See, for example, John Dewey, *Democracy and Education*, in *John Dewey: The Middle Works, 1899–1924*, volume 9, ed. Jo Ann Boydston (Carbondale: Southern Illinois University Press, 1985 [1916]); John Dewey, *Human Nature and Conduct*, in *John Dewey: The Middle Works, 1899–1924*, volume 14, ed. Jo Ann Boydston (Carbondale: Southern Illinois University Press, 1988 [1922]); and Paolo Freire, *Pedagogy of the Oppressed* (New York: Continuum, 1970 [1968]).

22. On the decentralized, power-leveled nature of slam, see especially Marc Smith and Joe Kraynak, *Take the Mic: The Art of Performance Poetry, Slam, and the Spoken Word* (Naperville, IL: Sourcebooks, 2009), 26.

23. PSI also organizes a Cross Training Poetry Camp with three days of workshops, discussions, open mics, feature performances, and slam competitions.

24. See, for example, Smith and Kraynak, *The Complete Idiot's Guide*, 20–26, 42, 282; McAllister et al., *A Bigger Boat*, 125.

25. See Glazner, "Poetry Slam: An Introduction," 13–14 and Smith and Kraynak, *The Complete Idiot's Guide*, 293. A full set of rules can be found at www.poetryslam.com.

26. The list of groups, businesses, political agencies, politicians, cities, counties, arts centers, radio stations, charitable groups, nonprofits, and a generic "all our fabulous volunteers" acknowledged for their role in helping sponsor the 2005 Albuquerque National Poetry Slam covers a full three single-spaced pages. See Susan McAllister, "Thank You and Acknowledgments," in McAllister et al., *A Bigger Boat*, 271–73.

27. Aptowicz, *Words in Your Face*, 38, 149–50.

28. See Mikaela Renz, "Aftermath: Organizing Community," in McAllister et al., *A Bigger Boat*, 319–20 on slam touring.

29. Harold Bloom, "The Man in the Back Row Has a Question VI," *Paris Review* 154 (Spring 2000): 379.

30. Smith and Kraynak, *The Complete Idiot's Guide*, 8.

31. Aptowicz, *Words in Your Face*, 240, 155.

32. Alix Olson, "Diary of a Slam Poet," *Ms. Magazine* 11, no. 1 (December 2000/January 2001): 68.

33. Smith and Kraynak, *The Complete Idiot's Guide*, 9–10, 15, 20.

34. Glazner, *Poetry Slam*, 14.

35. Smith and Kraynak, *The Complete Idiot's Guide*, 22.

36. Billy Collins, "Poems on the page, Poems in the air," in Eleveld, *The Spoken Word Revolution*, 4.

37. Olson, "Diary of a Slam Poet," 68.

38. Aptowicz, *Words in Your Face*, xx.

39. Daniel S. Solis, "Letter from the Chair of NPS 2005 (from the Event Program)," in McAllister et al., *A Bigger Boat*, 169.

40. Renz, "Aftermath," 320.

41. Mike Henry, "Group Discussion on the Group Piece," in Glazner, *Poetry Slam*, 216.

42. Genevieve Van Cleve, "Tour," in Glazner, *Poetry Slam*, 139. See again John Dewey, *Art as Experience* (1934), who emphasized the community-creating role of successful art.

43. For discussions of older, and newer liberal, forms of freedom, see Benjamin Constant, "The Liberty of the Ancients Compared with That of the Moderns," in *The Libertarian Reader: Classic and Contemporary Readings from Lao-Tzu to Milton Friedman*, ed. David Boaz (New York: Free Press, 1997 [1816]), 65–70; Isaiah Berlin, *Two Concepts of Liberty* (Oxford, UK: Clarendon Press,

1958); Gerald MacCallum, "Negative and Positive Freedom," *Philosophical Review* 76, no. 3 (1967): 312–34; and William Connolly, "The Idea of Freedom," in *The Terms of Political Discourse*, 2nd edition (Princeton, NJ: Princeton University Press, 1983), 139–78.

44. Barr, "American Poetry in the New Century," 3. The Poetry Foundation is a Brahmin organization.

45. Consider, for example, Ayn Rand's *Fountainhead* in which the protagonist, Howard Roark, is portrayed as achieving greatness as an architect only by separating and isolating himself from social influences. Ayn Rand, *The Fountainhead* (New York: Penguin Books, [1943] 2007).

46. Saul Williams, "The Future of Language," in Eleveld, *The Spoken Word Revolution*, 59.

47. Jerry Quickley, "Hip Hop Poetry," in Eleveld, *The Spoken Word Revolution*, 42. See also Aptowicz, *Words in Your Face*, 310.

48. Smith, "About Slam Poetry," 116.

49. Aptowicz interview with Susan Somers-Willett, in Aptowicz, *Words in Your Face*, 336; see also Somers-Willett, *The Cultural Politics of Slam Poetry*, 12–13.

Bibliography

Aptowicz, Cristin O'Keefe. *Words in Your Face: A Guided Tour through Twenty Years of the New York City Poetry Slam*. New York: Soft Skull, 2008.

Barr, John. "American Poetry in the New Century." *Poetry* 188, no. 5 (2006): 433–41. http://www.poetryfoundation.org/archive/print.html?id=178560.

Berlin, Isaiah. *Two Concepts of Liberty*. Oxford, UK: Clarendon Press, 1958.

Bloom, Harold. "The Man in the Back Row Has a Question VI." *Paris Review* 154 (Spring 2000): 370–402.

Collins, Billy. "Poems on the page, Poems in the air." In Eleveld, *The Spoken Word Revolution*, 3–5.

Connolly, William. "The Idea of Freedom." In *The Terms of Political Discourse*, 2nd ed, chap. 4. Princeton, NJ: Princeton University Press, 1983.

Constant, Benjamin. "The Liberty of the Ancients Compared with That of the Moderns." In *The Libertarian Reader: Classic and Contemporary Readings from Lao-Tzu to Milton Friedman*, edited by David Boaz, 65–70. New York: Free Press, 1997 [1816].

Dewey, John. *Democracy and Education*. In *John Dewey: The Middle Works, 1899–1924*, volume 9, edited by Jo Ann Boydston. Carbondale: Southern Illinois University Press, 1985 [1916].

———. *Human Nature and Conduct*. In *John Dewey: The Middle Works, 1899–1924*, volume 14, edited by Jo Ann Boydston. Carbondale: Southern Illinois University Press, 1988 [1922].

————. *Art as Experience*. Vol. 10 of *John Dewey: The Later Works, 1925–1953*, edited by Jo Ann Boydston. Carbondale: Southern Illinois University Press, 1989 [1934].

Eleveld, Mark, ed. *The Spoken Word Revolution: Slam, Hip Hop and the Poetry of a New Generation*. Naperville: Sourcebooks MediaFusion, 2003.

————. "Beat Remnants: Introduction." In Eleveld, *The Spoken Word Revolution*, 11–12.

————. *The Spoken Word Revolution, Redux*. Naperville: Sourcebooks MediaFusion, 2007.

Epstein, Joseph. "Who Killed Poetry?" *Commentary* 86, no. 2 (1988): 14–15.

Freire, Paolo. *Pedagogy of the Oppressed*. New York: Continuum, 1970 [1968].

Gioia, Dana. "Can Poetry Matter?" Reprinted in *Can Poetry Matter? Essays on Poetry and American Culture*, 10th anniversary edition, 1–22. St. Paul, MN: Graywolf Press, 2002 [1992].

Glazner, Gary Mex, ed. *Poetry Slam: The Competitive Art of Performance Poetry*. San Francisco: Manic D Press, 2000.

————. "Poetry Slam: An Introduction." In Glazner, *Poetry Slam*, 11–14.

Gonzalez, Guy Le Charles. "The Revolution Will Be." In Eleveld, *The Spoken Word Revolution, Redux*, 23–27.

Harms, Gregory. "Performance Art: Blood, Ice Skates, and Coyotes in the 20th Century." In Eleveld, *The Spoken Word Revolution*, 76–78.

Henry, Mike. "Group Discussion on the Group Piece." In Glazner, *Poetry Slam*, 214–20.

Holman, Bob. "The Room." In Glazner, *Poetry Slam*, 15–21.

Howard, Jean. "Performance Art, Performance Poetry—The Two Sisters." In Eleveld, *The Spoken Word Revolution*, 64–67.

Jacobus, Terry. "Poetic Pugilism." In Eleveld, *The Spoken Word Revolution*, 81–89.

Jancovich, Mark. *The Cultural Politics of the New Criticism*. Cambridge, MA: Cambridge University Press, 1993.

Kass, Jeff. "The 'Youuuuths': At base, we humans want to connect with each other." In Eleveld, *The Spoken Word Revolution, Redux*, 198–200.

Leitch, Vincent B., ed. *The Norton Anthology of Theory and Criticism*. New York: W. W. Norton & Company, 2001.

MacCallum, Gerald. "Negative and Positive Freedom." *Philosophical Review* 76, no. 3 (1967): 312–34.

MacNaughton, Anne. "The Taos Poetry Circus." In Eleveld, *The Spoken Word Revolution*, 101–04.

McAllister, Susan, Don McIver, Mikaela Renz, and Daniel S. Solis, eds. *A Bigger Boat: The Unlikely Success of the Albuquerque Poetry Slam Scene*. Albuquerque: University of New Mexico Press, 2008.

McAllister, Susan. "Slam Poetry Demystified." In McAllister et al., *A Bigger Boat*, 29–30.

———. "Thank You and Acknowledgments." In McAllister et al., *A Bigger Boat*, 271–73.

McNiece, Ray. "Cleveland Slam Team Championship Season and Other Reminiscences." In *Cleveland Poetry Scenes: A Panorama and Anthology*, edited by Nina Freedlander Gibans, Mary E. Weems, and Larry Smith, 111–18. Huron: Bottom Dog Press, 2008.

Nester, Daniel. Foreword. In Aptowicz, *Words in Your Face*, xiii–xiv.

Olson, Alix. "Diary of a Slam Poet." *Ms. Magazine* 11, no. 1 (December 2000/ January 2001): 66–73.

Prince, Richard. "Once a 'virgin, virgin' at the Green Mill." In Eleveld, *The Spoken Word Revolution*, 139–41.

Quickley, Jerry. "Hip Hop Poetry." In Eleveld, *The Spoken Word Revolution*, 38–42.

Rand, Ayn. *The Fountainhead*. New York: Penguin Books, 2007 [1943].

Renz, Mikaela. "Aftermath: Organizing Community." In McAllister et al., *A Bigger Boat*, 319–20.

Smith, Marc Kelly, with Joe Kraynak. *The Complete Idiot's Guide to Slam Poetry*. Indianapolis: Alpha Books, 2004.

Smith, Marc. "About Slam Poetry." In Eleveld, *The Spoken Word Revolution*, 116–20.

Smith, Marc, and Joe Kraynak. *Take the Mic: The Art of Performance Poetry, Slam, and the Spoken Word*. Naperville: Sourcebooks, 2009.

Solis, Daniel S. "Letter from the Chair of NPS 2005." In McAllister et al., *A Bigger Boat*, 168–69.

Van Cleve, Genevieve. "Tour." In Glazner, *Poetry Slam*, 135–39.

von Ziegesar, Cecily, ed. *Slam*. New York: Alloy Books, 2000.

Somers-Willett, Susan. "Can Slam Poetry Matter?" *Rattle* 13, no. 1 (2007): 85–90.

———. Interviewed by Cristin O'Keefe Aptowicz. In Aptowicz, *Words in Your Face*, 336.

———. *The Cultural Politics of Slam Poetry: Race, Identity, and the Performance of Popular Verse in America*. Ann Arbor: University of Michigan Press, 2009.

Williams, Saul. "The Future of Language." In Eleveld, *The Spoken Word Revolution*, 58–60.

Whitman, Walt. "Notes Left Over: Ventures, on an Old Theme." (1892), http:// www.bartleby.com/229/3003.html.

Chapter 7

Tragedy and Democracy

The Fate of Liberal Democratic Values in a Violent World

WAIRIMU NJOYA

Introduction

In the current climate of global insecurity, liberal democratic values have fallen into a crisis. Following the tragic events of September 11, 2001, lawmakers and the general public in the United States expressed their willingness to set aside concerns for liberty, justice, and human rights in the quest for greater security.[1] This chapter contends that the arts, and the art of tragedy in particular, have a crucial part to play in calling attention to the compromise of America's democratic values. At the same time, tragedy could provide vital resources for the reaffirmation of political and moral principles that have been set aside or discarded in the ongoing security crisis.

Tragic narratives, songs, musical odes, poetic lamentations, and other creative expressions of pain and loss offer a lens through which we can examine the hopes, failures, and possibilities of democracy in a violent world. The moments of decision in which communities or tragic heroes confront a clear and present danger with courage and moral integrity offer a useful guide for democratic decision-making. Artistic work that focuses on tragic dilemmas has been especially effective in demonstrating that there is no necessary opposition between liberty and security. The quest for physical security has been linked, in various tragic scenarios, to the types of action that reject the option of violence and physical aggression. Nowhere is this ethical vision more evident, I argue, than in the blues tradition in African American culture. Building on the insights of philosopher Cornel West, this chapter shows how representations of moral resistance against racial terror could reconfigure our understanding of the relationship between liberty and justice, on the one hand, and the need for security in a dangerous world.[2] I consider the contributions of classic blues singers of the 1920s and 1930s, and then trace the ethos of the blues through the creative writing of Toni Morrison, whose characters represent a commitment to freedom even in the most devastating circumstances.

The vision of the blues is sorely needed as a counter to the claim that the principles that support a vibrant democracy have no place in the high-risk operations of international politics. The "states of exception" arising from these claims pose a grave threat to human rights through the suspension of civil liberties and the enactment of authoritarian emergency measures.[3] Historically, such measures have opened the way for large-scale abuses and the denial of fundamental freedoms, inflicting particularly grievous harms on ethnic minorities and people with political views outside the mainstream.[4] The Alien and Sedition Acts of 1798, the internment of Japanese Americans during World War II, investigations of "un-American activities" during the Cold War, and the detention of Muslim immigrants after 9/11 are cases in point. Yet these lessons from history were quickly discarded in the context of the War on Terror, which was launched by the U.S. government in response to the terrorist attacks.[5] This war effort was accompanied by the retraction of long-standing commitments to civil liberties and access to justice. The "torture memos," which the Bush administration used to authorize interrogation techniques that violated international conventions, are a particularly egregious example of unprincipled actions that were taken to enable the aggressive pursuit of "national security."[6] Without democratic interventions that could expand public perceptions of the available options and bring rigorous scrutiny to policy-making in this field, the prospects for human rights and civil liberties will remain grim even after the drawdown of troops directly engaged in fighting the wars in Iraq and Afghanistan.

The discussion further on does not suggest that nothing at all should be done to enhance the physical security of citizens and minimize the risk of violence. Instead, I raise the question of how security threats are defined, and what kinds of responses can and should be supported by a democratic nation. Must one kind of tragedy—the devastating loss of human life—be followed by yet another loss—the renunciation of liberal democratic values? Put differently, might there be alternative ways of responding to human tragedy and global insecurity that do not reproduce the violence that democratic societies are struggling to combat? This is the question to which I believe the blues tradition could offer a response, making clear how principled commitments could be upheld in circumstances that call for decisive action. The argument here is not that a blues sensibility could provide a fail-safe blueprint for a "just war" against terror. However, the rich democratic traditions of blues people could help in empowering citizens to resist the deadening logic that pits liberty and justice against security prior to an integrated analysis of the physical, moral, and political dimensions of a particular threat.

While the art of tragedy as expressed in blues traditions could offer vital support for nonviolent responses in security emergencies, the discussion in this chapter also challenges the assumption that the arts will inevitably have this moderating influence. Indeed, aesthetic images have been used very prominently to support state violence, torture tactics, and preemptive strikes in the post-9/11 world. The War on Terror relied heavily on creative stories and imaginative models that "demonstrated" that normal human beings would, and actually *should*, privilege security in dangerous times, sacrificing freedom and justice in the process. The discussion here begins by considering this ambiguous relationship between tragedy and democracy, addressing the potential of art to be mobilized for democratic as well as antidemocratic purposes. Analyzing the literary images that were used to pit human rights and civil liberties against national defense in the course of the War on Terror, I show that the political message in art is not self-evident: the mobilization of artistic production for democratic purposes requires certain modes of judging artwork and linking those lessons to social action by specific groups who are struggling to make their voices heard in an ongoing policy debate.

The first and most crucial step in linking art to democratic participation, therefore, is to define the modes of judgment that would best support the efforts of marginalized groups to intervene in a policy environment that excludes them. Given the centrality of classified knowledge and strategic maneuvers in national security policy-making, it is an area of governance that is arguably the most resistant to democratic participation. The vast majority of ordinary citizens lack access to the forums where crucial decisions are made. Given the low likelihood that the voices of citizens will be incorporated into decision-making in real time during a national security emergency, it is especially important to define a mode of judgment that decision-makers could use to think from the standpoint of ordinary citizens who care about making ethical judgments in the midst of a crisis. I draw insights from Immanuel Kant's *Critique of Judgment* in order to highlight the moments of decision in which ordinary human beings find themselves in tragic circumstances, needing to take decisive action in order to respond to an imminent threat. Kant's *Critique* challenges conventional ideas regarding what human beings are capable of thinking, doing, and feeling in crisis situations. The view of humanity that we get here corresponds closely with the ethos of the blues and suggests specific methodologies for reading cultural texts in the African American tradition in terms of their critical dialogue with the aesthetic judgment espoused by European Enlightenment thinkers. The third section considers a number of blues women as cultural and political workers who put forward their visions of ethical resistance to racial terror using the artistic media of literature and music. In conclusion, I provide a rationale for continuing to hope that literature and the arts might reinvigorate democratic life and open up new possibilities for principled, participatory decision-making in the fight against terrorism.

Liberty vs. Security: A Tragic Dilemma?

In the various imaginative forms in which it is represented, tragedy deals with human vulnerabilities to violation, loss, terror, and unexpected devastation. Because it reflects on the human condition, tragedy appears in different cultures and different time periods from ancient Greece to the present. The heroes of Greek tragedy appealed to the imagination through actions that pitted free will against the vagaries of nature, history, and fate. In the eighteenth century, the tragic sensibility found new forms of expression within discourses on "the sublime," an aesthetic idea that continued a long conversation on the human capacity to think and act in ways that are greater than the limited circumstances in which individuals live from day to day.[7] Whereas ancient tragedy meditated on the unavoidable fate that snatched heroes like Oedipus or Antigone from their willfully chosen paths, the modern idea of the sublime placed the accent on the moment of resistance—the human will to determine one's own life and push against limitations even when the odds are overwhelming. This modern understanding of tragedy, which is explained more fully in the next section, illuminates what is at stake for democracy in the present moment when resistance against terror defines politics as much as it shapes everyday life.

In speaking of lessons for democracy that could be derived from tragedy and the blues, there is, however, a prior set of questions that must be dealt with. Where does the real world of politics end, and where does the creative imagination begin? How can we understand the relationship between democracy and creative arts such as poetry, music, and drama? Is there always a strong, affirmative relationship between tragedy and democratic values? How does it happen that the imagination sometimes becomes closed off from liberal ideals and is instead used as an alibi for violence?

The arenas in which dilemmas of national security have been defined have typically given little credence to aesthetic judgment as a practice of representing and defending ideals. Instead, literary images have been used to return a purportedly more "realistic" and "pragmatic" view to the policy questions at hand. The debate on the use of torture has been defined by precisely this rejection of ideals and concerns for human rights, which are seen as too "abstract" or "pure" to have any utility. To illuminate the tragic dilemmas and legal principles at stake in fighting terrorism, a commonly used imaginative device is the ticking bomb.[8] Details vary from one narration to the next, but the ticking bomb scenario is usually sketched in the following manner: A bomb has been planted somewhere in close proximity to a large number of people, perhaps in a city or near a school for young children. The authorities have apprehended a suspect who knows the location of the bomb, but the suspect does not provide the information upon routine interrogation. Many innocent lives are at risk and time is of the essence, as the bomb is set to detonate at any moment. Should the authorities be permitted to torture the suspect in order to obtain the information that would save lives?

Arguing from what he identifies as a "conditional normative" position, Alan Dershowitz infamously proposed that judges should be authorized to issue "torture warrants" in emergency situations.[9] He argued that security officers responding to an imminent threat would very likely employ torture methods to extract vital information from terrorism suspects, and that we are far better off regulating those interrogation procedures than not.[10] In the emergency situation created by the ticking bomb, Dershowitz contended, a cost-benefit analysis would suggest that "the lives of a thousand innocent people should be valued more than the bodily integrity of one guilty person."[11] According to this view of the dilemma, a requirement that security officers seek a warrant prior to using torture methods would insure some measure of judicial scrutiny and create a mechanism for accountability where none as yet exists.

The imaginative representation of the security crisis clearly conditions the argument that Dershowitz makes in this case, and the narrowness of the imagery reproduces itself in the limited range of legal options presented. There is a long list of assumptions underpinning arguments based on ticking bomb scenarios, not least of all the guilt of the suspect and the effectiveness of torture in producing true and actionable confessions. Years before the current torture debates, Henry Shue summed it up very nicely:

> Notice how unlike the circumstances of an actual choice about torture the philosopher's example is. The proposed victim of our torture is not someone we suspect of planting the device: he is the perpetrator. He is not some pitiful psychotic making one last play for attention: he did plant the device. The wiring is not backwards, the mechanism is not jammed: the device will destroy the city if it is not deactivated.[12]

But surely one of the most significant assumptions in relation to democratic politics is the notion that only one person—the suspected terrorist—would be harmed by human rights violations, while the rest of society retains its democratic character despite the fact that it has accepted torture as a necessary part of its common existence.[13]

Political philosopher Jean Bethke Elshtain has come out strongly against Dershowitz's proposal, calling torture warrants "a stunningly bad idea."[14] However, she does not offer any solutions that are stunningly different. Elshtain advances an approach to moral reasoning that acknowledges the need for "coercive interrogation" (also known as "torture lite"[15]) in emergencies, while simultaneously rejecting any move to normalize or sanction torture through law. She argues that a political leader should be willing to make difficult choices and incur moral guilt when necessary in order to save innocent lives; however, we should not seek to enshrine those exceptions in a legal framework. In a ticking bomb scenario, the rule prohibiting torture is overridden, but the rule itself still stands and torture somehow remains taboo. Elshtain is not far off from Dershowitz in stating: "Far greater moral guilt falls on a person in authority who permits the death of hundreds of innocents rather than choosing to 'torture' one guilty or complicit person."[16] Here again we find the assumption that torture can be carried out in dark places without affecting the general character of a society. The authorities take action while the society that authorized the use of force denies legitimacy to the acts that it allowed.

One gets the sense of having witnessed a theoretical sleight of hand. As James Ross has argued, based on an examination of historical evidence, no practice can be actively pursued by a state without becoming normalized and institutionalized.[17] The state cannot concede that torture is permissible under some special and rare conditions without creating an official sanction for torture. But Elshtain maintains that her objective is to address the short-term emergency, rather than the long-term effects, and to offer an account of the kind of moral reasoning that should guide action in a situation where there is something even more reprehensible than torture: inaction. Not all torture is very bad, in her view, and we could make some distinctions as to which methods are permissible and which ones we would not sanction. "To condemn outright . . . coercive interrogation [torture lite], is to lapse into a legalistic version of pietistic rigorism in which one's own moral purity is ranked above other goods," Elshtain claims. Preserving one's moral rectitude at the cost of innocent lives seems unconscionable under the circumstances, and she identifies the dangerous demand that we remain morally "pure" with Immanuel Kant's rule-driven moral philosophy. "This is also a form of moral laziness," she asserts. "One repairs to a code rather than grappling with a terrible moral dilemma."[18]

In making this claim, Elshtain picks up on Michael Walzer's famous discussion of "dirty hands" as a problem of political action. The reference to dirty hands comes from Jean-Paul Sartre's play by the same title, a many-sided inquiry into realism and idealism in politics that has generally been reduced to a few lines for the purposes of commentary. Caught up in a debate on the connection between means and ends in political decision-making, one of the central characters, a Communist leader named Hoederer, declares: "Purity is an idea for a yogi or a monk . . . I have dirty hands right up to the elbows. I've plunged them in filth and blood. But what do you hope? Do you think you can govern innocently?"[19] Although he is a rather unsavory character, Hoederer is still quoted with far greater frequency than any other character in the play because he has the advantage of being a "realist"—realism, of course, being highly desirable in ticking bombs and dirty hands theories. The *real* world, we are told, is highly imperfect and the choices are stark. Either defend your moral scruples or protect the lives of innocent children playing in the schoolyard: choose. Are you willing to stand by and watch others pay the price for your moral purity?

In framing the dilemmas, Walzer also borrows selectively from Albert Camus' tragic play, *The Just Assassins*.[20] In this play, a group of rebels in nineteenth-century Russia makes a commitment to end the despotic rule of the Grand Duke by assassinating him. "When we kill," the character Ivan Kaliayev asserts, "we're killing so as to build up a world in which there will be no more killing."[21] Toward this end, the group of terrorists is willing not only to incur moral guilt for spilling blood, but also to accept the punishment for their actions and to face execution for the crime of murder. They do not try to avoid legal responsibility or deny the moral burden they have taken up. Elshtain follows Walzer's interpretation of the play in making the argument that individual officers of the state can torture (litely) as long as they accept the moral burden that comes with doing the job as it must be done in those rare emergencies. Of course, there has to be a mechanism in place to ensure this accountability, and accountability becomes a new puzzle for moral and political theorists—assuming that they are willing to take up this next stage of the argument. In practical politics, however, there has not been much success in ensuring that officials answer for their actions, and, as Walzer at least acknowledges, "In most cases of dirty hands moral rules are broken for reasons of state, and no one provides the punishment."[22]

Given this accountability deficit, it might appear that Dershowitz's cynical solution, the torture warrant, is the last democratic hope for a state that has "no choice" but to resort to torture. However, in the next two sections, I make an argument for an alternative formulation of the ethical questions at hand, leading away from the false dilemmas that arise when liberty and justice are traded off against security as a matter of course. Narrowly drawn sketches of public emergencies, aesthetic judgments that work retrospectively to rationalize national security policy rather than present new alternatives, and selective borrowing from otherwise complex political dramas can only yield a limited vision for political action. No ideals can be defended in this manner. How, then, can creative imagination be brought to bear in policy deliberation that seeks to uphold liberal democratic ideals?

Acting "as if" We Were Free

Although given short shrift in dirty hands theories, Kant's account of the human capacity to act *as if* free when under severe constraint cannot be dismissed out of hand. To ignore these insights on account of the fact that human beings are not *in fact* free in any of the scenarios discussed earlier, or to limit freedom to yogis and monks, is to completely disregard histories of moral resistance by ordinary people who were enslaved or subjected to other forms of racial violence in the United States. Kant's writings on aesthetics not only help in explaining how such affirmations of the human spirit were possible under dehumanizing conditions, but they also provide an account of aesthetic judgment that prepares us to make sense of such actions whether we witness them directly or through artistic representation. Rejecting the one-dimensional view of humanity as simply a collection of bodies that could be annihilated through physical violence, Kant offers us a two-dimensional view of human freedom that touches on the body as well as moral personhood.

If Kant appears to be an insufficiently political thinker, lacking a sense of the concrete interest in the preservation of real breathing bodies, it is perhaps because his two-dimensional view of human personhood has been insufficiently explored in relation to the national security debates. As mentioned earlier, the modern interest in tragedy has not been concerned with the limitations on human freedom so much as it has been concerned with the sublime possibility of resisting—perhaps even transcending—those barriers. Thus fate, history, pain, loss, oppression, and insecurity are not occasions for despair in Enlightenment imaginaries, but the conditions out of which human beings attempt to make their lives in freedom. The tragedians of ancient Greece depicted such willfulness as a slippery slope that led even the most spirited heroes (precisely because they were so spirited) to fall into the pits of hubris. Taking the fallibility of human beings as one of the conditions out of which they act, modern sensibilities have instead focused on the assertion of the will by ordinary people facing extraordinary odds. The point is not simply to "win"—in many cases the opposing forces are overwhelming—but rather to conceive of what a "defeat without dishonor" would demand of those whose physical lives and moral principles are both equally at risk.[23]

The focus on resistance that is at the bottom of the modern idea of the sublime received its most clear articulation in the philosophy of

Immanuel Kant in the eighteenth century. During the Enlightenment, discourses on the sublime were incredibly diffuse, connecting a wide array of theoretical and aesthetic concerns through a common terminology and a shared sense that the sublime addressed the greatest challenge that human beings must face—the terrifying encounter with one's own death. Thus the sublime was often reduced to a set of objects or images that inspire terror by creating the illusion of impending death: cataracts, torrents, hurricanes, stormy seas, ragged mountain peaks, deserts, and rocky landscapes were declared sublime and frequently appeared in poetry and literary criticism.[24] Addressing this as a confusion in aesthetic judgment that mistook nature in all its terrifying grandeur for the subject of the sublime, Kant argued that only humanity is truly sublime.

By shifting the focus of the discourse on sublimity from physical objects to moral personhood, Kant reaffirmed the human capacity to negotiate between membership in the natural world, with all the fear that mortality inspires, and the truly sublime power to disregard this fear in making moral and aesthetic judgments. "[E]xternal nature is not aesthetically judged as sublime in so far as it arouses fear," Kant insisted, "but rather because it summons our power (one not of nature) to regard as small those things of which we are inclined to be solicitous (worldly goods, health, and life) . . ."[25] While he certainly recognized that human beings are conditioned by their material environments and level of physical well-being ("in these matters we are no doubt subjected," he wrote), Kant also argued that we are not entirely determined by these factors. Indeed, we can only fully claim our freedom when we recognize that we need not bow down to nature "once the question becomes one of our highest principles and our asserting or forsaking them."[26] Simply put, when we recognize that our dreams, values, and moral ideals are at stake, the presence of a physical threat need not compel us to abandon all these considerations in order to secure the natural body. The sense of the sublime, then, is that human interests extend beyond bare physical survival.

Kant's contribution to the clarification of aesthetic judgment is twofold: first, he created a philosophical language and a framework within which we can recognize the capacity of human beings to act *as if* free when they are actually in life-threatening positions. Kant wrote about freedom without discounting the inevitability of death or the very real threat of violence. Storms, volcanoes, and hurricanes *do* lead to the tragic losses of life, but that is not the sole importance of focusing attention on tragic scenes. If we are making the kinds of aesthetic judgments that the sublime calls for, a dual consideration becomes possible:

> the irresistibility of the might of nature forces upon us the recognition of our physical helplessness as beings of nature, but at the same time reveals a faculty of judging ourselves as independent of nature, and discovers a pre-eminence above nature that is the foundation of a self-preservation of quite another kind from that which may be assailed and brought into danger by external nature.[27]

When humanity is viewed from both of these perspectives, it becomes possible to understand self-preservation as a struggle for physical security as well as an effort to preserve the part of humanity that is concerned with moral values. From this standpoint, one can acknowledge the seriousness of a terrorist threat, for example, while at the same time making a case for upholding commitments to human rights. Defending ideals in such circumstances must always be judged as sublime because a principled course of action is prompted by respect for the two-dimensional character of humanity, which is both real and ideal. This idea of the sublime is what "saves humanity in our own person from humiliation, even though as human beings we would have to submit to external violence" in cases where force exceeds all principled efforts to combat it.[28] Evidence that ethical resistance to terror is not only theoretically but also practically possible will be presented later in consideration of African American creative arts that capture the stories of people who acted as if free when they were actually enslaved or otherwise brutalized.

Kant's second major contribution to the understanding of sublime resistance is that he was able to show the link between consciousness and action. His argument was that the experience of danger can call forth an audacity to think for oneself and to *imagine* things that the real world does not confirm, support, or allow. In one of its articulations, the Kantian sublime focuses on conscious resistance against the limits of what can be represented in thought or comprehended through the understanding.[29] Thus, besides the courage to confront physical violence with moral resistance, the sublime also addresses the capacity to visualize and represent the impossible. In the discussion further on, we will see how Morrison's novel *Beloved* presents images of black women fighting for bodily integrity precisely because they were engaged in an imaginative struggle to envision themselves differently from the ways in which they appeared in racist legal and social structures.

The Ethos of the Blues

As important as Kant's idea of the sublime has been in illuminating the two dimensions of humanity, physical and moral, the vision of the Enlightenment is itself limited by the range of experiences and the sets of interests that informed its political philosophy. At a crucial point in the escalation of the War on Terror, Cornel West contended that the most promising possibilities for the renewal of American democracy and the best ways of resisting the temptation of vengefulness could be found in the traditions of the "blues people" who resisted racial terror in America with courage as well as compassion. He called for a reaffirmation of democratic ideals not by returning to the Founding Fathers, who after all laid the groundwork for a limited racial democracy, but through the creative imagination of African Americans who nurtured a "deep democratic tradition" in their music, arts, and cultures.[30] West proceeded to offer a reconstruction of the critical dialogue between the Enlightenment and what it excludes at two levels: the political and the aesthetic. This critical exchange is captured in the idea of "tragicomic hope," an ethos that keeps alive a sense of possibility and moral agency among a people subjected to hatred and violence within a nation founded on the principles of democracy.

Tragicomic hope is not exclusive to the black radical tradition. As West explains, "A tragicomic view is one that, as Samuel Beckett and Franz Kafka made clear, locates human beings as already in 'the mess' of the world with no way to ever fully escape it."[31] The tragicomic view in the blues does, however, call for a special kind of reflection that emerges out of the historical specificity of the black experience in America: Classical blues music not only dealt with terror and resistance, but it also offered a meditation on what it means to be sorrowful, to grieve deeply, and to mourn. West describes the blues as a "lens" on the modern world that makes visible a third dimension of human experience, extending beyond physical embodiment and the moral interest in freedom:

When we see our lives through this lens, the stress is partly on what the Enlightenment also affirmed: the courage to think critically about one's situation. Yet it is also on what the

Enlightenment did not adequately articulate: the courage to care, to feel deep agony and anguish, to deal with the tears generated by the suffering that people experience—and this is not only a matter of following some objective and rational moral law, but is also rooted in the blood-drenched tear-soaked traditions of resistance, critique, and contestation—and in the agency of the wretched of the earth.[32]

In African American and African diaspora traditions, the sublime commitment to freedom and hope against the odds is inseparable from the critique of an Enlightenment vision that had no place for their humanity even in its affirmations of universal human rights.

The conditions out of which the blues emerged demanded that the art form have a capacity to hold body and spirit together in the context of deep suffering. The songs that emerged from the daily experiences of enslaved Americans were full of sorrow, conveying both the devastation and the fragile hope of a people who were subjected to unimaginable indignities. In his famous reflections on the "sorrow songs," W.E.B. Du Bois used the "rhythmic cry" of folksongs and spirituals to frame his exploration of what it meant to be black in America, with a particular focus on the period following the Civil War.[33] Songs that spoke of weariness and "the blood and dust of toil" arose from the daily struggles of enslaved blacks and continued to ring right through the Reconstruction era because the failure of economic restructuring meant that black farmers in the South were forced to live in conditions analogous to slavery.[34] Interpreting the melodies of their hopes as well as the depths of their despair, Du Bois concluded *The Souls of Black Folk* with the conviction that the spiritual strivings expressed in the sorrow songs represented the very best heritage of the nation. He characterized this music as a form of historical consciousness that grapples with America's worst atrocities without losing hope or the commitment to work toward the realization of the nation's best ideals.[35]

Arguably, what is most remarkable about the sorrow songs is not their content, but that they were sung at all. Amiri Baraka reminds us that the words and meaning of these songs were often obscured because sorrowful music was strictly forbidden by many slave owners. To express deep sorrow in defiance of the myth of the "happy slave" was seen, quite accurately, as a form of protest and a reassertion of a humanity denied.[36] To call attention to the mess in which one was struggling not only presented an image of the sublimity of a people who continually resisted oppression and dehumanization, but it also indicted the political order that so systematically and violently denied them their rights.

The rehumanization of black existence through music continued to be a provocative act even when hundreds of thousands of African Americans migrated to urban centers to escape the grinding poverty and racial prejudice of the rural South. As it turned out, there was to be no rest for the weary. Jim Crow laws secured white racial dominance through segregation and the denial of economic opportunities to blacks. The classic blues artists of the 1920s and 1930s—famous singers like Bessie Smith, Gertrude "Ma" Rainey, and Billie Holiday—achieved significant commercial success among black and some white audiences, but found that they could not gain admittance to many of the places where their music traveled.[37]

Being embedded in the difficult situations that they sang about, blues women remained close to folk music and gave voice to the problems blacks encountered on a daily basis. One of the roles they played in African American communities was that of "interpreters of the dreams, harsh realities, and tragicomedies of the black experience."[38] Thus Angela Davis invokes the legacies of blues women to discount claims made by white commentators at midcentury that the blues is an essentially apolitical art form that focuses on "complaining" about lost loves, sexual frustration, and being plain out of luck.[39] Davis emphasizes, instead, that "the personal relationship stands both for itself and for unrealizable social aspirations and failed dreams. The blues as aesthetic form and practice must be understood as a means of testifying to and registering the lack of real, objectively attainable possibilities of social transformation."[40] Blues singers of course gave voice to something more than the experience of devastation; there was also a denormalization of social inequalities and an implicit demand that the social and political order be transformed in line with an ethical vision of the world. Thus Davis concludes that "while there may not be a direct line to social activism, activist stances are inconceivable without the consciousness such songs suggest."[41] Music became a way of gathering people together in social spaces, defining political issues for action, forging solidarity, commemorating losses, and holding out hope when there was none in sight, thus foregrounding democratic ideals that were as yet unrealized.[42]

Consider, for example, the famous song "Strange Fruit," which Billie Holiday recorded in 1939 and performed before live audiences for many years.[43] At the time of the recording, Holiday was exceedingly conscious of the impossibility of representing the full horror of lynching to an unreceptive, mostly white public. "I worked like the devil on it," she later reflected, "because I was never sure that I could put it across or that I could get across to a plush nightclub audience the things that it meant to me."[44] The song, written by Jewish American composer Abel Meeropol (pen name Lewis Allan), took on in her performances the ineffable quality of a pain that vibrates powerfully just below the surface but never quite breaks out of the sustained depths of her voice.

> Southern trees bear a strange fruit,
> Blood on the leaves and blood at the root,
> Black bodies swinging in the Southern breeze,
> Strange fruit hanging from the poplar trees.
>
> Pastoral scene of the gallant South,
> The bulging eyes and the twisted mouth,
> Scent of magnolia sweet and fresh,
> Then the sudden smell of burning flesh.
>
> Here is a fruit for the crows to pluck,
> For the rain to gather, for the wind to suck,
> For the sun to rot, for the tree to drop,
> Here is a strange and bitter crop.[45]

These images of tortured, violated bodies are at the same time a call to return dignity to African Americans and address the devastation. The victims of lynching are rehumanized through the evocation of their pain and accorded their proper last rites, if only in song. Through this musical commemoration of what they suffered, an appeal is made for compassionate solidarity in order to resist hatred and violence.[46]

Ultimately, what the blues sensibility calls for is a refusal to cover up the pain of injustice. The ethos of the blues is infused in and transmitted through music, but it has also come to define the politics of African American political protest more broadly. For West,

> The high point of the black response to American terrorism (or niggerization) is found in the compassionate and courageous voice of Emmet Till's mother, who stepped up to the lectern at Pilgrim Baptist Church in Chicago in 1955 at the funeral of her fourteen-year-old son, after his murder by American terrorists, and said: "I don't have a minute to hate. I'll pursue justice for the rest of my life."[47]

By holding an open-casket funeral service for her son, Mamie Till Mobley presented to the world the extreme brutality of America's racial order and the violence that her son and other African Americans were subjected to in a racist environment; however, she also affirmed the possibility of pursuing justice in the midst of pain and insecurity. "That is the essence of the blues," West concludes: "to stare painful truths in the face and persevere without cynicism or pessimism."[48]

The Slave Sublime

Keeping painful truths in sight requires nothing less than a tragic disposition and a propensity to gaze unstintingly into abysmal depths of suffering. At the same time, blues performers set their audiences to dreaming, hoping, working, and loving with a broken heart. Thus the blues entails the development of a "productive rapport with death," or a readiness to confront pain and mortality without masking the devastation caused by violence. And yet hope remains that freedom is coming. Using the term "slave sublime" to describe the highly improbable sense of possibility that was sustained despite daily encounters with death during slavery, Paul Gilroy places the tragicomedies of the black experience in a dialogue with the Enlightenment discourse on the sublime.[49] In addition to the two dimensions of real and ideal personhood described by Kant, the slave sublime is shaped by the experience of sorrow, mourning, and the presence of the ghosts of those who are dead but not gone. The slave sublime thus represents the experience of violence, the recognition of its deadly force, and the resistance of the spirit that refuses to be killed even after the body is overwhelmed by violence. All these representations appear simultaneously, for hope and spirited resistance do not entirely erase violence or make it less devastating; but hope does motivate principled action and create the conditions for political activism to overcome violence.

The slave sublime captures important elements of the cultural production of people of African descent within structures of thinking, creating, and remembering that Gilroy calls the black Atlantic world.[50] The black Atlantic forges connections among different historical experiences of racial terror in the New World slavery and on the continent, creating a sense of rootedness along the routes that people and ideas have traveled in deepest yearning for freedom and in search of community. Aesthetic sensibilities circulate not only between continents, but also between different artistic genres and from one historical period to the next. If the focus is maintained on music alone, then the heirs to the classic blues singers can be found among some of the jazz, rhythm and blues, hip hop, and neo-soul artists of the past few decades who give voice to stark social truths with an honesty that resists nihilism.[51] Of even more interest than the survival of blues elements in new musical styles, however, is the vibrancy of the blues sensibility beyond the art form that initially gave it a broad popular audience. The rise of the novel as a form of African American cultural expression with wide appeal is particularly important in this respect, as the writer Toni Morrison explains:

> For a long time, the art form that was healing for black people was music. That music is no longer exclusively ours; we don't have exclusive rights to it. Other people sing and play it; it is the mode of contemporary music everywhere. So another form has to take its place, and it seems to me that the novel is needed. . . . now in a way that it was not needed before.[52]

In her own writing, Morrison has made a deliberate effort to reconstruct the spirituals, blues, and jazz in the intricacy of all their rhythms, cadences, and tones, which gives her use of language its characteristic style.[53]

There are additional dimensions to the musicality of Morrison's writing, dimensions that speak even more directly to the philosophical and existential problems expressed in the idea of the slave sublime. Gilroy shows how she and several other creative writers of the black Atlantic, much like blues singers, have found ways to represent the slave sublime through "imaginative proximity to forms of terror that surpass understanding and lead back from contemporary racial violence, through lynching, towards the temporal and ontological rupture of the middle passage."[54] The sublimity that he asks us to attend to is the struggle to represent in language the ineffable suffering and unspeakable loss that draws a thread through past and present in the black experience. Morrison's writing grapples with the kinds of existential despair and cognitive failure that are occasioned by the experience of unremitting violence and the devastating losses of slavery.

The focus on memory and excavation in Morrison's novels is not intended to glorify suffering for its own sake, nor does her work suggest that suffering is redemptive in and of itself. Indeed, Morrison reminds us with characteristic directness that the blues is not about "whining."[55] The confrontation with death in her powerful historical novel, *Beloved*, moves instead toward an affirmation of the very humanity and dignity that blacks were denied through racial terror, gendered violence, and endemic sexual abuse. The understanding of the relationship between moral idealism and physical security that is already expressed in Enlightenment thought gains new inflections and a third dimension in Morrison's narration of the histories of black women in the United States who confronted racial terror with courage and hope. What would freedom and security have meant for women who survived through and rebelled against their enslavement? What did they value most highly in the midst of great insecurity, and what were they willing to sacrifice for those values?

Imminent Threat Revisited

In *Beloved*, Morrison creates a fictional narrative around the life of Margaret Garner, a nineteenth-century woman who escaped from slavery along with her family and struggled to preserve her children's freedom against all odds. As slave catchers were closing in on the house where the family had taken refuge, Garner slit the throat of her two-year-old daughter and fully intended to kill her three other children; she was stopped in the very act.[56] What notion of freedom could possibly cause a mother to put her own child to death?

In order to explicate the moral dilemmas that Garner faced in that critical moment, Morrison depicts her protagonist, Sethe, in a classic ticking bomb scenario. Here is the scene: a number of white men bearing arms are approaching a house in which a family they had formerly enslaved has managed to find freedom. The inhabitants of the house are three generations of black women, the youngest of whom is a baby who has just learned to crawl. The leader of the armed slave catchers is a known member of a planter class that has held millions of blacks in abject slavery. We have seen him torture in ways that clearly exceed the dubious "torture lite" threshold. The evidence of his cruelty is spread across Sethe's back in scars that will never heal. We also know that he has recruited young men, his nephews, into his household and instructs them in racial hatred and various torture methods—hence the name "Schoolteacher." He is producing a treatise full of his ideologies and he presumably intends to disseminate it widely. The villain is, as Elshtain might remark, thoroughly villainous. We are as certain as any reader could be in such circumstances that a return to slavery would mean not only the loss of freedom for Sethe and her children, but also a painful death through slow, continuous exploitation and degradation. Is Sethe permitted to kill in order to save the lives of her little children?

The bomb begins to tick as Schoolteacher and his party advance steadily on the house where Sethe, her two daughters, and two sons have lived as free persons for only a few short days. At that crucial juncture, Sethe is faced with dilemmas of freedom and security that people subjected to hatred and terror have struggled with for generations. Although Margaret Garner is a unique individual, Morrison's retelling of her story evokes the memory of the "Sixty Million and more" to whom *Beloved* is dedicated. How Sethe finds agency in that situation therefore has important implications for moral reasoning in the face of terror.

We learn that Sethe acted swiftly when she looked up and caught sight of Schoolteacher's hat:

> And if she thought anything, it was No. No. Nono. Nonono. Simple. She just flew. Collected every bit of life she had made, all the parts of her that were precious and fine and beautiful, and carried, pushed, dragged them through the veil, out, away, over there where no one could hurt them. Over there. Outside this place, where they would be safe.[57]

Thus we know that she had a notion of security that guided her actions, however impulsive her response may have seemed. But what kind of safety involves a dead child and a mother soaked in the blood she herself has drawn? As Morrison confirmed in an interview, the question at the heart of the novel is how something as "grotesque" as the murder of the child could spring from a mother's love—and the circumstances under which that would have moral legitimacy. "While I was writing it," Morrison explains, "I was sort of trying to think of situations in which that would be a good thing to do; I couldn't come up with anything. And then I thought the person who ought to answer that question would be the girl she killed. Nobody else had that legitimacy."[58]

Thus the child that was killed returns to Sethe and haunts her home and her life with unrelenting force. What this haunting signifies is a reckoning with history, with death, moral responsibility, and the meaning of freedom and safety in the shadow of slavery. Whereas Sethe had found only a skeptical audience among her neighbors, the return of her child's ghost in the body of a fully grown woman gives her a new opportunity to explain her actions. Sethe wants to explain to the woman–child,

Beloved, that she slit her throat in order to save her from the violence suffered by the entire community of Sethe's friends and family:

> [W]orse than [having her throat cut]—far worse—was what Baby Suggs died of, what Ella knew, what Stamp saw and what made Paul D tremble. That anybody white could take your whole self for anything that came to mind. Not just work, kill, or maim you, but dirty you. Dirty you so bad you forgot who you were or couldn't think it up. And though she [Sethe] and others lived through and got over it, she could never let it happen to her own.[59]

In placing her daughter outside Schoolteacher's reach, Sethe's assurance was that she saved her daughter from losing her spirit and sense of worth, not just her bodily integrity.

The affirmation of her child's spirit was clearly a central consideration in Sethe's decision-making in an emergency situation. It would be meaningless, however, to claim that Sethe thought only of abstract values of dignity and freedom and paid no mind to the child's physical security. Considerations of bodily integrity were clearly at play in Sethe's claim that she wanted to keep the little girl's body safe from a slow death, continuous exploitation, and almost certain sexual violation. Spiritual and physical notions of security are seen to have equal importance in Sethe's actions, which present security as a kind of freedom from the physical torture that breaks the human *spirit*. Saving the body from harm is critically important, but dignity is what gives embodied living its incomparable worth.[60]

The question nevertheless remains: Did Sethe really do the right thing in killing her child? Morrison's novel draws a moral distinction that Elshtain and Walzer approached but ultimately fell short of because they did not have the strong conception of responsibility that is presented in *Beloved*.[61] Morrison is very conscious that what Sethe did was "the right thing to do, but she had no right to do it," and creates a situation in her novel that prompts reflection on how this could be the case.[62] There are antecedents to Morrison's notion of responsibility, as represented in this novel, and other reflections on moral dilemmas within and beyond the blues tradition. In Camus' *Just Assassins*, for example, the assassinator of the Grand Duke submits to the law he has violated and is executed for his crime. The redemption lies in the rebel's submission to the very law he has broken. We can think here, too, of Martin Luther King Jr.'s "Letter from Birmingham Jail," in which he lays out the argument for civil disobedience against segregation laws even as he upholds the institution of law by his presence in jail. Similarly, in *Beloved*, Sethe is determined to take responsibility for killing her child even if it means accepting death as the punishment. She dedicates herself entirely to making amends to Beloved, including giving up every last scrap of food to the embodied ghost who thrives as Sethe shrinks to a shadow of her former self. But unlike the scenario in Camus' play, death of the protagonist does not present a final resolution to the moral dilemmas of killing other human beings in the quest for freedom. Sethe's endless torment and soul-searching suggest that a willingness to accept punishment is not redemptive in itself. The cycles of justification and retribution between Sethe and her resurrected child remain excruciatingly unproductive, and the real rapport with death only begins with the intervention of a community that recalls Sethe to moral humility and a blues sensibility.

What Sethe must accept in order to end her battle with Beloved is her own limitations in bringing justice into this world, or even the next.[63] The ethos of the blues demands courage in resisting degradation, but also reminds us that there are limits to our capacity to protect ourselves and our loved ones from harm and insulate ourselves from mortality. Efforts to secure our physical existence in an unjust world will not be successful in every single case or without fail—indeed, the attempt to transcend all limitations leads inevitably to a loss of our humanity in the quest for total invulnerability. More courageous, perhaps, than facing death for the sake of freedom was the determination Sethe eventually found to continue to live with hope in a world full of hatred and violence that could not be completely overcome by killing her child or giving up her own life. The ethos of the blues is not a promise of an end to all struggles, but a way of sustaining hope, dignity, and continuing to struggle for justice within "the mess" that we are in. It is a call to work for justice without reproducing violence, and its final transcendence is not the overcoming of death, but the rejection and despair of nihilism

From Individual Morality to Political Decision-Making

Beloved indicts structures of racial violence while presenting the possibility of moral action by individuals caught up in the security crises of slavery and the immediate post-Emancipation era. Although these individuals are never presented as isolated from the communities and social structures in which they are embedded, a further elaboration of the blues sublime is needed in order to make the link between aesthetic representations of individual morality and the unique dilemmas of political decision-making. How might aesthetic images add power to ordinary people who seek to be included in defining national security strategies? As Supreme Court Justice Ruth Bader Ginsburg warned in 2004, "On important issues like the balance between liberty and security, if the public doesn't care, then the security side is going to overweigh the other."[64] This problem might appear to become less urgent as the U.S. military disengages from conflicts abroad, but the long-term prospects for democracy still remain dependent on citizens' participation in defining the nation's responses to present and future security threats.

Morrison's assessment of America's response to the challenges of a post-9/11 world should dispel any illusion that prospects for democracy no longer hang in the balance. "The notion that we're the best, the strongest—that we run the world. It's depressing. There's always an enemy somewhere—somebody to fight," she observes. The focus of politics ought to be, instead, on the ethical and social commitments that the United States makes to its citizens and the world: "The power of the United States ought to be in its democratic principles. Its health. Its education," she argues.[65] Although it would be highly reductive to see her writing simply as an imaginative expression of her political position, Morrison's 1997 novel, *Paradise*, very starkly depicts the conflicts between national security and ethical citizenship that would come to define politics in the decade after the novel's publication.

At issue in *Paradise* is the fate of a small, insular community of African Americans who established their own town on the plains of Oklahoma after a harrowing migration westward during the 1880s. Along their way from Mississippi to Oklahoma, the founding families of Ruby braved impossible hardships and faced discrimination across the board, the most painful being the denial of hospitality by other pioneering black communities who saw the migrants as unsuitable for their newly established towns. Generations later, in the 1970s, the residents of Ruby have achieved relative prosperity and "freedom," which they guard zealously against all perceived threats to their community. The founding narratives of injury, hardship, and endurance that gave the residents of Ruby their communal identity now become justifications for violence against any persons or ideas that seem to endanger this community. Strangers, women who defy traditional roles, or women who try but fail to meet cultural expectations are seen as the biggest threat, becoming a lightning rod for other anxieties and rifts within the community. A changing national environment and intergenerational conflicts that shake Ruby are dealt with indirectly through attempts to shut out people seen as Other. A motley group of women occupying an abandoned Convent near the town becomes the target for various fears and a generalized hostility, setting the stage for the terrorist incident with which Morrison opens her novel.

"They shoot the white girl first. With the rest they can take their time. . . . They are nine, over twice the number of women they are obliged to stampede or kill and they have the paraphernalia for either requirement . . ."[66] This is our introduction to *Paradise.* The group of men from Ruby hunts down the women in the Convent with the self-assurance and sense of righteous purpose of a people defending themselves against an existential threat. The tragic irony is that the women they pursue down the hallways and room by room, guns drawn, are already in flight from violence, pain, and loss in their individual lives. Through a series of vignettes, we become familiar with the life histories of each of the Convent's occupants, and the catastrophes that drove them to seek refuge and recovery among an unlikely but ultimately supportive group of women. The devastation of this fragile community just as the women were beginning to recollect themselves constitutes the shattering scenario around which the novel turns. Morrison crafted this work with a very clear vision in mind: to unsettle simplistic ideas about what can be justified in the name of preserving a community. She explained further: "I also wanted to explore unpopular ideas about the difference between liberation and conservation. The liberation movement, the movement to free oneself to be completely independent—as a community not as an individual—is marvelous. But how one moves from liberation to conservation is what I want to explore. How you can make a liberationary gesture and how it can make you end up as the world's most static conservative."[67] This is a powerful warning against the continued deployment of nationalist narratives that preserve freedom by mandating its sacrifice, and it is an important lesson for a world still grappling with real and present dangers.

Conclusion

With the threat of global terrorism now extending into the second decade of the new millennium, the political commitment to defending ideals must continue to be affirmed. The role of art and public culture in these efforts remains highly contingent on the provision of an interpretive framework and a mode of aesthetic judgment that would privilege concerns of dignity and freedom. The good news is that these resources are not in short supply. The tragic sensibility may be nurtured through attentiveness to histories of moral resistance against racial terror, many of which are being presented in art forms that have grown out of the musical genre in which the tradition originated. Art and literature in the blues tradition not only present the stories of past generations that fought injustice, but they also demonstrate the kinds of aesthetic judgments that are called for in bearing witness to those struggles and making contemporary sense of historical images.

The potential of tragic literature and images of the sublime to reinvigorate democratic politics is demonstrated by the role that a blues sensibility has played in African American political activism. When images of freedom gained currency in the cultural life of black communities, as in the singing of the blues, or were taken up by social movements, as in the strong response of civil rights activists to the protest of Mamie Till Mobley, the possibilities for principled political action in those times of crisis were seen to expand significantly. Art and images of the sublime provided an accessible entry point for popular participation in deliberating on pressing public problems and envisioning the most appropriate course of action. For African Americans who were excluded from formal structures of political participation through the denial of citizenship rights and assaults on their humanity, the social spaces in which blues music and personal narratives were presented offered important venues in which their experiences could become visible. Expressions of pain and visions of freedom exposed the hollowness and lack of promise in American democracy. At the same time, musical and narrative cultures acted as a repository for dreams that were as yet unrealized, creating images of freedom that strongly motivated action through their contrast against the pervasive indignities of daily life. With a vision of what social relations *could* become, political activism to realize this vision gained momentum. Mobley's call to the public to bear witness to the brutalized body of her son added power to the movement for civil rights not simply by portraying the enormity of the violence they stood against, but also by giving moral resistance a nonviolent form through the act of mourning. The need for physical security and struggles for justice for the brutalized black body were placed squarely in the context of a yearning for freedom.

The preservation and reaffirmation of blues traditions through literature, as in Morrison's creative writing, ensures that images of the slave sublime can be transmitted to an audience beyond the communities that participate directly in creating these cultural forms. The blues tradition insists that human beings *can* act in accordance with ethical principles when their lives are at risk. To the degree that we can find safety in a very dangerous world, it must lie in the protection and affirmation of what Kant defined as the "unconditional, incomparable worth" of humanity and not in the mere perpetuation of physical existence.[68] This calls us not only to take full responsibility for difficult choices that cause harm to others in defending our security, but also to come to terms with vulnerability, fallibility, and finitude in the post-9/11 era. It is not simply life that matters, but the meaning and the values that we attach to life and our common existence in a democracy and in a globalized world.

Notes

1. Darren K. Carlson, "Liberty vs. Security: Public Mixed on Patriot Act," *Gallup Daily News*, July 19, 2005, http://www.gallup.com/poll/17392/liberty-vs-security-public-mixed-patriot-act.aspx. In this poll, 41 percent of Americans said the USA Patriot Act, which expanded the powers of law enforcement and reduced privacy protections, was "about right" in restricting civil liberties in order to investigate suspected terrorism. Twenty-one percent of respondents said the Patriot Act "does not go far enough."

2. Cornel West, *Democracy Matters* (New York: Penguin Books, 2004).

3. Giorgio Agamben, *State of Exception*, trans. Kevin Attel (Chicago: University of Chicago Press, 2005).

4. Some connections between these situations are highlighted in Tram Nguyen, *We Are All Suspects Now: Untold Stories from Immigrant Communities after 9/11* (Boston: Beacon Press, 2005). Also see Nina Bernstein, "Echoes of '40s Internment Are Seen in Muslim Detainees' Suit," *New York Times*, April 3, 2007, B1.

5. For a critical analysis of the War on Terror in relation to practices of authoritarianism and the concern for democratic processes, see Carl Boggs, *Imperial Delusions: American Militarism and Endless War* (Lanham, MD: Rowman & Littlefield, 2005); Stephen Eric Bronner, *Blood in the Sand: Imperial Fantasies, Right-Wing Ambitions, and the Erosion of American Democracy* (Lexington: University Press of Kentucky, 2005); Cynthia Enloe, *Globalization and Militarism: Feminists Make the Link* (Lanham, MD: Rowman & Littlefield, 2007).

6. See "A Guide to the Memos on Torture," *New York Times*, http://www.nytimes.com/ref/international/24MEMO-GUIDE.html. Relevant human

rights conventions are the United Nations Convention against Torture (1984), the Universal Declaration of Human Rights (1948), and the Geneva Conventions (1949), especially Common Article 3. Also relevant is the United States Uniform Code of Military Justice.

7. The modern discourse on sublimity is based on a post-classical Greek text attributed to Longinus. For a comparison between tragedy and the sublime, and the relation of both to the experience of terror, see Terry Eagleton, "Commentary," *New Literary History* 35, no. 1 (2004): 151–59. A concise history of the idea of the sublime can also be found in Jonathan Lamb, "The Sublime," in *The Cambridge History of Literary Criticism: The Eighteenth Century*, eds. George Alexander Kennedy, Hugh Barr Nisbet, and Claude Rawson (Cambridge, UK and New York: Cambridge University Press, 1997), 394.

8. See the description of the "ticking bomb" scenario in Jean Bethke Elshtain, "Reflection on the Problem of 'Dirty Hands,'" in *Torture: A Collection*, ed. Sanford Levinson (Oxford, UK: Oxford University Press, 2006), 77–89.

9. Alan Dershowitz, "Should the Ticking Bomb Terrorist Be Tortured?," in *Why Terrorism Works* (New Haven, CT: Yale University Press, 2002), 132–63, and "Tortured Reasoning," in *Torture: A Collection*, ed. Sanford Levinson (Oxford, UK: Oxford University Press, 2006), 257–80.

10. Dershowitz, "Tortured Reasoning," 257.

11. Dershowitz, "Should the Ticking Bomb Terrorist Be Tortured?," 144. Although he characterizes this cost-benefit analysis as a "simple and simple-minded" approach, it certainly factors into his consideration of how a security officer would likely assess the situation and therefore his proposal for how the law should institute checks on that officer's response.

12. Henry Shue, "Torture," *Philosophy and Public Affairs* 7, no. 2 (1978): 142. Also see Elaine Scarry, "Five Errors in the Reasoning of Alan Dershowitz," in *Torture: A Collection*, ed. Sanford Levinson (Oxford, UK: Oxford University Press, 2006), 281–90.

13. For a development of this critique and an explication of the societal impact of torture, see James Ross, "A History of Torture," in *Torture: Does It Make Us Safer? A Human Rights Perspective*, eds. Kenneth Roth and Minky Worden (New York: The New Press and Human Rights Watch, 2005), 3–17.

14. Jean Bethke Elshtain, "Reflection on the Problem of 'Dirty Hands,'" in *Torture: A Collection,* ed. Sanford Levinson (Oxford, UK: Oxford University Press, 2006), 83.

15. The term was coined by Mark Bowden in "The Dark Art of Interrogation," *The Atlantic*, October 2003, http://www.theatlantic.com/magazine/archive/2003/10/the-dark-art-of-interrogation/2791.

16. Elshtain, "Reflection on the Problem of 'Dirty Hands,'" 87.

17. Ross, "A History of Torture."

18. Elshtain, "Reflection on the Problem of 'Dirty Hands,'" 87–88.

19. Jean-Paul Sartre, *Dirty Hands*, in *No Exit and Three Other Plays* (New York: Vintage, 1989), 218.

20. Michael Walzer, "Political Action: The Problem of Dirty Hands," *Philosophy and Public Affairs* 2, no. 1 (1973): 160–80; Albert Camus, *The Just Assassins*, in his *Caligula and 3 Other Plays* (New York: Random House, 1958), 233–302. The reference to "dirty hands" in Walzer's essay comes from Jean-Paul Sartre's play by the same title.

21. Camus, *Just Assassins*, 245.

22. Walzer, "Political Action," 179. Note, also, the warning issued by Camus' character Dora, who stated: ". . . I fear for the future. Others, perhaps, will come who'll quote our authority for killing; and will *not* pay with their lives" (*Just Assassins*, 296 [emphasis in original]).

23. The theme of "defeat without dishonor" that runs through the discourse of the sublime is discussed by Michel Deguy, "The Discourse of Exaltation: Contribution to a Rereading of Pseudo-Longinus," in *Of the Sublime: Presence in Question*, trans. Jeffrey S. Librett (Albany: State University of New York Press, 1993), 5–24. Although focused on an ancient text, Deguy's interpretation has a greater affinity with modern sensibilities.

24. See Andrew Ashfield and Peter de Bolla, eds., *The Sublime: A Reader in British Eighteenth-Century Aesthetic Theory* (Cambridge: Cambridge University Press, 1996).

25. Immanuel Kant, *Critique of Judgment*, trans. James Creed Meredith, ed. Nicholas Walker (Oxford, UK: Oxford University Press, 2007), 92.

26. Ibid.

27. Ibid.

28. Ibid.

29. Kant calls this the "mathematically sublime." *Critique of Judgment*, 78–90.

30. Cornel West, *Hope on a Tightrope: Words and Wisdom* (New York: Smiley Books, 2008), 189.

31. Cornel West, "Celebrating *Tikkun* and Tragicomic Hope," *Tikkun* 19, no. 6 (2004): 53.

32. Ibid., 53–54.

33. W.E.B. Du Bois, *The Souls of Black Folk* (New York: Fawcett Publications, 1961), 181–90.

34. Du Bois reported, as the nineteenth century came to a close, "in well-nigh the whole rural South the black farmers [were] peons, bound by law and custom to an economic slavery from which the only escape [was] death or the penitentiary." Ibid., 41.

35. Ibid., 189–90.

36. Amiri Baraka [LeRoi Jones], *Blues People: The Negro Experience in White America and the Music That Developed from It* (New York: William Morrow and Company, 1963), 78–79. Also see Du Bois, *Souls of Black Folk*, 183.

37. See Lawrence W. Levine, *Black Culture and Black Consciousness* (Oxford, UK: Oxford University Press, 1977), 217–97.

38. Daphne Duval Harrison, *Black Pearls: Blues Queens of the 1920s* (New Brunswick, NJ: Rutgers University Press, 1988), 10, quoted in Angela Davis, *Blues Legacies and Black Feminism: Gertrude "Ma" Rainey, Bessie Smith, and Billie Holiday* (New York: Pantheon Books, 1998), xviii.

39. Davis comments on misconstructions of the blues in the work of Samuel Charters and Paul Oliver, among others. Ibid., 92–94.

40. Ibid., 106.

41. Ibid., 119.

42. For a detailed discussion of the connection between music, democratic theory, and political contestation, see Mark Mattern, *Acting in Concert: Music, Community and Political Action* (New Brunswick, NJ: Rutgers University Press, 1998) and Nancy S. Love, *Musical Democracy* (Albany: State University of New York Press, 2006).

43. "Strange Fruit," words and music by Lewis Allan. Recorded by Billie Holiday, Commodore 526, April 20, 1939.

44. Although there is no evidence that Holiday ever witnessed a lynching, her memoir reveals that thoughts of her own father's death were foremost in her mind as she worked to recreate the song in performance. Her father fought in World War I and sustained permanent lung damage during combat. In the crucial weeks before his death, he was unable to receive treatment from segregated hospitals in the South and his health deteriorated beyond the possibility of recovery. Billie Holiday with William Dufty, *Lady Sings the Blues* (New York: Penguin, 1984) as quoted in Davis, *Blues Legacies*, 183.

45. "Strange Fruit," words and music by Lewis Allan. Copyright © 1939 (Renewed) by Music Sales Corporation (ASCAP). All rights for the United States controlled by Music Sales Corporation (ASCAP). International copyright secured. All rights reserved. Used by permission of Music Sales Corporation and Edward B. Marks Music Company.

46. For a brief discussion of what solidarity meant in progressive movements of the 1930s, see Davis, *Blues Women*, 190–92. Meeropol's union activism and the long life of his famous composition as a protest song are documented in Joel Katz's film, *Strange Fruit* (California Newsreel, 2001).

47. West, *Democracy Matters*, 20–21.

48. Ibid.

49. Paul Gilroy, "'Not a Story to Pass On': Living Memory and the Slave Sublime," in *The Black Atlantic: Modernity and Double Consciousness* (Cambridge, MA: Harvard University Press, 1993), 187–233.

50. Ibid., 3.

51. The challenge of maintaining artistic integrity in today's corporate-controlled music industry is of course considerable; classic blues singers encoun-

tered similar problems, but not to the same degree (Levine, *Black Culture*, 228). For studies that follow the legacy of the blues women up to the present, see Guthrie P. Ramsey, *Race Music: Black Cultures from Bebop to Hip-Hop* (Berkeley: University of California Press, 2003) and Buzzy Jackson, *A Bad Woman Feeling Good: Blues and the Women Who Sing Them* (New York: W. W. Norton Company, 2005).

52. Mari Evans, ed., *Black Women Writers: Arguments and Interviews* (London: Pluto Press, 1983), 340, quoted in Gilroy, *Black Atlantic*, 219.

53. See Paul Gilroy, "Living Memory: An Interview with Toni Morrison," in *Small Acts: Thoughts on the Politics of Black Cultures* (London: Serpent's Tail, 1993), 175–82, portions of which are quoted in *Black Atlantic*, 78.

54. Gilroy, *Black Atlantic*, 222.

55. Toni Morrison and Cornel West, "Blues, Love and Politics," *The Nation*, May 24, 2004, 18.

56. See Julius Yanuck, "The Garner Fugitive Slave Case," *Mississippi Valley Historical Review* (Now *Journal of American Historians*) 40, no. 1 (1953), http://www.michiganopera.org/mg_ed/educational/Garner%20Slave%20Case.pdf.

57. Toni Morrison, *Beloved* (New York: Vintage Books, 1987), 192.

58. Interview with Toni Morrison, *BBC World Book Club*, first broadcast January 3, 2009, http://www.bbc.co.uk/worldservice/arts/2009/03/000000_worldbookclub.shtml.

59. Morrison, *Beloved*, 295–96.

60. This understanding of dignity has much in common with Kantian moral philosophy.

61. The inadequacy of Elshtain and Walzer's theories is all the more pronounced because they explicitly took up ideas from Camus' *Just Assassins*, which approaches responsibility in much the same way as Morrison's *Beloved*.

62. Interview with Toni Morrison, *BBC*.

63. Sethe's agony intensifies as Beloved recounts her experience of sexual violation by "men without skin" beyond the grave. The injustices of this world are carried into the next.

64. Quoted in West, *Democracy Matters*, 6.

65. Ariel Leve, "Toni Morrison on Love, Loss and Modernity," *The Telegraph*, http://www.telegraph.co.uk/culture/books/authorinterviews/9395051/Toni-Morrison-on-love-loss-and-modernity.html.

66. Toni Morrison, *Paradise* (New York: Penguin, 1997), 3.

67. Carolyn Denard, "Blacks, Modernism, and the American South: An Interview with Toni Morrison," *Studies in the Literary Imagination* 31, no. 2 (Fall 1998): 12.

68. Immanuel Kant, *Groundwork of the Metaphysics of Morals*, in his *Practical Philosophy*, ed. and trans. Mary J. Gregor (New York: Cambridge University Press, 1996), 84–85.

Bibliography

Agamben, Giorgio. *State of Exception*. Translated by Kevin Attel. Chicago: University of Chicago Press, 2005.

Allan, Lewis. "Strange Fruit." Copyright © 1939 Music Sales Corporation (ASCAP) and Edward B. Marks Music Company.

Ashfield, Andrew, and Peter de Bolla, eds., *The Sublime: A Reader in British Eighteenth-Century Aesthetic Theory*. Cambridge: Cambridge University Press, 1996.

Baraka, Amiri [LeRoi Jones]. *Blues People: The Negro Experience in White America and the Music That Developed from It*. New York: William Morrow and Company, 1963.

Bernstein, Nina. "Echoes of '40s Internment Are Seen in Muslim Detainees' Suit." *New York Times*, April 3, 2007, B1.

Boggs, Carl. *Imperial Delusions: American Militarism and Endless War*. Lanham, MD: Rowman & Littlefield, 2005.

Bowden, Mark. "The Dark Art of Interrogation." *The Atlantic*, October 2003, http://www.theatlantic.com/magazine/archive/2003/10/the-dark-art-of-interrogation/2791.

Bronner, Stephen Eric. *Blood in the Sand: Imperial Fantasies, Right-Wing Ambitions, and the Erosion of American Democracy*. Lexington: University Press of Kentucky, 2005.

Camus, Albert. *The Just Assassins*. In *Caligula and 3 Other Plays*, 233–302. New York: Random House, 1958.

Carlson, Darren K. "Liberty vs. Security: Public Mixed on Patriot Act." *Gallup Daily News*, July 19, 2005, http://www.gallup.com/poll/17392/liberty-vs-security-public-mixed-patriot-act.aspx.

Davis, Angela. *Blues Legacies and Black Feminism: Gertrude "Ma" Rainey, Bessie Smith, and Billie Holiday*. New York: Pantheon Books, 1998.

Deguy, Michel. "The Discourse of Exaltation: Contribution to a Rereading of Pseudo-Longinus." In *Of the Sublime: Presence in Question*, translated by Jeffrey S. Librett, 5–24. Albany: State University of New York Press, 1993.

Denard, Carolyn. "Blacks, Modernism, and the American South: An Interview with Toni Morrison." *Studies in the Literary Imagination* 31, no. 2 (Fall 1998): 1–16.

Dershowitz, Alan. "Should the Ticking Bomb Terrorist Be Tortured?" In *Why Terrorism Works*, 132–63. New Haven, CT: Yale University Press, 2002.

Du Bois, W.E.B. *The Souls of Black Folk*. New York: Fawcett Publications, 1961.

Eagleton, Terry. "Commentary." *New Literary History* 35, no. 1 (2004): 151–59.

Elshtain, Jean Bethke. "Reflection on the Problem of 'Dirty Hands.'" In *Torture: A Collection*, edited by Sanford Levinson, 77–89. Oxford, UK: Oxford University Press, 2006.

Enloe, Cynthia. *Globalization and Militarism: Feminists Make the Link*. Lanham, MD: Rowman & Littlefield, 2007.

Evans, Mari, ed. *Black Women Writers: Arguments and Interviews*. London: Pluto Press, 1983.

Gilroy, Paul. "Living Memory: An Interview with Toni Morrison." In *Small Acts*, 175–82. London: Serpent's Tail, 1993.

———. "'Not a Story to Pass On': Living Memory and the Slave Sublime." In *The Black Atlantic: Modernity and Double Consciousness*, 187–233. Cambridge, MA: Harvard University Press, 1993.

"A Guide to the Memos on Torture." *New York Times*, http://www.nytimes.com/ref/international/24MEMO-GUIDE.html.

Harrison, Daphne Duval. *Black Pearls: Blues Queens of the 1920s*. New Brunswick, NJ: Rutgers University Press, 1988.

Holiday, Billie, with William Dufty. *Lady Sings the Blues*. New York: Penguin, 1984.

Jackson, Buzzy. *A Bad Woman Feeling Good: Blues and the Women Who Sing Them*. New York: W. W. Norton Company, 2005.

Kant, Immanuel. *Groundwork of the Metaphysics of Morals*. In *Practical Philosophy*, edited and translated by Mary J. Gregor, 37–108. New York: Cambridge University Press, 1996.

Katz, Joel. *Strange Fruit*. California Newsreel, 2001.

Lamb, Jonathan. "The Sublime." In *The Cambridge History of Literary Criticism: The Eighteenth Century*, edited by George Alexander Kennedy, Hugh Barr Nisbet, and Claude Rawson, 394–418. Cambridge: Cambridge University Press, 1997.

Leve, Ariel. "Toni Morrison on Love, Loss and Modernity." *The Telegraph*, http://www.telegraph.co.uk/culture/books/authorinterviews/9395051/Toni-Morrison-on-love-loss-and-modernity.html.

Levine, Lawrence W. *Black Culture and Black Consciousness*. Oxford, UK: Oxford University Press, 1977.

Levinson, Sanford, ed. *Torture: A Collection*. Oxford, UK: Oxford University Press, 2006.

Love, Nancy S. *Musical Democracy*. Albany: State University of New York Press, 2006.

Mattern, Mark. *Acting in Concert: Music, Community and Political Action*. New Brunswick, NJ: Rutgers University Press, 1998.

Morrison, Toni. *Beloved*. New York: Vintage Books, 1987.

———. *Paradise*. New York: Penguin 1997.

———. Interview. *BBC World Book Club*, January 3, 2009, http://www.bbc.co.uk/worldservice/arts/2009/03/000000_worldbookclub.shtml.

Morrison, Toni, and Cornel West. "Blues, Love and Politics." *The Nation*, May 24, 2004, 18–28.

Nguyen, Tram. *We Are All Suspects Now: Untold Stories from Immigrant Communities after 9/11*. Boston: Beacon Press, 2005.

Ramsey, Guthrie P. *Race Music: Black Cultures from Bebop to Hip-Hop*. Berkeley: University of California Press, 2003.

Ross, James. "A History of Torture." In *Torture: Does It Make Us Safer? A Human Rights Perspective*, edited by Kenneth Roth and Minky Worden, 3–17. New York: The New Press and Human Rights Watch, 2005.

Sartre, Jean-Paul. *Dirty Hands*. In *No Exit and Three Other Plays*, 125–222. New York: Vintage, 1989.

Scarry, Elaine. "Five Errors in the Reasoning of Alan Dershowitz." In Levinson, *Torture*, 281–90.

Shue, Henry. "Torture." *Philosophy and Public Affairs* 7, no. 2 (1978): 124–43.

Walzer, Michael. "Political Action: The Problem of Dirty Hands." *Philosophy and Public Affairs* 2, no. 1 (1973): 160–80.

West, Cornel. *Democracy Matters*. New York: Penguin Books, 2004.

———. "Celebrating *Tikkun* and Tragicomic Hope." *Tikkun* 19, no. 6 (2004): 53–54.

———. *Hope on a Tightrope: Words and Wisdom*. New York: Smiley Books, 2008.

Yanuck, Julius. "The Garner Fugitive Slave Case." *Mississippi Valley Historical Review* (Now *Journal of American Historians*) 40, no. 1 (1953): 1–19. http://www.michiganopera.org/mg_ed/educational/Garner%20Slave%20Case.pdf.

Discography

Holiday, Billie. "Strange Fruit." Words and music by Lewis Allan. Commodore 526, April 20, 1939.

Part V

Music

Chapter 8

"You're an American rapper, so what do you know?"

The Political Uses of British and U.S. Popular Culture by First-Time Voters in the United Kingdom

SANNA INTHORN AND JOHN STREET

Introduction

The election of President Barack Obama in 2008 provided a vivid illustration of the intimate link between popular culture, especially popular music, and politics. The campaign was marked by will.i.am's musical reworking of Obama's "Yes We Can" speech, and the inauguration celebrations were led by the good and great of Hollywood and the music industry.[1] Something similar took place with his reelection in 2012, when the president was pictured frequently in the company of Bruce Springsteen. In such moments, and many others besides, the crude distinction between serious politics and frivolous entertainment breaks down. Politics becomes culture, and culture politics. But while this mingling of the realms of the political and the aesthetic may be a commonplace of our time, it receives less detailed attention than it deserves. In particular, we

Our chapter draws on research funded by the United Kingdom's Economic and Social Research Council (RES-000-22-2700). We are very grateful for this support, for the contribution made by our research assistant Martin Scott, and for the comments and advice of the editors of this volume.

know surprisingly little about how the juxtaposition of politics and popular culture affects political thought and action, about what popular culture, in its commercial, everyday form, contributes to "doing democracy."

In this chapter, we take up the question of how and when forms of popular culture—from music to entertainment television—may shape the capacities of individuals and groups to act effectively in the world. This is not simply an opportunity to reflect upon the possible ways in which art—in our case, mass-produced art—may enable people to move toward a more democratic politics. It is asking for hard evidence of real contributions to this process. We focus on the example of young people in the United Kingdom. We report on research in which we have explored how first-time voters use popular culture to engage politically with the wider world, particularly how they employ it to imagine their collective identities and the interests attendant upon them.

We are not the first to do this. There is now a substantial, and growing, literature on the way popular television—whether in the guise of late-night satire, soaps, television drama (like *The West Wing*), or reality television shows—affects political engagement.[2] There are also studies devoted to the impact of "celebrity politicians."[3] What we offer, however, is different to the extent that we look at more than television and we concentrate on the words and thoughts of a particular category of cultural consumer, the first-time voter.

Our argument is that the capacity to act democratically (or indeed undemocratically) depends upon three key elements: knowledge of the wider world, a sense of shared community with others in it, and an ethical and emotional concern for it. Our question, therefore, becomes how and when does popular culture contribute to these dimensions of political action? What sense of "community" do the pleasures of popular culture afford and articulate? Put simply, what "world"—how narrow or broad, how inclusive or exclusive, how mean or generous—do young people imagine and experience through popular culture? We argue that any claim for culture's political impact must at some point engage with the routine realities and banalities of fandom and the pleasures which, at root, ground culture's meanings and its ways of mattering. This chapter concentrates upon one of the three elements: the use of popular culture to create a sense of community. Our assumption is that democratic engagement depends fundamentally upon a notion of common interests and of collective identity. And our question is, therefore, how does popular culture, if at all, enable such identities and interests to emerge? Can a form of culture designed to entertain and to make money also act to create the conditions for democracy?

In a series of group and individual interviews with young people in the United Kingdom, we raised the questions described earlier. And while the resulting data do not provide a simple or an unambiguous answer, they do help to illustrate the ways in which popular culture is used to sustain and articulate forms of democratic engagement. But before we turn to the specifics, it is important to fill in the background and to refine our argument.

Background: Politics and Popular Culture

There is a long tradition, deriving from a diverse range of disciplines and fields, that links art and culture to political engagement. It stretches from Plato through Rousseau to Adorno and beyond. It finds expression in arguments about the role of culture in education, in debates about censorship and state regulation, and in the use of art to promote causes and movements. At its heart, this tradition addresses the question of how and why art and culture matter, a question that is often sharply focused in debates about the public funding of the arts or the public regulation of broadcasting, debates which in turn connect to wider issues of democracy and the public sphere.[4]

While this long-established tradition has touched on all aspects and forms of art and culture, it has more recently been focused upon popular culture. This is a consequence of the commercial and social impact of popular culture, and of the polemics and panics it has provoked.[5] These negative responses have been matched by more positive ones, which have dwelt upon, for example, popular culture's capacity to mobilize political action, especially the role of music in social movements,[6] or upon popular culture's ability to give voice to political resistance.[7] Popular culture has featured, too, in studies of political ideology, where films or music are seen to convey ideas that reconcile peoples to their domination or awaken them to their subservience.[8] The recent phenomenon of the celebrity politician, typically incarnated in the guise of Bob Geldof or Bono or Arnold Schwarzenegger, has provided a new peg upon which to hang claims (and counterclaims) about the emergent forms of political leadership and representation enabled through popular culture.[9] What these various examples have in common is the suggestion that popular culture (or culture more generally) has the capacity to shape political thought and action.

By contrast, others have viewed popular culture as a symptom of a wider political malaise. Illustrations of this latter view are to be found in Colin Crouch's account of the post-democratic state in which democratic politics are enacted as a popular spectacle that is more show than substance,[10] or in David Marquand's portrait of the "hollowing out" of the public sphere or Danilo Zolo's of the "spectacularisation of politics."[11] Crouch, Marquand, and Zolo see democratic politics as being emptied of substance and replaced with a superficial display. Politics becomes, as a result, a version of popular culture and condemned as a consequence.

These dystopian accounts typically lack detailed empirical support. There is one notable exception to this rule, Robert Putnam's *Bowling Alone*, in which the consumption of popular culture is linked directly to political disengagement.[12] According to Putnam, the answer to the question as to whether popular culture enables people to promote democracy is a resounding "no." As is well known, Putnam contends that privatized cultural consumption not only takes time away from communal activity and erodes the networks that sustain social capital, but also that the messages contained within entertainment television reinforce the processes of disengagement. It encourages a sense of fatalism and a perception of a mean world.[13]

Putnam's claims have divided commentators. There are those who have disputed the evidence upon which his thesis rests, arguing that, in fact, television-watching enhances civic engagement, while others have suggested that his claims do not apply to countries outside of the United States.[14] The specifics of Putnam's case have also been examined, raising questions about the time-displacement effect and seeking to differentiate between the effects of contrasting types of entertainment television.[15]

But while the Putnam argument has been much debated, it has tended to reinforce an underlying general assumption, one which is shared by the more positive perspectives, that popular culture has a place in our understanding of the mechanisms of political engagement. This common ground only takes us so far. It suggests that popular culture has a role in political engagement, but it begs questions about why such different effects are observed: when and why does popular culture lead to positive forms of political engagement, and when and why does it lead to disengagement? These are large questions, and we do not pretend to offer definitive answers here. However, we do propose that the key to any answer is a detailed observation of how popular culture signifies for fans and audiences. In the last part of this chapter, we present the results of such observations. But first we consider in more detail what it might mean for popular culture to increase people's capacity to engage democratically in the world.

Popular Culture and Political Engagement

In focusing on popular culture, as opposed to "art" more generally, we are not proposing to challenge those who see popular culture as a lesser form of culture and thereby deleterious in its social and political consequences.[16] Nor do we wish to argue with those who see no significant or coherent distinction to be drawn between popular and "high" culture.[17] Rather we want to adopt a relatively neutral position, in which "popular culture" is understood as one form of art, albeit one that is commercially produced for the purpose of entertaining a mass market. The contrast we are making here is between entertainment and news coverage. The latter is typically seen to hold the key to mass media's role in democratic political engagement. Conventionally, popular culture is not assigned such a role, and what we are asking here, like others before us, is whether popular entertainment can also engage people politically.

The more pressing definitional questions turn on what we mean by democratic (or indeed, undemocratic) political engagement. We are aware of the danger of advancing an account of "political engagement" that is so inclusive as to make everything done by an individual or group a form of political engagement. If everything counts, then all forms of cultural consumption become acts of political engagement—a claim that is both banal and devoid of analytical value. There is a further danger to not tackling this definitional question. This is that, in circumstances where there is growing anxiety about political disengagement, there needs to be clarity about what engagement entails and how it might be advanced.[18]

In his own work on youth political engagement and television, David Buckingham argues forcefully against an all-inclusive definition, in which the public and the private are wholly elided: "Ultimately, we need to sustain meaningful distinctions between the 'personal' and the 'political,' or the 'private' and the 'public,' if we wish to avoid lapsing into political incoherence. The central educational issue remains that of building connections between these domains—between the 'micro-politics' of everyday life and the 'macro-politics' of political institutions and of collective political action."[19] Buckingham proposes that the "political" be captured in the way in which people identify themselves with others and with the public realm.[20] His notion of politics involves, as a minimum, collective attempts to affect the exercise of public power.

Buckingham's approach is echoed—in a more elaborated form—in a recent study of public engagement and media consumption. Like Buckingham, Nick Couldry and his colleagues want to avoid the elision of the public and the private, the personal and the political, and argue for a notion of the public that refers not to a designated space but rather to common decisions. Expressions of "social belonging" or "common identity" do not in themselves constitute democratic political participation.[21] They have to be accompanied by some intention to act upon this collective sensibility. We cannot assume that use of mass-mediated culture automatically connects people to others or to the public realm.[22] This means that, for Couldry and his colleagues, the question of how and when popular culture contributes to an ability to act effectively depends on the extent to which it is perceived to provide an "orientation to *any* of those issues affecting how we live together that require common resolution."[23] In other words, as with Buckingham, the issue is whether media or cultural consumption prompts collective engagement in the exercise of public power. But while Buckingham and others want to avoid presuming too much about political engagement, their default position tends to be that engagement, when it occurs, is democratic in character, that it represents the voices and interests of "the people." We need to be wary of this presumption, not only because populism is not itself necessarily democratic, but also because political engagement may be directed at suppressing democracy. In our research, we have tried to allow for the possibility that popular culture's pleasures may yield anti-democratic sentiments.

First, however, we need to consider how popular culture might contribute to a capacity to engage politically, whatever the form of that politics. As we indicated earlier, we suggest that there are three possible ways in which popular culture might connect people to politics. First, it may be seen to give an account of, or represent, the wider (political) world in which people are expected to engage. In other words, popular culture may be regarded as describing a "real" public world rather than a purely fictional one. Secondly, it might contribute to the formation of collective identities that can constitute the basis of political action. This is the thought behind Liesbet van Zoonen's comparison of fan communities and political communities.[24] And thirdly, popular culture might motivate or mobilize those communities of identity to act on their (or others') behalf. Audiences or fans might be persuaded or induced to care about the wider world as a result of their consumption of popular culture. As we show briefly further on, the existing literature supports the suggestion that, in principle, popular culture can enable all three.

Representing the Wider World

This refers to the way in which culture is held to (literally) re-present the world to its audiences. The form of this representation also explicitly or implicitly gives an account of how that world works. Many researchers have analyzed culture in these terms, including Putnam, reading political narratives into films, television programs, and music. Van Zoonen argues, for example, that there are four narratives that organize popular culture's representation of politics (quest, conspiracy, bureaucracy, and soap).[25] Jeffrey Jones concentrates upon the satirical representations of politics.[26] These representations are seen as enabling or disabling forms of political engagement by the way that politics is mediated.

Constituting Identities and Actors

The narratives that represent the world and its driving forces can be seen to place the viewer, listener, or reader in a particular relationship to that world. The plotlines trace the movement of power, creating a sense of "them" and "us," and establishing possibilities of intervention. Both Jones and Van Zoonen argue that the narratives that they identify in popular culture's representation of politics position the audience in relation to power and suggest possibilities for change. Van Zoonen contrasts the telling of politics as a "quest," in which individual success is possible, with the narrative of politics as a "conspiracy," in which engagement is pointless.

Other writers, rather than looking to the text to reveal its relationship to political engagement, have turned to the context. Typically, this context has been created by social and political movements.[27] Popular culture acts to counter the logic of collective action by articulating a sense of collective purpose. Closely linked to this is the suggestion that culture acts to constitute forms of collective identity. Benedict Anderson's "imagined communities," for example, are constructed through cultural activity.[28] And finally, there are those who would suggest that the stars of popular culture can assume leadership or representation of these communities in the guise of "celebrity politics."[29]

Mobilizing Action

Being invited to see the world in a particular way, or being situated within specific relationships, are both important conditions for political engagement. But arguably a third element is required. This is the energy or motivation to act. One of Putnam's concerns about television is the passivity it induces.[30] Others point to the invigorating effects of music. Lawrence Grossberg, for example, focuses on the affective power of popular music to account for political action, while Jane Bennett points to the capacity of rhythm to "energize" moral commitments.[31] More generally, social movement theorists are increasingly aware of the place played by culture, not just in conveying the movement's political message, but in animating those who share it.[32]

Existing literature, then, suggests that popular culture might be implicated in political engagement in at least three ways: to represent the world to us, to help forge identities of interest, and to animate these communities to act in pursuit of these interests. However this research does not, for the most part, demonstrate how and when this happens in particular cases, whether that be particular forms of popular culture or particular audiences. This is a crucial step, and one to which the rest of this chapter is devoted. It means focusing on how audiences themselves connect popular culture to political engagement.

A growing number of writers have started to conduct audience research to explore the potential of cultural consumption to facilitate an orientation toward issues of public concern. In his study of television programs like *The Daily Show*, Jones reveals how audiences use them to connect to public life and to express an affinity toward their civic community.[33] The humor of these programs, together with their representation of "ordinary citizens," is crucial in helping audiences to make these connections. Similarly, Kevin Barnhurst has shown how young people use "commercials and magazine ads, fictional TV shows and films, and sports or gaming to give form to their dreams, personal and collective, and . . . to create their own styles and express themselves as political beings."[34] While these writers have successfully made the case for an "entertainment effect" upon political dispositions, an important question remains as to how particular forms of popular culture provide audiences with the capacity to act upon these dispositions. This is the issue upon which we report here, drawing on research into young people's discussion of different forms of popular culture and its relevance to the wider world.

In reporting our evidence, we concentrate primarily on the way young audiences draw on national and international popular culture to explore the geographic and cultural boundaries of their political community and its interests. This is to focus on only one of the conditions of political engagement (the sense of collective identity), but it touches on the others. In consuming popular culture, we ask, do young people see themselves as part of a particular national or global constituency, and does this generate a concern for political action in pursuit of their common interests? This is to tap into a familiar debate about the extent to which global popular culture provides a platform for an inclusive cosmopolitanism (what might be called "the Live 8 effect"), or as the source of a destructive homogeneity and the erosion of distinct national and local identities. The evidence of cultural consumption is that fears of a homogenous global culture are unfounded, although dissenting voices remain, pointing to the need to place all responses to culture in their context.[35] The question is whether, in their specific contexts, audiences see the culture they consume as fueling parochial national interests or cosmopolitan compassion. What sorts of national or global citizenship is constructed in cultural consumption, and what is its implication for the way people may act in the world? Do the celebrities who claim to speak on their behalf have any legitimacy with their audience?

Researching Popular Culture and Political Engagement

Our evidence derives from conversations among young people about popular culture. We examined these conversations to see what they reveal about the role that popular culture plays in political engagement with the wider world. The decision to concentrate on seventeen- to eighteen-year-olds was a response to the increasing concern with their perceived political disengagement, a perception that is not confined to the United Kingdom.[36]

Our research was based on students from five schools in three UK counties (Norfolk, Suffolk, and Essex). They were representative of a particular cohort—those who had remained in education beyond the period required by law (that is, sixteen years of age). There was a rough balance between boys (43%) and girls (57%). They were predominantly white British in ethnicity, but there was a small proportion of other ethnicities. This was characteristic of the region from which the sample was drawn. Two of our thirteen focus groups were educated in the private sector, the rest were from the public sector.

The research itself involved a brief questionnaire, designed primarily to identify their cultural preferences. This was followed by a series of focus groups in the sample schools and subsequent interviews with individual students. Our aim was to facilitate conditions in which students could talk with relative freedom about their cultural pleasures. We did, however, steer their talk toward those cultural artifacts that they themselves had identified in their questionnaire responses, and we did press for further clarification of their views where they made links to politics or to celebrity politicians. We should stress that our method is based on the assumption that talk about popular culture is revealing of both the value and the meaning culture has for people.[37] In what we report here, we concentrate primarily on how our respondents used popular culture to articulate some notion of a national and international community and their relation to it. This allows us to see how popular culture might be implicated in how, in Henrik Bang's words, individuals "can develop political commonality from their political individuality."[38]

Creating Communities, Drawing Boundaries

Reviewing the many hours of recorded conversation that we collected, we looked for examples of talk about popular culture that, either explicitly or implicitly, connected the pleasures—and the displeasures—of popular culture to regional, national, and global others, and what kinds of political communities were (or were not) thereby evoked. While we noted that our respondents saw music and television as ways of introducing themselves to the realities of the wider world—"TV and music . . . make me think about the international world" (Interview 9)[39]—we were more concerned with how popular culture was linked to imagined collectivities. We noted two distinct ways in which this occurred. First, it was revealed in the comparisons made between national popular cultures; and secondly, it emerged in the critical evaluation of those cultures.

Comparing Culture and Constructing National Identities

Much of the popular culture that our respondents consumed derived from the United States—television programs such as *Heroes* or *Friends*, music by Kanye West or Metallica or Eminem. The other main source of their culture was the United Kingdom. Video games were one exception to this rule, many of them being Japanese imports (for example, Super Mario Bros.). But while the United States and the United Kingdom were the main sources of cultural pleasure, we also spoke to young people who, for a variety of reasons, listened to French hip hop or Asian pop. However, the majority of respondents were not exposed, for the most part, to cultural goods from politically and economically marginalized countries. Such tastes might be expected to lead either to "Americanization" or to the reinforcement of national identities.[40] We might have expected, in other words, an "imagined community" that was Anglo-American in character. The reality—at least as revealed by the conversations of our sample—was more confused and complicated.

In their conversations about their cultural tastes, many of our respondents seemed to work with a traditional mapping of the world where national and local cultures offer the strongest points of identification. Respondents valued the role played by local news in giving visibility to ordinary citizens like themselves and to their community. They found reassurance in the media's recognition of their local existence. But significantly this reassurance came in the form of local news and reports of events to which they had a connection. As one participant said: "I think those things, like, make you feel important don't they?"; and another added that it "brings people together" (Focus Group 13). Entertainment rarely, if ever, featured in such conversations about local communities and identities, although they did mention the pride they felt if someone from their area appeared on national television talent shows (Focus Group 6). There was a contrast to be drawn between the community they imagined in their engagement with news and that which they imagined through their entertainment.

Entertainment was a feature of discussion of national identity and community. One form of this was the use of domestically produced entertainment to establish a basis for national pride. British situation comedies, for example, were compared favorably ("a more intelligent comedy") to those of other nations. The main contrast was made with the United States: "The difference is that in America, people just watch stuff. So people can just churn out stuff, and people will still watch it. But in England, if you want to make a sitcom, then you actually have to have a decent proposal to do it. You can't just go in and make one" (Focus Group 7). Although this might be read as a judgment of rival tastes or of rival television systems, it entailed more than this. It was a statement about how they saw themselves, and how they used popular culture in establishing this identity.

The concept of a national community emerged across focus groups and interviews as respondents suggested the existence of collectively shared national values and cultural practices. While many of our respondents located themselves quite comfortably and positively within a national community, for some it was more complex and difficult. Complexity emerged in conversations about regional identity. For several of our respondents popular culture offered a way of identifying not only with a national collectivity, but also with a concept of the region. For example, respondents in one of our focus groups agreed that seeing someone from one's own region on a television talent show, such as *Britain's Got Talent* or the *X Factor* (Focus Group 6), would make them more likely to participate in the public vote. The identification with the concept of a region was particularly noticeable among respondents from Norfolk and Suffolk (or East Anglia). These respondents expressed appreciation of moments when national television referred to cultural life and, in particular, the popular music scene in their region. But they also reported that they felt ignored by the rest of the nation. Seeing cities and people of one's region on television programs, as one respondent put it, is "quite cool" as "most people, all they see East Anglia as, [is] a place to go on holiday. But people actually live here" (Interview 24). The standard concept of "the nation" was not always embraced by our respondents, who negotiated other collective identities through popular culture. But sometimes this sense of collective self was more traditional and less global than that which one might expect of young people who consume a lot of international (and especially U.S.) media.

When they made distinctions between their country and the countries of others, they might be seen simply as expressing crude stereotypes or prejudices. Certainly, our respondents could appear very jingoistic. Americans were described as people who were "a bit dim" and who "think America is the world" (Interview 22). But behind these crude characterizations, there was a sense of differences of another kind, ones that might be classified as political. Criticism of the U.S. television industry was, for example, couched in terms of its democratic populism. In contrast, the British television industry was held up as an example of regulated, quality programming (Interview 24). This was not a universal view, however. Such views were challenged on the grounds that American television "is always better" and generally more widely known than British programming (Focus Group 5).

Underlying these judgments, and the crude stereotypes used to articulate them, there is a more substantial political debate about what television should do and how it should be regulated. It was not just the country of origin that mattered, but the quality of the cultural product, which was used to code for particular identities and values. The soap opera *EastEnders* was appreciated for the fact that it represented "British values" (Interview 10).

What all the comments we elicited had in common, regardless of whether they praised or criticized American programming, was that they all "imagined" concepts of a national self and an Other through discourses about television audiences and production. In this process, identity was tied to particular cultural values. Although the latter might, on the surface, appear to entail aesthetic judgments (and prejudices), they can be seen to have significance for relations to a wider world, to the extent that they represent views about what audiences are capable of understanding and deserve. These might not constitute fully realized political ideas, but they could be seen as "proto-political" in the sense that they propose a set of values for their different "imagined communities."

Judging Culture and Constructing Communities and Representatives

National differences, and their associated values, did not just derive from discussion of production values. One other source of distinction was perceived in the content. This extended from storylines to jokes. Echoing what other writers on globalization and television have observed, our respondents claimed that, in order for gags and punch lines to work, they need to appeal to local cultural traditions and knowledge.[41] Such perceptions were used to reinforce a sense of national identity and to see popular culture as implicated in this. Jokes were understood to derive from a national context and to reinforce national identity. As one respondent noted, U.S. television makes "jokes about some kind of person that obviously us in Britain don't really know about" (Interview 24).

Shared cultural proximity between a media text and its audience was also crucial in determining the extent to which respondents were willing to engage with its meaning. This sensitivity to national origins and context is not simply a function of culture; it also has political dimensions. It has implications for who is perceived to speak credibly about politics and to have valid claims to represent political interests. Drawing on the example of the celebrity politician, we asked our respondents about which entertainers they would listen to on the subject of politics. One typical response was this: "if you hear an American, like a typical, stereotypical . . . American girl, talking about politics, you'd sort of be, like, 'seriously, they've been told to say that.' Like, I don't know, Britney Spears, if she talked about politics, I'd be, like, 'seriously, what the hell?'" (Focus Group 9) Such statements suggest all manner of prejudice (not least sexism), but what they also reveal is the extent to which judgments about popular culture elide into political views. Insofar as entertainers and forms of entertainment are able to speak for people, their success as representatives depends upon the credibility and legitimacy that they are assigned. These factors are partly a product of the perceived authenticity of the artists—does Britney Spears speak for herself? Just as our respondents filtered their sense of national identity through their perception of the culture industry, so did they with judgments of celebrity politicians. Britney Spears was viewed as the product of the music industry, someone who was dictated to by her managers and others, and to this extent she was deemed not to be able to speak for her fans.

It is interesting to contrast the discussion of Britney Spears with that of Kanye West. The U.S. rap artist was seen by UK fans as someone whose views they respected (Focus Group 12). His "American-ness" did not feature in the conversation. He had earned their respect as a performer, and that was sufficient. He was deemed to be "authentic" and autonomous in a way that Britney Spears was not. Such judgments serve to show how, insofar as popular culture identifies communities and interests, a range of mediating factors are brought to bear and used in the process. Among these factors is a perception of control that artists exercise over their career and their work. Another factor is a perception of the star's integrity and the incentives to which they respond.

This was evident when we asked our young people what they thought of the efforts of rock stars to bring attention to developing country debt and other such issues. They complained that either "they [the rock stars] get paid to say it [talk about debt]," or "they are just doing it for themselves," or they do it "to promote their fame," or that they are "hypocrites" who do nothing about global warming (Focus Group 8). Again by way of contrast, a Kanye West fan spoke of how such artists could talk authoritatively about Africa because of their background and of their visits to the continent. By contrast, the same respondent doubted Madonna's authority as a commentator because she "had not been through as much" as West and "doesn't really know what she's talking about" (Interview 13).

In judging between the ability of stars to pronounce on politics, our respondents voiced a similar suspicion of those who lacked direct experience of conventional politics. As one of them explained to us, Eminem could not speak on politics because "I wouldn't trust him, but I would listen. If he told me what to do, I would be, like, 'you don't know what you're talking about, you're an American rapper'" (Interview 21). In a similar vein, asked if Justin Timberlake could conceivably be U.S. president, another respondent said: "No, because he's more of an entertainer" (Interview 16). And even those celebrities who have proved successful as business people, like the entrepreneur Alan Sugar, who acts as a judge on the reality show *The Apprentice*, are treated with suspicion because business and political competence are seen as different (Interview 24). Our participants reproduced familiar stereotypes of the characteristics required of leaders: "Yeah, politicians, I think, are just, like, above the normal people. I don't think they live the lives that you and me do" (Interview 5).

The judgment of credibility, legitimacy, and integrity did not just derive from judgments of the "authenticity" or the expertise of the celebrities; it also derived, once again, from evaluations of the system of cultural production itself. The U.S. system is seen as less able to represent "the people" because of its commercial character. By contrast, programs produced by the British public service broadcasting system are approached initially with a degree of trust: "Oh yeah, I think I probably would trust the BBC a bit more because you know it is paid for by the people for the people. . . . I would trust the BBC more [than U.S. television]" (Interview 23). However much we might question these evaluations, the point is that they operate not just as forms of cultural discrimination but as the basis for political judgments about possible collective identities and about how those identities might be represented and expressed.

In focusing on the way our respondents discuss the rival claims of U.S. and UK popular culture, we have tried to show how in comparing and judging them they implicitly and explicitly constructed collective identities that were political in character. What might, at first sight, look like straightforward expressions of cultural taste, turn out to have wider resonances. They summon up imagined communities, which are not only differentiated culturally, but in terms of the values they constitute and how those values can be represented. We cannot claim that these conversations about culture lead directly to political action, but they do help to construct the collectivities that underpin such action.

Discussion

We began this chapter by noting the widespread assumption that, for good or ill, there is a link between popular culture and political engagement. We also noted that the details of this connection tend to receive less close attention than the general assumption would seem to warrant. We contended that for popular culture to form the basis for some kind of political engagement, it might be expected to do three things: to provide a picture of the wider world, to help constitute communities with an interest in acting on the world, and to engender the political passion necessary to action. We have concentrated here on the second of these elements. Our concern has been with whether the pleasures of popular culture help to forge the sense of common identity and interests that underlie democratic politics. To see whether this was possible, we conducted focus groups and interviews, in order to give young people the opportunity to talk about their experience of popular culture, and to see if these conversations revealed evidence of its capacity to constitute fans and audiences as communities of interest.

Our respondents typically expressed little or no concern for traditional politics. Conventional party politics were regarded as irrelevant or with disdain. The majority of our respondents declared themselves to have little interest in government politics and even less trust in politicians. Nonetheless, we found that their response to popular culture often appealed to, or depended upon, a sense of community (and of the interests that attached to it). It is true that this community was more parochial than it was cosmopolitan, but then this would be more consistent with the UK population and their media use.[42] To this extent, we concluded that popular culture may help to constitute a sense of community, but not that it offers a radically different one.

Our respondents demonstrated a similarly traditional view of politics in their reflections on how "celebrity politics" might, or might not, provide a way to represent their identities and interests. They trusted Kanye West over Britney Spears. They thought that the pop industry tycoon Simon Cowell might make a good politician, not so much for his knowledge of the wider world, but because of his business success and his willingness to pass judgment (Focus Group 10).

While these specific views are interesting and revealing, they do not represent the only lessons that we wish to draw from our research. We would also suggest that the routine responses to popular culture—what is liked and disliked, what is valued and not valued—are themselves part of a process by which political identities and values are articulated. The movement between aesthetic and political judgments is what, we would argue, contains the key to understanding how and when popular culture engages audiences and fans with politics. Popular culture does not just contain "messages" about politics; it also constitutes a possible site of democratic life.

To put this yet more starkly, the typical way in which popular culture has been linked to politics has been through the texts, through what they seem to "say" about the world. Close reading of media texts has been seen to reveal political ideologies that position audiences in relation to the "real" world of politics. There is clearly importance and value in such work. However, there is a danger, in concentrating on the text, of ignoring how these texts actually signify for audiences, particularly given the huge variety of contexts in which they are consumed. It was for this reason that we determined to focus on the conversations that young people had about popular culture. These revealed how aesthetic and cultural judgments—what was good, what was rubbish—shaded into political ones.

Arguments about the relative merits of Kanye West or Britney Spears might seem to revolve around crude dichotomies of taste, of assertions of "good" or "bad," that allow for no further discussion and admit of no deeper insights. What we have suggested, and what we hope our evidence has supported, is that such debates are expressions of wider concerns and considerations. Encoded in them, and experienced through them, are competing notions of who "we" are, revealed both in what "we" like or dislike and in how "we" account for presence or absence of the qualities "we" value—where it is produced, in what kind of media system. In other words, judgments of taste articulate judgments of other kinds, ones that we suggest are—at least—"proto-political" in their appeal to rationale of how things should be organized and what people deserve.

There is a further insight that might be garnered from the conversations we recorded. Not only are distinctions made within forms of popular culture, they are also made between them. Listening back to our focus groups and interviews, it is notable how often the conversation turns to music, at least when talking about things that seem to matter most to our respondents. They were acute observers of television and enthusiastic players of video games, but it was music that tended to animate them. This might suggest that music is different in its capacity to inspire or mobilize political thought and action, to create and animate communities of interest.

Finally, we do not mean for our concern with young fans and their talk about popular culture to replace the other connections to be made between political engagement and popular culture. The links made via close textual reading and through research into social movements are also vital to the full picture, as is analysis of the political economy of the cultural industry. What we do want to claim, however, is that the research reported here, and the arguments that underlie it, make a contribution to our ability to determine when and how art and culture can contribute to the capacity to promote democratic engagement.

In particular, we have suggested that the capacity to act effectively is tied to the collective entities with which people associate themselves, with the judgments they make of others, and with the judgments they make of those who should be empowered to represent those collectivities. It is no surprise that our respondents use popular culture to articulate or express their sense of identity. What is more surprising is how the judgments they make of culture—of its source, of its performers, and of its system of production—are revealing of the political dimensions of those identities. This suggests that engagement with popular culture inspires ideas and values that are important to the capacity to act effectively in the world, even for those who appear to take no interest in traditional forms of politics.

Notes

1. http://www.youtube.com/watch?v=jjXyqcx-mYY&feature=related.

2. Geoffrey Baym, "*The Daily Show*: Discursive Integration and the Reinvention of Political Journalism," *Political Communication* 22, no. 3 (2005): 259–76; Dhavan V. Shah, "Civic Engagement, Interpersonal Trust, and Television Use: An Individual-Level Assessment of Social Capital," *Political Psychology* 19, no. 3 (1998): 469–96; Robert Putnam, *Bowling Alone: The Collapse and Revival of American Community* (New York: Simon & Schuster, 2000); Liesbet van Zoonen, "Audience Reactions to Hollywood Politics," *Media, Culture and Society* 29, no. 4 (2007): 531–47; Todd Graham and Auli Hajru, "Reality TV as a Trigger of Everyday Political Talk in the Net-Based Sphere," *European Journal of Communication* 26, no. 1 (2011): 18–32.

3. David Jackson and Thomas Darrow, "The Influence of Celebrity Endorsements on Young Adults' Political Opinions," *Harvard International Journal of Press/Politics* 10, no. 3 (2005): 80–98.

4. Tim Blanning, *The Triumph of Music: Composers, Musicians and Their Audiences, 1700 to the Present* (London: Allen Lane, 2008); Jürgen Habermas, *The Structural Transformation of the Public Sphere: An Inquiry into a Category of Bourgeois Society* (Cambridge, UK: Polity, 1992); D. L. LeMahieu, *A Culture for Democracy:*

Mass Culture and the Cultivated Mind in Britain between the Wars (Oxford, UK: Oxford University Press, 1998); Nancy S. Love, *Musical Democracy* (Albany: State University of New York Press, 2006).

5. See, for example, Linda Martin and Kerry Segrave, *Anti-Rock: The Opposition to Rock'n'Roll* (New York: Da Capo Press, 1993).

6. Ron Eyerman and Andrew Jamison, *Music and Social Movements: Mobilizing Traditions in the Twentieth Century* (Cambridge: Cambridge University Press, 1998); Mark Mattern, *Acting in Concert: Music, Community, and Political Action* (New Brunswick, NJ: Rutgers University Press, 1998); Brian Ward, *Just My Soul Responding: Rhythm and Blues, Black Consciousness and Race Relations* (London: University College London Press, 1998).

7. John C. Scott, *Domination and the Arts of Resistance: Hidden Transcripts* (New Haven, CT: Yale University Press, 1990).

8. Theodor Adorno and Max Horkheimer, *Dialectic of Enlightenment* (London: Verso, 1979); Paul Cantor, *Gilligan Unbound: Pop Culture in the Age of Globalization* (New York: Rowman & Littlefield, 2003); Douglas Kellner, *Media Culture* (London: Routledge, 1995).

9. Darrell M. West and John Orman, *Celebrity Politics* (Upper Saddle River, NJ: Prentice Hall, 2003).

10. Colin Crouch, *Post-Democracy* (Cambridge, UK: Polity, 2004).

11. David Marquand, *The Decline of the Public: The Hollowing Out of Citizenship* (Cambridge, UK: Polity, 2004); Danilo Zolo, *Democracy and Complexity* (Cambridge, UK: Polity, 1992).

12. Putnam, *Bowling Alone*.

13. Ibid., 242ff.

14. Pippa Norris, *Virtuous Circle: Political Communication in Post-Industrial Societies* (Cambridge: Cambridge University Press, 2000); Peter Hall, "Social Capital in Britain," *British Journal of Political Science* 29, no. 3 (1999): 417–61.

15. John Besley, "The Role of Entertainment Television and Its Interaction with Individual Values in Explaining Political Participation," *Harvard International Journal of Press/Politics* 11, no. 2 (2006): 41–63; Marc Hooghe, "Watching Television and Civic Engagement," *Harvard International Journal of Press/Politics* 7, no. 2 (2002): 84–104.

16. Allan Bloom, *The Closing of the American Mind* (New York: Simon & Schuster, 1987); Roger Scruton, *An Intelligent Person's Guide to Modern Culture* (London: Duckworth, 1998).

17. John Storey, *Cultural Theory and Popular Culture* (London: Prentice Hall, 2000).

18. Jonathan Tonge and Andrew Mycock, "Citizenship and Political Engagement among Young People: The Workings and Findings of the Youth Citizenship Commission," *Parliamentary Affairs* 63, no. 1 (2010): 182–200; see also, Colin Hay, *Why We Hate Politics* (Cambridge, UK: Polity, 2007).

19. David Buckingham, *The Making of Citizens: Young People, Politics and News* (London: Routledge, 2000), 34.

20. Ibid., 175.

21. Nick Couldry, Sonia Livingstone, and Tim Markham, *Media Consumption and Public Engagement: Beyond the Presumption of Attention* (Houndmills, UK: Palgrave Macmillan, 2007), 6–8.

22. Ibid., 3.

23. Ibid., 6, their emphasis.

24. Liesbet van Zoonen, *Entertaining the Citizen: When Politics and Popular Culture Converge* (New York: Rowman & Littlefield, 2005), 53–68.

25. Ibid., 105–22.

26. Jeffrey P. Jones, *Entertaining Politics: New Political Television and Civic Culture* (New York: Rowman & Littlefield, 2005).

27. See Eyerman and Jamison, *Music and Social Movements*, and Mattern, *Acting in Concert*.

28. Benedict Anderson, *Imagined Communities: Reflections on the Origins and Spread of Nationalism* (London: Verso, 2006).

29. John Street, "Celebrity Politicians: Popular Culture as Political Representation," *British Journal of Politics and International Relations* 6, no. 4 (2004): 435–52.

30. Putnam, *Bowling Alone*, 240.

31. Lawrence Grossberg, *We Gotta Get Out of This Place: Political Conservatism and Popular Culture* (New York: Routledge, 1992); Jane Bennett, *The Enchantment of Modern Life* (Princeton, NJ: Princeton University Press, 2001); Love, *Musical Democracy*, 87–108.

32. See Eyerman and Jamison, *Music and Social Movements*, and Mattern, *Acting in Concert*; Marc Steinberg, "When Politics Goes Pop: On the Intersection of Popular and Political Culture and the Case of the Serbian Student Protests," *Social Movement Studies* 3, no. 1 (2004): 3–29; Jeff Goodwin, James M. Jasper, and Francesca Polletta, eds., *Passionate Politics: Emotions and Social Movements* (Chicago: University of Chicago Press, 2001).

33. Jones, *Entertaining Politics*.

34. Kevin Barnhurst, "Politics in the Fine Meshes: Young Citizens, Power and Media," *Media, Culture & Society* 20, no. 2 (1998): 216.

35. Ramaswami Harindranath, *Perspectives on Global Cultures* (Maidenhead, UK: Open University Press, 2006); Paul Nee, "Television and Global Culture: The Role of Television in Globalization," in *The New Communications Landscape: Demystifying Media Globalization*, edited by Georgette Wang, Anura Goonasekera, and Jan Servaes (London: Routledge, 2000), 194; Des Freedman, "Who Wants to Be a Millionaire? The Politics of Television Exports," *Information, Communication & Society* 6, no. 1 (2003): 26.

36. Russell Dalton, "Citizen Norms and the Expansion of Political Participation," *Political Studies* 56, no. 1 (2008): 76–98.

37. Peter Dahlgren, *Media and Political Engagement: Citizens, Communication and Democracy* (Cambridge: Cambridge University Press, 2008); Sonia Livingstone, ed., *Audiences and Publics: When Cultural Engagement Matters for the Public Sphere* (Bristol, UK: Intellect Books, 2005).

38. Henrik Bang, "'Yes we can': Identity Politics and Project Politics for a Late-Modern World," *Urban Research & Practice* 2, no. 2 (2009): 21.

39. We conducted thirteen focus groups and twenty-four one-to-one interviews. All respondents are anonymous and represented by capital letters (the facilitators appear as "I"), and the reference indicates the system of numbering we used to identify our data. The data from the research will be available through the ESRC Data Archive.

40. Daniel Biltereyst and Philippe Meers, "The International Telenovela Debate and the Contra-Flow Argument: A Re-Appraisal," *Media, Culture & Society* 22, no. 4 (2000): 393–413; David Hesmondhalgh, *The Cultural Industries*, 2nd edition (London: Sage, 2007).

41. Sharon Lockyer and Michael Pickering, eds., *Beyond a Joke: The Limits of Humour* (Houndmills, UK: Palgrave Macmillan, 2005).

42. Martin Scott, *The World in Focus: How UK Audiences Connect with the Wider World and the International Content of News in 2009* (London: Department for International Development, 2010).

Bibliography

Adorno, Theodor, and Max Horkheimer. *Dialectic of Enlightenment*. London: Verso, 1979.

Anderson, Benedict. *Imagined Communities: Reflections on the Origins and Spread of Nationalism*. London: Verso, 2006.

Bang, Henrik. "'Yes we can': Identity Politics and Project Politics for a Late-Modern World." *Urban Research & Practice* 2, no. 2 (2009): 1–21.

Barnhurst, Kevin. "Politics in the Fine Meshes: Young Citizens, Power and Media.'" *Media, Culture & Society* 20, no. 2 (1998): 201–18.

Baym, Geoffrey. "*The Daily Show*: Discursive Integration and the Reinvention of Political Journalism." *Political Communication* 22, no. 3 (2005): 259–76.

Bennett, Jane. *The Enchantment of Modern Life*. Princeton, NJ: Princeton University Press, 2001.

Besley, John. "The Role of Entertainment Television and Its Interaction with Individual Values in Explaining Political Participation." *Harvard International Journal of Press/Politics* 11, no. 2 (2006): 41–63.

Biltereyst, Daniel, and Philippe Meers. "The International Telenovela Debate and the Contra-Flow Argument: A Re-Appraisal." *Media, Culture & Society* 22, no. 4 (2000): 393–413.

Blanning, Tim. *The Triumph of Music: Composers, Musicians and Their Audiences, 1700 to the Present.* London: Allen Lane, 2008.

Bloom, Allan. *The Closing of the American Mind.* New York: Simon & Schuster, 1987.

Buckingham, David. *The Making of Citizens: Young People, Politics and News.* London: Routledge, 2000.

Cantor, Paul. *Gilligan Unbound: Pop Culture in the Age of Globalization.* New York: Rowman & Littlefield, 2003.

Couldry, Nick, Sonia Livingstone, and Tim Markham. *Media Consumption and Public Engagement: Beyond the Presumption of Attention.* Houndmills, UK: Palgrave Macmillan, 2007.

Crouch, Colin. *Post-Democracy.* Cambridge, UK: Polity, 2004.

Dahlgren, Peter. *Media and Political Engagement: Citizens, Communication and Democracy.* Cambridge: Cambridge University Press, 2008.

Dalton, Russell. "Citizen Norms and the Expansion of Political Participation." *Political Studies* 56, no. 1 (2008): 76–98.

Eyerman, Ron, and Andrew Jamison. *Music and Social Movements: Mobilizing Traditions in the Twentieth Century.* Cambridge: Cambridge University Press, 1998.

Freedman, Des. "Who Wants to Be a Millionaire? The Politics of Television Exports." *Information, Communication & Society* 6, no. 1 (2003): 24–41.

Goodwin, Jeff, James M. Jasper, and Francesca Polletta, eds. *Passionate Politics: Emotions and Social Movements.* Chicago: University of Chicago Press, 2001.

Graham, Todd, and Auli Hajru. "Reality TV as a Trigger of Everyday Political Talk in the Net-Based Sphere." *European Journal of Communication* 26, no. 1 (2011): 18–32.

Grossberg, Lawrence. *We Gotta Get Out of This Place: Political Conservatism and Popular Culture.* New York: Routledge, 1992.

Habermas, Jürgen. *The Structural Transformation of the Public Sphere: An Inquiry into a Category of Bourgeois Society.* Cambridge, UK: Polity, 1992.

Hall, Peter. "Social Capital in Britain." *British Journal of Political Science* 29, no. 3 (1999): 417–61.

Harindranath, Ramaswami. *Perspectives on Global Cultures.* Maidenhead, UK: Open University Press, 2006.

Hay, Colin. *Why We Hate Politics.* Cambridge, UK: Polity, 2007.

Hesmondhalgh, David. *The Cultural Industries,* 2nd edition. London: Sage, 2007.

Hooghe, Marc. "Watching Television and Civic Engagement." *Harvard International Journal of Press/Politics* 7, no. 2 (2002): 84–104.

Jackson, David, and Thomas Darrow. "The Influence of Celebrity Endorsements on Young Adults' Political Opinions." *Harvard International Journal of Press/Politics* 10, no. 3 (2005): 80–98.

Jones, Jeffrey P. *Entertaining Politics: New Political Television and Civic Culture.* New York: Rowman & Littlefield, 2005.

Kellner, Douglas. *Media Culture.* London: Routledge, 1995.

LeMahieu, D. L. *A Culture for Democracy: Mass Culture and the Cultivated Mind in Britain between the Wars.* Oxford, UK: Oxford University Press, 1998.

Livingstone, Sonia, ed. *Audiences and Publics: When Cultural Engagement Matters for the Public Sphere.* Bristol, UK: Intellect Books, 2005.

Lockyer, Sharon, and Michael Pickering, eds. *Beyond a Joke: The Limits of Humour* Houndmills, UK: Palgrave Macmillan, 2005.

Love, Nancy S. *Musical Democracy.* Albany: State University of New York Press, 2006.

Marquand, David. *The Decline of the Public: The Hollowing Out of Citizenship.* Cambridge, UK: Polity, 2004.

Martin, Linda, and Kerry Segrave. *Anti-Rock: The Opposition to Rock'n'Roll.* New York: Da Capo Press, 1993.

Mattern, Mark. *Acting in Concert: Music, Community, and Political Action.* New Brunswick, NJ: Rutgers University Press, 1998.

Nee, Paul. "Television and Global Culture: The Role of Television in Globalization." In *The New Communications Landscape: Demystifying Media Globalization,* edited by Georgette Wang, Anura Goonasekera, and Jan Servaes, 191–201. London: Routledge, 2000.

Norris, Pippa. *Virtuous Circle: Political Communication in Post-Industrial Societies.* Cambridge: Cambridge University Press, 2000.

Putnam, Robert. *Bowling Alone: The Collapse and Revival of American Community.* New York: Simon & Schuster, 2000.

Scott, John C. *Domination and the Arts of Resistance: Hidden Transcripts.* New Haven, CT: Yale University Press, 1990.

Scott, Martin. *The World in Focus: How UK Audiences Connect with the Wider World and the International Content of News in 2009.* London: Department for International Development, 2010.

Scruton, Roger. *An Intelligent Person's Guide to Modern Culture.* London: Duckworth, 1998.

Shah, Dhavan V. "Civic Engagement, Interpersonal Trust, and Television Use: An Individual-Level Assessment of Social Capital." *Political Psychology* 19, no. 3 (1998): 469–96.

Steinberg, Marc. "When Politics Goes Pop: On the Intersection of Popular and Political Culture and the Case of the Serbian Student Protests." *Social Movement Studies* 3, no. 1 (2004): 3–29.

Storey, John. *Cultural Theory and Popular Culture.* London: Prentice Hall, 2000.

Street, John. "Celebrity Politicians: Popular Culture as Political Representation." *British Journal of Politics and International Relations* 6, no. 4 (2004): 435–52.

Tonge, Jonathan, and Andrew Mycock. "Citizenship and Political Engagement among Young People: The Workings and Findings of the Youth Citizenship Commission." *Parliamentary Affairs* 63, no. 1 (2010): 182–200.

Ward, Brian. *Just My Soul Responding: Rhythm and Blues, Black Consciousness and Race Relations.* London: University College London Press, 1998.

West, Darrell M., and John Orman, *Celebrity Politics.* Upper Saddle River, NJ: Prentice Hall, 2003.

Zolo, Danilo. *Democracy and Complexity.* Cambridge, UK: Polity, 1992.

Zoonen, Liesbet van. *Entertaining the Citizen: When Politics and Popular Culture Converge.* New York: Rowman & Littlefield, 2005.

———. "Audience Reactions to Hollywood Politics." *Media, Culture and Society* 29, no. 4 (2007): 531–47.

Chapter 9

Playing with Hate

White Power Music and the Undoing of Democracy

NANCY S. LOVE

It is a hard thing to live haunted by the ghost of an untrue dream;
to see the wide vision of empire fade into real ashes and dirt.

—W.E.B. Du Bois, *The Souls of Black Folks*

Music speaks to us at a deeper level than books or political rhetoric:
music speaks directly to the soul. Resistance Records . . . will be the
music of our people's renewal and rebirth.

—William Pierce, quoted in "Deafening Hate:
The Revival of Resistance Records"

Early versions of this essay were presented at the 2006 American Political Science Association Convention, the 2008 Global Studies Association Convention, and the 2012 University of Virginia, Department of Politics, Political Theory Colloquium. My thanks to Lawrie Balfour, Charles Hersch, Mark Mattern, Molly Scudder, Stephen K. White, and the anonymous reviewers for their useful comments. Thanks as well to graduate and undergraduate students Coty Hogue, Tausif Khan, and Travis Smart, who assisted with the research for this chapter.

Introduction

The official biography of Ian Stuart Donaldson, lead singer of the racist skinhead band Skrewdriver, opens with the following description of how the band's music affected its author, who is known only as Benny:

> Ian Stuart opened my eyes, and many others to the Whiteman's cause. I can still remember the first time I heard his voice come growling out of my speakers, sending a shot of adrenalin through my body and from that day on my life changed. In track after track of hard hitting, boot stomping rock he sang of truth, of clenched White fists, and the pride of our people's past, and the promise of a bright and glorious future for the youth who dared to dream and dared to fight.[1]

Benny's experience is more common than some might suppose. The challenges globalization poses to the economic security and cultural identity of western liberal democratic nation-states have prompted a rise in right-wing extremism.[2] A growing white power music scene increasingly supports efforts of the radical right to recruit youth.[3] Variously described as the "soundtrack to the white revolution," "a common language and a unifying ideology," and, in the case of Ian Stuart Donaldson's band Skrewdriver, "'the musical wing' of the National Front," hate music now fuels and funds white supremacist groups across the globe.[4]

A key question in defining hate music is, "when does hatred toward *an* other become hatred toward *the* other?"[5] Although many country, folk, and pop songs express anger, grief, pain, and even hatred toward individuals, two main features distinguish hate music from these other musical genres. Hate music is: 1) overtly racist and/or ultranationalist; and 2) directly associated with violence toward historically oppressed groups.[6] The labels "white rock," "white power," or "white noise," the name of the British National Front recording company that produced Skrewdriver's music, usually refer to racist skinhead music, along with national socialist black metal and fascist experimental music. Ian Stuart Donaldson preferred to call his music White Rock, and, as we will see, it clearly qualifies as hate music by both of the aforementioned criteria.

I argue here that current increases in right-wing extremism are best understood as part of a longer cultural-political project of racial hegemony in western liberal democracies.[7] By situating racist skinhead music in this larger context, I would show how it reproduces the historical ties between liberal democracy and white supremacy. In the process, I would also redirect attention from external threats to liberal democracy, such as international terrorists and Muslim extremists, to its internal tensions, especially its history of racism. Although many liberal democrats may see racist skinheads as quasi-outsiders or "lone wolves" surviving on the margins of society, I argue that racialized hatred has shaped and continues to shape the history of liberal democracy.[8] Among other things the racist skinhead music scene reveals deep ties between the political aesthetic of liberal democracy and an emerging form of neo-fascism that Sheldon Wolin calls "inverted totalitarianism."[9]

My title phrase, "playing with hate," characterizes this complex, ongoing relationship between white supremacy and liberal democracy. The white power music scene, I argue, shows how liberal democrats and white supremacists are both "playing with hate," though in very different ways. Racist skinhead musicians, who reproduce a cultural politics of identity-based aversion to nonwhites, often deny the seriousness of their musical messages. By attributing this hate-filled music to individual pathologies, liberal democrats also deny how the rhetoric of rights and toleration obscures the complicity of hegemonic liberalism with white supremacy.[10] I ask liberal democrats to consider instead how the hate music of racist skinheads might manifest the inner demons of hegemonic liberalism. I conclude that only by recognizing the troubled relationship between liberal democracy and white supremacy can the potential for (re)doing democracy be realized.

My argument begins with a discussion of "inverted totalitarianism," Sheldon Wolin's term for the new form of fascism emerging in western liberal democracies today. Next, I turn to the story of Ian Stuart Donaldson, who is widely regarded as the "godfather of racialist music the world over," and his three white power bands.[11] I analyze two key features of Ian Stuart's racist skinhead music that exemplify the aesthetic politics of inverted totalitarianism: global hybridity and cellular networks. In my final section, I return to the problems that "playing with hate" poses for liberal democracy and assess the prospects for "doing democracy" anew.

Inverted Totalitarianism and Cultural Politics

Although the cultural politics of racist skinheads is arguably fascist, it differs from classical fascism in important ways. Sheldon Wolin's concept of "inverted totalitarianism" provides a useful starting point for understanding those differences. For Wolin, "an inversion is conventionally defined as an instance of something's being turned upside down."[12] An inverted order is not created through revolutionary changes; instead it emerges "imperceptibly, unpremeditatedly and in seeming unbroken continuity with the nation's political traditions."[13] Wolin argues that "an inversion is present when a system, such as a democracy, produces a number of significant actions ordinarily associated with its antithesis."[14] According to Wolin, all democratic orders are sustained by two interrelated political imaginaries: 1) a constitutional imaginary prescribes the procedures, such as elections and laws, through which state authority is legitimated and limited; 2) a power imaginary continually attempts to expand state capacities, often beyond these constitutional limits. An animating myth and providential mission justify these expansionist efforts as required, for example, by struggles against communism, fascism, and now terrorism. These mythic struggles to defend liberal democracy from all-powerful and evil enemies provide the rationale for suspending constitutional limits and expanding government powers, and result eventually in an inverted totalitarian order.

Wolin contrasts the new and inverted form of totalitarianism emerging in contemporary American politics with classical fascism. The latter emanated from self-conscious and deliberate decisions; mobilized support from the masses; advocated strongly for public unity; relied on centralized, charismatic leadership; expanded state power; distinguished Homeland from foreign lands; and invoked a collective identity against known enemies. However, inverted totalitarianism barely distinguishes elected leaders from corporate managers and reduces democratic citizens to consumers and clients of the state. Inverted totalitarianism is also characterized by pervasive tendencies toward pragmatic decision-making, a fragmented public sphere, privatized basic services, significant reductions in rights, generalized amnesia, and civic compliance. Unlike classical fascism, "inverted totalitarianism is only in part a state-centered phenomenon. Primarily, it represents the *political* coming of age of corporate power and the *political* demobilization of the citizenry."[15]

Wolin's extensive analysis of the gradual emergence of inverted totalitarianism in post-9/11 America is compelling and, at times, chilling. However, he somehow misses or, at least, minimizes the ongoing mobilization of right-wing extremists within the passive citizenry he depicts. Although Wolin asks whether "persistent racism" is the inverted totalitarian analogue to Nazi genocide, he concludes that a deep public ambivalence blocks much contemporary racist—and antiracist—activism.[16] Wolin's perception of public disengagement is probably influenced, in part, by his sense of the "fugitive character of democracy," his conviction that democracy is generally better understood as an "ephemeral phenomenon" than a "settled system."[17] Although he acknowledges that fugitive movements can mobilize citizens across the political spectrum, Wolin gives radical right-wing movements relatively little attention.[18]

This conspicuous absence may be further explained by Wolin's emphasis on inversions of political and economic institutions. Like many democratic theorists, Wolin tends to downplay the political importance of the arts and popular culture. He separates politics from aesthetics and treats the latter as a matter of individual choice, taste, or will. For example, he regards the culture wars in American politics as a distraction from strong democracy; they are an "antipolitics" or a "separatist politics," not a cultural politics.[19] Regarding the symbolic politics of myth-making, Wolin seems to assume that political elites continue to manipulate the mass media as they always have. In response to a Bush administration remark, "We're an empire now, we create our own reality," Wolin writes,

> It would be difficult to find a more faithful representative of the totalitarian credo that true politics is essentially a matter of "will," of a determination to master the uses of power and to deploy them to reconstitute reality. The statement is a fitting epigraph to Riefenstahl's *Triumph of the Will*—is it a possible epitaph for democracy in America?[20]

By invoking Leni Riefenstahl, Adolf Hitler's documentary filmmaker, along with Friedrich Nietzsche, Wolin acknowledges that inverted totalitarianism has an aesthetic politics; the political will of its leaders continues to be "staged." Yet he does so without exploring fully how fascist aesthetics may have changed since the Third Reich.

In her brilliant review of Riefenstahl's films, Susan Sontag summarizes the key features of classical fascist aesthetics: "National Socialism— more broadly, fascism—. . . stands for an ideal or rather ideals that are persistent today under other banners: the ideal of life as art, the cult of beauty, the fetishism of courage, the dissolution of alienation in ecstatic feelings of community; the repudiation of the intellect; the family of man (under the parenthood of leaders)."[21] Although Sontag does not use the descriptive term "inversion," she claims that a deep longing for this "romantic ideal" persists even among liberal democrats. Their romantic longings can be seen "in such diverse modes of cultural dissidence and propaganda for new forms of community as the youth/rock culture, primal therapy, anti-psychiatry, Third World camp-following, and belief in the occult."[22] Sontag fears that citizens of contemporary liberal democracies are woefully limited in their ability to "detect the fascist longings in their midst," a limitation she also traces to the liberal tendency to separate politics and aesthetics.[23] With their attempts to depoliticize the arts and popular culture, liberal democrats tend to minimize the vulnerability of many citizens to contemporary versions of fascist aesthetics. In the process, they also undermine democratic citizens' capacity to engage critically with cultural-political projects, including the racial formation of liberal democracy itself.

Sontag identifies a potentially serious problem within liberal democracy, one that suggests Wolin's concept of inverted totalitarianism is at best incomplete. Some important questions remain: Is classical fascist aesthetics also experiencing an inversion? What are the aesthetic politics of inverted totalitarianism? How might this inversion relate to the politico-economic changes Wolin describes? Does the racist skinhead music scene exemplify such an aesthetic politics? If so, why do committed democrats minimize the significance of these white supremacist groups mobilizing in their midst? In other words, how are racist skinheads and liberal democrats both "playing with hate"? I return to this final question after discussing Ian Stuart Donaldson and his racist skinhead music.

The Story of Ian Stuart Donaldson and His Bands

Ian Stuart Donaldson was the founder and lead singer of Skrewdriver, the longest-lived racist skinhead band and one of few known to the mainstream music industry. When Ian Stuart died in 1993 from injuries sustained in a car accident, many followers thought that the British secret police had murdered him due to the growing popularity of his music and his outspoken support for the neo-Nazi terrorist group Combat 18.[24] At the time, Ian Stuart was facing trial for a street fight with patrons of a gay pub, and Skrewdriver, his primary band, was scheduled to play at the largest white nationalist music festival in European history. He had recently told Combat 18 members that he might soon be assassinated, a remark supporters later took as evidence that his car was sabotaged.

Although he died a martyr, Ian Stuart was born in relative obscurity in 1957 to working-class parents in Blackpool, England. He left school in 1974 with "a couple of O levels" and worked low-paying, dead-end jobs as an apprentice coach trimmer, a car washer, and then a clerical assistant.[25] In 1975, he formed his first band, which he named the Tumbling Dice after the Rolling Stones' song. Its members came from his teenage street gang, and their music combined the sounds of popular rock bands—the Clash, the Who, and the Stones—with skinhead culture. The Tumbling Dice was short-lived, but Ian Stuart formed a new band in 1976, with some of the same members and began to compose his own music. Inspired by a Sex Pistols' concert, he wrote several punk numbers that the band successfully performed at local pubs. A British recording company, Chiswick Records, heard the group perform, offered them a contract for the song "All Skrewed Up," and gave the band its name, Skrewdriver. Under the Chiswick label the band relocated to London where they developed a following of loyal fans, many of them skinheads.

In 1976, Rock Against Racism (RAR) and the Anti-Nazi League began organizing concerts in London featuring prominent punk and reggae bands, including the Clash. RAR wanted to fuel an antiracist, working-class cultural and political rebellion. Skrewdriver officially became a skinhead band in 1977 and soon afterward faced increasing pressure to denounce the racism of their fans, many of whom supported the neo-fascist National Front (NF) and British Movement (BF) parties.[26] Although many skinhead bands capitulated to RAR and wider media pressure, Skrewdriver refused to modify their racist image. As a result, Chiswick Records dropped the band, and Skrewdriver was banned from performing at clubs and concerts in Britain. Ian Stuart complained bitterly about punk "turning a bit left-wing" and associated RAR with what he regarded as the "Marxist dominated music media."[27] In a revealing interview, he describes how Skrewdriver gradually "became political":

> I wasn't really political at all to be honest, I didn't like blacks because I'd never seen one till I went down London, and there I met lots, and they all seemed to have a chip on their shoulder, I didn't like the lefties funny enough, because they all reminded me of students being all Anti-British and that put me off them. Most of our mates that came to our gigs were political, they were either NF (National Front—Club 28 addition) or BM (British Movement-Club 28 addition) and in the end what happened was the press ordered us along with Sham 69 to denounce those people in the audience, or get banned. We refused and Sham 69 said OK. So Sham 69 became

very big and we got banned from everywhere, they banned
all of our adverts from the music papers and everything. All
this was in 1977.[28]

The pressure on the band was ultimately too much, and in the
late 1970s Skrewdriver again broke up. Ian Stuart used this hiatus to
strengthen his political ties with the NF Party. With support from the
Young National Front (YNF), Skrewdriver briefly regrouped in 1979 and
recorded "Built Up, Knocked Down" with Tony Johnson Music. However, major media continued to ban Skrewdriver's music and the band
dissolved again in 1980. Ian Stuart spent the next four years working in
his father's tool shop and traveling to NF rallies throughout Britain. Then,
in 1984, Skrewdriver released two new and very successful songs, "Back
with a Bang" and "Boots and Braces." Increased skinhead demand for
their music resurrected the band yet again. Seeing the recruiting potential
of Skrewdriver's music, the NF created its own record label, White Noise
Records, and produced the band's first explicitly political songs: "White
Power," "Smash the I.R.A.," and "Shove the Dove."

Skrewdriver now began to attract large audiences and their concerts
often provoked violent clashes between RAR and supporters of Rock-
Against Communism (RAC), a counter-organization. The band again
faced club and media bans, but this time continued NF support meant
they could still perform. The international white supremacist movement
now also became interested in Skrewdriver. Stories about the band began
to appear in white nationalist publications in the United States. Then
the German label Rock-O-Rama offered a new recording contract, and
Skrewdriver began marketing their music in Europe. In 1985 Rock-O-
Rama released the LP *Hail the New Dawn*, which included a popular
single, "Free My Land." It was soon followed by a second LP, *Blood &
Honour*. Shortly thereafter, Ian Stuart was jailed for twelve months due to
a street fight with a group of blacks. His experience in prison inspired
the songs "Where Has Justice Gone" and "Behind the Bars" on the band's
next Rock-O-Rama LP, *White Rider*. Skrewdriver was now an established
racist skinhead band and ready to break with the NF Party, which they
claimed had mismanaged funds from their British record sales. In 1987
Ian Stuart launched his own social movement, called Blood & Honour.
Along with its fan magazine, Blood & Honour continues to maintain
an internet site and produce records under the label White Power. It
sponsored Skrewdriver's final concerts and now also supports other white
rock bands.

Although Skrewdriver was Ian Stuart's primary band, he also formed two spin-off groups, The Klansmen and White Diamond. The Klansmen's first release was "Fetch the Rope" in 1989. They cultivated a rock-a-billy sound and specifically targeted audiences in the American South. Benny (quoted earlier) describes their sound as "pure Rock and Roll Nationalism with a deep south flavour for those with quiffs and confederate flags."[29] The Klansmen recorded two more albums: *Rebel with a Cause*, a tribute to Robert Jay Mathews, the National Alliance leader killed by U.S. government forces at his western compound in 1984; and *Rock & Roll Patriots*, which was released in 1991, to celebrate the fall of communism. During the early 1990s, Blood & Honour formed strong ties with a number of white supremacist groups in the United States, including Tom Metzger's White Aryan Resistance (WAR) and William Pierce's National Alliance, the owner of Resistance Records. Both groups continue to promote Skrewdriver's music and the music of other racist skinhead bands.

Ian Stuart also formed a third band, White Diamond, that performed fascist experimental music and targeted a biker audience. He explained the creation of White Diamond as follows: "Basically we are just spreading our wings and trying to appeal to everybody, not just skinheads."[30] White Diamond songs convey the messages of white supremacy with greater clarity, maturity, and urgency. When *Last Chance* magazine asked Ian Stuart in 1991, "What can you envision yourself doing in 5 or 10 years?," he replied, "Probably being in prison. They're bringing in so many new laws in this country. Or dead!"[31] Before Ian Stuart's death in 1993, Skrewdriver, which remained his primary band, would also release three more explicitly political CDs, *Live at Waterloo*, *Freedom What Freedom*, and *Hail Victory*.

Inverting Fascist Aesthetics:
Global Hybrids and Cellular Networks

In analyzing how Ian Stuart creates an inverted fascist aesthetic with his music, I distinguish political ideologies from framing devices. Definitions of "ideology" vary and are often themselves ideologically charged. However, widespread agreement exists that ideologies are coherent, consistent belief systems that inform, justify, and motivate political action.[32] By comparison "framing" involves more dynamic, fluid, and unstable processes of meaning creation; it also employs a variety of devices that shift codes with changing audiences and contexts.[33] In their analysis of hate music, Corte and Edwards suggest how ideologies and frames relate: "Ideology functions as a cultural resource from which social actors draw ideas, values, and beliefs to construct meaning through framing processes and framing devices."[34]

Music is much more than its lyrics, though, even when lyrics are understood as speech acts, that is, as forms of action, behavior, or conduct. To a greater extent than speech, music involves nonverbal communication, including bodily movements, vocal melodies, and emotional expressions. In order to analyze these nonverbal aspects of racist skinhead music, I adopt what is called a "performative aesthetic." Roland Barthes contrasts this musical aesthetic with formal aesthetics: "Let the first semiology manage, if it can, with the system of notes, scales, tones, chords, and rhythms; what we want to perceive and follow is the effervescence of the beats . . . a second semiology, that of the body in a state of music."[35] I argue that the affective, corporeal effects of music are as important as its ideological messages, perhaps even more important. Activist musicians mobilize audiences with their sounds as well as their lyrics. Along with music, loyal fans use attire, dance, gestures, insignia, posters, videos, and more, to express their cultural connections and group identities. Unlike more formal analyses, a performative aesthetic shows how music scenes bridge the distinction between form and content, including how form can even become content.

In the next two sections, I first discuss how Ian Stuart's song lyrics reframe classical fascism into a global hybrid white supremacy appropriate for an inverted totalitarian order. Then, I move beyond song lyrics to argue that racist skinheads' inverted fascist aesthetic appears even more clearly in the cellular networks fostered by their performances.

Inversion I: White Supremacy as Global Hybrid[36]

Ian Stuart's song lyrics modify classical fascist ideology for a global audience, creating a complex hybrid of regional, national, and pan-Aryan meanings. This inversion is best described as turning liberal democracy inside out rather than upside down. Like neoliberal, corporate capitalism, racist skinhead music "knows no country" and flows freely between nations. Multiple Skrewdriver songs extol pan-Aryan racial community and the expansionist politics of empire, even as they condemn immigration. For example, "White Power" attacks Asian immigrants and promotes "Paki-bashing," a common activity among American, British, and German skinheads.[37] In "Free My Land," Skrewdriver joins immigrant, communist, and Jewish threats to British empire: "I stand and watch my country today / It's easy to see that it's being taken away / All the immigrants and all the left wing lies / Why does no one ever ask the reason why?" The chorus concludes, "Once a nation, and now we're run by who? / We want our country back now!"[38] Country here stretches well beyond a territorial nation-state to the blood, soil, and spirit of pan-Aryan empire. A strong sense of an epic struggle between the races emerges in many of Skrewdriver's songs, such as "Excalibur," "Blood of the Kings," "Road to Valhalla," or "God of Thunder." One of Ian Stuart's favorite songs, "Tomorrow Belongs to Me," appeals to future generations and offers a vision of a once and future (white) British empire. With their allusions to ancient warriors, mythic foundings, and imagined communities, these songs are not only transnational but also transtraditional in scope.[39]

Economic decline, marked by unemployment, dead-end jobs, and capitalist corruption, also figures prominently in multiple Skrewdriver songs. These themes converge in the chorus of "Power from Profit": "It's power from profit, they're buying our souls / It's power from profit, puts you on the dole / It's power from profit, a good job's hard to find / It's power from profit, they'll soon own our minds."[40] In "Thunder in the Cities," the thoroughly corrupt Zionist Occupational Government (ZOG) is blamed for Britain's continued decline: "We see corruption at all levels, / we know the end is not in sight / Our government is dealing with the devil and his men, / they've set out to sell out all Whites."[41] Whites who do speak out and stand up to the government confront the racial double standard of the so-called British law machine. Shortly after his first prison term for a street fight with a group of blacks, Ian Stuart composed "Where Has Justice Gone?" with its chorus: "It seems we stand convicted, accused of being White / It seems that we are criminals, for we're not scared to fight / There'll be no surrender, to all our people's foes / We'll fight until the victory, we'll find the way to go."[42]

Two additional themes—praise for heroic racial warriors and concern for the working poor—reveal how Ian Stuart shifts his lyrics, folding local heroes and symbols into his global hybrid white supremacy. Explicit references to Adolf Hitler, Rudolf Hess, and more recent neo-Nazi heroes frequently appear in Skrewdriver songs. Some include alternate, more explicit language (occasionally in German) for live performances. Nazi references also occur in songs by the Klansmen, Ian Stuart's band that targets audiences in the American South. Instead of allusions to Camelot, Valhalla, and Norse Gods—all of which play well in Britain—the

Klansmen's racial heroes are Confederate soldiers or gray riders, especially Robert E. Lee. For his American audience, Ian Stuart also shifts the rebel images in his songs from skinheads' antisocial behavior to direct political action. The lyrics "Be a man, be a man, and join the Klan" and "Fetch the Rope" with its chorus—"I said, don't give up hope / Well they can cope / Don't give up hope / Fetch that rope"—sound a call for white vigilante violence.[43] Only one Skrewdriver song explicitly refers to the Klan, suggesting that Ian Stuart knew "the Southern cause," like the Klansmen's rock-a-billy sound, would have limited appeal in Britain.

Concern for the working poor also takes culturally, economically, and politically specific forms in Skrewdriver and Klansmen songs. Multiple Klansmen songs link white poverty with skinheads' standard antisocial outlaw and rebel themes. In the American South, though, white trash confronts Yankee carpetbaggers: "They call me White trash, 'cos my hair hangs long / My baggy pants with no buttons on / My teeth are black, my shoulder's lack, but I fly—the Confederate flag."[44] Some songs also link Civil War heroes with more indirect pleas to save a disappearing Southern way of life: "They were Outlaws / Never vowed to the blue / In the civil war the Southern flag they flew / Outlaws, never vowed to the blue / In the civil war to the South they were true."[45] Klansmen songs also temper pan-Aryanism and racial nationalism with a greater emphasis on states' rights. References to Hitler and the Nazis persist, but Klansmen songs redirect white working-class anger from anti-Semitism to anticommunism and focus racial hatred on blacks and Asians, especially Vietnamese immigrants, all of whom take American jobs.

In the songs of White Diamond, Ian Stuart's third and last band, his white supremacist message comes through loud and clear. Foreign immigrants, race-mixers, and corrupt politicians together pose an imminent threat to "our culture, our identity." A raw, stark quality marks the lyrics of songs like "Politician": "Politician, are you really sane? / Politician, the country's going down the drain? / Politician, who's putting money in your hands? /Politician, you're a traitor to the land."[46] "The Power and the Glory" concludes with the refrain "Never ask you what the people think, they just act on how they think / If this is called democracy, I think your system stinks."[47] In "The Only One" race-mixers or "zebras" are bringing "our nation down," and in "Refugee" immigrants on welfare are impoverishing "the people of our own lands."[48] With a sense of impending doom—"Now its system rules here, the warrior seems now dead / Its creed is called deception, the nation has been bled"—White Diamond songs announce the racial apocalypse when northern warriors from across the globe will rise again: "Take no Prisoners / This is war / Expect no mercy / 'Cause you know what you're fighting for."[49]

The global hybrid that Ian Stuart creates reframes fascist ideology for listeners with varied—Nazi, KKK, and racist skinhead—cultural and political histories of white supremacy. Through subtle and some not so subtle shifts in emphasis, his song lyrics position regional and national struggles as part of a larger global struggle that threatens to destroy the white race. A final example powerfully illustrates the hybrid quality of Ian Stuart's song lyrics. The Klansmen's "Rock 'n' Roll Patriots" weaves together the U.S. flag, "our" freedoms, white America, and antigay, antired, antigreen politics around the world:

> Some play for Lenin, for others it's Marx, as long as it's red
> Some play for Greenpeace, lettuce and cress, I like meat
>   with my bread
> 'Cos they play for anything, just as long as it's financing
>   their own
> We fight for freedom and pride of our race, we're gonna
>   reclaim that goal.
> 'Cos we're Rock 'n' roll Patriots now, red, white and blue
> Rock 'n' roll patriots yeah, and we're playing for you.[50]

As if to confirm the global reach of pan-Aryan empire, Skrewdriver thanks supporters from "America, Australia, Austria, Bavaria, Belgium, Denmark, England, Finland, France, Germany, Greece, Holland, Hungary, Italy, Poland, Rhodesia, Scotland, South Africa, Sweden, Switzerland, Ulster and Wales" on the back of the *White Rider* CD.[51]

Inversion II: Cellular Networks and White Supremacy

In addition to his hybrid lyrics, Ian Stuart's performative aesthetic—the images, rhythmic movements, and sounds associated with his music—promotes a cellular network of racist skinheads across the globe. Most of Ian Stuart's songs have "catchy" tunes, simple refrains, and, unlike some skinhead bands whose music is unintelligible growls, his lyrics are easily understood. All these features make it easy for listeners to sing or shout along. Many Klansmen songs also borrow traditional southern folk tunes that are familiar to their audiences.[52] As the term "catchy" suggests, many listeners cannot resist these songs that produce visceral responses in primal regions of the human brain.[53] George Burdi, lead singer for another white power band, Racial Holy War (RaHoWa), confirms that the musicians intend to "infect" their listeners through repetition: "We hear the slogan 'White people awake, save our great race' twice per chorus, eight times per total throughout an entire song, and if they play the tape five times a week, and just listen to that one song, they are listening to [the slogan] 40 times in one week, which means 160 times a month. You do the math behind that."[54]

Ian Stuart's pounding guitar chords, frequent strong modulations, and thundering drum beats also have a physical impact on the audience. In "Ain't Got the Time," he denounces cabaret, disco, and rap, and explicitly avows his musical aesthetic: "Give me a loud guitar and a blood-red bass /And drums that fill your head / Give me a screaming lead to make your ear holes bleed / And a riff that knocks you dead."[55] Many listeners echo the experience Benny described—"a shot of adrenalin through my body"—in the opening quote. The poor quality of much recorded white power music seems irrelevant here. According to Dave, an Ian Stuart fan, "The first time I heard Skrewdriver was it. Every skinhead can tell you about that. It was a bootleg of a bootleg of a bootleg and the sound wasn't worth shit, but it was still magical. It was instantaneous."[56] The "magic" of Skrewdriver's music arguably invited the spontaneous violence that often accompanied their live performances. Concerts frequently spilled over into the streets and triggered fights between RAC supporters and RAR protesters, or between fans of the band and blacks and gays. Today racist skinhead performances usually include circle and slam dances that enhance listeners' visceral reactions to the music. Concert crowds often get out of control and injure participants and bystanders. Recognizing this phenomenon, German government sources describe racist skinhead music as "'Gateway Drug #1' to violence."[57]

The violence of racist skinheads' performative aesthetic also takes more symbolic forms. The official story of Skrewdriver omits the origins of skinhead music in West Indian and African culture. Along with punk, ska and reggae heavily influenced skinhead musicians' distinct genre, "Oi!," which is named after the cockney greeting. "Oi!" mirrors African American call and response songs, often employed by civil rights activists in the sixties, as well as British pub sing-alongs. When racist skinhead bands, like Skrewdriver, politicized "Oi!," they deleted these West Indian, African, and African American influences from the(ir) story. As Timothy Brown attests: "With the emergence of Oi!, a skinhead, could, in theory, completely avoid or negate the question of the subculture's black roots."[58]

Like their sound, British skinhead fashion was a complex mix of West Indian immigrant and white working-class cultures. The skinheads' "clean, hard look" combined the "Rude-boy" fashion that originated in the Kingston ghettos with a "caricature of the model worker: cropped hair, braces, short, wide levi jeans or functional sta-prest trousers, plain or striped button-down Ben Sherman shirts and highly polished Doctor Marten boots."[59] Dick Hebdige claims that the "Black man" served as a "past master in the gentle arts of escape and subversion" for British working-class skinheads and argues that this cultural hybrid would eventually "'dissolve,' . . . into a concern with race, with the myth of white ethnicity, the myth, that is, that you've got to be white to be British."[60]

Racist skinheads' distinctive sounds and fashions also create a powerful collective aspect to their music scene. Like military and church music, racist skinhead music promotes "muscular bonding," an experience of coordinated group action that neutralizes the individual's sense of physical vulnerability.[61] We have already seen that white supremacists' global community is not nativist or nationalist in the traditional sense of patriotic loyalty to a territorial state. Unlike classical fascists, racist skinheads also challenge centralized leadership and hierarchical organizations. The embodied solidarity characteristic of their inverted fascist aesthetic best resembles what Michael Hardt and Antonio Negri call "swarm intelligence." A swarm is "a mobilization of the common that takes the form of an open, distributed network, in which no center exerts control and all nodes express themselves freely."[62] Drawing on Rimbaud's poetry, Hardt and Negri describe the "music of the swarm" as "the reawakening and reinvention of the senses in the youthful body . . . that takes place in the buzzing and swarming of the flesh."[63] To describe how swarms function they further extend the musical metaphor: "Such instances of innovation in networks might be thought of as an orchestra with no conductor—an orchestra that through constant communication determines its own beat and would be thrown off and silenced only by the imposition of a conductor's central authority."[64] Hardt and Negri recognize the importance of content as well as form, and they note that swarms are not necessarily democratic or nonviolent. However, they also tend to contrast the innovative networks of swarm movements with traditional terrorist groups—from Al Qaeda to the radical right—that employ now outmoded forms of top-down authority.

I would argue that the cellular networks of racist skinheads mirror "swarm intelligence" more closely than these traditional terrorist organizations. In "Leaderless Resistance," the white nationalist Louis Beam contrasts the "phantom cells" of contemporary right-wing extremists with the "pyramid type groups" led by Hitler, Mussolini, and even Stalin. Beam writes: "Let the coming night be filled with a thousand points of resistance. Like the fog which forms when conditions are right and disappears when they are not, so must the resistance to tyranny be."[65] In an analogous passage, Tom Metzgar explains how his White Aryan Resistance (WAR) inverts classical fascist aesthetics: "WAR wears no uniform, carries no membership card, takes no secret oath. WAR doesn't require you to march around a muddy street. WAR works the modern way, with thousands of friends doing their part behind the scene, within the system, serving their race."[66] Many racist skinheads are seemingly "normal" citizens, a point often made by their unwitting neighbors in the wake of hate crimes. According to Metzgar, this "embedded" quality keeps the movement secure and strong: "The movement will not be stopped. . . . We're too deep! . . . They've got the program. We planted the seeds. Stopping Tom Metzgar is not going to change what's going to happen in this country now."[67] Whether the metaphor is rolling fog, swarming flesh, or embedded seeds, racist skinheads are joined today through a network of house parties, closed bars, restricted festivals, and internet sites. Their inverted fascist aesthetic, which Kathleen Blee labels "anarcho-proto-fascist," no longer requires the centralized leadership and hierarchical institutions of classical totalitarianism.[68] Although many white supremacist elders are now deceased, including Ian Stuart and William Pierce, the movement continues to thrive on the spontaneous, visceral hatred funded and fueled by its global music scene.

Playing with Hate, Playing with Democracy

Racist skinheads' inverted totalitarian aesthetic turns liberal democracy inside out (global hybrids) and upside down (cellular networks), while continuing to celebrate a romanticized (white) racial community. I argue that both sides in this troubled relationship between liberal democracy and white supremacy are "playing with hate."

Many racist skinhead bands have intentionally left the political questions their music poses open. Although punk musicians often wear swastikas, some scholars argue that their use of the symbol no longer connotes fascism, but instead introduces chaos or noise into everyday life.[69] For punk bands that denounce fascism and racism, the swastika may have little meaning beyond its shock effect. Yet it strains credulity to think the hand-drawn swastikas on the shirts of Skrewdriver's band members were merely intended to shock. What of the Confederate flags and white-robed figures on the covers of the Klansmen's CDs? Or the grim reaper prominently featured on the White Diamond label? When asked to describe Ian Stuart, Grinny, an original band member, said, "Ian was funny to be around, a piss taker." Along with their more serious political lyrics, Skrewdriver songs include "(OH NO) Here Comes a Commie" with its refrain "Won't you give it a rest?" and "This Little Piggy," with the chorus "This little piggy says that he's the boss / Listen piggy, we don't give a toss."[70] Grinny also said Ian "could talk anyone round to his point of view. He was definitely charismatic and once you met him you didn't forget him."[71]

As Grinny implies, Ian Stuart was not above using the so-called punk defense—"It was a joke. It wasn't serious. We didn't mean it"— while advocating global white revolution.[72] Such "playful hatred" can protect a racist band by creating ambiguity about their political stance. Meanwhile provocative lyrics, sounds, and symbols attract critical attention, create political controversy, and help sell their music. Ian Stuart repeatedly denied that money motivated him musically, and he arguably paid a high price for his racist convictions. Yet claims to artistic integrity and racial authenticity are also marketing tools, as a major white power music distributor's website reveals: "You are not merely consumers of a product, and we are not merely distributors of a product. Together we are fighting a war to awaken the survival instincts in a dying people ['the white race']. You, our supporters, are our most valuable ally in that war."[73]

"Playing with hate," also refers to the tendency of many liberal democrats to overlook the white supremacists organizing in their midst and to deny the racist history of hegemonic liberalism. Linking the 9/11 attacks to the 1995, Oklahoma City bombing, Timothy Baysinger asks the relevant question here: "While our collective consciousness prioritizes radical Islamists as the preeminent threat, should individuals and groups that encompass the radical right be viewed as having a reduced capacity to perform acts of terrorism?" He concludes that "[t]o safeguard our nation from future acts of terrorism, a constant awareness of right-wing extremist beliefs, activities, and adherents must be maintained."[74] A recent example makes the connection to music explicit: Wade Michael Page, the alleged shooter at the Sikh temple, played in several white power bands sponsored by the neo-Nazi organization Hammerskin Nation.[75] Increased awareness must go beyond legal action, though, and not only because of First Amendment and other Constitutional protections. The racist skinhead music scene raises a deeper problem within liberal democracy: its hate-filled swarms cannot be effectively managed by political and economic institutions, including those of the inverted totalitarian order Wolin depicts.

We have already seen the tendency of liberals to depoliticize the arts and popular culture, a tendency that can limit the capacity of democratic citizens to recognize and respond to racist cultural-political projects. Another related tendency is also important here. According to Wendy Brown, liberal democrats tend to assume that individuals *choose* their culture, and less civilized, less reasonable "others"—fundamentalists and traditionalists—*have* a culture or even *are* their culture.[76] It is this distancing from culture that arguably allows liberal democrats to tolerate the diverse cultures in their midst. However, it may also let the seemingly "normal" citizens of liberal democracies off the culture hook and position right-wing extremists as disturbed or psychotic individuals. If, as Sontag suggests, deep longings for the romantic ideals of fascist aesthetics persist in liberal democracy, then perhaps its ordinary citizens can also be *had* by their culture. Racist skinheads' inverted totalitarian aesthetic retains important aspects of the fascist aesthetic Sontag describes, especially its emphasis on heroic warriors and racial community. This largely unacknowledged cultural politics may remain attractive on some level to many liberal democratic citizens. If so, recent rises in hate group membership may reflect a sort of heyday or, more appropriately, nadir of white cultural politics. Indeed liberal tolerance, and perhaps even liberal democracy itself, increasingly seem to be coming undone.

The challenge is to create the awareness among liberal democrats of this right-wing cultural politics as a largely unacknowledged part of their constitutional history and national identity. The cultural roots of liberal democracy include conquest and genocide along with freedom and equality. In the face of such persistent racism, why assume that fugitive movements or youthful swarms will mobilize on behalf of democratic ideals? Such assumptions move too quickly past the troubled origins of liberal democracy in white supremacy. When western democracy is seen as a racial project of hegemonic liberalism that involves exterminating Native Americans, disenfranchising women, enslaving Africans, interring Japanese Americans, deporting Hispanics, the list continues, then the vulnerability of liberal democrats to right-wing cultural politics is arguably less surprising. A largely unacknowledged investment in whiteness—political, economic, and cultural—pervades the history of liberal democracy from Britain to America and beyond.[77]

Only an analysis of inverted totalitarianism that reunites aesthetics and politics can fully recognize and begin to redeem this cultural history of liberal democracy. In his recent reflections on late-modern citizenship, Stephen White takes up the question of cultural politics where Wolin leaves off. He explores liberal democrats' rush to position otherness as difference-to-be-controlled-and-dominated.[78] And, he urges greater awareness of our shared human vulnerabilities to pain, suffering, and death as the basis for a less hostile and more generous ethos of democratic citizenship. For White, democracy ideally becomes a continual presencing and absencing of the *demoi*, an ongoing politics of enactment that is attuned both to democracy and difference. According to White, this democratic politics occurs primarily through deliberative discourse. However, I maintain that the arts and popular culture also contribute to the politics he describes by providing opportunities for diverse citizens to experience beauty and creativity, even to reimagine democracy itself. I agree with White that an "ethos of presumptive generosity" cannot offer policy responses to the problem of right-wing extremists mobilizing in democratic societies. Yet it may suggest how democratic citizens—individually and collectively—can begin to transform their history of white supremacy and, with it, the arrogance of hegemonic liberalism.[79]

I began with two epigraphs. The first comes from W.E.B. Du Bois, who prefaces each chapter of *The Souls of Black Folks* with a sorrow song that hovers over his text, setting its tone, speaking what cannot be said. The second is from William Pierce of Resistance Records, who invokes this capacity of music to capture the soul on behalf of white supremacy. Elsewhere I have argued that what Martin Luther King Jr. called the power of musical song to "meet physical force with soul force," can inspire good or evil, a moral choice for which democratic citizens bear the primary responsibility.[80] Today many citizens in western democracies are avoiding or denying this responsibility, even as others unleash their fear and rage. If the African American educator and civil rights activist W.E.B. Du Bois could empathize with white slave owners in the defeated South, can the contemporary citizens of western liberal democracies do anything less than face their inner cultural-political demons?[81] The future of democracy may depend on it, and any undoing also offers an opportunity to begin "doing democracy" anew.

Notes

1. Benny, *Ian Stuart Donaldson: Diamond in the Dust*, 2001, 2, http://www. Skrewdriver.org/diamond.html. For more testimonials to Skrewdriver's music see: Pete Simi and Robert Futrell, *American Swastika: Inside the White Power Movement's Hidden Spaces of Hate* (New York: Rowman & Littlefield, 2010), 62–63.

2. Right-wing extremist groups increased 40 percent in the United States during 2009. This figure includes an 80 percent surge in anti-immigration nativist groups and a 244 percent increase in active Patriot groups. U.S. Patriot groups, mostly paramilitary organizations, have mobilized in anger against changing demographics, rising public debt, declining economic opportunities, and a series of Obama initiatives perceived as "socialist" or even "fascist" (Mark Potok, "Rage on the Right," *Intelligence Report* 141 [Spring 2010], http://www.splcenter.org/). For additional historical context see: Leonard Zeskind, *Blood and Politics: The History of the White Nationalist Movement from the Margins to the Mainstream* (New York: Farrar, Straus and Giroux, 2009); Peter H. Merkl and Leonard Weinberg, eds., *The Revival of Right-Wing Extremism in the Twenty-First Century* (London: Frank Cass, 2003); Betty A. Dobratz and Stephanie L. Shanks-Meile, *The White Separatist Movement in the United States* (Baltimore, MD: Johns Hopkins University Press, 2000).

3. Approximately 350 white power bands perform in the United States, western Europe, and postcommunist nations, 120 of them based in America. This music industry provides millions of dollars annually to white supremacist movements and National Front parties. Anti-Defamation League (ADL), "Neo-Nazi Hate Music: A Guide," 2004, http://www.adl.org/main_Extremism/hate_music.

4. Resistance Records, quoted in Ugo Corte and Bob Edwards, "White Power Music and the Mobilization of Racist Social Movements," *Music and Arts in Action* 1, no. 1 (June 2008): 5; Southern Poverty Law Center, "White Pride Worldwide: The White Power Music Industry Is Helping to Drive the Internationalization of Neo-Nazism," *Intelligence Report* 103 (Fall 2001), http://www.splcenter.org/intel/intelreport/article; Anton Shekhovtsov, "*Apoliteic* Music: Neo-Folk, Martial Industrial and 'metapolitical fascism,'" *Patterns of Prejudice* 43, no. 5 (December 2009): 431.

5. Keith Kahn-Harris, "The Aesthetics of Hate Music," Institute for Jewish Policy Research, 2003, 4, http://www.axt.org.uk/HateMusic/KahnHarris.htm.

6. Shekhovtsov, "*Apoliteic* Music," 434.

7. Michael Omi and Howard Winant, *Racial Formation in the United States, from the 1960s to the 1990s* (New York: Routledge, 1994), chap. 4.

8. See for example: John Avalon and Tina Brown, *Wingnuts: How the Lunatic Fringe Is Hijacking America* (New York: Beast Books, 2010); Louis Theroux, *Call of the Weird: Travels in American Subcultures* (London: Macmillan, 2005).

9. Sheldon Wolin, *Democracy Incorporated: Managed Democracy and the Specter of Inverted Totalitarianism* (Princeton, NJ: Princeton University Press, 2008).

10. Wendy Brown, *Regulating Aversion: Tolerance in the Age of Identity and Empire* (Princeton, NJ: Princeton University Press, 2006).

11. Paul Burney, "A Tribute to Ian Stuart," September 1993, http://www.Skrewdriver.org/html.

12. Wolin, *Democracy Incorporated*, 45.

13. Ibid., 46.

14. Ibid.

15. Ibid., x.

16. Sheldon Wolin, *Politics and Vision: Continuity and Innovation in Western Political Thought*, expanded edition (Princeton, NJ: Princeton University Press, 2006), 591–92.

17. Ibid., 602.

18. Wolin regards Huey Long's Share-the-Wealth movement, the Townsend movement for old-age pensions, and Father Coughlin's National Union for Social Justice as "versions of a 'fugitive' democracy," because each mobilized outside the political parties to challenge the legitimacy of mainstream democracy. Wolin, *Democracy Incorporated*, 23.

19. Ibid., 111–12.

20. Ibid., 3.

21. Susan Sontag, "Fascinating Fascism," in *Under the Sign of Saturn: Essays* (New York: Farrar, Straus and Giroux, 1980), 95–96. For other discussions of fascist aesthetics today see: Morton Schoolman, *Reason and Horror: Critical Theory, Democracy, and Aesthetic Individuality* (New York: Routledge, 2001); Andrew Hewitt, *Fascist Modernism: Aesthetics, Politics, and the Avant-Garde* (Stanford, CA: Stanford University Press, 1996).

22. Sontag, "Fascinating Fascism," 96.

23. Ibid.

24. The number 18 here refers to Adolf Hitler's initials, the first and eighth letters of the alphabet.

25. Ian Stuart Donaldson, "Interview," *Last Chance Skinzine*, 1991–1992, http://www.bloodandhonour.com/modules.php?name=Ian.Interviews.

26. On tensions between racist and antiracist skinheads, see: Roger Sabin, "'I won't let that dago by': Rethinking Punk and Racism," in *White Riot: Punk Rock and the Politics of Race*, eds. Stephen Duncombe and Maxwell Tremblay (New York: Verso, 2011), 57–68; Mike Roberts and Ryan Moore, "Peace Punks and Punks against Racism: Resource Mobilization and Frame Construction in the Punk Movement," *Music and Arts in Action* 2, no. 1 (2009): 21–36.

27. Donaldson, "Interview," *Last Chance Skinzine*; quoted in Benny, *Diamond in the Dust*, 8.

28. Donaldson, "Interview," *Last Chance Skinzine*.

29. Quoted in Benny, *Diamond in the Dust*, 30.

30. Donaldson, "Interview," *Last Chance Skinzine*.

31. Ibid.

32. Nancy S. Love, *Understanding Dogmas and Dreams: A Text*, 2nd ed. (Washington, DC: CQ Press, 2006), chap. 1.

33. Judith Butler, *Frames of War: When Is Life Grievable?* (New York: Verso, 2010).

34. Corte and Edwards, "White Power Music," 9.

35. Quoted in Barbara Engh, "Loving It: Music and Criticism in Roland Barthes," in *Musicology and Difference: Gender and Sexuality in Music Scholarship*, ed. Ruth A. Solie (Berkeley: University of California Press, 1993), 73–74.

36. This discussion is based on a content analysis of 120 Skrewdriver songs from 9 LPs or CDs from 1982–1994, 35 Klansmen songs from 3 CDs from 1989–1991, and 22 White Diamond songs from 3 CDs in 1992. These songs continue to be released in commemorative compilations. Lyrics were coded for references to anti-Semitism; Odinism; violence; nature; Nazi names, symbols, rhetoric; KKK names, symbols, rhetoric; nationalist rhetoric and symbols; heroes and martyrs; state's rights and the Southern cause. These categories were adapted from Helene Lööw's "White Power Rock 'n' Roll: A Growing Industry," in *Nation and Race: The Developing Euro-American Racist Subculture*, eds. Jeffrey Kaplan and Tore Ojorgo (Boston: Northeastern University Press), 126–74.

37. Ian Stuart Donaldson, "White Power," White Noise, WTN1, 1983.

38. Ian Stuart Donaldson, "Free My Land," on *Hail the New Dawn*, Rock-O-Rama, LP, 1984.

39. Benedict Anderson's term "imagined communities" refers to earlier processes of nation-building in Europe. However, it arguably also applies to the transnational and cyber-based networks now being created by white supremacist groups. Benedict Anderson, *Imagined Communities: Reflections on the Origin and Spread of Nationalism*, 2nd ed. (New York: Verso, 2006). The term "transtraditional" refers to the hybrid rituals and symbols employed by globalizing movements today. Mattias Gardell, *Gods of the Blood: The Pagan Revival and White Separatism* (Durham, NC: Duke University Press, 2003), 70.

40. Ian Stuart Donaldson, "Power from Profit," on *Hail the New Dawn*.

41. Ian Stuart Donaldson, "Thunder in the Cities," on *White Rider*, Rock-O-Rama, LP, 1987.

42. Ian Stuart Donaldson, "Where Has Justice Gone," on ibid.

43. Ian Stuart Donaldson, "Fetch the Rope," on ibid. and "Join the Klan," on *Rebel with a Cause*, Klan Records, CD, 1989.

44. Ian Stuart Donaldson, "White Trash," on *Fetch the Rope*, Klan Records, LP, 1983.

45. Ian Stuart Donaldson, "Outlaws," on ibid.

46. Ian Stuart Donaldson, "Politician," Glory Discs Label, 1992.

47. Ian Stuart Donaldson, "The Power and the Glory," on ibid.

48. Ian Stuart Donaldson, "The Only One," on ibid.

49. Ian Stuart Donaldson, "Take No Prisoners," on ibid.

50. Ian Stuart Donaldson, "Rock 'n' Roll Patriots," on *Rock 'n' Roll Patriots*, Klan Records, CD, 1991.

51. Benny, *Diamond in the Dust*, 21.

52. For discussions of folk traditions see: Eyerman and Jamison, *Music and Social Movements: Mobilizing Traditions in the Twentieth Century* (Cambridge: Cambridge University Press, 1998); Karl Hagstrom Miller, *Segregating Sound: Inventing Folk and Pop Music in the Age of Jim Crow* (Durham, NC: Duke University Press, 2010).

53. On the neurological effects of music see: Daniel J. Levitin, *This Is Your Brain on Music: The Science of a Human Obsession* (London: Dutton, 2006); Oliver Sacks, *Musicophilia: Tales of Music and the Brain* (New York: Vintage Books, 2007).

54. Quoted in Corte and Edwards, "White Power Music," 9.

55. Ian Stuart Donaldson, "Ain't Got the Time," Glory Discs Label, 1992.

56. Quoted in Simi and Futrell, *American Swastika*, 62.

57. Timothy S. Brown, "Subcultures, Pop Music and Politics: Skinheads and Nazi Rock in England and Germany," *Journal of Social History* 38, no. 1 (Autumn 2004): 171.

58. Ibid., 163.

59. Cohen quoted in Dick Hebdige, *Subculture: The Meaning of Style* (New York: Methuen & Co., 1979), 55.

60. Hebdige, *Subculture*, 54; Hebdige quoted in Brown, "Subcultures," 162.

61. William H. McNeill, *Keeping Together in Time: Dance and Drill in Human History* (Cambridge, MA: Harvard University Press, 1995).

62. Michael Hardt and Antonio Negri, *Multitude: War and Democracy in the Age of Empire* (New York: Penguin, 2004), 218.

63. Ibid., 92–93.

64. Ibid., 338.

65. Louis Beam, "Leaderless Resistance," *The Seditionist* 12 (February 1992), http://www.louisbeam.com/leaderless.htm.

66. Quoted in Elinor Langer, *A Hundred Little Hitlers: The Death of a Black Man, the Trial of a White Racist, and the Rise of the Neo-Nazi Movement in America* (New York: Henry Holt and Company, 2003), 181.

67. Quoted in ibid., 350.

68. See: Kathleen Blee, *Inside Organized Racism: Women in the Hate Movement* (Berkeley: University of California Press, 2002).

69. Hebdige, *Subculture*, 114–16.

70. Ian Stuart Donaldson, "Here Comes a Commie" and "This Little Piggy," on *Freedom What Freedom*, Rock-O-Rama, CD, 1992.

71. Alex Gottschalk, "Better Off Crazy: An Interview with Grinny from Skrewdriver," *Nihilism on the Prowl*, http://www.geocities.com/interviews2/Skrewdriver.html?20066.

72. Langer, *Hundred Little Hitlers*, 49.

73. Quoted in Corte and Edwards, "White Power Music," 11.

74. Timothy G. Baysinger, "Right-Wing Group Characteristics and Ideology," *Homeland Security Affairs* 11, no. 2 (July 2006): 1, 15.

75. Robert Futrell and Pete Simi, "The Sound of Hate," *New York Times*, August 9, 2012, http://www.nytimes.com/2012/08/09/opinion/the-sikh-temple-killers-music-of-hate.html?_r=0.

76. Wendy Brown, *Politics of Aversion*, chap. 6.

77. Tim Wise, *White Like Me: Reflections on Race from a Privileged Son* (Berkeley, CA: Soft Skull Press, 2011).

78. Stephen K. White, *The Ethos of a Late-Modern Citizen* (Cambridge, MA: Harvard University Press, 2009), chap. 5. In "The Virtual Patriot Syndrome: Tea Partyers and Others," White counters characterizations of the Tea Party and Minutemen as "proto-fascist" and claims they instead represent a protective republican strain in American political history. The lingering question, of course, is what might motivate them to ally with the more radical right-wing extremists depicted here. Stephen K. White, "The Virtual Patriot Syndrome: Tea Partyers and Others," unpublished manuscript.

79. White, *Ethos of a Late-Modern Citizen*, 110.

80. Quoted in Nancy S. Love, *Musical Democracy* (Albany: State University of New York Press, 2006), 100.

81. I am indebted to Lawrie Balfour for suggesting the opening epigraph from Du Bois. I also want to acknowledge her argument that Du Bois came to see education as a necessary but insufficient response to the tangled history of democracy with slavery in America and beyond. Economic development, including reparations, gratitude for African Americans' contributions to the nation, and recognition of "the black world" are also needed. Indeed, Du Bois' "committed empathy" is yet another gift to a "white nation" struggling to redeem its past. See Lawrie Balfour, *Democracy's Reconstruction: Thinking Politically with W.E.B. Du Bois* (Oxford, UK: Oxford University Press, 2010), 10, chap. 6.

Bibliography

Anderson, Benedict. *Imagined Communities: Reflections on the Origin and Spread of Nationalism*, 2nd ed. New York: Verso, 2006.

Anti-Defamation League (ADL). "Deafening Hate: The Revival of Resistance Records, Anti-Defamation League." http://archive.adl.org/resistance%20 records/print.asp.

———. "Neo-Nazi Hate Music: A Guide." 2004. http://www.adl.org/main_ Extremism/hate_music.

Avalon, John, and Tina Brown. *Wingnuts: How the Lunatic Fringe Is Hijacking America*. New York: Beast Books, 2010.

Balfour, Lawrie. *Democracy's Reconstruction: Thinking Politically with W.E.B. Du Bois.* Oxford, UK: Oxford University Press, 2011.

Baysinger, Timothy G. "Right-Wing Group Characteristics and Ideology." *Homeland Security Affairs* 2, no. 2 (2006): 1–19.

Beam, Louis. "Leaderless Resistance." *The Seditionist* 12, 1992 (February), http://www.louisbeam.com/leaderless.htm.

Benny. *Ian Stuart Donaldson: Diamond in the Dust*, 2001. http://www.Skrewdriver.org/diamond.html.

Blee, Kathleen. *Inside Organized Racism: Women in the Hate Movement.* Berkeley: University of California Press, 2002.

Brown, Timothy S. "Subcultures, Pop Music and Politics: Skinheads and Nazi Rock in England and Germany." *Journal of Social History* 38, no. 2 (Autumn 2004): 157–78.

Brown, Wendy. *Regulating Aversion: Tolerance in the Age of Identity and Empire.* Princeton, NJ: Princeton University Press, 2006.

Burney, Paul. "A Tribute to Ian Stuart." September 1993. http://www.Skrewdriver.org/html.

Butler, Judith. *Frames of War: When Is Life Grievable?* New York: Verso, 2010.

Corte, Ugo, and Bob Edwards. "White Power Music and the Mobilization of Racist Social Movements." *Music and Arts in Action* 1, no. 1 (June 2008): 4–20.

Dobratz, Betty A., and Stephanie L. Shanks-Meile. *The White Separatist Movement in the United States.* Baltimore, MD: Johns Hopkins University Press, 2000.

Donaldson, Ian Stuart. "Interview." *Last Chance Skinzine.* 1991–1992. http://www.bloodandhonour.com/modules.php?name=Ian.Interviews.

Du Bois, W.E.B. *The Souls of Black Folks.* New York: Oxford University Press, 2007 [1903].

Engh, Barbara. "Loving It: Music and Criticism in Roland Barthes." In *Musicology and Difference: Gender and Sexuality in Music Scholarship*, edited by Ruth A. Solie, 66–82. Berkeley: University of California Press, 1993.

Eyerman, Ron, and Andrew Jamison. *Music and Social Movements: Mobilizing Traditions in the Twentieth Century.* Cambridge: Cambridge University Press, 1998.

Futrell, Robert, and Pete Simi. "The Sound of Hate." *New York Times*, August 9, 2012. http://www.nytimes.com/2012/08/09/opinion/the-sikh-temple-killers-music-of-hate.html?_r=0.

Gardell, Mattias. *Gods of the Blood: The Pagan Revival and White Separatism.* Durham, NC: Duke University Press, 2003.

Gottschalk, Alex. "Better Off Crazy: An Interview with Grinny from Skrewdriver." *Nihilism on the Prowl.* http://www.geocities.com/interviews2/Skrewdriver.html?20066.

Hardt, Michael, and Antonio Negri. *Multitude: War and Democracy in the Age of Empire.* New York: Penguin, 2004.

Hebdige, Dick. *Subculture: The Meaning of Style.* New York: Methuen & Co., 1979.

Hewitt, Andrew. *Fascist Modernism: Aesthetics, Politics, and the Avant-Garde.* Stanford, CA: Stanford University Press, 1996.

Kahn-Harris, Keith. "The Aesthetics of Hate Music." Institute for Jewish Policy Research, 2003. http://www.axt.org.uk/HateMusic/KahnHarris.htm.

Langer, Elinor. *A Hundred Little Hitlers: The Death of a Black Man, the Trial of a White Racist, and the Rise of the Neo-Nazi Movement in America.* New York: Henry Holt and Company, 2003.

Levitin, Daniel J. *This Is Your Brain on Music: The Science of a Human Obsession.* London: Dutton, 2006.

Lööw, Helene. "White Power Rock 'n' Roll: A Growing Industry." In *Nation and Race: The Developing Euro-American Racist Subculture,* edited by Jeffrey Kaplan and Tore Ojorgo, 126–74. Boston: Northeastern University Press.

Love, Nancy S. *Understanding Dogmas and Dreams: A Text,* 2nd edition. Washington, DC: CQ Press, 2006.

———. *Musical Democracy.* Albany: State University of New York Press, 2006.

McNeill, William H. *Keeping Together in Time: Dance and Drill in Human History.* Cambridge, MA: Harvard University Press, 1995.

Merkl, Pete H., and Leonard Weinberg, eds. *The Revival of Right-Wing Extremism in the Twenty-First Century.* London: Frank Cass, 2003.

Miller, Karl Hagstrom. *Segregating Sound: Inventing Folk and Pop Music in the Age of Jim Crow.* Durham, NC: Duke University Press, 2010.

Omi, Michael, and Howard Winant. *Racial Formation in the United States, from the 1960s to the 1990s.* New York: Routledge, 1994.

Potok, Mark. "Rage on the Right." *Intelligence Report* 141 (Spring 2010). http://www.splcenter.org/.

Roberts, Mike, and Ryan Moore. "Peace Punks and Punks against Racism: Resource Mobilization and Frame Construction in the Punk Movement." *Music and Arts in Action* 2, no. 1 (2009): 21–36.

Sabin, Roger. "'I won't let that dago by': Rethinking Punk and Racism." In *White Riot: Punk Rock and the Politics of Race,* edited by Stephen Duncombe and Maxwell Tremblay, 57–68. New York: Verso, 2011.

Sacks, Oliver. *Musicophilia: Tales of Music and the Brain.* New York: Vintage Books, 2007.

Schoolman, Morton. *Reason and Horror: Critical Theory, Democracy, and Aesthetic Individuality.* New York: Routledge, 2001.

Shekhovtsov, Anton. "*Apoliteic* Music: Neo-Folk, Martial Industrial and 'metapolitical fascism.'" *Patterns of Prejudice* 43, no. 5 (December 2009): 431–57.

Simi, Pete, and Robert Futrell. *American Swastika: Inside the White Power Movement's Hidden Spaces of Hate.* New York: Rowman & Littlefield, 2010.

Sontag, Susan. "Fascinating Fascism." In *Under the Sign of Saturn: Essays,* 73–108. New York: Farrar, Straus and Giroux, 1980.

Southern Poverty Law Center. "White Pride Worldwide: The White Power Music Industry Is Helping to Drive the Internationalization of Neo-Nazism." *Intelligence Report* 103 (2001), http://www.splcenter.org/intel/intelreport/article.

Theroux, Louis. *Call of the Weird: Travels in American Subcultures.* London: Macmillan, 2005.

White, Stephen K. *The Ethos of a Late-Modern Citizen.* Cambridge, MA: Harvard University Press, 2009.

Wise, Tim. *White Like Me: Reflections on Race from a Privileged Son.* Berkeley, CA: Soft Skull Press, 2011.

Wolin, Sheldon. *Politics and Vision: Continuity and Innovation in Western Political Thought,* expanded edition. Princeton, NJ: Princeton University Press, 2006.

————. *Democracy Incorporated: Managed Democracy and the Specter of Inverted Totalitarianism.* Princeton, NJ: Princeton University Press, 2008.

Zeskind, Leonard. *Blood and Politics: The History of the White Nationalist Movement from the Margins to the Mainstream.* New York: Farrar, Straus and Giroux, 2009.

Discography

Donaldson, Ian Stuart. "Outlaws." On *Fetch the Rope.* Klan Records, LP, 1983.

————. "White Power." White Noise, WTN1, 1983.

————. "White Trash." On *Fetch the Rope.* Klan Records, LP, 1983.

————. "Free My Land." On *Hail the New Dawn.* Rock-O-Rama, LP, 1984.

————. "Power from Profit." On *Hail the New Dawn.*

————. "Fetch the Rope." On *White Rider.* Rock-O-Rama, LP, 1987.

————. "Thunder in the Cities." On *White Rider.* Rock-O-Rama, LP, 1987.

————. "Where Has Justice Gone." On *White Rider.* Rock-O-Rama, LP, 1987.

————. "Join the Klan." On *Rebel with a Cause.* Klan Records, CD, 1989.

————. "Rock 'n' Roll Patriots." On *Rock 'n' Roll Patriots.* Klan Records, CD, 1991.

————. "Here Comes a Commie." On *Freedom What Freedom.* Rock-O-Rama, CD, 1992.

————. "Ain't Got the Time. Glory Discs Label, 1992.

————. "The Only One." Glory Discs Label, 1992.

————. "The Power and the Glory." Glory Discs Label, 1992.

————. "Politician." Glory Discs Label, 1992.

————. "Take No Prisoners." Glory Discs Label, 1992.

————. "This Little Piggy." On *Freedom What Freedom.* Rock-O-Rama, CD, 1992.

Part VI

Theater

Chapter 10

Betrayed by Democracy

Verbatim Theater as Prefigurative Politics

MARK CHOU AND ROLAND BLEIKER

Introduction

Times of war are often times when democratic debates are under siege. The apparent necessity to ward off an enemy and secure the nation's survival can trigger a state of exception: a partial suspension of crucial democratic rights and practices for the sake of national security. In the context of the War on Terror that followed the terrorist attacks of September 11, 2001, the U.S. government curtailed civil rights and censored critical information about its wartime intentions and strategy. The mainstream media, especially in the early phases of war, likewise stifled the brand of critical debate fundamental to a vibrant democratic society. In such an environment, conventional democratic forms and forums can quickly become complicit in the problem and incapable of discussing and solving important social and political problems. When this happens, other less conventional avenues for debates may be required to fill the democratic deficit.

The purpose of our chapter is to examine systematically the potential and limits that theater has to offer an alternative forum for public debate in contexts where freedom of speech is limited. In particular, we explore the dual hypothesis that theater is able to: first, deploy fiction as a means to sidestep political censorship and, second, give expression to a range of voices and perspectives that would otherwise remain silenced or sidelined during a state of exception. The latter can be seen as a form of prefigurative politics: a genre of activism that is small in scale and limited in impact but nevertheless can show the way toward a more democratic political community.

To examine the issues at stake we focus on George Packer's *Betrayed*: an award-winning play that premiered in early 2008 at New York's Culture Project.[1] Packer's play was one of several notable political dramas that scrutinized the political practices of the War on Terror at the peak of hostilities. Others to do so have included Richard Norton-Taylor's *Justifying War* (2003), Victoria Britain and Gillian Slovo's *Guantanamo: Honor Bound to Defend* (2004), and Lawrence Wright's *My Trip to Al-Qaeda* (2007).

Packer's play is based on meticulous journalistic research he had initially conducted for a feature article in *The New Yorker* magazine.[2] He wrote about the predicament of a little-known and yet highly symbolic group of Iraqis: interpreters employed by U.S. forces as mediators and as informants during the war.[3] Scattered throughout Iraq, these young women and men became central to the coalition's war effort. Underprepared for the skirmishes that ensued, the Americans employed local Iraqis to act as their eyes and ears in a hostile and unpredictable environment. But by stepping forward to aid the coalition's mission, these Iraqis soon found themselves the targets of intimidation and ostracism, even of torture and murder. They were deeply mistrusted both by the Iraqis, who suspected them of being American collaborators, and by the Americans, many of whom never managed to see their Iraqi colleagues as anything other than potential threats.

Though it substantially influenced public debates, Packer's *New Yorker* article did not, as he would later acknowledge, adequately empower the Iraqis to speak for themselves.[4] Because of this, Packer felt compelled to push further. Using techniques drawn from Verbatim Theater, a style of documentary theater that dramatizes real people, their words, and their situations, he returned to the stories of betrayal that had first inspired his journalistic effort. But this time, his objective was to offer a group of individuals who had been denied political franchise the ability to express themselves—through their own unique and often multiple voices—in a communal setting.

We compare Packer's journalism with his play and identify what precisely theater can add to democratic debates. We advance a two-tiered argument in support of the dual hypothesis with which we began this chapter.

First we argue that certain forms of theater have the potential to sidestep censorship during a time of war more effectively than journalism. It is well recognized that both in the lead-up to and early phases of the Iraq War the Bush administration controlled information and curtailed civil liberties in a way that made it difficult for mainstream media sources to express critical views.[5] Against this backdrop, the fictional and seemingly less serious realm of theater offered an alternative space to raise issues that might otherwise have remained silenced. One could even say that the fictional techniques of theater paradoxically provided a more realistic account of reality than factual representations. That, at least, is what Packer believed. For him, it was theater, not journalism, that captured best the chaotic realities of current-day Iraq.[6]

Second we argue that theatrical explorations like Packer's can give voice to a multitude of real characters and underrepresented perspectives. *Betrayed* is a play full of marginalized and forgotten voices that provide diverging views on the situation in Iraq; perspectives different from those mediated by bureaucrats, politicians, and the news media. Allowing these and other marginalized voices to enter democratic debates is important if the United States is to contribute to a fair, stable, and secure political order in Iraq.

Packer's play can thus be seen as an ideal form of a prefigurative politics: an activist engagement that prefigures a more democratic politics to come. Such an engagement is inevitably small scale and limited in its direct impact. Only very few people will actually be able to see a play like *Betrayed*. Add to this that most viewers are well educated and perhaps already aware of the need to critically investigate and debate political issues. This is why the political significance of a play like *Betrayed* does not lie in its direct political impact but in the prefigurative model it can offer of a more democratic and just political community—one that, in this particular case, searches for open and critical discussion of the coalition's war effort in Iraq.

The Iraqis Who Trusted America the Most: How Journalism Can Expose the Undersides of War

Packer's well-known *New Yorker* article, "Betrayed: The Iraqis Who Trusted America the Most," was published in March 2007. In it, he drew attention to a group of Iraqis, mostly in their twenties and thirties, who had been employed—and in some cases were still employed—as interpreters for the United States during the Iraq War.

Having come of age under Saddam Hussein's rule, many of these interpreters welcomed the war and the prospect of change.[7] Ba'athist rule had curtailed their lives in almost every aspect. Even so, they grew up listening secretly to American music, watching American movies, and reading all genres of western literature. This is why they welcomed change when it came in 2003. And, more importantly, this is why they became so valuable to the coalition following the fall of Baghdad. Underprepared for the challenges that followed, the coalition was rapidly made aware of its limitations on the ground. Chief among them were its lack of local knowledge and the inability to communicate effectively with local inhabitants.

Thousands of young Iraqis found employment this way: as interpreters or mediators between coalition forces and Iraqi inhabitants. Being uniquely suited to advise the Americans on cultural, intelligence, and policy matters, they quickly became indispensible to the war effort.[8]

But more than this, what Packer's article did was to expose the double lives and the double-edged sword that soon confronted the Iraqis who found employment as interpreters for the United States. In a country beset with suspicion, antipathy, and violence, these interpreters became caught in between the frontlines of conflict. Insurgents often suspected them of being American agents and treated them as such, subjecting them to intimidation, torture, and even murder.[9] The United States, in turn, offered little if any formal protection against these threats. Ali, one Iraqi interpreter whom Packer met and interviewed, said that the Iraqis "aren't trusting you, and the Americans don't trust you from the beginning. You became a person in between."[10] Unwanted by their own, Ali and many of his colleagues were subsequently denied the legal rights that would enable them to access humanitarian assistance from their supposed liberators. Politically, legally, and morally, these individuals became betrayed by a war whose outcomes failed to match many or any of its original guarantees. Toward the end of his article, Packer concludes that a part of the U.S. legacy in Iraq will be the "thousands of Iraqis who, because they joined the American effort, can no longer live in their own country."[11]

Given the impassioned case Packer put forward, the piece quickly generated widespread political debate and even influenced policy responses. As Packer would later comment, though there were always particular Americans who were fighting for these Iraqis, the initial response from their government left a lot to be desired. "Individual Americans cared," a point Packer labors to make clear, "but institutionally, the U.S. government was washing their hands of this terrible problem."[12] In this regard, Packer's article formed part of a small but dedicated chorus rallying for a more humane governmental response. By making a point of identifying how, under similar circumstances, President Ford had felt morally obligated to offer refuge to those Vietnamese affected by the Vietnam War all those years ago, Packer's article perhaps had the effect of shaming more than a few figures within the Bush administration into a less hesitant response.[13] Specifically, his article, read by many State Department officials, was instrumental in influencing the department's decision to expedite visas for Iraqis in most need of help.[14] Like other coalition nations that had already made exit plans for their Iraqi contractors, the United States soon adopted the so-called Kennedy Special Immigrant Visa Program, the purpose of which was to increase the U.S. visa quota—predominately aimed at Iraqi but also Afghani interpreters—from five hundred to five thousand cases per year.[15]

Unfortunately, even conservative estimates as early as 2007 suggested that there were at least some nine thousand interpreters officially employed by the U.S. forces in Iraq alone.[16] This number did not include the tens of thousands of other Iraqis employed by the United States—many on an informal, ad hoc basis—nor did it include the members of their families. In actual fact, the number of Iraqis clamoring for asylum today in order to escape the danger and violence resulting from their association with the United States lies somewhere in the hundreds of thousands.[17]

Betrayed: From Journalism to Theater

Despite being widely read by influential policy-makers in Washington, and even despite having played a role in helping to shape the state's official policy response, Packer felt that his article had only just etched the surface of the issue. Even the most thorough journalistic accounts, in this respect, leave important things unsaid. What frustrated Packer in particular was the inability of the prevailing media coverage to "see past the abstractions to what the war meant in people's lives."[18] As he learned, the daily challenges of most Iraqis had little to do with "democracy," "totalitarianism," or any of the other abstract concepts that dominated political debates within the United States.[19] Instead, the key issue was more rudimentary: "to stay or to leave."[20]

Hoping to find a way of conveying these important but largely neglected struggles in Iraq, Packer pushed further, supplementing his journalism with a political play that re-presented the very characters and stories he had written about. Premiering at New York's Culture Project in 2008, less than a year after the publication of his *New Yorker* article, the play *Betrayed* offered American audiences a more realistic and more personal account of the motivations and predicaments faced by Iraqi interpreters who risk their lives to help rebuild a new Iraq.[21] It conveyed the individual stories that Packer's informants had regaled him with: stories that "most Americans hadn't really heard of" but which nevertheless evoked the larger political decisions, actions, and consequences that, even today, are reverberating throughout Iraq and the rest of the world.[22] *Betrayed*, in short, politicizes what politics had rendered unpolitical.

Centering on a series of dialogues and flashbacks, the play weaves together three distinct stories of three different Iraqis who would come to find themselves defined by one thing: their profession as U.S.-employed interpreters. The first of these interpreters is Adnan, whose introduction comes by a frank confession: "I read mostly philosophy and adventure books. To be totally frank with you, even some porn books. And this helped a lot to improve my English, because it's an interesting subject so you really make an effort to understand."[23] The English he commands— self-taught—he treasures dearly. Savvy yet prudent, he does what he must to survive—under and after Saddam. But what sets him apart is his self-confession as a "non-belonger." This was Adnan's experience under Saddam. But by play's end, having been cast out by the Iraqis and the Americans, it also becomes his future.[24] Intisar, Adnan's colleague and former classmate at Baghdad University, is "another non-belonger."[25] Strong willed and independent, Intisar knew that what she desired would never be realized under Saddam's rule. Yet, even post-Saddam, her struggles as an Iraqi and as a woman persist. In a telling passage, she conveys the anguish she feels every day working as an interpreter for a cause that she believes is worth fighting and dying for:

> It's something unbelievable to be a target every day, to be wanted, and you just have a feeling that people are looking for you and you're on the street in the middle of them, you are not hiding. It is crazy. . . . But the Americans cannot have the feeling what it is to take these risks. They cannot understand.[26]

The play's third interpreter is Laith. Of the three, Laith is the most pragmatic and least idealistic. Not that this diminishes the connection he feels toward his job interpreting for the Americans. Like so many other interpreters, his employment with the United States quickly consumed his life and, when his job ended, it was as if he "fell in between heaven and hell."[27]

Set in a derelict room in a near-abandoned hotel in central Baghdad, the play opens as Adnan enters the darkened stage. There, he meets Laith. Together they speak with an invisible reporter: the audience. They tell stories of the last four years in war-torn Iraq: stories about their colleague Intisar, their American supervisor and friend, Bill Prescott, and about a war that, for Iraqi and American alike, has produced expectations and betrayals of trust, respect, and commitment.

Audiences of *Betrayed* quickly learn that employment as an interpreter for the United States is not without risks. In a country divided along ethnic, religious, and political lines, any sign of partisanship can be a cause for contempt, retribution, and exclusion. However, as mouthpieces of the coalition, the eyes and ears of the foreign occupier, the dangers are even greater. Indirect as well as direct threats became common for interpreters like those dramatized by Packer, often being inseparable from the job itself. "Why do you work as an agent of the occupier? There is no safe place for traitors in Iraq."[28]

This is the very nature of the threats that unite Laith and Adnan. Following his unjust dismissal from the embassy, Laith finds himself targeted by local insurgents seeking inside U.S. intelligence. Unable to satisfy their demands and fearful of their threats, he meets with Adnan in a desperate effort to secure international asylum in the United States. Having exhausted what limited official channels were available to him, Adnan informally contacts Prescott, their former supervisor at the American embassy. "Bill," Adnan appeals over the telephone, "Laith has a very serious situation. Last week he had a direct threat. If there is any way to get him out of Iraq . . ." But Laith snatches the phone from Adnan, almost in embarrassment, saying: "He is exaggerating, Bill. You know how Iraqis love to exaggerate."[29] Having been shunned by the Americans in charge, Laith is reticent, even embarrassed, to strain his personal relationship with Prescott. He asks no favors despite the injustices and risks he faces.

Told by two ordinary Iraqis, this story is about those who supported the war, even before it began. Now it is they who need America's support. To have come so close, having lost family, friends, and colleagues along the way, having had their pleas for assistance heard and summarily rejected by the American officials in command, they plead directly to the American public. Even Prescott, an American working within the embassy, soon realizes just how the coalition's bureaucratic morass and moral certitude can strangely belittle the pleas for help from the Iraqis who trusted them the most.

Both Packer's article and play, in this regard, expose the tragic realities faced by Iraqi interpreters. In both versions an otherwise unknown situation and people are divulged for the American public. Understanding the life of these non-belongers is central to understanding the fragmented and fraying politics of current-day Iraq. Such an understanding is precisely what is needed to free Iraq from sectarian violence and hatred. If we are to recognize, assist, and free people who are caught "in between" then we must willingly become the same: people willing to live "in between" languages, cultures, and ethnicities; "in between" competing goals and aspirations for the present and future; and "in between" moral absolutes in that vast chasm of uncertainty and struggle.

Betrayed the play never strays far from the spirit of "Betrayed" the article. Because of this, it is perhaps necessary to explore in greater detail the question just what does Packer's play achieve that his journalistic account had not already done? What does a theatrical dramatization add to an in-depth political analysis already read by numerous influential actors in Washington and around the country? In what follows, we offer two suggestions: the first having to do with the potential of fiction to sidestep the political restrictions imposed through censorship and the second with the ability of political theater such as Packer's *Betrayed* to bring out multiple voices that might not otherwise reach a democratic constituency.

The Democratic Potential of Theater in a Time of War (I): The Ability of Fiction to Sidestep Censorship

Our first argument stipulates that the fictional nature of theater enables it to sidestep some of the pernicious aspects of censorship. This is particularly important in times of war when censorship practices invariably intensify. By censorship, we mean not just the obvious attempts to curtail media and civil liberties, but also the underlying and far more powerful tendency to determine what constitutes realistic representations of war—an ability that yields considerable power and determines how political discourses are waged and public policies made. Censorship of this variety, as David Dadge writes, entails three crucial elements.[30] The first involves senior administration officials, including the president himself, portraying dissent of any form as perilous to national security and, indeed, as unpatriotic. The second requires the administration to rally the American public behind its cause through any means available so that they come to see the national interest as no different from their own personal interest. And the final element is the need to police the media to ensure that what they publicize supports, or at the very least does not oppose, the administration's position.

Numerous scholars and policy analysts have already drawn attention to the results of this censorship, especially during the early phases of the War on Terror: the deception, misinformation, and civil rights infringements that characterized the Bush administration's domestic and foreign policies after 9/11.[31] Equally well discussed is how the ensuing situation stifled crucial information and prevented it from reaching the American public. We will not rehearse these debates here, but only sketch out their main thrust.

Following the terrorist attacks of September 11, 2001, the Bush administration responded by restricting access to information under the Freedom of Information Act and by legislating into law the USA Patriot Act (2001).[32] Empowered by these emergency measures, the U.S. government could legitimately deny heads of state, the media, as well as the American public access to crucial information pertaining to issues of national security. In addition, the government was given extensive powers to invade the privacy of everyday citizens and employ excessive interrogation techniques.[33]

Such forms of censorship are common and sometimes warranted in times of war during so-called states of exception.[34] But there are intrinsic dangers involved. Precisely during times of war it is necessary to explore the full spectrum of perspectives and possible solutions to difficult challenges. Yet this cannot be done when democratic debates and public dissent are stifled—as they were in the wake of the War on Terror. By rousing nationalistic sentiment and fueling an irrational fear of Islamic terrorism, the American public was quickly mobilized behind an administration adamant on waging war in Iraq.[35] For its part, the media also lost much of its traditional political function as an independent and critical source of information.[36] Mass media reports of Iraq, from NBC to CNN, saturated the public with information, but only rarely did they provide insights that truly challenged the prevailing governmental line. Views from the periphery, such as the pleas of assistance from Iraqi interpreters, were easily drowned out. This is why Packer lamented that the reality of faraway war-torn Iraq was "never closer" but, paradoxically, also "never more out of reach."[37]

In this context, the need for alternative forums of public debate was never more important. Theater became one such forum. Operating at a level that, ostensibly, is more artistic than political, theater can be viewed as another site of democratic deliberation; a forum where critical perspectives about the events of the day can be aired without fear of political reprisal. That, at least, is the spirit in which *Betrayed* was conceived: as an attempt to provide a democratic forum where the Iraqis could speak directly to the American public.

Packer used Verbatim Theater to achieve his objectives. This is a theatrical technique inspired by real life issues, characters, and the stories they tell. Verbatim Theater uses facts to create fictional representations. Its main aim is to allow audiences to see reality anew. As such, it relies heavily on the "taping and subsequent transcription of interviews with 'ordinary' people, done in the context of research into a particular region, subject area, issue, event, or combination of these things."[38] Having done that, the dramatist amalgamates the characters she or he encountered and the language spoken to weave together a dramatic play.

Verbatim Theater can become particularly important in contexts where public discourses are dominated by an omnipresent media that is, at the same time, heavily censored or self-censored. By moving deeply painful and tense matters to the realm of fiction, they can be analyzed and reflected upon more openly and away from the constraints of censorship and political correctness. It is in this sense that theater scholars have noted how Verbatim Theater can expose the "democratic deficit" in societies where political repression and censorship abound.[39] What is too difficult, too dangerous, and too restrictive to discuss in reality can be put on stage hopefully as a "rehearsal for reality."[40]

Yet the political role that theater plays can go beyond sidestepping governmental interferences with the flow of information. It also addresses deeper forms of censorship that manipulate how we perceive the realities of war: what we accept as real and reasonable from what we dismiss or do not even manage to see in the first place.

Verbatim Theater offers a mechanism to problematize how we represent war—what we see as real or how we draw the boundaries between truth and untruth. As Packer lamented, the more images we saw about the war in Iraq and the more messages we heard, the more our grasp of truth and reality became "flickering and formless."[41] By providing an alternate frame of reference, Verbatim Theater offers audiences a means to reassess political reality freed from the distortions of censorship and misinformation.[42] To say so is not to claim that theater can offer representations that are free of bias and political values. But what good theater can do is bring into public view a range of sensitive and neglected issues, such as the predicament of Iraqi interpreters and their implications for the War on Terror. Doing so leads audiences to question their own views about the purpose, direction, and legitimacy of the war in Iraq.

Unlike real-life politics and political forums, where norms, conventions, and official discourses too frequently impede dialogue, there is a sincerity and simplicity in the way *Betrayed* presents its issues. What would have been problematic to convey in reality only became probable when presented as fiction. Without it, American audiences who went to see *Betrayed* may not have otherwise been made aware of the situation that confronts the war effort in Iraq. They may have remained oblivious to how the decision to go to war became arbitrarily fused with the promotion of democracy. Nor would they have truly appreciated how dangerous the newfound democracy could become. By stepping forward to aid the coalition's mission in Iraq, these young Iraqi men and women embraced the new freedoms without reservations. Sharing many of the values and goals of their American liberators, they soon became the Americans' political compass and linguistic mediators. Yet to speak on behalf of both the Iraqis and the Americans meant that, as the situation deteriorated and divisions intensified, they were distinguishing themselves as neither. This is the tragedy at the heart of *Betrayed*: the fate of those who are genuinely committed to the breaking down of barriers in a country whose recent history has only known suspicion, antipathy, and violence. In the confusion and chaos that followed after the fall of Saddam, interpreters like Adnan, Laith, and Intisar translated the uncertain and factious reality for their American employers and their Iraqi countrymen and women. But unable or unwilling to deal with complex and contingent scenarios, what they said only fueled frustration and became a cause for suspicion. Losing trust on both sides, the individuals who Packer brought to the stage began to understand how hypocritical and dangerous an idea democracy can be and how quickly their newfound freedoms could be revoked in the name of security.

An apt example of both the democratic dangers and how Packer moved between fact and fiction in order to get at them is the story, which he first recounted in his article, that would go on to inspire the scene within the play where Adnan, Laith, and Prescott plead with the U.S. ambassador and the regional security officer (RSO) for the badge that would allow the interpreters direct entry into the Green Zone. This was what Packer initially documented in his *New Yorker* article:

According to the Iraqis, they asked Frese [the RSO] for green badges, which were a notch below the official blue American badges. These allowed the holder to enter through the priority lane and then be searched inside the gate.

"I can't give you that," Frese said.

"Why?"

"Because it says 'Weapon permit: yes.'"

"Change the 'yes' to 'no' for us."

Frese's tone was peremptory: "I can't do that."

Ahmed made another suggestion: allow the Iraqis to use their Embassy passes to get into the priority lane. Frese again refused. Ahmed turned to one of his colleagues and said, in Arabic, "We're blowing into a punctured bag."

"My top priority is Embassy security, and I won't jeopardize it, no matter what," Frese told them, and the Iraqis understood that this security did not extend to them—if anything, they were part of the threat.

After the meeting, a junior American diplomat who had sat through it was on the verge of tears. "This is what always calmed me down," Firas said. "I saw Americans who understand me, trust me, believe me, love me. This is what always kept my rage under control and kept my hope alive."[43]

As Packer would later say in an interview, "The badge is the key symbol."[44] The "yellow" badge these Iraqi interpreters possessed meant they were neither American nor Iraqi. They were something "in between." And that was precisely what they were employed to be: mediators between the occupier and the occupied. They were trusted by neither side; unable to remain in Iraq, unwanted by the United States.

Drawing from this experience, Packer's play captured something of the tormented anguish, on the one hand, and the unfeeling rationalization, on the other. Nothing that Adnan, Laith, nor Prescott can say really matters. Only the RSO's and the U.S. ambassador's words count, and they are final:

RSO: No way I can upgrade yellow badges to green. Anything else sir?

Ambassador: I believe that's it. Thank you gentlemen. My door is always open.[45]

The use of fiction appeals to the senses and, in this instance for example, the dramatized hypocrisy, conceit, and desperation can have the potential to affect audiences as few other media do. This way of communicating emotions is important not least because war is one of the most emotional phenomena possible: almost all of its dimensions, from the reasons that lead to conflict to the suffering and political reactions it causes, are inherently emotional. Prevailing social scientific ways of understanding conflict offer few if any tools to understand and communicate these important emotional dimensions.[46] Theater does, as Jeremy Gerard observed of one performance he attended: "I noted something I've rarely heard in a lifetime of theatergoing: the sound of audience members weeping."[47] But that, for Packer at least, is what a dramatic representation can do. It can "grab you by the throat" and implicate all those who have witnessed the event.[48]

By crisscrossing reality with fiction then, *Betrayed* enacts for an American audience a little-known crisis about a little-known group of individuals that together are evocative of many of the larger problems faced in Iraq. Seen this way, the play becomes much more than just a night at the theater. Instead, it is a democratic channel for accessing the real-life Iraqi stories behind what we see broadcast on the nightly news.[49]

Still, there are clear limitations to what theater can achieve. For one, Verbatim Theater remains after all a form of representation that is inevitably subjective and mediated.[50] It cannot authentically represent the realities of war-torn Iraq. What it can and does do, though, is to problematize the very politics of representation: to correct and publically display what has been obfuscated or deemed false.[51] No account of war, no matter how neutral or objective it professes to be, can genuinely present all the facts as they are. As such, challenging the political nature of this process can itself make an important contribution to democratic debates. This is why Packer's fictional yet all-too-real reproduction of reality can help audiences to question what really happened in Iraq and how prevailing media sources portrayed the related facts.

The Democratic Potential of Theater in a Time of War (II): Validating Multiple Voices as a Form of Prefigurative Politics

The second, related reason why political theater can potentially be a democratic source of insight is that it provides a venue for multiple perspectives to be heard and debated. As a play, *Betrayed* went further than Packer's political journalism to highlight multiple voices: to allow the Iraqis he had met to speak for themselves about their existence to those audiences in America eager for more than official statements and mainstream news. Through the medium of theater, those who had been denied political franchise or restrained by civil rights infringements, both in Iraq and the United States, began to speak their minds about a war that, till then, had largely remained beyond question. The play, as such, was pitched as a dialogue—between everyday Iraqis and Americans in an open community forum.

To illustrate this point, we emphasize two examples where *Betrayed* brings to the stage a multitude of otherwise marginalized stories, characters, and voices. The first arises within the play itself and the second as part of one post-performance audience discussion that occurred at Berkeley's Aurora Theater on February 6, 2009.

Toward the play's end, when contacted by Adnan and Laith, Prescott is finally made aware of the extent of the situation facing Iraqi interpreters employed by the United States. While it is too late for many of their colleagues, Intisar being among them, Prescott makes it his personal cause to fight for those he still can—even if against the reproach of an administration that willingly turns a blind eye to those in need. He asks Adnan and Laith to forward the contacts and petitions of any other Iraqi interpreter to him. In scene 21 the audience hears firsthand several of these petitions, read in different voices over theater speakers, overlapping at the edges, as if to affirm their distinct yet connected predicaments. Each explains to Prescott their situation, reiterating anew what Adnan, Laith, and Intisar have said all along. Two examples are especially evocative:

> The whole neighborhood cannot forget that I worked with U.S. Army sometime in the past and I feel that someday a close-minded neighbor will reflect his anger toward the U.S. troops on me. . . . I am willing to leave Iraq forever and find a safer place for my family as I am living in a society that looks at me as a betrayer and should be outcasted.
>
> Three weeks ago I received a threat from the Sadr militia and I tried to hide for some time but just a week ago my brother was kidnapped by a militia group belongs to a new elected democratic government of Iraq which is supported by the U.S. government and the President Bush.

Distinctly heard are the voices of people with no direct channel of communication or appeal to the Americans they worked for or to the

American public at large. There is little that the play does with them, with the entire scene, except to let them speak. After they do, the stage fades to black.

Betrayed illustrates the difference between reality theater as text and performance. The play has now been staged in New York, Berkeley, Washington, DC, and Stanford. For each of these productions the audience was invited to discuss the issues they had seen onstage. In each instance, the directors hoped that by opening the floor up to audiences, in a forum removed from the reaches of political correctness and censorship, they would speak freely without fear of retribution. And that was what they did, at least during one particular performance on February 6, 2009, at Berkeley's Aurora Theater.[52] At the conclusion of the play, audience members spoke generally of political misinterpretations and cultural misunderstandings. More specifically, they spoke about their relation, or lack thereof, to the Iraqis they had seen onstage. One audience member, in particular, noted that: "Sometimes I couldn't relate to the translators, despite the fact they try so hard to be like us. But this is perhaps because they are not us. This is something to recognize and cultivate." The telling point here seems to be that even Iraqis who so clearly embrace the American project are uniquely different and cannot always be easily understood by those Americans with whom they claim affinity. How much less, then, can the United States make crude assumptions and estimations for the whole of Iraq and for the millions who do not share its vision at all? Where we cannot relate, because of our mutual difference, is where recognition and cultivation are most needed. Another audience member agreed, stating that these are the "voices we need to hear more in our society." As an example, one audience member pointed to Intisar, stating that she "spoke for women silenced by religion, tradition, and politics." But despite all that is said through *Betrayed*, another audience member asked, "Who is listening? Not the regional security officer in Baghdad, not the ambassador, not most American people." If these sentiments are correct, then efforts to bring a variety of—otherwise marginalized—stories, characters, and voices onto the public stage become even more important. The dialogue that took place that night between the Iraqis dramatized onstage and the American audience offstage—through the conduit of *Betrayed*—provides a model of how this can take place.

A play like *Betrayed* can best be seen as a form of prefigurative politics: a small prototype of a democratic community that might one day play a more important role at a national or even international level. In this sense it is more about democratic potential than about actual political engagement. The latter will always be very limited. Local productions of a play can never reach the mass audience that a television program can. They are unable to have an immediate and widespread impact. In addition to this, reactions to a play depend invariably on the locality of the performance. Packer fully acknowledged that audience reactions would have been very different had his play been staged in Baghdad and not New York or Berkeley for instance.[53] The impact of the play would still have been political, but for different reasons. Staging *Betrayed* in an Iraq that remains highly "sensitive and raw" would have asked a lot of an audience.[54] But that would have also been the case had the play not been staged in Washington or Stanford but in more conservative American communities where the audience might have less liberal and cosmopolitan outlooks. There is one final impediment: the price of theater admissions, an issue that several audience members alluded to with regard to the democratic potential of theater. This, if nothing else, broaches the question of inclusiveness. Who are the people actually attending these productions? Are they really those who are marginalized within society, those who are most politically disenfranchised? In both regards the answer would probably be no. Again, the question of "who is listening," or watching as it were, poses real barriers to the supposed democratic potential of theater.

The impact of a prefigurative democratic politics can be illuminated through the so-called efficacy debate: the ability to gauge the precise political effects of a play. The links between performance, political attitudes, and political actions are always multifarious and tenuous.[55] The claim that a performance will affect political attitudes and actions in this or that way remains contingent on a diverse range of variables, from the particular audience member's background, the quality of the production, the direction of the production, issues of performance location, accessibility, affordability, and outreach, to the complicated nature of politics itself. In addition to this, the task of gauging audience responses post-performance, the basis for conducting such research, is an undertaking that, at best, can only "restore some of [the performance's] main principles and not the authentic event."[56] Because of this, drawing simple, quantitative cause-and-effect conclusions will always remain fraught.

The form of agency that takes place through theater and prefigurative politics operates in tactical, rather than strategic terms. This is to say that its political impact is indirect. There is no concrete causal relationship between a theater performance and a political target—such as a particular policy. Tactical actions cannot be autonomous from their target. But they can nevertheless exert agency and have a political impact. They might do so over an extended period of time, by shaping the attitudes of viewers and, indirectly and eventually, the societal values that surround them.[57]

Political theater like Packer's *Betrayed* offers us more of a model than a definitive example of community engagement. As a model, *Betrayed* can be viewed as democratic in two ways. The first is the way in which it enables audiences to enter into direct dialogue with each other and with the lives of the individuals dramatized onstage. According to Marianne Paget, dramatic performances are dialogical to the extent that they open a channel of communication between what takes place on and off stage, between what appears in the text and what is subsequently performed.[58] Texts come to life when they are performed and they can begin to privilege repressed emotions and political imaginaries that have been smudged out by social scientific analyses or the prevailing political mood. The second way that theater can be seen to be democratic is in the way that it helps to constitute a "human subject and their relations with the world."[59] If nothing else, theater typically captures social relations and the relations between various actors. It offers these individuals a form of and forum for representation. "The politics of representation is the politics of multiple relations," because, argues E. J. Westlake, "[b]eing able to see those relationships, and hopefully the possible consequences of forming them, leads to an opening where political change can take place."[60] By watching a performance within the theater, "you [become] part of a community of watchers."[61] And, as Paul Woodruff writes, "[p]art of our need to watch theater grows from our need to care about other people. . . . Caring about people in the make-believe world of mimetic theater may strengthen your ability to care about people offstage."[62] This is an intrinsically democratic trait, even if it occurs within a theater.

Concluding Reflections

Theater puts on stage otherwise invisible individuals, issues, and sensations, and confers them with "a social, historical meaning and context" that can help to incite recognition, evaluation, and judgment.[63] Using real human beings and crises to embody historical, societal, and political abstractions, theater engages individuals in dialogue. It can put on stage real-life stories, characters, and voices—those that may not be known or important enough to warrant the media's, the politicians', the government's, or even one's own attention.

There is no doubt that such theatrical political engagements are limited in their direct impact. Performances of plays reach only a limited audience and often one that is already sensitive to the political issues the playwright seeks to address. Add to this that plays like *Betrayed* are more of an aberration to the common and commercially based brands of theater that exist today—those that are highly entertaining yet largely apolitical.

The political significance of political plays thus does not lie in their direct and immediate impact. It lies in the fact that they are a form of prefigurative politics. They are microcosms of democratic experiments. They demonstrate how it is possible to create a forum for public debate at a time when censorship inhibited critical discussions of important political issues. As a democratic forum that explicitly tries to incorporate its audiences into the performance, *Betrayed* shows us that "[a] political struggle on the part of democracy requires the involvement of the public, not as frightened spectators but as active participants."[64] The struggle for true freedom requires conflict and demands a toleration of uncertainty by the entire community. That is what democracy is and requires: that we become individuals capable of living "in between" reality and fiction so that we can learn to harbor the dynamic, complex, and paradoxical realities that exist. By asking questions of its audiences, *Betrayed* came to resemble what, as one audience member put it, "a town hall meeting, a place where we can hear about the lives and concerns of others." Perhaps, then, theater can potentially dramatize key political issues that might otherwise remain sidelined in public debates. This is the case both because the seemingly fictional and apolitical nature of plays allows them to sidestep at least some of the prevailing censorship issues and because good theater can elicit multiple voices and perspectives in a real, if not authentic, manner. By seeing the dichotomy between reality and fiction as inherently fluid, we confront those stories, characters, and voices marginalized by factual accounts. What is recovered through these aesthetic practices is no less real than the reality in which we live our lives.

Notes

1. See the Culture Project, http://cultureproject.org/index.php?option=com_content&task=view&id=64.

2. George Packer, "Betrayed: The Iraqis Who Trusted America the Most," *The New Yorker*, March 26, 2007, http://www.newyorker.com/reporting/2007/03/26/070326fa_fact_packer.

3. Ibid. See also George Packer, ed., *The Fight Is for Democracy: Winning the War of Ideas in America and the World* (New York: Harper Perennial, 2003); George Packer, *The Assassins' Gate: America in Iraq* (New York: Farrar, Straus and Giroux, 2005).

4. George Packer interview, *Gothamist*, February 1, 2008, http://gothamist.com/2008/02/01/george_packer_p.php; Charles Isherwood, "Seduced and Abandoned by Promises of Freedom," *New York Times*, February 7, 2008, http://theater.nytimes.com/2008/02/07/theater/reviews/07betr.html?ref=theater; Ken Bullock, "Aurora Presents Packer's 'Betrayed,'" *Berkeley Daily Planet*, February 4, 2009, http://www.berkeleydailyplanet.com/issue/2009-02-05/article/32167?headline=Aurora-Presents-George-Packer-s-Betrayed-.

5. See David Dadge, *The War in Iraq and Why the Media Failed Us* (Westport, CT: Praeger, 2006), 31, 59.

6. George Packer, "KQED's Forum Program Hosted by David Iverson," January 30, 2009, accessed March 4, 2009, http://www.auroratheater.org/index.php. See also Stephen Bottoms, "Putting the Document into Documentary: An Unwelcome Corrective," *The Drama Review* 50, no. 3 (2006).

7. Editorial, "The Road Home," *New York Times*, August 22, 2007, http://www.nytimes.com/2007/07/08/opinion/08sun1.html?_r=1.

8. Packer, "Betrayed."

9. Ibid.

10. Ibid.

11. Ibid. Also see David Ignatius, "Will We Leave Iraqi Allies Behind?," *Washington Post*, January 3, 2007, http://www.washingtonpost.com/wp-dyn/content/article/2007/01/02/AR2007010200942.html; Samantha Power, "Access Denied," *Time*, September 26, 2007, http://www.time.com/time/world/article/0,8599,1665921,00.html.

12. George Packer cited in Steve Fyffe, "Stanford Performance of *Betrayed*," *Stanford Report*, May 17, 2011, http://news.stanford.edu/news/2011/may/packer-betrayed-play-051711.html.

13. George Packer, "Ask the Author: George Packer," *The New Yorker*, April 2, 2007, http://www.newyorker.com/online/2007/04/02/070402on_ask_packer.

14. Ibid.

15. James B. Foley and Lori Scialabba, "Briefing on Developments in the Iraqi Refugee Admissions and Assistance Programs," U.S. State Department, September 12, 2008, https://digitalndulibrary.ndu.edu/cdm4/document.php?CISOROOT=/merln&CISOPTR=13187&REC=14; Alissa J. Rubin, "U.S. Expands Visa Program for Iraqis," *New York Times*, July 25, 2008, http://www.nytimes.com/2008/07/25/world/middleeast/25visa.html?_r=2&hp&oref=login.

16. Anwa Damon, "Iraqi Interpreter: 'Now I have no future,'" CNN.com, August 10, 2007, http://www.cnn.com/2007/WORLD/meast/08/09/iraqi.interpreters/index.html.

17. Packer, interview, *Gothamist*.

18. Packer, *The Assassins' Gate*, 6–7.

19. George Packer, Introduction, in *Interesting Times: Writings from a Turbulent Decade* (New York: Farrar, Straus and Giroux, 2009), xii.

20. George Packer, "The Lessons of Tal Afar," in *Interesting Times: Writings from a Turbulent Decade* (New York: Farrar, Straus and Giroux, 2009), 90.

21. Isherwood, "Seduced and Abandoned by Promises of Freedom."

22. Julianne Hiffenberg of the Culture Project cited in Dexter Filkins, "A Reporter Finds Drama in Iraqis' Heartbreak," *New York Times*, February 3, 2008, http://www.nytimes.com/2008/02/03/theater/03filk.html; George Packer, Introduction, in *Betrayed: A Play* (New York: Faber and Faber, 2008), viii.

23. Adnan in Packer, *Betrayed: A Play*, 11.

24. Adnan in ibid., 107.

25. Adnan in ibid., 30.

26. Intisar in ibid., 42.

27. Laith in ibid., 90.

28. Laith in ibid., 22.

29. Adnan and Laith in ibid., 93–94.

30. Dadge, *The War in Iraq and Why the Media Failed Us*, 52–53.

31. James Bamford, *A Pretext for War: 9/11, Iraq, and the Abuse of America's Intelligence Agencies* (New York: Anchor Books, 2005); Noam Chomsky, *Failed States: The Abuse of Power and the Assault on Democracy* (New York: Metropolitan Books, 2006); David Corn, *The Lies of George W. Bush: Mastering the Politics of Deception* (New York: Crown, 2003); John W. Dean, *Worse Than Watergate: The Secret Presidency of George Bush* (New York: Little, Brown & Co., 2004); Raimond Gaita, ed., *Why the War Was Wrong* (Melbourne, Australia: Text, 2003); Amy Goodman (with David Goodman), *The Exception to the Rulers: Exposing Oily Politicians, War Profiteers, and the Media That Love Them* (New York: Hyperion 2004); Seymour M. Hersh, *Chain of Command: The Road from 9/11 to Abu Ghraib* (Camberwell, UK: Allen Lane, 2004); Dilip Hiro, *Secrets and Lies: Operation 'Iraqi Freedom' and After* (New York: Nation Books, 2004); Molly Ivins, *Bushwhacked: Life in George W. Bush's America* (New York: Random House, 2003); Danny Schechter, *Embedded—Weapons of Mass Deception: How the Media Failed to Cover the War on Iraq* (Amherst, MA: Prometheus Books, 2003); Christopher Scheer, Robert Scheer, and Lakshmi Chaudhry, *The Five Biggest Lies Bush Told Us about Iraq* (Crows Nest, Australia: Allen & Unwin, 2004); Bob Woodward, *Plan of Attack* (New York: Simon and Schuster, 2004); Bob Woodward, *State of Denial* (New York: Simon and Schuster, 2006).

32. See Dadge, *The War in Iraq and Why the Media Failed Us*, 36–37; Michael Freeman, *Freedom or Security: The Consequences for Democracies Using Emergency Powers to Fight Terror* (Westport, CT: Praeger, 2003), 1; Richard Ashby Wilson, "Human Rights in the 'War on Terror,'" in *Human Rights in the 'War on Terror,'* ed. Richard Ashby Wilson (Cambridge: Cambridge University Press, 2005), 26; Didier Bigo and Anastassia Tsoukala, eds., *Terror, Insecurity and Liberty: Illiberal Practices of Liberal Regimes after 9/11* (Milton Park, UK: Routledge, 2008).

33. Geoffrey Stone, "Liberty," *Democracy: Journal of Ideas* 11 (2009), n.p. http://www.democracyjournal.org/article.php?ID=6664.

34. See, for instance, Carl Schmitt, *The Nomos of the Earth in the International Law of the Jus Publicum Europaeum*, trans. G. L. Ulmen (New York: Telos Press, 2003); Giorgio Agamben, *The State of Exception* (Chicago: University of Chicago Press, 2005) for general discussion of states of exception and emergency powers.

35. Dadge, *The War in Iraq and Why the Media Failed Us*, 52–53.

36. Ibid., 33, 44, 52–53; Paul Rutherford, *Weapons of Mass Deception: Marketing the War against Iraq* (Toronto: University of Toronto Press, 2004), 39.

37. Packer, Introduction, in Packer, *Interesting Times*, xi.

38. Derek Paget, "'Verbatim Theater': Oral History and Documentary Techniques," *New Theater Quarterly* 3, no. 12 (1987): 317.

39. Jenny Hughes, "Theater, Performance and the 'War on Terror': Ethical and Political Questions Arising from British Theatrical Responses to War and Terrorism," *Contemporary Theater Review* 17, no. 2 (2007): 152.

40. International Theatre of the Oppressed Organisation Declaration of Principles, paragraph 9, http://www.theatreoftheoppressed.org/en/index.php?nodeID=23.

41. George Packer, "The Lessons of Tal Afar," in *Interesting Times*, 156.

42. See, for instance, Hughes, "Theater, Performance and the 'War on Terror.'" 151–52.

43. Packer, "Betrayed: The Iraqis Who Trusted America the Most."

44. Packer, KQED's "Forum" Program.

45. RSO and Ambassador in Packer, *Betrayed: A Play*, 57.

46. Roland Bleiker and Emma Hutchison, "Fear No More: Emotions and World Politics," *Review of International Studies* 34, no. 1 (2008): 115–35; Emma Hutchison and Roland Bleiker, "Emotions in the War on Terror," in *Security and the War on Terror*, eds. Alex Bellamy, Roland Bleiker, Sara Davis, and Richard Devetak (London: Routledge, 2008), 57–70.

47. Jeremy Gerard, "Packer's 'Betrayed' Brings Abandoned Iraqis to TV: Interview," *Bloomberg*, October 20, 2008, http://www.bloomberg.com/apps/news?pid=newsarchive&refer=muse&sid=a6dzm5wejyLA.

48. Ibid.

49. See Justin Bertin, "George Packer Translates Interpreters' Tale," *San Francisco Chronicle*, February 11, 2009, http://articles.sfgate.com/2009-02-11/entertainment/17187388_1_new-yorker-betrayed-iraqis.

50. Bottoms, "Putting the Document into Documentary," 58.

51. Hughes, "Theater, Performance and the 'War on Terror,'" 151–52; Donna Soto-Morettini, "Trouble in the House: David Hare's *Stuff Happens*," *Contemporary Theater Review* 15, no. 3 (2005): 313–14.

52. The authors were present at the performance that night and recorded several interviews and comments made by the audience members.

53. Packer, "KQED's Forum Program."

54. Ibid.

55. See David A. Schlossman, *Actors and Activists: Politics, Performance, and Exchange among Social Worlds* (New York: Routledge, 2002).

56. Patrice Pavis, *Analyzing Performance: Theater, Dance, and Film*, trans. David Williams (Ann Arbor: University of Michigan Press, 2003), 10–11.

57. See Michel de Certeau, *Arts de Faire*, vol. 1 of *L'Invention du Quotidien* (Paris: Gallimard, 1990).

58. Marianne A. Paget, "Performing the Text," *Journal of Contemporary Ethnography* 19, no. 1 (1990): 151.

59. Rachel Fensham, *To Watch Theater: Chapters on Genre and Corporeality* (Brussels: PIE Peter Lang, 2009), 11.

60. E. J. Westlake, "Mapping Political Performances: A Note on the Structure of the Anthology," in *Political Performances: Theory and Practice*, eds. Susan C. Haedicke, Deirdre Heddon, Avraham Oz, and E. J. Westlake (Amsterdam: Rodopi, 2009), 8.

61. Paul Woodruff, *The Necessity of Theater: The Art of Watching and Being Watched* (Oxford, UK: Oxford University Press, 2008), 17.

62. Ibid., 20.

63. John McGrath, foreword, in Raymond Williams, *A Good Night Out: Popular Theater Audience, Class and Form* (London: Nick Hern Books, 1996), 83.

64. George Packer, "A Democratic World," in *Interesting Times: Writings from a Turbulent Decade* (New York: Farrar, Straus and Giroux, 2009), 54.

Bibliography

Agamben, Giorgio. *The State of Exception*. Chicago: University of Chicago Press, 2005.

Ashby Wilson, Richard. "Human Rights in the 'War on Terror.'" In *Human Rights in the "War on Terror*," edited by Richard Ashby Wilson, 1–36. Cambridge: Cambridge University Press, 2005.

Bamford, James. *A Pretext for War: 9/11, Iraq, and the Abuse of America's Intelligence Agencies*. New York: Anchor Books, 2005.

Bertin, Justin. "George Packer Translates Interpreters' Tale." *San Francisco Chronicle*, February 11, 2009, http://articles.sfgate.com/2009-02-11/entertainment/17187388_1_new-yorker-betrayed-iraqis.

Bigo, Didier, and Anastassia Tsoukala, eds. *Terror, Insecurity and Liberty: Illiberal Practices of Liberal Regimes after 9/11*. Milton Park, UK: Routledge, 2008.

Bleiker, Roland, and Emma Hutchison. "Fear No More: Emotions and World Politics." *Review of International Studies* 34, Special Issue: International Relations and the Challenges of Global Communication (2008): 115–35.

Bottoms, Stephen. "Putting the Document into Documentary: An Unwelcome Corrective." *The Drama Review* 50, no. 3 (2006): 56–68.

Bullock, Ken. "Aurora Presents Packer's 'Betrayed.'" *Berkeley Daily Planet*, February 4, 2009, http://www.berkeleydailyplanet.com/issue/2009-02-05/article/32167?headline=Aurora-Presents-George-Packer-s-Betrayed-.

Chomsky, Noam. *Failed States: The Abuse of Power and the Assault on Democracy.* New York: Metropolitan Books, 2006.

Corn, David. *The Lies of George W. Bush: Mastering the Politics of Deception.* New York: Crown, 2003.

The Culture Project. http://cultureproject.org/index.php?option=com_content&task=view&id=64.

Dadge, David. *The War in Iraq and Why the Media Failed Us.* Westport, CT: Praeger, 2006.

Damon, Anwa. "Iraqi Interpreter: 'Now I have no future.'" CNN.com, August 10, 2007, http://www.cnn.com/2007/WORLD/meast/08/09/iraqi.interpreters/index.html.

Dean, John W. *Worse Than Watergate: The Secret Presidency of George Bush.* New York: Little, Brown & Co., 2004.

de Certeau, Michel. *Arts de Faire*, vol. 1 of *L'Invention du Quotidien.* Paris: Gallimard, 1990.

Editorial. "The Road Home." *New York Times*, August 22, 2007, http://www.nytimes.com/2007/07/08/opinion/08sun1.html?_r=1.

Fensham, Rachel. *To Watch Theater: Chapters on Genre and Corporeality.* Brussels: PIE Peter Lang, 2009.

Filkins, Dexter. "A Reporter Finds Drama in Iraqis' Heartbreak." *New York Times*, February 3, 2008, http://www.nytimes.com/2008/02/03/theater/03filk.html.

Foley, James B., and Lori Scialabba. "Briefing on Developments in the Iraqi Refugee Admissions and Assistance Programs." U.S. State Department, September 12, 2008, https://digitalndulibrary.ndu.edu/cdm4/document.php?CISOROOT=/merln&CISOPTR=13187&REC=14.

Freeman, Michael. *Freedom or Security: The Consequences for Democracies Using Emergency Powers to Fight Terror.* Westport, CT: Praeger, 2003.

Fyffe, Steve. "Stanford Performance of *Betrayed.*" *Stanford Report*, May 17, 2011, http://news.stanford.edu/news/2011/may/packer-betrayed-play-051711.html.

Gaita, Raimond, ed. *Why the War Was Wrong.* Melbourne: Text, 2003.

Gerard, Jeremy. "Packer's 'Betrayed' Brings Abandoned Iraqis to TV: Interview." *Bloomberg*, October 20, 2008, http://www.bloomberg.com/apps/news?pid=newsarchive&refer=muse&sid=a6dzm5wejyLA.

Goodman, Amy (with David Goodman). *The Exception to the Rulers: Exposing Oily Politicians, War Profiteers, and the Media That Love Them.* New York: Hyperion, 2004.

Hersh, Seymour M. *Chain of Command: The Road from 9/11 to Abu Ghraib.* Camberwell, UK: Allen Lane, 2004.

Hiro, Dilip. *Secrets and Lies: Operation "Iraqi Freedom" and After.* New York: Nation Books, 2004.

Hughes, Jenny. "Theater, Performance and the 'War on Terror': Ethical and Political Questions Arising from British Theatrical Responses to War and Terrorism." *Contemporary Theater Review* 17, no. 2 (2007): 149–64.

Hutchison, Emma, and Roland Bleiker. "Emotions in the War on Terror." In *Security and the War on Terror*, edited by Alex Bellamy, Roland Bleiker, Sara Davis, and Richard Devetak, 57–70. London: Routledge, 2008.

Ignatius, David. "Will We Leave Iraqi Allies Behind?." *Washington Post*, January 3, 2007, http://www.washingtonpost.com/wp-dyn/content/article/2007/01/02/AR2007010200942.html.

International Theatre of the Oppressed Organisation Declaration of Principles, paragraph 9, http://www.theatreoftheoppressed.org/en/index.php?nodeID=23.

Isherwood, Charles. "Seduced and Abandoned by Promises of Freedom." *New York Times*, February 7, 2008, http://theater.nytimes.com/2008/02/07/theater/reviews/07betr.html?ref=theater.

Ivins, Molly. *Bushwhacked: Life in George W. Bush's America.* New York: Random House, 2003.

McGrath, John. Foreword. In Raymond Williams, *A Good Night Out: Popular Theater Audience, Class and Form.* London: Nick Hern Books, 1996.

Packer, George, ed. *The Fight Is for Democracy: Winning the War of Ideas in America and the World.* New York: Harper Perennial: 2003.

———. *The Assassins' Gate: America in Iraq.* New York: Farrar, Straus and Giroux, 2005.

———. "Betrayed: The Iraqis Who Trusted America the Most." *New Yorker*, March 26, 2007, http://www.newyorker.com/reporting/2007/03/26/070326fa_fact_packer.

———. "Ask the Author: George Packer." *The New Yorker*, April 2, 2007, http://www.newyorker.com/online/2007/04/02/070402on_ask_packer.

———. Interview, *Gothamist.* February 1, 2008, http://gothamist.com/2008/02/01/george_packer_p.php.

———. *Betrayed: A Play.* New York: Faber and Faber, 2008.

———. *Interesting Times: Writings from a Turbulent Decade.* New York: Farrar, Straus and Giroux, 2009.

———. George Packer: "KQED's Forum Program Hosted by David Iverson." January 30, 2009, http://www.auroratheater.org/index.php.

Paget, Derek. "'Verbatim Theater': Oral History and Documentary Techniques." *New Theater Quarterly* 3, no. 12 (1987): 317–336.

Paget, Marianne A. "Performing the Text." *Journal of Contemporary Ethnography* 19, no. 1 (1990): 136–55.

Pavis, Patrice. *Analyzing Performance: Theater, Dance, and Film*, translated by David Williams. Ann Arbor: University of Michigan Press, 2003.

Power, Samantha. "Access Denied." *Time*, September 26, 2007, http://www.time.com/time/world/article/0,8599,1665921,00.html.

Rubin, Alissa J. "U.S. Expands Visa Program for Iraqis." *New York Times*, July 25, 2008, http://www.nytimes.com/2008/07/25/world/middleeast/25visa.html?_r=2&hp&oref=login.

Rutherford, Paul. *Weapons of Mass Deception: Marketing the War against Iraq*. Toronto: University of Toronto Press, 2004.

Schechter, Danny. *Embedded—Weapons of Mass Deception: How the Media Failed to Cover the War on Iraq*. Amherst, MA: Prometheus Books, 2003.

Scheer, Christopher, Robert Scheer, and Lakshmi Chaudhry. *The Five Biggest Lies Bush Told Us about Iraq*. Crows Nest: Allen & Unwin, 2004.

Schlossman, David A. *Actors and Activists: Politics, Performance, and Exchange among Social Worlds*. New York: Routledge: 2002.

Schmitt, Carl. *The Nomos of the Earth in the International Law of the Jus Publicum Europaeum*, translated by G. L. Ulmen. New York: Telos Press, 2003.

Soto-Morettini, Donna. "Trouble in the House: David Hare's *Stuff Happens*." *Contemporary Theater Review* 15, no. 3 (2005): 309–19.

Stone, Geoffrey. "Liberty." *Democracy: Journal of Ideas* 11 (2009): n.p. http://www.democracyjournal.org/article.php?ID=6664.

Westlake, E. J. "Mapping Political Performances: A Note on the Structure of the Anthology." In *Political Performances: Theory and Practice*, edited by Susan C. Haedicke, Deirdre Heddon, Avraham Oz, and E. J. Westlake, 7–16. Amsterdam: Rodopi, 2009.

Woodruff, Paul. *The Necessity of Theater: The Art of Watching and Being Watched*. Oxford, UK: Oxford University Press, 2008.

Woodward, Bob. *Plan of Attack*. New York: Simon and Schuster, 2004.

———. *State of Denial*. New York: Simon and Schuster, 2006.

Chapter 11

Political Actors

Performance as Democratic Protest in Anti-Apartheid Theater

EMILY BEAUSOLEIL

What happens in theater *happens*. Representation has the effect of action.

—David B. Coplan, "Ideology and Tradition in
South African Black Popular Theater"

Pluralist democracies take as given that difference is the very stuff of politics—that dominant meanings, values, and ways of life and the political relations they maintain do not account for all citizens, and alternative possibilities might yet prove legitimate, viable, even preferable. As such, democracy requires that we not only make space for diverse ways of life, or simply contain enough difference—as if this were possible—but also remain open and receptive to the changes implied by such differences.[1] In short, it demands both a *care for difference*—an attentiveness to and agonistic care for the complexity of identity, partiality of prevailing accounts, and the persistent murmur and occasional shout of the difference that exceeds them—and *receptive generosity*[2] toward "others" within the unsettling terrain of politics. Further, it requires forms of affiliation and coalition that work *through* rather than in spite of difference—where intensity of resonance is not premised on identification, where difference "converges but is not conflated."[3] And yet, as critics of feminism, truth commissions, and multiculturalism have shown in various ways, these challenges are difficult to meet even within those policies and practices designed for these very purposes.

It is in precisely these ways that artistic performance has been a pivotal, if still largely overlooked, site of democratic engagement. In theory, the salience of this claim is not difficult to argue. When, as so many critical theorists have observed, power is understood as embodied and maintained through the discourses, practices, and sites of the everyday as well as formal institutions, artistic performance quickly comes to the fore as a context for the contestation of power. Moreover, given the basic democratic demand to remain attentive and responsive both to difference and the various forms of its exclusion within prevailing terms for identity, action, and relation—what Jacques Rancière calls the "distribution of the sensible"—those everyday practices that seek to unsettle, interrogate, and broaden these terms are shown to be democratic and pluralizing gestures.[4]

But artistic performance is not a potential site of democratic engagement merely insofar as it resembles more conventional political practices. It remains distinct among these sites, and, interestingly, it is precisely the most *unruly* of its characteristics—those that have led political theorists to handle performance gingerly, if at all—that allow it to serve as a site of democratic practice in powerful ways. Indeed, structured to represent meaning as complexly and persuasively as possible, artistic performance has developed communicative techniques that are not necessarily available to or used within other instances of civil society.

Here, in contrast to conventional modes of communication that all too easily lapse into static terms of identity politics, meaning is expressly conveyed as multimodal, multivalent, and nonexhaustive. And here, while declarative modes of discourse conventionally used in politics tend to deny their own performativity or erase their own absences—by implicitly claiming direct, bounded, and stable referents; by grammatically asserting faithful accounts of the factual; by presumed opposition to and ostensible absence of rhetorical or aesthetic modalities—the *evocative* nature of artistic performance draws reflexive attention to the interpretive and partial nature of its account. And here, too, are practices found that expressly and artfully cultivate receptivity even as they challenge deeply held and often latent beliefs and values. It is this potential that this chapter will explore, using the case of South African protest theater, where a form of artistic engagement became a broad-sweeping national phenomenon widely recognized for its political influence against an oppressive state, to do so. In fact, here we find an extreme case where, despite experiences of state and more insidious antidemocratic pressures, artistic performance was able to challenge effectively monolithic discourses and the antidemocratic political systems they sustain, and even flourish as alternative sites of democratic engagement in the face of such repression.

Protest Theater in Apartheid South Africa:
Historical Background

With segregation laws, mass removals, and profound state violence and suppression of all opposition making democratic practices all but impossible, black South Africans[5] and their allies increasingly turned to artistic performance. Throughout the history of apartheid in South Africa, "cultural struggle has always formed an integral part of efforts of the oppressed in the fight for democracy and national liberation."[6] Theater in particular was considered its most powerful vehicle, to some extent taking the place of open dissent during apartheid's darkest years.[7]

The apartheid state, of course, was not oblivious to this use of theater for democratic ends. The few public venues available within black communities were subject to aggressive censorship and police interference; in fact, until the 1980s the control of these spaces was the predominant means through which the state limited and contained artistic expression in the townships and was able to dramatize its own strength.[8] Segregation legislation made interracial interaction and collaboration increasingly difficult, and producers, playwrights, and actors of contestatory theater were repeatedly detained, arrested, exiled, intimidated, and harassed.[9] During the state's short-lived "reform" policies of 1978, resistant theater may have passed safely under this watchful eye, but only if it proved prohibitive to black communities through the use of arcane dramatic codes, high admission costs, or "intimate" urban experimental theaters that predominantly preached to a converted choir and served as a safety valve rather than a fulcrum for resistant energies.[10] The state's keen understanding of the subversive power of art was succinctly expressed by a security police officer while threatening the founder of Workshop 71, Robert (Kavanagh) McLaren, who in reference to Maoist China described art as an "organizational and agitational weapon."[11] Beyond such overt state suppression, subtler but no less powerful forces of racism and segregation at play among theater establishments, critics, academics, publicity agencies, and publishers worked to devalue and marginalize such theater either by scathing critiques or absenting them from records altogether, so that these acts of opposition were subject to both legal bannings and "hegemonically induced absences and erasures."[12]

Certainly, this had significant impact: interracial groups such as the Dorkay House, United Artists, and the Phoenix Players, and Black Consciousness groups such as People's Experimental Theatre (PET) and Theatre Council of Natal (TECON) were forced to fold; numerous artists fled in exile, or were too shaken by state intimidation to continue writing politically, as in the case of Gibson Kente. Many plays even if documented could not be published, while the few published works were, until recently, extremely difficult to obtain.[13]

However, despite these instances of effective state and socioeconomic repression, the phenomenon of theater as democratic resistance persisted and, at times, thrived: (Kavanagh) McLaren has counted no less than 150 separate known productions throughout South Africa between 1953 and 1977, most of them original works, not to mention the proliferation of resistant theater notably after the 1976 Soweto Uprising. Indeed, in some of the strictest years of apartheid during the 1960s and 1970s black theater actually came into its own as an artistic genre and political forum, while interracial or white liberal-facilitated resistant theater persisted. Despite overt, targeted, and violent suppression of oppositional expression, despite bannings, arrests, harassment, and socioeconomic restraints, such theater was produced more frequently, and became far more aggressively positioned against the apartheid state, than ever before, emerging as a force "that the white South African hegemony could no longer afford to ignore."[14]

(En)Acting Protest: Theater as Democratic Practice

This ability of theater to function as a forum for democratic engagement, in the very teeth of an antidemocratic and aggressive state, can be understood in relation to its use of two aesthetic resources in particular: *polyphony* and *transience*. *Polyphony* is, as the word implies, "multi-leveledness and semantic multi-voicedness"[15]—performance's multiple communicative modes, including the visual, kinetic, sonic, spatial, affective, and symbolic. For the purposes of this analysis, I examine polyphony of three kinds: linguistic, nonverbal (including visual, aural, dramatic, and physical), and what I will be calling "creative." *Transience* of representation refers to the ephemerality of performance's medium; as process rather than object, performance dissolves even as it renders visible, leaving few traces. Though inherent to all performance, this might be augmented by minimizing dependence on physical sets and props, relying upon orality rather than textuality, or incorporating greater improvisation rather than pregiven scripts. Both polyphony and transience have been used throughout the history of South African resistant theater, to varying degrees and in different ways, to enable performance to resignify identities, ideas, and values; expose and challenge the prevailing political and ideological system; empower and mobilize subordinated groups; and cultivate new alliances and differently structured publics, all despite profound state efforts of suppression. In the South African context, these aesthetic strategies were consciously and continually employed within political performance, demonstrating in various ways that it is not merely what, but *how* performers communicate that enables performance to function as a site of democratic engagement.

Polyphony and Transience:
Performing Identity, Challenging Authority

As so many critical theorists have argued, identity is inherently complex, multiple, contingent, and in process. By communicating through multiple modes, polyphony holds together in apparently impossible simultaneity what so often becomes simplified, reified, or conflated in other forms of representation. As such, it enables the articulation and exploration of identity beyond tight scripts of fixed social categories or restrictive discourses, through a "multifaceted polylog" that can reveal and contend with multiple themes, connections, and contradictions, and intersectional identities in their complexity.[16] In the context of a racist and totalitarian state, this proved especially significant by enabling alternative significations of subordinated groups beyond prevailing racist discourses and the asymmetrical relations they sustained.

But in facilitating rather than explicitly defining meaning, by presenting such multiplicity without its negation or resolution, such polyphony does something more: it makes impossible claims that such meaning is fixed, exhaustive, or unmediated. Like the opacity and thus "unfinalizability" of meaning Bakhtin sees due to Dostoevsky's multiple characters, this polyphony of artistic modalities makes difficult any totalizing claims to a final "resting place" for meaning.[17] This is due to the inevitable and explicit "excess" and "absence" of meaning such polyphony generates. Art always conveys more than it intends; and it is never totalizing. The "excess" meaning conveyed by representation creates a supplement that makes multiple and resistant readings possible. Despite the excess, representation produces ruptures and gaps; it fails to reproduce the real exactly. Precisely because of [its] supplemental excess and its failure to be totalizing, close readings of . . . representation can produce psychic resistance and, possibly, political change.[18]

In this way, this explicit artfulness can work to cultivate a tolerance for ambiguity and complexity, and for the limits of one's own understanding. As we will see, in the South African context this proved vital to the task of challenging the authority of monolithic discourses and the political order they legitimized—rather than, as Martha Nussbaum has argued, preventing such resistance.[19]

Likewise, *transience* draws attention to the process of meaning-making behind ostensibly stable and authoritative meanings; by making overt the making and unmaking of identities on stage, this transience can contribute to agency-building by rendering meanings constructed and contestable. Similarly, it enables the communication of meaning while simultaneously alluding to the limitations of such accounts: performance "becomes itself through disappearance" and cannot be saved or recorded.[20] Just as polyphony makes difficult attempts to claim the authority of one aspect or reading of a piece over another, transience makes it possible to dwell but not rest within the various moments of the moving image. As such, performance effectively resists efforts or claims to exhaustively name, contain, and possess that which it represents.

In the context of South African protest theater, the exploration of "the whole gamut of expression" available within aesthetic, dramatic, and physical codes helped crystallize and condense meaning, as well as creatively disrupt and move beyond "constricted apartheid-determined relationships and modes of expressiveness."[21] Given the inadequacy of language to capture the complexities and contradictions of both apartheid and the meanings, experiences, and identities suppressed by it, it is no wonder the polyphony of artistic performance became a pivotal site of communication and collective inquiry. In this context, as Mark Fleishmann also observes, "A complex subject requires a complex treatment and gives rise to a complex text in which the written word, the spoken word, and the transformative material body amongst others are in a constant state of dynamic dialogue."[22]

The creative play of linguistic polyphony facilitated this project in a number of ways. Beyond the use of English, these plays used various Indigenous languages, as well as *tsotsitaal*, the urban polyglot slang spoken in the streets at the time, offering "an immensely rich mine" for playwrights. This use of language "exactly as . . . in real life" represented such marginalized experience as not only lived reality but something of value.[23] Moreover, the interjection of Indigenous languages served to contest the presumed authority of colonial languages and the primacy of certain modes of discourse. The strategic use of specific languages for intertribal jokes, exclamations, sexual content, and songs not only invoked local knowledge but served purposes of inclusion and exclusion: acting as a secret code, African languages could assert the linguistic proficiency of those who tended to understand more languages than white South Africans, as well as enable communication past white audience members directly to African populations to create a sense of shared knowledge and struggle. Even the use of colonial languages in these contexts, particularly when spoken in their localized *tsotsitaal* form, functioned as "colonial mimicry" that undermined the ostensible authority of the Afrikaans state by turning "the gaze of the discriminated black upon the eye of power." Moreover, the slip between and subversive play of languages in these productions functioned to draw attention to the role of language as an instrument of domination and the linguistic power structures that exist in South African society as a result.[24]

Nonverbal aspects of polyphony served similar purposes, not least the repeated disruption of established dramatic codes. This, in the South African apartheid context, was enacted in two ways: first, by the interjection of traditional African modes of performance, and second, by innovating new dramatic codes. The use of Indigenous aesthetic codes, apart from their particular nature, was in itself an act of defiance of apartheid and its legitimizing narratives on two fronts: such acts not only reclaimed lost heritage and asserted its worth and place, but also reconfigured and expanded available aesthetic vocabularies and in so doing undermined the universality and legitimacy such discourses claim.

More than this, in the South African context the precise nature of these traditional dramatic codes provided further resources for unsettling the authority and stability of prevailing meanings and values. David Coplan's extensive work on the subject finds these codes to be defined by their "interconnection, visibility, imagery, and efficacy." South African traditional aesthetics have routinely used representative forms that are synesthetic, fluidly transitioning from one meaning to another and simultaneously coordinating expression of visual, aural, and tactile media. In so doing, they draw connections between communicative modes—such as the rhythm of the feet echoing that of the voice—which further reinforces conveyed meaning. Here very clearly is the employment of polyphony, made doubly effective as a means of subversion by its invocation of traditional values and concepts. By using aspects of these traditional performative codes, playwrights such as Matsemela Manaka and Maishe Maponya and plays such as *Sizwe Bansi Is Dead* (1972) and *The Blood Knot* (1962) were not only able to invoke suppressed history and meaning but in so doing to discover a revitalizing resource for democratic practices.[25]

Beyond this invocation of traditional artistic culture, resistant theater in South Africa has also innovatively transformed established dramatic codes as a means of contesting received knowledge and the dictated parameters of possible thought and action. Breaking with established conventions became a means of rejecting white theater and with it, white dominance: Mthuli Shezi's *Shanti* (1973), for example, the only play published from the Black Consciousness movement, is one of the many plays to deliberately break with conventions of naturalism and realism. Having each actor move between multiple characters, using stage narration of scenes, dream sequences, flashbacks, and numerous other devices, allowed these plays simultaneously to make a political statement concerning the primacy of received aesthetic codes, assert the agency of black artists to create in their own right, and signify to their audiences the mutability of dominant codes and possibilities for intervention. Others, such as *Sizwe*, moved away from the use of the proscenium arch and, with it, the traditional divide between performer and audience that was seen as crucial to bourgeois theater: this was done by directly addressing the audience and demanding their active participation through devices such as call and response, songs, and improvised dialogue with audience members.[26]

Other techniques pioneered by Workshop 71 and used in plays such as *The Hungry Earth* (1979) broke with conventions by dissolving the boundary separating art and reality, through the use of the day's newspaper headlines, deliberate slippage to actors' real names, or actors introducing themselves directly to the audience before taking on their characters.[27] In a context of daily oppression and violence, these theater practitioners often sought to dissolve the suspension of disbelief so integral to western theater and instead use performance as a means by which, as Martin Orkin observes, to directly link actors and audiences, "and situate all, in turn, directly within the processes within which they are lodged in common."[28] However, despite these acts of coimplication to provoke reflexivity and critical analysis, these disruptions of traditional codes simultaneously resisted the creation of equally seamless, manageable constructions based on their own complex significations. As a result, these complex engagements challenged the viewer to problematize not only prevailing discourse but the manner in which monolithic discourses of racism and apartheid distort complex meaning. In these ways, disruptions of dramatic form served to transform the representation of event into event, or what Richard Schechner calls "actuals," where something consequential happens to contribute to social and political change.[29]

The body provided yet another mode of communication within such work. The prolific use of physical language in South African resistant theater ranged from formal dance choreography to elaborate gestures to complement dialogue, to sculpted physical imagery, to the body completely replacing verbal communication where words are simply insufficient. Following traditional Indigenous aesthetic codes, often the body was also used to metaphorically render musical and verbal images such that it did not merely accompany but was itself integral to meaning. This proved politically significant given the containment and regulation of the body in the context of domination. More than merely conveying what cannot be adequately captured in words, the performative use of the body experiments with the creative expression of one's identity through the very form most intimate with it and, in the context of domination, alienated from it. In so doing, it actively contests inscriptions on the body and explodes the possibilities for signification. As Mark Fleishmann observes in his account of such practices, "the physical image is multivalent, ambiguous, complex. It leads to the proliferation of meaning which demands an imaginative response from the spectator."[30]

A poignant example of this is the gradual transition enacted during *Bopha!* from the physical training routines of political academies to traditional Zulu dance, which effectively uses the body to speak to the difficulties of black policemen in South Africa. In the words of playwright Percy Mtwa, "that body which you have can be anything, can be a piece of sculpture, it can sing, it can be a song, it can be movement, can be sound, can be anything, that body."[31] Moreover, the body provided poor and subordinated communities with, as the creator of worker theater Ari Sitas states, "powers and talents that are rich despite our predicaments."[32] Here the "excess" of the living body strains against and creatively plays with the prevailing terms of the social body, before the eyes of audiences; as Moira Gatens, Rosalyn Diprose, and others argue, the individual body "contains its own logic" that can expose, interrogate, and possibly transform the norms of inclusion, exclusion, and asymmetry within the social body.[33]

As may already be apparent, these strategies are effective forms of democratic resistance not only because of their polyphony, but also due to the transience they necessarily entail. Transitions from one mode of communication to another, or within a modality from one meaning to the next, create a slippage that signals the constructedness and mutability of established discourses that have been naturalized and internalized. Whether one actor moves seamlessly from playing one character to another in front of the audience with merely the exchange of a simple prop or piece of clothing—as epitomized in *Woza Albert, Asinamali,* and *Bopha!*—or transforms one movement or sound into another—such as the prophet-turned-automaton with merely the repeated use of a shovel in *Prophets in a Black Sky*—or the continual shift from dramatic action to song to dance and back, such transience foregrounds the ever-mutable process of meaning-making, and can challenge the fixed categories and scripted relations of dominant culture and explore new forms of self-identification. Moreover, they serve to shatter the spectator's illusion of "dominant specularity"—psychic distance, assurance of firm understanding—by performing "discontinuity, contradiction, the fact of mobility in process, and the impossibility of a sure and centrally embracing view."[34]

In these ways, such theater made the most of the subversive potential of such aesthetic dimensions to articulate and develop "counteridentifications" that exposed and interrogated existing conditions, experimented with alternatives, and made explicit the capacity to do so beyond the performative frame.[35] Here, polyphony and transience provided the means to represent otherwise suppressed realities and positions, and do so in ways that did not restrict such meanings to fixed or bounded terms; rather, by engaging meaning and identity through these evocative modalities, such practices enacted and fostered a *care for difference* that democracy demands. As Schutzman and Cohen-Cruz state, rather than preclude political representation, mobilization, and coalition,

> the potency of in-between (or open space) and ambiguity (or paradox) [are] strategies of resistance . . . playful, unpredictable, improvisatory, shape-shifting, and yet empowering means to challenge fixed, centralized, hierarchical, and often oppressive circumstances and/or readings.[36]

Whether challenging apartheid discourses or overt state control, the *unruliness* of performance proved the very means through which such monoliths could be effectively challenged and transformed. Moreover, as we will see, these aesthetic dimensions are largely responsible for making theater in the South African apartheid context "the most accessible and forceful medium" in which to do so.[37]

Polyphony: Connecting Across Difference

Democracy, as I have argued, requires not only the engagement of identity as complex and nonexhaustive—and so realizes and fosters what I call a care for difference—but also dispositions toward "others" defined by *receptive generosity* if such difference is to unsettle and transform the terms of politics in ever-democratizing ways. Moreover, it demands forms of affiliation and coalition that are not premised on erasure but rather work through and across difference. Performance's polyphony helps to cultivate receptivity by opening up multiple points of contact: one might connect with, be affected by, find resonance or meaning through art's multiple "modes of inhabitation," however divergent one's own experience may be from that of the creator or other observers. Through its explicit excess and absence—enhanced by the move away from verbal to more symbolic, visual, and embodied forms—the aesthetic creates a space through which the "multiple, conflictual axes of identity/difference" that pose such a challenge to conventional forms of political representation can be the very means for communication and coalition.[38] In fact, due to their aesthetic and affective dimensions, artistic modalities can often provoke responses denied to other ostensibly "rational" fora of democratic engagement, precisely because they can reach past our usual psychological defenses through these alternative channels. The "concrete relational density" of artistic performance's polyphony and the great pressure this creates of, to borrow Altieri's phrase, "the whole on the particular" can generate intensive affective encounters that move beyond, between, and beneath habitual patterns of interpretation and response; this is, as many theorists have argued, an inherently democratic moment, in which our "partitions of the sensible" are dissembled and we may "figure the newly thinkable."[39]

However, even as this polyphony allows for the generation of multiple axes of affiliation across seemingly insurmountable differences, its explicit "excess" and "absence" also foreground the interpretive nature of the meanings it generates, and so even in moments of intense affective resonance it can foster "a feeling for another that entails an encounter with something irreducible and different, often inaccessible." In so doing, it can guard against a crude empathy that confuses affiliation with identification by substituting "the 'you' with the 'as-if-it-were-me.'"[40] This was certainly true in the case of South African protest theater, where polyphony enabled communication and a sense of solidarity among diverse and far-flung communities in all-too-rare forms of "non-identical kinship."[41]

The use of both verbal and nonverbal forms of polyphony enabled protest theater to broaden its impact, both in terms of drawing and holding audience attention, and generating multiple points of contact. In the first instance, as David Coplan also notes, "[t]he relevance and effectiveness of this theatre depends upon whether it can be popular in the best sense," and the strategic use of both traditional and township performative styles, as well as the central role of dance and song, mime and tableau often gave these potentially heavy-handed performances mass appeal among black audiences unfamiliar with formal theater as well as outside communities.[42] The use of slang and local languages, beginning with the musical plays of Gibson Kente, also gave performances a markedly greater appeal among township communities, whose political education and mobilization the apartheid state was most determined to prevent.

Moreover, performance's multivalence was used consciously and strategically by various playwrights and directors to generate multiple possibilities for connection and resonance across significant cultural and linguistic differences both locally and abroad. Linguistically, English was the preferred *lingua franca* of resistant theater, as it was seen to be an essential tool in struggles against cultural isolation and state control of communicative channels. And yet the strategic use of different local languages, as with the translation of Fatima Dike's *The Sacrifice of Kreli* into multiple regional languages along the tour circuit, also helped performance to reach linguistically isolated communities. Further, the role of visual cues such as images, mime, and physical metaphor often spoke "more strongly than the words," while dance and music would often "carry the burden of the performance." Such aesthetic devices are far from trivializing: they prove vital to the constant challenge to, in the words of Ngeme, "communicate with anyone anywhere in the world, [to] bridge the barriers of language and culture." Due to these affective, aesthetic, and dramatic strategies, theater was able to become one of South Africa's most visible exports and contributed to the struggle against apartheid by sensitizing diverse audiences to injustices at home.[43]

As well as broadening the reach of such work, the use of aesthetic and affective codes also deepened a performance's impact, making audiences, in the words of actor, director, and playwright John Kani, "cross the barriers of illusory distance, to feel [another's] plight as [their own]." Dramatic techniques and notably the use of song prompted emotional responses from audiences, who at times spontaneously joined in song from their seats or, on the rare occasion, on stage, but far more often expressed their affective identification with and responses to various performances. Gibson Kente's musical melodramas, despite their often temperate politics on the spectrum of resistant theater, were seen to be among the most threatening of such performances precisely because of their music, which seemed the source of black audiences' deep connection with his work: in Kente's words, "people carry it home, they sing about it because it is in musicals. It's very dangerous."[44]

Polyphony also played a role in forging coalitions and enabling alternative models to do so behind and beyond the veritable curtain. These artistic spaces by definition entail a degree of collaboration, or *creative polyphony*, as each participant interprets the work at hand and contributes their role. Black and alternative companies and collectives created spaces for marginalized voices and all-too-rare sites of democratic engagement not only on stage, but also through the creative process, facilitating the practice of critical inquiry, creative agency, and democratic citizenship among cast and crew. For instance, the creation, direction, and production of pieces of theater by black artists became a primary means of wresting the modes of production away from dominant forces and enabling self-determination. During the Black Consciousness period, groups such as the Music, Drama, Arts and Literature Institute (MDALI), the first radical theater group to work in townships to promote black-run theater; TECON, who in 1973 banned white audiences; or PET, who resisted creative collaboration with white artists, used theater as both a symbol and enactment of black capacity, solidarity, and perspective. As one practitioner stated, "we are a movement which announces a real democracy on this land—where people like you and me can control for the first time our productive and creative power."[45]

Where projects were multiracial, the creative process often enabled cross-racial engagement altogether absent in almost all other spheres of civil society. *King Kong*, the play often earmarked as the beginning of resistant theater in South Africa, was the most important example of multiracial collaboration and was used as the model of such theater for years to come. This was developed later by companies like the world-renowned Market Theatre, which defied segregation laws at the time and forged a new multiracial direction for South African theater despite its own fraught dimensions.[46] Within the context of segregation, whether legally or socially enforced, these creative endeavors helped to bridge barriers in experience and understanding in the very ways they sought to represent on the stage. Indeed, these collaborations opened up spaces radically different from the surrounding sociopolitical climate, providing "a glimpse within the space of the theater itself, intimations of an alternative South Africa."[47]

Recognizing the political potential of the creative process, many theater practitioners of all races moved toward the "workshop" creative method started by Union Artists in the 1950s that was consciously grounded in the collaboration of all artists involved. Barney Simon, playwright and cofounder of the Market Theatre, used to ask his performers to research their own environments to make artistic depictions more robust and realistic. Other practitioners, such as in the Junction Avenue Theatre Company (JATC) post-1976 and Workshop 71, required active, equal participation of all artists involved, at times even encouraging the audience to interrupt the performance and discuss the issues presented in the work. It is of significance that some theater groups consciously became multilingual to facilitate this cross-cultural dialogue. The most extreme form of such collaborative creation took place in worker theater, used by trade unions and performed by and for workers within factory walls during breaks: Ari Sitas, initiator of this form of resistant theater, describes their use of the workshop method as requiring "each participant . . . to become a performer, thinker, planner, and storyteller," holding one another's narratives to account and combining their individual perspectives with full creative agency.[48]

In this way, the workshop method enhanced the polyphony of performance's creative process, enabling subordinated artists to become creative agents in their own right and in so doing bridged gaps in, and offered alternate forms of, cross-racial engagement from those created by apartheid. In the words of Will Kentridge of the JATC, at least in principle and often in practice, "the workshop space in South Africa is a space where South Africans can momentarily leave the monster of apartheid behind them and meet as equals, without prejudice, to work creatively together."[49] At a time when sites for democratic citizenship and engagement across the lines set by racist discourse and the apartheid state were altogether absent in South African society, theater offered the means through which such democratic engagement and practices of citizenship were possible, not only modeling on stage but also enacting democratic alternatives to the prevailing system.

There were, however, several occasions when this ideal was not realized and collaborations went sour, due to unequal power relations, artistic exploitation, and failure to acknowledge contributions of black practitioners.[50] The line between democratic and antidemocratic practices is neither clear nor fixed, and even within these resistant spaces, aspects of the apartheid system found their way in. However, on many occasions these spaces created the all-too-rare conditions for greater understanding of perspectives and struggles both "overlooked" and "overdetermined" by racism and apartheid, the transformation of one's own perspectives in light of this exposure, and the creation of contexts in which one could not only discuss or represent but also experience aspects of an alternative political order, preparing the way for "a more democratic South Africa—one freer and more able to tolerate both difference and dialogue."[51]

Polyphony and Transience:
Slipping through the Grasp of a Totalitarian State

While these dimensions of performative engagement might play a role in any democratic project, in the context of an antidemocratic state, such practices must also possess the basic capacity to continue despite forces of counter-resistance. Here too, performance's polyphony and transience proved vital in bypassing censure and other forms of state control in ways denied most other forms of democratic engagement in oppressive societies. Polyphony assisted with this in several ways: the multiple faces of performance—in straddling both commercial entertainment spheres and public political fora—creates a certain spaciousness in which the former dimension might effectively veil the latter. Further, the transience of performance—dissolving even as it renders visible—means these forums are far more difficult to control. In the context of the South African apartheid state, this proved vital in enabling theater to function—even flourish—as the primary form of cultural resistance, during even the most aggressive and targeted periods of state censorship.

In the first instance, the multiplicity of possible readings of performance made it possible to mask political content as mere entertainment. Indeed, performances were at times able to function as crucial organizing and conscientizing sites precisely through their avoidance of overtly political dimensions.[52] For those performances that could not disguise their political meaning, however, companies in both townships and cities would work through a system of entertainment clubs requiring "membership" and inviting audience members as "guests" with donations at the door to bypass segregation laws and assembly restrictions of state-controlled public spaces. In this way, Workshop 71 was able to usher in the reinstatement of mixed-race audiences and casts, banned since the early 1960s. Similarly, these companies were able to rehearse through affiliations with private drama clubs, youth clubs, volunteer organizations, and educational institutions.[53]

Moreover, the use of African languages and urban township slang allowed for the communication of subversive messages despite the presence of superintendents, police, and other figures of state control during performances. Meanwhile, contemporary issues could be addressed obliquely through the use of metaphor, such the Antigone myth in *The Island* (1973) or the harvest as euphemism for the need to reclaim land in *Pula* (1982); likewise, critique could be masked under the veil of songs, dance, melodrama, and other aesthetic devices, or the use of cultural code only understood in full by its intended audience. Much as prose writers turned progressively to poetry during the 1960s as a means of continuing to write despite increased government censorship, the aesthetic and symbolic codes of drama were a vocabulary with which to disguise antiapartheid criticism. This led to plays once or potentially banned by the Publications Control Board successfully escaping censure, as their meanings could be, as with Zakes Mda's collected volume of scripts, misunderstood or, if understood, perceived to pose no real threat.[54]

Furthermore, here transience comes to the fore as a vital resource in resisting containment, regulation, and cooptation by the apartheid system in terms of either the state or the market, through four different means: spatial and temporal transience, or the impermanence of place and event; physical transience, or the limited use of physical aids, whether props, costumes and sets, or technical equipment; the employment of orality over text; and the role of improvisation over script. Indeed, the degree to which performance is made of such strategies corresponds in this case to the state's inability to suppress its presence.

Control over public space continued to be the most effective form of state regulation of artistic production throughout the apartheid era. Consequently, while certain established theaters like the Market Theatre in Johannesburg and the People's Space Theatre in Cape Town provided much-needed spaces for rehearsal, training, collaboration, and performance, they were also the most easily targeted and greatly affected by the tentacles of the state, and due to high maintenance costs were more vulnerable to manipulation by investors from the business sector and the demands of the market. By contrast, those performances that capitalized on their capacity for transience were able to perform within brief windows of opportunity amid pervasive state control as well as move away from the "economy of display" and demands of the market. Kente's companies, for instance, traveled by bus throughout the country for one-night-only performances, their impromptu promotional banners hastily posted during the day. A great deal of such unscripted, minimally rehearsed, and quickly convened and dismantled performance occurred during times of the strictest repression of political resistance.[55]

An example at the farthest end of this spectrum was "guerrilla theater," such as that by Peter Makhari, which took place during political rallies, demonstrations, and mass protests: materializing somewhere amid a crowd nervously anticipating confrontation, these performances would enact confrontations ending in the retreat of police. At the arrival of the actual police, these "rehearsals" would then dissolve into the crowd, only to appear elsewhere to incite, encourage, and mobilize other sectors of the group. As of the mid-1980s, there were literally hundreds of such "hastily assembled but energetic" performances, attesting to the capacity such transience gives potentially threatened political performance.[56]

Certain performances also chose to limit their dependence upon material objects. "Propertyless theater," such as *The Long March* (1986), *The Reed* (1975), or *The Sacrifice of Kreli* (1976), not only cut down on costs to enable longer performance runs and more affordable tickets for poor black audiences but also made these performances extremely mobile, able to set up and dissolve quickly in response to cracks and closures in the armor of the state. This tactic of minimizing material constraints opened up greater opportunities for touring as well as performance in transient spaces such as political rallies, as was increasingly the case during the 1980s; this ability to function within such overtly political sites in turn helped to undermine the ability of censors to "gloss their role with 'tolerant' or 'reformist' qualities" as was the current rhetoric of the time.[57]

Stemming from the use of traditional African performance codes and consequent emphasis on orality, but also very consciously in response to state restrictions, most resistant theater also refrained from writing their plays down, or, if they did, this was often done after the fact as a testament to a significant performance rather than a prescriptive document.

Instead, works such as *Egoli* (1979), *The Hungry Earth* (1978), and JATC's *Sophiatown* (1986) emerged from improvisation within rehearsal workshops. By relying on oral memory rather than text, these plays were therefore not subject to detailed government scrutiny as demanded by the Publications Control Board.[58] Similarly, in relying upon improvisation rather than fixed script, performances were malleable enough to not only respond to the particular demands of a given performative context but also avoid censure by leaving no paper trail, nor even a fixed oral agenda.[59] In these ways, because such theater was less a physical artifact than a moving image, it "lent itself readily to devious practices" despite intense and targeted state suppression.[60]

Concluding Remarks

By maximizing performance's polyphony and transience in strategic ways, South African protest theater found the means to expose and challenge the discourses and practices of apartheid, explore and enact alternative possibilities and differently structured publics, and cultivate a sense of agency and possibility for change. Moreover, these artistic resources enabled communication and resonance across profound cultural and linguistic differences, and the ability to do so despite aggressive and targeted attempts by the state to suppress them. It is significant that most political leaders emerging from oppressed communities at this time began as theater practitioners; similarly, the conscientizing and mobilization of the trade union movement has often been directly linked to preceding worker theater performances.[61] Resistant theater provided political education and practices of democratic citizenship to a vast number of people where both were scarce, and both on and off stage explored, modeled, and enacted more democratic alternatives to the apartheid system. Even where its effects were more subtle and indirect, such theater proved a crucial catalyst and conduit for broader sociopolitical change, to such an extent that scholars and artists who have witnessed South Africa's transition to democracy repeatedly claim that "theatre . . . has long been ahead of political events, has pioneered society."[62]

These aesthetic resources contributed to this capacity of performance to foster the conditions for a democratic politics, opening up both alternative democratic fora and alternatives to how such fora might be structured. The very aspects of artistic performance that defy the prevailing discourse of political legitimacy—a discourse that renders the arts irrational, messy, unquantifiable—are, in this case, the very resources that made such democratic practices possible and effective. In the process, they gesture not only to the legitimacy of artistic practices as sites of democratic engagement but to how identity may be communicated, meaning may be contested, and coalitions may be formed beyond static forms of identity politics that persist in the policies, theories, and practices of democratic pluralism. Indeed, the very *unruliness* of such aesthetic practices offers the means to engage identity and difference in ways that more conventional political sites find most challenging: with a *care for difference* as complex and nonexhaustive, and with *receptivity* toward the unsettling of meaning, identity, and relation this necessarily introduces. Through creatively subversive strategies so intimately understood and finely honed within the arts, such performance effectively challenges not only its *political* context but also the theoretical terrain within which it is understood.

Notes

1. Claude Le Fort, *Democracy and Political Theory*, trans. David Macey (Minneapolis: University of Minnesota Press, 1988); Chantal Mouffe, "Democracy, Power, and the 'Political,'" in *Democracy and Difference: Contesting the Boundaries of the Political*, ed. Seyla Benhabib (Princeton, NJ: Princeton University Press, 1996), 245–65; Bonnie Honig, "Difference, Dilemmas and the Politics of Home," in *Democracy and Difference: Contesting the Boundaries of the Political*, ed. Seyla Benhabib (Princeton, NJ: Princeton University Press, 1996), 257–77; Iris Marion Young, *Inclusion and Democracy* (Oxford, UK: Oxford University Press, 2000); Davide Panagia, *The Political Life of Sensation* (Durham, NC: Duke University Press, 2009).

2. Romand Coles, *Rethinking Generosity: Critical Theory and the Politics of Caritas* (Ithaca, NY: Cornell University Press, 1997).

3. Chandra Mohanty and Biddy Martin, "What's Home Got to Do with It?," in *Feminism Without Borders: Decolonizing Theory, Practicing Solidarity* (Durham, NC: Duke University Press, 2003), 100.

4. Jacques Rancière, *The Politics of Aesthetics*, trans. Gabriel Rockhill (New York: Continuum, 2004), 12.

5. While this chapter will focus on the experiences and struggles of black communities under the apartheid system, this is by no means a full account of the racial discrimination in policy and practice within South Africa

at the time. The division of South Africans into three racial categories—Bantu (black African), white, or Coloured (mixed race), with a fourth, Indian, added later—under the Population Registration Act of 1950 enabled the implementation of apartheid policies affecting all aspects of society for nonwhites. Likewise, political resistance in theater by nonwhites also included key leaders such as Ronnie Govender, whose plays *The Lahnee's Pleasure*, *Offside*, and *At the Edge* both marked the emergence of a distinctive Natal Indian theater and political engagement of issues of Indian and Coloured marginalization, manipulation, and forced and violent eviction, and were often met by "heavy-handed action by security police." Govender, in Rolf Solberg, *Alternative Theatre in South Africa: Talks with Prime Movers since the 1970s* (Pietermaritzburg, South Africa: Hadeda Books, 1999), 150–55; Ismael Mahomed, whose satirical critique of traditional Indian family values in *Purdah* caused community uproar; Ari Sitas and the Natal Worker's Theatre Movement mentioned briefly in this chapter, which emerged out of the social and industrial struggles in Natal and produced *The Long March* and *Bambatha's Children*; and theater companies such as the Durban Academy of Theatre Artists and the Shah Theatre Academy. For more detail on these dimensions of antiapartheid struggle, see Geoffrey V. Davis and Anne Fuchs, eds., *Theatre and Change in South Africa* (Netherlands: Overseas Publishers Association, 1996) and Muthal Naidoo, *The Search for a Cultural Identity: A Personal Odyssey*, Indic Theatre Monograph Series No. 1 (Durban, South Africa: Asoka Theatre Publications, 1993). This chapter is limited to a discussion of apartheid's targeting of black communities in particular, though the acts of creative resistance it includes speak to this diversity of experience and struggle under the apartheid system.

6. Peter Horn, "What Is Tribal Dress? The *Imbongi* and the People's Poet," in Davis and Fuchs, *Theatre and Change in South Africa*, 116.

7. Marcia Blumberg and Dennis Walder, Introduction, *South African Theatre as/and Intervention*, eds. Marcia Blumberg and Dennis Walder (Atlanta: Rodopi, 1999), 5. Although a distinct force, such theater was by no means a homogenous phenomenon: always emerging from and in response to changing political, ideological, and sociocultural conditions, resistant theater in this context has manifested along wide spectrums with regard to form, content, audience, and inherent ideology. Ranging from a liberal national discourse to more militant ideas of the Black Consciousness movement; from the use or radical innovation of European aesthetic codes to the use of traditional or contemporary African aesthetic codes and cultural forms; from narrations of collective history and individual morality to direct challenges to the contemporary political context—performances varied in relation to political position, intended audience, and the demands and limits of changing political circumstances. Within this vast range, resistant theater was used to address a wide range of issues related to apartheid, examine their nature and consequences, and explore political and ideological alternatives. Pass arrests, petty bureaucracy, police violence, prison conditions, racial discrimination, struggles of migrant workers, the breakdown of moral and cultural values in the

townships, and the need for solidarity within black communities are only a few of the most common themes from this period. For more detail on this range, see Bhekizizwe Peterson, "Apartheid and the Political Imagination in Black South African Theatre," *Journal of Southern African Studies* 16, no. 2 Special Issue: Performance and Popular Culture (June 1990): 235.

8. J. C. W. van Rooyen, *Censorship in South Africa* (Cape Town, South Africa: Juta, 1987), 7; Peterson, "Apartheid and the Political Imagination in Black South African Theatre," 232–34; Martin Orkin, "Whose Popular Theatre and Performance?," in *Theatre and Change in South Africa*, eds. Geoffrey V. Davis and Anne Fuchs (Netherlands: Overseas Publishers Association, 1996), 55; Martin Orkin, *Drama and the South African State* (Manchester, UK: Manchester University Press, 1991), 150–52.

9. The author of *Shanti*, one of the most influential resistant plays of the period, was thrown in front of a train before the first night of performance, while cast members were arrested and charged with treason under the Terrorism Act. Gibson Kente, responsible for the creation of a distinctly black popular theater, was arrested and detained while trying to film his play *How Long*, while Black Consciousness playwright Reverend Julius Maqina, increasingly popular in the townships from 1976 on, was harassed, detained, and put under house arrest. In 1975, along with political Black Consciousness organizations, the People's Experimental Theatre (PET) and the Theatre Council of Natal (TECON) were put on trial for "inflammatory, provocative, anti-white, racialistic, subversive and/or revolutionary" activities. For more detail, see Orkin, *Drama and the South African State*, 1–2, 214; T. Philemon Wakashe, "'Pula': An Example of Black Protest Theatre in South Africa," *The Drama Review: TDR* 30, no. 4 (Winter 1986): 41; Davis and Fuchs, "Introduction," *Theatre and Change in South Africa*, 7; Rolf Solberg, *Alternative Theatre in South Africa: Talks with Prime Movers since the 1970s*, 17; and Davis and Fuchs, "An Interest in Making Things: An Interview with William Kentridge," *Theatre and Change in South Africa*, 7.

10. Van Rooyen, *Censorship in South Africa*, 118; Peterson, "Apartheid and the Political Imagination in Black South African Theatre," 235. One illustration of the state's targeted and overt repression of grassroots theater is the arrest of Gibson Kente for filming *How Long* in 1976, while the more politically radical Workshop 71's *Survival* was touring the United States. When *Survival* began to attract larger audiences in townships, it was banned in 1978; this was also the case for Reverend Maqina's *Give Us This Day* (1974) and Khayalethu Mqhayisa's *Confused Mhlaba* (1975). For more on such state practices, see Robert Mshengu Kavanagh, *South African People's Plays* (London: Heinemann, 1981), 125–72; Coplan, "Ideology and Tradition in South African Black Popular Theater," 169.

11. Robert McLaren, "'The Many Individual Wills.' From *Crossroads* to *Survival*. The Work of Experimental Theatre Workshop 71," in Davis and Fuchs, *Theatre and Change in South Africa*, 33.

12. Orkin, *Drama and the South African State*, 250.

13. Kavanagh, *South African People's Plays*, xxiii; Coplan, "Ideology and Tradition in South African Black Popular Theater," 168, 209, 220; Solberg, *Alternative Theatre in South Africa: Talks with Prime Movers since the 1970s*, 8, 17; Peter Larlham, "Theatre in Transition: The Cultural Struggle in South Africa," *TDR* 35, no. 1 (Spring 1991): 201.

14. Kavanagh, *South African People's Plays*, xvii; David B. Coplan, *In Township Tonight! South Africa's Black City Music and Theatre* (New York: Longman Group, 1985), 210; Solberg, *Alternative Theatre in South Africa: Talks with Prime Movers since the 1970s*, 20–22; Orkin, *Drama and the South African State*, 209; Linn I. Dalrympie, "Explorations in Drama, Theatre and Education: A Critique of Theatre Studies in South Africa," PhD thesis, University of Zululand, 1987, 146.

15. Mikhail Bakhtin, *Problems of Dostoevsky's Poetics*, ed. and trans. Caryl Emerson (Minneapolis: University of Minnesota Press, 1984), 20.

16. Nikos Papastergiadis, "And: An Introduction into the Aesthetics of Deterritorialization," *Art and Cultural Difference: Hybrids and Clusters*, guest-edited by Nikos Papastergiadis (London: Academy Editions, 1995), 8; Ella Shohat and Robert Stam, "The Politics of Multiculturalism in a Postmodern Age," *Art and Cultural Difference: Hybrids and Clusters*, 12.

17. Bakhtin, *Problems of Dostoevsky's Poetics*.

18. Peggy Phelan, *Unmarked: The Politics of Performance* (London: Routledge Press, 1996), 2.

19. Martha Nussbaum, "The Professor of Parody," *The New Republic Online*, November 28, 2000, http://www.akad.se/Nussbaum.pdf.

20. Phelan, *Unmarked: The Politics of Performance*, 146; Diana Taylor, *The Archive and the Repertoire: Performing Cultural Memory in the Americas* (Durham, NC: Duke University Press, 2003), 9.

21. David Alcock, "Somatic Emphasis in South African Theatre: Intervention in the Body Politic," in *South African Theatre as/and Intervention*, eds. Marcia Blumberg and Dennis Walder (Atlanta: Rodopi, 1999), 51; Doreen Mazibuko, "Theatre: The Political Weapon of South Africa," in Davis and Fuchs, *Theatre and Change in South Africa*, 17; Mark Fleishmann, "Physical Images in the South African Theatre," in Davis and Fuchs, *Theatre and Change in South Africa*, 181.

22. Fleishmann, "Physical Images in the South African Theatre," 174.

23. Christopher Balme, "The Performance Aesthetics of Township Theatre: Frames and Codes," in Davis and Fuchs, *Theatre and Change in South Africa*, 77; Temple Hauptfleisch, "Citytalk, Theatretalk: Dialect, Dialogue, and Multilingual Theatre in South Africa," *English in Africa* 16, no. 1 (May 1989): 78; Loren Kruger, "Review: Staging South Africa," *Transition* 59 (1993): 122; Robert Mshengu Kavanagh, *Theatre and Cultural Struggle in South Africa* (London: Zed Books, 1985), 214.

24. Balme, "The Performance Aesthetics of Township Theatre: Frames and Codes," 77–78; Yvette Hutchison, "Barney Simon: Brokering Cultural Interven-

tions," *Contemporary Theatre Review* 13, no. 3 (2003): 4–15, 11; Homi Bhabha, *The Location of Culture* (New York: Routledge, 1994), 85–92.

25. Coplan, "Ideology and Tradition in South African Black Popular Theater," 153–54, 158.

26. Orkin, *Drama and the South African State*, 157.

27. Coplan, *In Township Tonight! South Africa's Black City Music and Theatre*, 221–22.

28. Orkin, *Drama and the South African State*, 159–60.

29. Richard Schechner, *Essays on Performance Theory, 1970–1976* (New York: Drama Book Specialists, 1977), 8; Coplan, "Ideology and Tradition in South African Black Popular Theater," 157.

30. Fleishmann, "Physical Images in the South African Theatre," 175, 182; Coplan, "Ideology and Tradition in South African Black Popular Theater," 155.

31. Balme, "The Performance Aesthetics of Township Theatre: Frames and Codes," 80; Percy Mtwa, with Eckhard Breitinger, "I've Been an Entertainer throughout My Life . . . : Interview with Percy Mtwa," *Matatu* 2, nos. 3/4 (1988): 170.

32. Ari Sitas, "The Workers' Theatre in Natal," in Davis and Fuchs, *Theatre and Change in South Africa*, 133.

33. Fleishmann, "Physical Images in the South African Theatre," 179; Moira Gatens, *Imaginary Bodies: Ethics, Power, and Corporeality* (London: Routledge, 1996), 120; Rosalyn Diprose, *Corporeal Generosity: On Giving with Nietzsche, Merleau-Ponty, and Levinas* (Albany: State University of New York Press, 2002), 172.

34. Fleishmann, "Physical Images in the South African Theatre," 177–79; Orkin, *Drama and the South African State*, 229.

35. Orkin, *Drama and the South African State*, 18.

36. Mary Schutzman and Jan Cohen-Cruz, Introduction, *A Boal Companion: Dialogues on Theatre and Cultural Politics*, eds. Jan Cohen-Cruz and Mary Schutzman (New York: Routledge, 2006), 8.

37. Keyan Tomaselli, "South African Theatre: Text and Context," *English in Africa* 8, no. 1 (1980): 45–73.

38. Jill Bennett, *Empathic Vision: Affect, Trauma, and Contemporary Art* (Stanford, CA: Stanford University Press, 2005), 12; Rita Felski, "The Doxa of Difference," *Signs* 23, no. 1 (Autumn 1997): 12.

39. Rancière, *The Politics of Aesthetics*, 12; Panagia, *The Political Life of Sensation*, 16; Theodor Adorno, *Aesthetic Theory* (Minneapolis: University of Minnesota Press, 1997), 187; Charles Altieri, *The Particulars of Rapture: An Aesthetics of the Affects* (Ithaca, NY: Cornell University Press, 2003), 14; bell hooks, *Art on My Mind: Visual Politics* (New York: The New Press, 1995).

40. Bennett, *Empathic Vision: Affect, Trauma, and Contemporary Art*, 10; Diana Taylor, "Border Watching," in *The Ends of Performance*, eds. Peggy Phelan and Jill

Lane (New York: New York University Press, 1998), 10; Doris Sommer, "Taking a Life: Hot Pursuit and Cold Rewards in a Mexican Testimonial Novel," *Signs* 20, no. 4, Special Issue: Postcolonial, Emergent, and Indigenous Feminisms (summer 1995): 925.

41. Avtar Brah, "The Scent of Memory: Strangers, Our Own and Others," in *Hybridity and Its Discontents: Politics, Science, Culture*, ed. Avtar Brah and Annie E. Coombes (London: Routledge, 2000), 273.

42. Coplan, *In Township Tonight! South Africa's Black City Music and Theatre*, 210; Coplan, "Ideology and Tradition in South African Black Popular Theater," 151, 174; Peterson, "Apartheid and the Political Imagination in Black South African Theatre," 237.

43. Coplan, *In Township Tonight! South Africa's Black City Music and Theatre*, 208; Coplan, "Ideology and Tradition in South African Black Popular Theater," 168–69; Balme, "The Performance Aesthetics of Township Theatre: Frames and Codes," 78; Wakashe, "'Pula': An Example of Black Protest Theatre in South Africa," 45; Zakes Mda, "Politics and the Theatre: Current Trends in South Africa," in Davis and Fuchs, *Theatre and Change in South Africa*, 216; Blumberg and Walder, Introduction, *South African Theatre as/and Intervention*, 6; Fleishmann, "Physical Images in the South African Theatre," 176.

44. Kani, qtd. in Coplan, *In Township Tonight! South Africa's Black City Music and Theatre*, 215; Coplan, "Ideology and Tradition in South African Black Popular Theater," 174; Solberg, *Alternative Theatre in South Africa: Talks with Prime Movers since the 1970s*, 14; Gibson Kente, in Solberg, *Alternative Theatre in South Africa: Talks with Prime Movers since the 1970s*, 84.

45. Orkin, *Drama and the South African State*, 155–58, 193; Solberg, *Alternative Theatre in South Africa: Talks with Prime Movers since the 1970s*, 16.

46. The Market Theatre was heavily critiqued by some for its funding by the Johannesburg City Council as well as white businessmen and professionals, and looked upon as a site defined by liberal condescension. Further, its continued ability to produce radical work has been scrutinized much as internationally touring theater at the time: as a tokenist strategy by the government to demonstrate its reasonableness and to create what Yvette Hutchison calls "a false illusion of a democratic environment, with healthy doses of freedom of expression." While these factors complicate any facile reading of the resistant effects of ostensibly resistant theater, they do not undermine the Market Theatre's oppositional character, as it remained one of the few spaces defined by an antiapartheid ethos. See Hutchison, "Barney Simon: Brokering Cultural Interventions," 8; Solberg, *Alternative Theatre in South Africa: Talks with Prime Movers since the 1970s*, 21; Mda, "Politics and the Theatre: Current Trends in South Africa," 205; Kruger, "Review: Staging South Africa," 125–26; and Orkin, *Drama and the South African State*, 185.

47. Coplan, "Ideology and Tradition in South African Black Popular Theater," 166; Orkin, *Drama and the South African State*, 159, 185.

48. Astrid von Kotze, "Workshop Plays as Worker Education," *South African Labour Bulletin* 9, no. 8 (1984): 93; Hilary Burns, "The Market Theatre of Johannesburg in the New South Africa," *New Theatre Quarterly* 18, no. 4 (November 2002): 362; Hutchison, "Barney Simon: Brokering Cultural Interventions," 5, 13; Malcolm Purkey, "*Tooth and Nail:* Rethinking Form for the South African Theatre," in Davis and Fuchs, *Theatre and Change in South Africa*, 228; Orkin, *Drama and the South African State*, 192–93; McLaren, "'The Many Individual Wills.' From *Crossroads* to *Survival.* The Work of Experimental Theatre Workshop 71," 29; Sitas, "The Workers' Theatre in Natal," 136.

49. Davis and Fuchs, "An Interest in Making Things: An Interview with William Kentridge," *Theatre and Change in South Africa*, 156.

50. Solberg, *Alternative Theatre in South Africa: Talks with Prime Movers since the 1970s*, 21; Hutchison, "Barney Simon: Brokering Cultural Interventions," 6.

51. Bhabha, *The Location of Culture*, 236; Solberg, *Alternative Theatre in South Africa: Talks with Prime Movers since the 1970s*, 20; Orkin, *Drama and the South African State*, 185, 252.

52. Balme, "The Performance Aesthetics of Township Theatre: Frames and Codes," 34. This, like the temperate political content and radical political effect of Gibson Kente's musicals, gestures to an important, though difficult, dimension of democratic resistance, the counterpart to which is exemplified in the previous discussion of radical theater on international tour and in experimental urban theaters. What appears noncontentious might prove incredibly resistant, perhaps due in part to this very temperance, while what appears resistant might in fact be harmless, or even counter-resistant, insofar as it can cathartically relieve productive discomfort among apologist audiences, siphon potentially mobilized energies, and demonstrate both the power and legitimacy of the prevailing powers it resists.

53. Hutchison, "Barney Simon: Brokering Cultural Interventions," 8; McLaren, "'The Many Individual Wills.' From *Crossroads* to *Survival.* The Work of Experimental Theatre Workshop 71," 30; Balme, "The Performance Aesthetics of Township Theatre: Frames and Codes," 30; Coplan, "Ideology and Tradition in South African Black Popular Theater," 165; Solberg, *Alternative Theatre in South Africa: Talks with Prime Movers since the 1970s*, 22.

54. Wakashe, "'Pula': An Example of Black Protest Theatre in South Africa," 43; Orkin, *Drama and the South African State*, 160, 204, 214; Solberg, *Alternative Theatre in South Africa: Talks with Prime Movers since the 1970s*, 22.

55. Kruger, "Review: Staging South Africa," 125, 127; Orkin, *Drama and the South African State*, 150.

56. Orkin, *Drama and the South African State*, 233; Coplan, "Ideology and Tradition in South African Black Popular Theater," 169.

57. Kruger, "Review: Staging South Africa," 129; Coplan, *In Township Tonight! South Africa's Black City Music and Theatre*, 209; Peterson, "Apartheid and the Political Imagination in Black South African Theatre," 237.

58. Alcock, "Somatic Emphasis in South African Theatre: Intervention in the Body Politic," 49–50; Solberg, *Alternative Theatre in South Africa: Talks with Prime Movers since the 1970s*, 22.

59. Wakashe, "'Pula': An Example of Black Protest Theatre in South Africa," 42.

60. Tomaselli, "South African Theatre: Text and Context," 51; Solberg, *Alternative Theatre in South Africa: Talks with Prime Movers since the 1970s*, 22; Mshengu (Robert Kavanagh), "South Africa: Where Mvelinqangi Still Limps," *Yale/Theatre* 8, no. 1 (1976): 45.

61. Mazibuko, "Theatre: The Political Weapon of South Africa," 221; Orkin, *Drama and the South African State*, 197.

62. Schechner, *Essays on Performance Theory, 1970–1976*, 76; Davis and Fuchs, Introduction, *Theatre and Change in South Africa*, 2.

Bibliography

Adorno, Theodor. *Aesthetic Theory.* Minneapolis: University of Minnesota Press, 1997.

Alcock, David. "Somatic Emphasis in South African Theatre: Intervention in the Body Politic." In *South African Theatre as/and Intervention*, edited by Marcia Blumberg and Dennis Walder, 49–58. Atlanta: Rodopi, 1999.

Altieri, Charles. *The Particulars of Rapture: An Aesthetics of the Affects.* Ithaca, NY: Cornell University Press, 2003.

Bakhtin, Mikhail. *Problems of Dostoevsky's Poetics.* Edited and translated by Caryl Emerson. Minneapolis: University of Minnesota Press, 1984.

Balme, Christopher. "The Performance Aesthetics of Township Theatre: Frames and Codes." In *Theatre and Change in South Africa*, edited by Geoffrey V. Davis and Anne Fuchs, 65–84. Netherlands: Overseas Publishers Association, 1996.

Benhabib, Seyla, ed. *Democracy and Difference: Contesting the Boundaries of the Political.* Princeton, NJ: Princeton University Press, 1996.

Bennett, Jill. *Empathic Vision: Affect, Trauma, and Contemporary Art.* Stanford, CA: Stanford University Press, 2005.

Bhabha, Homi. *The Location of Culture.* New York: Routledge, 1994.

Blumberg, Marcia, and Dennis Walder, eds. *South African Theatre as/and Intervention.* Atlanta: Rodopi, 1999.

———. Introduction. In *South African Theatre as/and Intervention*, edited by Marcia Blumberg and Dennis Walder, 1–22. Atlanta: Rodopi, 1999.

Brah, Avtar. "The Scent of Memory: Strangers, Our Own and Others." In *Hybridity and Its Discontents: Politics, Science, Culture*, edited by Avtar Brah and Annie E. Coombes, 272–90. London: Routledge, 2000.

Burns, Hilary. "The Market Theatre of Johannesburg in the New South Africa." *New Theatre Quarterly* 18, no. 4 (November 2002): 359–74.

Cohen-Cruz, Jan, and Mary Schutzman, eds. *A Boal Companion: Dialogues on Theatre and Cultural Politics.* New York: Routledge, 2006.

Coles, Romand. *Rethinking Generosity: Critical Theory and the Politics of Caritas.* Ithaca, NY: Cornell University Press, 1997.

Coplan, David B. *In Township Tonight! South Africa's Black City Music and Theatre.* New York: Longman Group, 1985.

———. "Ideology and Tradition in South African Black Popular Theater." *The Journal of American Folklore* 99, no. 392 (April/June 1986): 151–76.

Dalrympie, Linn I. "Explorations in Drama, Theatre and Education: A Critique of Theatre Studies in South Africa. PhD thesis, University of Zululand, 1987.

Davis, Geoffrey V., and Anne Fuchs, eds. *Theatre and Change in South Africa.* Netherlands: Overseas Publishers Association, 1996.

———. Introduction. In *Theatre and Change in South Africa,* edited by Geoffrey V. Davis and Anne Fuchs, 1–12. Netherlands: Overseas Publishers Association, 1996.

———. "An Interest in Making Things: An Interview with William Kentridge." In Davis and Fuchs, *Theatre and Change in South Africa,* 140–54.

Diprose, Rosalyn. *Corporeal Generosity: On Giving with Nietzsche, Merleau-Ponty, and Levinas.* Albany: State University of New York Press, 2002.

Felski, Rita. "The Doxa of Difference." *Signs* 23, no. 1 (Autumn 1997): 1–21.

Fleishmann, Mark. "Physical Images in the South African Theatre." In Davis and Fuchs, *Theatre and Change in South Africa,* 173–82.

Gatens, Moira. *Imaginary Bodies: Ethics, Power, and Corporeality.* London: Routledge, 1996.

Hauptfleisch, Temple. "Citytalk, Theatretalk: Dialect, Dialogue, and Multilingual Theatre in South Africa." *English in Africa* 16, no. 1 (May 1989): 71–92.

Honig, Bonnie. "Difference, Dilemmas and the Politics of Home." In Benhabib, *Democracy and Difference,* 257–77.

hooks, bell. *Art on My Mind: Visual Politics.* New York: The New Press, 1995.

Horn, Peter. "What Is Tribal Dress? The *Imbongi* and the People's Poet." In Davis and Fuchs, *Theatre and Change in South Africa,* 115–31.

Hutchison, Yvette. "Barney Simon: Brokering Cultural Interventions." *Contemporary Theatre Review* 13, no. 3 (2003): 4–15.

Kavanagh, Robert Mshengu. *South African People's Plays.* London: Heinemann, 1981.

———. *Theatre and Cultural Struggle in South Africa.* London: Zed Books, 1985.

Kruger, Loren. "Review: Staging South Africa." *Transition* 59 (1993): 120–29.

Larlham, Peter. "Theatre in Transition: The Cultural Struggle in South Africa." *TDR* 35, no. 1 (Spring 1991): 200–11.

Le Fort, Claude. *Democracy and Political Theory.* Translated by David Macey. Minneapolis: University of Minnesota Press, 1988.

Mazibuko, Doreen. "Theatre: The Political Weapon of South Africa." In Davis and Fuchs, *Theatre and Change in South Africa,* 219–24.

McLaren, Robert. "'The Many Individual Wills.' From *Crossroads* to *Survival.* The Work of Experimental Theatre Workshop 71." In Davis and Fuchs, *Theatre and Change in South Africa,* 25–48.

Mda, Zakes. "Politics and the Theatre: Current Trends in South Africa." In Davis and Fuchs, *Theatre and Change in South Africa,* 193–218.

Mohanty, Chandra, and Biddy Martin. "What's Home Got to Do with It?" In *Feminism Without Borders: Decolonizing Theory, Practicing Solidarity,* 85–105. Durham, NC: Duke University Press, 2003.

Mouffe, Chantal. "Democracy, Power, and the 'Political.'" In Benhabib, *Democracy and Difference,* 245–56.

Mshengu (Robert Kavanagh). "South Africa: Where Mvelinqangi Still Limps." *Yale/Theatre* 8, no. 1 (1976): 38–48.

Mtwa, Percy, with Eckhard Breitinger. "I've Been an Entertainer throughout My Life . . . : Interview with Percy Mtwa." *Matatu* 2, nos. 3/4 (1988): 160–75.

Naidoo, Muthal. *The Search for a Cultural Identity: A Personal Odyssey,* Indic Theatre Monograph Series No. 1. Durban: Asoka Theatre Publications, 1993.

Nussbaum, Martha. "The Professor of Parody." *The New Republic Online,* November, 28, 2000. http://www.akad.se/Nussbaum.pdf.

Orkin, Martin. *Drama and the South African State.* Manchester, UK: Manchester University Press, 1991.

———. "Whose Popular Theatre and Performance?" In Davis and Fuchs, *Theatre and Change in South Africa,* 49–64.

Panagia, Davide. *The Political Life of Sensation.* Durham, NC: Duke University Press, 2009.

Papastergiadis, Nikos, ed. *Art and Cultural Difference: Hybrids and Clusters.* London: Academy Editions, 1995.

———. "And: An Introduction into the Aesthetics of Deterritorialization." In Papastergiadis, *Art and Cultural Difference,* 7–8.

Peterson, Bhekizizwe. "Apartheid and the Political Imagination in Black South African Theatre." *Journal of Southern African Studies* 16, no. 2 Special Issue: Performance and Popular Culture (June 1990): 229–45.

Phelan, Peggy *Unmarked: The Politics of Performance.* London and New York: Routledge Press, 1996.

Purkey, Malcolm. "*Tooth and Nail:* Rethinking Form for the South African Theatre." In Davis and Fuchs, *Theatre and Change in South Africa,* 155–72.

Rancière, Jacques. *The Politics of Aesthetics.* Translated by Gabriel Rockhill. New York and London: Continuum, 2004.

Schechner, Richard. *Essays on Performance Theory, 1970–1976.* New York: Drama Book Specialists, 1977.

Schutzman, Mary, and Jan Cohen-Cruz. Introduction. In *A Boal Companion: Dialogues on Theatre and Cultural Politics*, eds. Jan Cohen-Cruz and Mary Schutzman. New York: Routledge, 2006.

Shohat, Ella, and Robert Stam. "The Politics of Multiculturalism in a Postmodern Age." In Papastergiadis, *Art and Cultural Difference*, 10–16.

Solberg, Rolf. *Alternative Theatre in South Africa: Talks with Prime Movers since the 1970s.* Pietermaritzburg, South Africa: Hadeda Books, 1999.

Sommer, Doris. "Taking a Life: Hot Pursuit and Cold Rewards in a Mexican Testimonial Novel." *Signs* 20, no. 4 Special Issue: Postcolonial, Emergent, and Indigenous Feminisms (Summer 1995): 913–40.

Taylor, Diana. "Border Watching." In *The Ends of Performance*, eds. Peggy Phelan and Jill Lane, 178–85. New York: New York University Press, 1998.

———. *The Archive and the Repertoire: Performing Cultural Memory in the Americas.* Durham, NC: Duke University Press, 2003.

Tomaselli, Keyan. "South African Theatre: Text and Context." *English in Africa* 8, no. 1 (1980): 45–73.

van Rooyen, J. C. W. *Censorship in South Africa.* Cape Town, South Africa: Juta, 1987.

von Kotze, Astrid. "Workshop Plays as Worker Education." *South African Labour Bulletin* 9, no. 8 (1984): 92–111.

Wakashe, Philemon. "'Pula': An Example of Black Protest Theatre in South Africa." *The Drama Review: TDR* 30, no. 4 (Winter 1986): 36–47.

Young, Iris Marion. *Inclusion and Democracy.* Oxford, UK: Oxford University Press, 2000.

Part VII

Festival and Spectacle

Chapter 12

Art in the House

Cultural Democracy in a Neighborhood

Bruce Baum

Art should be part of the creative process of changing the world.

—Melanie Joseph, artistic director of the Foundry Theater,
quoted in Felicia R. Lee, "Cut, Baste, Stitch, Sing!"

The moment of true volition [in artistic creation] . . . is mediated through nothing other than the form of the work itself, whose crystallization becomes an analogy of that other condition which should be. As eminently constructed and produced objects, works of art, including literary ones, point to a practice from which they abstain: the creation of a just life.

—Theodor W. Adorno, "Commitment"

Melanie Joseph's comment summarizes one influential view of the relationship between art and politics—the activist's view that in the twentieth century was closely associated with the German playwright Bertolt Brecht, among others.[1] As I began this essay, Joseph was involved in a theater production in Brooklyn, New York, that was in the Brechtian

Thanks to Nancy Love, Mark Mattern, and Minelle Mahtani for helpful comments on earlier versions of this chapter.

vein: *Furee in Pins & Needles*.[2] Comprised of sketches and songs, it was a revival of the 1930s show *Pins and Needles*, which was created to benefit the International Ladies' Garment Workers' Union—a powerful union with 250,000 workers in 1936. The original show became a Broadway hit.[3] The revival was a joint project of Joseph's "Obie-winning Foundry Theater and Families United for Racial and Economic Equality (Furee), which since 2001 has worked to increase access to housing, jobs and services for low-income families."[4]

Melanie Joseph's vision of art as world-changing is politically appealing, although such "committed art" often risks failure *as art*. In its efforts to instruct people about worldly wrongs or rally people behind a cause, committed art can be overly preachy—more like pamphleteering than art. As Theodor Adorno says with reference to Brecht's tendency to be didactic in his plays,

> Bad politics becomes bad art, and vice versa. But the less the more telling they become in their own right; and the less they need a surplus of meaning beyond what they are. . . . The gravest charge against commitment is that even right intentions go wrong when they are noticed, and still more so, when they try to conceal themselves.[5]

While Adorno criticizes didacticism in committed art, he does not reject the idea of committed art outright. Thus, discussing Jean-Paul Sartre's ideas of "engaged" art, Adorno says that committed art "in the proper sense is not intended to generate ameliorative measures, legislative acts or practical institutions—like earlier propagandistic plays against syphilis, duels, abortion laws or borstals—but to work at the level of fundamental attitudes."[6] Adorno emphasizes the importance of *form* rather than *content* in committed art "in the proper sense": "It is not the office of art to spotlight alternatives, *but to resist by its form alone the course of the world*, which permanently puts a pistol to men's heads. In fact, as soon as committed works of art do instigate decisions at their own level, the decisions themselves become interchangeable."[7]

In what follows I take my lead from Adorno regarding the relative significance of form over content in committed art.[8] Yet I follow Adorno in this regard, as I will explain shortly, without adopting all aspects of his aesthetic theory. I am going to consider the political promise for "doing democracy" in a performance art event that is decidedly nondidactic in its politics: the annual (since 2003) In the House Festival in Vancouver,

British Columbia.[9] On the surface, the In the House Festival is largely nonpartisan, even apolitical, in much (if not most) of its *content*. I contend, however, that it is edifying and democratizing in its *form*. I focus my discussion on the recent 2011 (eighth) incarnation of the festival, which was typical, in June 2011.[10]

One of the festival's distinguishing features is that it is set in people's houses and backyards in a Vancouver neighborhood, and it opens people's houses to the public.[11] Another distinguishing feature is that the festival, in contrast to music and theater festivals, includes a variety of performance art genres—dance, cabaret, spoken word, circus acts, magicians, children's shows, backyard film screenings, and several types of music (for example, singer-songwriters, jazz, gospel and blues, classical, alt rock, country/folk rock, and hip hop). While parts of the In the House Festival might be considered in their own right, I will consider its parts in relation to the whole. For my purposes, although a few of the performances were expressly political in their content, as a politically consequential work of art, the whole of the festival is greater—more innovative in its character and spirit—than its parts.

As a whole, In the House is countercultural (or counterhegemonic, in Antonio Gramsci's sense) with respect to the experience of performance art that it facilitates: it showcases artistic performances that are not chiefly commercial (and in some cases not commercially viable) in the intimacy of the backyards and living rooms of houses in an urban residential neighborhood. It provides alternative venues for performing artists in a city that, like many, has relatively few small and medium size venues given the number of performers. Likewise, it provides an alternative to how most people typically produce, distribute, and consume (or experience) artistic performance in contemporary capitalist societies, filtered through the major media of the capitalist "culture industries."[12] That is, it gives artists and audiences an alternative to how they usually encounter each other: through TV, radio, and Hollywood films; corporate production and distribution of music; access to music through YouTube and other major internet sites; and "live" concerts in large auditoriums, arenas, and stadiums. As the originator of In the House, Daniel Maté says, the basic idea has been to join "community relatedness and delightful self-expression" such that people might enjoy "art and each other in revelatory new ways."[13]

Regarding the politics of the In the House Festival, the festival's current artistic director and guiding spirit, Myriam Steinberg, says that she does not choose performers with a definite political agenda in mind. She seeks to showcase artists with a wide range of styles, talents, and voices, with the caveat that she will exclude performers whose works are expressly racist or misogynist. Steinberg says that insofar as the festival manifests an overarching politics, it is a "politics of generosity."[14] This politics is manifest in the festival's neighborliness, diversity, and inclusiveness.[15] Bringing performing arts to private living rooms and backyards in a Vancouver neighborhood, the festival embodies a buoyant communitarian sensibility; its communitarianism is characterized by mutuality among diverse people who share experiences of art in shared spaces rather than by an integral community with a shared conception of the good life.

The idea of a "politics of generosity" captures well the ethos of In the House, the festival's welcoming, democratic spirit in its effort to support performing arts while breaking down barriers between performers and audiences, professionals and amateurs. Additionally, I suggest that it also manifests a postmodern version of medieval European carnival. At the same time, taken as a whole, In the House through its carnivalesque character conveys something akin to Adorno's notion of "autonomous art"—that is, artistic work that offers intimations of a humane world "beyond the mutilating sway of exchange, profit and false needs."[16]

The Russian literary critic Mikhail Bakhtin describes carnival as a "certain pattern of play" during a discreet time period that is neither "a purely artistic form nor a spectacle. . . . It belongs to the borderline between art and life."[17] The imaginative and oppositional character of carnival responds to the rigid hierarchies of the medieval church, the feudal class and political structure, and "official" feasts that were "a consecration of inequality."[18] Against this backdrop, the medieval carnival marked a "temporary suspension, both ideal and real, of hierarchical rank." In carnival, "all were considered equal," Bakhtin says, and "the new mode of man's relation to man is elaborated."[19]

Certainly, care is due in an effort to apply ideas from Adorno and Bakhtin to an idiosyncratic contemporary event like the In the House Festival. My appeal to Adorno might seem especially puzzling given that he excluded "all varieties of applied art and mass art" from his category of autonomous art.[20] Reading Adorno against the grain of his own particular aesthetic judgments, my contention is twofold: his notions of culture industry and autonomous art, once slightly revised, continue to illuminate the difficulties of and possibilities for emancipatory or edifying art; and these concepts shed light on the counterhegemonic and emancipatory possibilities of the In the House Festival. For present purposes, the key limitation of Adorno's aesthetics, as Lorenzo Simpson elaborates, is hermeneutical—his failure to understand popular cultural forms, such as jazz, to grasp what they offer in their own terms.[21] To be fair to Adorno, this limitation has its roots in an overriding theme of Adornian aesthetics that I leave aside here: his interest, writing "after Auschwitz," in the possibilities for art to (in Russell Perkins' words) "bear witness to violence . . . [that] has been rendered inscrutable."[22]

With respect to Bakhtin's account of medieval carnival, Michael Holquist explains, "Bakhtin leaves no doubt that the give-and-take between the medieval church/state nexus on the one hand and the carnival on the other was a very real power struggle. The state had its temporal and spatial borders as did carnival."[23] The world of contemporary democratic capitalist culture and politics is far removed from that of the medieval European world. This is why I call In the House a postmodern version of carnival. There are real power struggles in the contemporary world in which In the House is staged, but these are more fragmentary and contradictory than the rigid, almost Manichean, feudal power struggle. Furthermore, the subversive or carnivalesque character of In the House is more fragmentary and ambiguous than the oppositional character of the medieval carnival. Still, In the House creatively recaptures some key aspects of carnival: folksiness, subversive play, immediacy, egalitarianism. In actualizing Steinberg's sense of a "politics of generosity," In the House intimates a "new mode" of people's relationships to each other through performance art that is both an artistic expression of and cultural resource for "doing democracy" more deeply and inclusively.

In the next section, I situate the In the House Festival within current Vancouver civic life and cultural politics. I then discuss the overall character of the festival along with a few characteristic performances. Finally, borrowing insights from Bakhtin and Adorno, I discuss In the House's way of "doing democracy" through its combination of carnivalesque subversiveness and a prefigurative cultural politics of generosity.

Context and Character

Whereas medieval carnival took place in the context of feudal hierarchies and official festivities, the In the House Festival takes place in a radically different context. Two features of this context are especially salient: the political economic and cultural (artistic performance) context of Vancouver, British Columbia, Canada; and the latest permutations of the encompassing "democratic" capitalist culture industries in North America. I will discuss each of these elements briefly.

Regarding local public culture, it is noteworthy that Vancouver, with support from local businesses, was the host city for the 2010 Winter Olympics—part of Vancouver's bid for recognition as a "world class" city.[24] Thousands of Vancouverites cheered the Olympics and enjoyed official Olympic festivities. These included the Cultural Olympiad 2010, with commissioned projects, such as Robert Lepage's *The Blue Dragon/Le Dragon Bleu*, a version of Joni Mitchell's ballet *The Fiddle and The Drum*, cutting-edge music, visual art exhibitions, interactive art and animation, and concerts featuring popular performers like Steve Earle and Wilco.[25]

The Vancouver Olympics also drew vigorous protests concerning the unjust, corporate-oriented allocation of public resources in a city that— like other big cities in North America—is marked by sharp inequalities of income, wealth, and well-being. As Jules Boykoff reports in the *New Left Review*, anti-Olympic activists in Vancouver "produced a spirited critique: taxpayer money was being squandered on a two-and-a-half week sports party rather than going to indispensable social services; civil liberties were being threatened by a massively militarized police force; the Olympics were taking place on unceded aboriginal (Coast Salish) land."[26] Local groups mobilized against the games included No One Is Illegal, the Anti-Poverty Committee, Streams of Justice, the Power of Women Group, No 2010 Olympics on Stolen Native Land, Van.Act!, and Native Youth Movement. These groups brought together "indigenous dissidents, anti-poverty campaigners, environmentalists, anarchists, civil libertarians and numerous combinations thereof."[27] Although the International Olympic Committee (IOC) chose to hold the Winter Games on unceded Coast Salish territory, First Nations groups lined up both in support of and in opposition to the Vancouver Olympics.[28] The events went off with a veneer of public unity under the steady gaze of heavy surveillance—with close to one thousand closed-circuit TV cameras in greater Vancouver— and active efforts to keep homeless people off the streets and out of sight in the poor Downtown Eastside neighborhood and elsewhere.[29]

The protests included an activist art component. Boykoff notes that a "counter-space" to the official Olympic cultural activities

> was forged at the artist-run VIVO Media Arts Centre, whose "Safe Assembly Project" featured "Afternoon School" workshops, screenings, art productions and a pirate-radio poetry project. A vital contribution was the "Evening News" forum . . . which occurred every other night for the duration of the Games. At Evening News events, video activists showed raw protest

footage, practising artists responded to the Olympics industry and its effects, and panels of activists and scholars debated particular themes.[30]

A pirate-radio program, *Short-Range Poetic Device*, ran shows periodically during the Olympics. *Poetic Device* "featured readings and discussions with local poet-activists."[31] Activists in the Vancouver Media Co-op news also worked to circulate information and political art concerning the Olympics that the corporate media considered "unfit to print."[32]

The Vancouver Olympics was expensive. The cost "was originally estimated at $1 billion; by the month before the Games, costs had ballooned to $6 billion, and post-Olympics estimates soared into the $8–10 billion range."[33] The City of Vancouver followed a common public-private partnership model to finance the event, with the support of Vancouver mayor Gregor Robertson, of the center-left Vision Vancouver municipal party. (Robertson is also a cofounder of the Happy Planet Juice Company.)[34]

While the Vancouver Olympics was supported with substantial public funding, other social needs like health care and education faced funding cuts. In 2010, after the Olympics, the "Vancouver School Board announced an $18 million funding shortfall for the 2010–11 school year, which translated into reduced music programmes and hundreds of Vancouver teachers receiving pink slips."[35] Funding for BC Arts Council grants was cut 50 percent from the 2008–09 level.[36] This has had a significant impact on the work of small community organizations such as Vancouver's Public Dreams Society and the In the House Festival.[37] For 2011, In the House absorbed an overall funding cut of $11,000 from the previous year; the BC Arts Council cut to zero its funding for In the House, and Heritage Canada substantially reduced its financial support for the festival. The City of Vancouver remains the festival's biggest funding source.[38]

Given the distinguishing "in the house" (or in the backyard) character of In the House, it is notable that Vancouver is Canada's most expensive city for housing, and it is one of the most expensive cities in North America. According to the statistics released in January 2011, by the Real Estate Board of Greater Vancouver, the benchmark price for all three categories of housing in Vancouver—detached, attached, and apartments—had by then reached $585,068 (in Canadian dollars).[39] According to a citywide estimate, as of June 2011, the "average" listing for a four-bedroom, two-full-bathroom home in Vancouver was $1,546,475.[40] Housing prices are lower (but hardly inexpensive) in Vancouver's Eastside, the home of In the House; and by North American standards, festival houses are relatively modest "middle-class" or upper-middle-class dwellings.

Relatedly, one of the major fissures in current Vancouver politics concerns zoning and development. Developers and their political allies are on one side, winning most of the battles; on the other side, community groups, activists, and some members of the Coalition of Progressive Electors (COPE) have worked to prioritize neighborhood concerns, sustainable development, and affordable "social housing."[41] The city's poor, drug-riddled Downtown Eastside neighborhood is being squeezed by gentrification.

Turning to the wider political economy of cultural production and distribution, Fredric Jameson locates recent cultural production and consumption in relation to "the emergence in full-blown and definitive form of that ultimate transformation of late monopoly capitalism variously known as the *société de consummation* or as post-industrial society."[42] Jameson reconsiders Theodor Adorno's and Max Horkheimer's idea that the "cultural industry" in contemporary capitalism constitutes a "'total system,' which expressed [their] sense of the increasingly closed organization of the world into a seamless web of media technology, multinational corporations, and international bureaucratic control."[43] Jameson notes problems with this totalizing theory, which seems to deny the possibility of any meaningful cultural and political resistance to dominant modes of politics and culture. Yet he says, aptly, that

> we may at least agree with Adorno that in the cultural realm, the all-pervasiveness of the system, with its "culture" or . . . its "consciousness-industry," makes for an unpropitious climate for any of the older, simpler forms of oppositional art. . . . The system has a power to co-opt and to defuse even the most potentially dangerous forms of political art by transforming them into cultural commodities.[44]

Jameson wrote this in the 1970s. Since then continuing concentration of media conglomerates (with substantial control of TV, radio, movies, music distribution, and book, newspaper, and magazine publishing) has been joined by the development of the internet as a major—and similarly corporate capitalist mediated—vehicle of cultural distribution and consumption. While the internet significantly has altered the ways in which people produce, distribute, encounter, and consume cultural objects—such as books, newspapers, and music—it is doubtful that this has undermined Jameson's basic assessment of the pervasive commodification of art and culture. For instance, almost anyone with computer access and other rudimentary technologies can post something on YouTube or on Facebook; but these are also major corporations, and few works of art that are put out to the world in this manner will "go viral" and reach large audiences.[45]

Moreover, Canada boasts many notable artists (for example, musicians Oscar Peterson, Joni Mitchell, Neil Young, the Guess Who, Leonard Cohen, Bruce Cockburn, Jane Siberry, Sarah McLachlan, Alanis Morissette, Barenaked Ladies, and Drake, among others), a distinctive sports culture (for example, Canadian Broadcasting Corporation [CBC] TV's *Hockey Night in Canada*), and other independent cultural outlets (for example, CBC radio and the Toronto-based *Globe and Mail* newspaper). Yet Canadian popular culture (especially in Canada outside of Quebec) is significantly shaped by U.S. culture industry imports, such as pop music, movies, and TV.

The In the House Festival is, in part, a response to the limitations of how performing arts circulate through North American culture industries. It is a bare-bones nonprofit operation that survives on public funding, ticket and merchandise sales, committed volunteers, and a dedicated artistic director, Steinberg, who works year-round on a meager income.[46] All of the performers are paid, but the venues (living and dining rooms; backyards) are loaned to the festival by homeowners; and In the House also relies partly on loaned equipment, such as speakers. In recent years, in addition to the festival, the projects of In the House have included a monthly performance series from August through May (since 2005) and a haunted house for Halloween (since 2009). The monthly performance series may be cut due to the recent funding cuts.[47]

When he started In the House in 2003, Daniel Maté aimed to introduce something novel to the Vancouver art scene. He wanted to accomplish two things with the festival: "(1) to bring together and cross-pollinate various artistic disciplines in one festival; (2) to give people a whole new experience of making, sharing and enjoying the arts, outside of their normal venues and 'scenes' and comfort zones."[48] Bringing performing arts directly into homes in a neighborhood, he says, "struck me as the perfect way to accomplish these aims."[49] Building on these issues, In the House outlines its three-part "mandate" on its website:

1) Increase audience awareness of the immense variety and talent of performers in Vancouver through culturally and stylistically varied acts.

2) Create strong communities by getting home owners to open their homes as venue hosts and bringing together people from both the neighborhood and the rest of the city in the intimate setting of the home.

3) Bring recognition and exposure to artists based in the Lower Mainland in a non-traditional way.[50]

The Lower Mainland, the region surrounding Vancouver, is home to a considerable number of performance artists. This makes In the House viable. Yet in this regard the Vancouver region is probably not much different from other metropolitan areas of comparable size in North America. Therefore, In the House probably could be replicated in many other cities.[51]

Theory and Event

The In the House Festival operates, then, amid ongoing contestation in Vancouver over zoning, sustainable development, and affordable housing, and in juxtaposition to deepening corporate capitalist commodification of civic cultural life.[52] As a grassroots project of cultural democracy, In the House enacts carnivalesque subversion and a prefigurative politics of generosity in the way that its particular performance elements fit within the festival as a whole. With respect to the festival's mode of "doing democracy," its carnivalesque and prefigurative features are integrally related.

For 2011, the In the House Festival was comprised of ten different performance slots or sets, with two different performances running concurrently in most of the time slots for a total of nineteen performances: Friday night, and Saturday and Sunday, afternoons and evenings.[53] Each performance is about one hour and forty-five minutes with a few individual or group performers, or acts, in each performance slot. For instance, a dance performance might include three or four groups of dancers; a music show might include three or four solo performers or musical groups.

The performances that I saw over the weekend varied both in genre and quality, reflecting the overall character of the festival.

Friday

"The World in Music" (7 p.m.): with the Raha Ensemble, a three-person, Vancouver-based Persian music group; Kurai and Friends, featuring Zimbabwe-born mbira (thumb piano) player Kurai Blessing, who now lives in Vancouver, and two other local musicians; and Shine, an Australian didgeridoo player. "Cabaret So Mignon" (9 p.m.): including Little Woo, a multidisciplinary artist who performed a fairly tale with shadow puppets; Travis Bernhardt, a local magician who was quite funny; Lalu, dancer/actor/clown Nayana Filkow in an unsettling contact dance-clown performance; Luciterra, featuring two women from the four-woman "fusion belly dance company"; and the Hastings, a musical group that blends jazz, soul, and hip hop.

Saturday

"Worlds of Dance" (2 p.m.): with a Vancouver-based Cuban Salsa group; a small modern dance group; a blues dancing duo; four members of the stand-out break dancing group, the Now or Never Crew; and local Flamenco group, Flamenco Rosario. "Sirens of Song" (4 p.m.): with singer-song writers Yvette Narlock, Kate Reid, and Jess Hill. "Thundering Word" (7 p.m.): a spoken-word session with five writer/storytellers. "Backyard Films" (9 p.m.): two short films and a longer documentary, "Scared Sacred," in which the filmmaker, Velcrow Ripper, traces his travels looking for hope in several places in the world that have experienced tragedy (Afghanistan, Bhopal, post-9/11 New York, Bosnia, Hiroshima, Israel, and Palestine).

Sunday

"Mundo Latino" (2 p.m.): three groups, featuring Latin jazz and Salsa, dance, and Spanish guitar, gypsy violin, and Afro Latin percussion. "Banjo Boogies" (4 p.m.): three groups, each of which featured an occasional banjo accompaniment (a folk-country rock group, a string band, and a New Orleans-style jazz band). "Spring Evening Doom Lounge—A Celebration of Destruction and Renewal" (7 p.m.): a set of percussive soundscapes produced collectively by six musicians who have their own individual projects (King Ore, olo J. Milkman, David Gowman, Sacha Levin, Curtis Mathewson, and the Mythical Man). Grand Finale: "Blues Circus" (9:30 p.m.). Another nine shows were performed concurrently with the shows I attended, including a children's show, with a puppeteer and a storyteller-saxophonist duo.

A few performers and performances exemplified the overall spirit of the In the House Festival. The "World in Music" set on Friday highlighted the multicultural aspects of Vancouver. The Raha Ensemble had a distinctive Persian instrumental sound and featured a song of love with words by Rumi, the thirteenth-century Persian-Muslim poet, jurist, and theologian. During the performance of Kurai and Friends, Kurai Blessing explained that his instrument, the mbira (with keys set inside a calabash, or gourd), has been used in Zimbabwean traditional ceremonies. He told the audience that the use of the mbira was made "uncool," and was disrespected and driven underground, due to antipagan sentiments in the era of white Christian rule in British colonial Rhodesia. Then Shine, a white Australian, pointedly acknowledged the First Nations peoples of Australia and Canada as he explained how to play the didgeridoo; he also discussed how for aboriginal people of Australia singing has been a way to honor nature and engage its rhythms.

On one level, the earnestness of these performances yielded a domesticated version of multiculturalism, like the array of "ethnic" restaurants on nearby Commercial Drive; and from an Adornian aesthetic perspective the accompanying stories arguably were too literal to bear witness adequately to the colonialist violence that they recounted.[54] Yet the performance set introduced the audience (about thirty-five people in a modest backyard) to varied musical forms and histories, and it built a sense of peaceful communion, with varied, openhearted rhythms.

The "Sirens of Song" music session included two of the most expressly political performances at this year's festival. Yvette Narlock and Kate Reid are both lesbian and feminist-identified singer-songwriters who explore political dimensions of personal life in distinct folk styles. Narlock, who has retreated from the music recording business to work full time with drug-addicted and sexually exploited youth, has an intensely expressive and graceful style.[55] Her songs range from "If Your Man Doesn't Man," a slyly subversive, quasi-love song about erotic longing for a married female friend, to "One Drop," a stirring song about moments or "drops" of hope that regularly offer us glimpses into the possibility of a more just world. In the tradition of the best artful political pop rock music, in "One Drop" Narlock ranges melodically across terrains of children, song, moral and political apathy, and the connections (and disconnections) between human beings and nonhuman nature.[56]

Reid, who has interviewed LGBTQ families in Canada and in the United States and written songs based on their stories, is more whimsical. Her 2011 compact disc is titled *Doing It for the Chicks*.[57] Reid's work has roots in, among other things, the North American tradition of "talking blues," or talking folk songs. One of her humorous songs is "Co-op Girlz," which tells about (in her words) trying to "pick up chicks" at the Kootenay Co-op Health Food Store in Nelson, BC, while passing through the produce, deli, and herbal supplement sections.[58]

The "Thundering Word" set, on Saturday night, was one of the performances that joined amateur (or hobbyist) artists with more professional artists. In this case, a successful younger professional performer, C. R. Avery, joined with several older writer-performers—Rosemary Nowicki, Mary Gavan, Bryant Ross, and host Bill McNamara. They performed in a rotation. Nowicki read a series of reflective poems, including one about her mother's death. She poignantly expressed her fear of losing her mother and of witnessing her mother's own impending death. Gavin, a registered yoga teacher, told a couple of stories, one of which was "storytelling yoga"; it involved the audience doing "yoga in a chair"—with Gavin punctuating her story with changing yoga directions. Ross, a fireman by profession, is a particularly vivid storyteller. He told a moving parable about boxing, respect, and mortality. It concerned his father, who managed a boxing ring for forty-two years, taught Ross to box (at age five), and insisted that boxing was fundamentally about respect, expressed chiefly through each boxer respecting his or her opponent. His boxing story centered on his father's last two rounds of boxing, while ill with cancer at age sixty-five. His two rounds ended (at least so the story goes) with him knocking out an arrogant young (twenty-five-year-old) boxer who refused to show him (the father) due respect. Like the Sirens of Song, these writers all communicated a spirit of generosity.

Avery, the professional, plays banjo, piano, harmonica, and does beatboxing, which involves using one's mouth for percussive beats and rhythms. His performance style carries echoes of Bob Dylan, Jack Kerouac, Bruce Springsteen, Tom Waits, and hip hop. He began with a beatbox version of Dylan's song "Maggie's Farm." He followed this with a spoken-word piece and then a harmonica-accompanied, solo version of the Beatles song "Blackbird."

Of the performances I attended, the "Spring Evening Doom Lounge" was the most avant-garde. For an hour and a half the musicians developed a contemplative soundscape that gathered the audience into a communal experience of sound and energy. One of their pieces included an audience-participation element: audience members were asked to repeat loud vowel sounds. We participated with gusto, at least for a short while, and some of these sounds were recorded and later played back to us as an integral part of the piece. The Doom Lounge group used lots of percussion and several other instruments, including apparently homemade wind instruments. Another piece was more distinctly melodic, with a striking vocal performance; its lyrics, which beckoned a new day and "new dreams," might sound hokey out of context but had a galvanizing effect *in context*.

The finale, which this year had a "Blues Circus" theme, was especially festive and popular. More than one hundred people filled two adjoining backyards. The theme was expressed in a storyline that was set in the late nineteenth century and adopted from the fable of how the blues musician Robert Johnson sold his soul to the devil at the crossroad to become a blues sensation. The story was lowbrow, but its purpose was to frame a set of folk-blues (guitar and drum) accompanied performances in juggling, crystal ball contact juggling, clowning, and hoop performance.[59]

In addition to this year's performances, two acts from the evening cabaret performance at last year's In the House Festival (June 2010) memorably embodied a carnivalesque spirit. Diana David, a dancer, performed an expressive solo dance, with mime and shadow puppet elements, to a recorded monologue about a young man who bargained with his parents for permission to attend a Michael Jackson concert in the early 1980s. Part of David's performance involved mimicking Jackson's dance moves. Set alongside the storytelling and puppetry, David's performance indicated the expressive possibilities of modern dance: the storytelling, dance, and puppetry worked together to convey both the combination of excitement and angst that mark adolescent longings in North America and the specific cultural-historical moment when Michael Jackson was the "king of pop." A second act, the Wet Spots, was a married cabaret duo (Cass King and John Woods) that travels widely to perform what they aptly call "sophisticated sex comedy."[60] With Woods playing guitar, they perform funny songs about oral sex and other modes of sexual pleasuring. King explains on their website, "The aim of our show is to entertain people with the notion that sexual expression is healthy and beautiful . . . and funny."[61] Their performance style, which plays off of their intimacy, counteracts common, unhealthy tendencies in North America either to avoid frank discussions of sex or to romanticize and fetishize it.

Overall, the variety of genres is one of the things that give the festival a carnival character. Other carnivalesque elements are cabaret performance segments, the mixture of more professional and (selectively) more hobbyist performers, multiculturalism, the circus-like Grand Finale performance, and the intimate performance settings—in the living rooms and backyards of private homes that put performers and audiences in close proximity. The "in the house" performance settings make the festival carnival-like in Bakhtin's sense by blurring the line between art and life such that the festival (to borrow Bakhtin's words) is neither "a purely artistic form nor a spectacle."[62]

This intimate, welcoming quality is central to In the House's politics of generosity. And concerning this politics of generosity, the festival's form was not completely separate from the content of the performances. This was especially evident in the performances by Kurai Blessing and Friends, Yvette Narlock and Kate Reid, the "Spring Evening Doom Lounge" in 2011, and the Wet Spots in 2010 (see earlier discussion). There appears to be some self-selection among artists who perform at In the House—who tend to exude an inclusive politics of generosity—along with the conscious selection of artists by Myriam Steinberg, the festival's artistic director. So, the festival tends to convey a liberal democratic multicultural humanism (loosely understood); but it does so from many angles, without being didactic and without following any fixed aesthetic-political guidelines.[63]

The politics of generosity, manifest in performer-audience rapport in the neighborly spaces, offers modest intimations of—and moments of mutual participation in—what for Bakhtin characterized carnival: a new mode of human being-together in the world. Bakhtin explains that the carnival and marketplace festivals of the European Middle Ages, because of their playfully subversive, life-affirming character,

> were the second life of the people, who for a time entered the utopian realm of community, freedom, equality, and abundance. . . . People were, so to speak, reborn for new, purely human relations. These truly human relations were not only a fruit of imagination or abstract thought; they were experienced. The utopian ideal and the realistic merged in this carnival experience, unique to its kind.[64]

Bakhtin adds that carnival laughter "builds its own world in opposition to the world, its own church versus the official church, its own state versus the official state."[65]

It may seem a bit of a stretch to claim that In the House is carnivalesque in this way. Nonetheless, I contend that In the House achieves a small measure of this, providing a vision of, and spaces for, an inclusive, reciprocal practice of cultural freedom and empowerment. Michael Holquist explains that Bakhtin's vision of carnival has been "widely appropriated in the west by folklorists, literary critics, and intellectual historians," but it has wider significance than these particular uses of it.[66] Bakhtin's account of carnival "is finally about freedom, the courage to establish it, the cunning required to maintain it, and—above all—the horrific ease with which it can be lost."[67] Krystyna Pomorska remarks of Bakhtin's idea of carnival, "The inherent features of carnival that he underscores are its emphatic and purposeful 'heteroglossia' (*raznogolosost'* [diverse and conflicting voices]) and its multiplicity of styles (*mnogostil'nost'*)."[68]

My point is not that the In the House Festival recapitulates carnival in its original medieval European character. Rather, In the House enacts something like a postmodern version of carnival.[69] As I said at the outset, in contrast to medieval carnival, In the House enacts cultural and political subversion in fragmentary and indirect ways. While carnival countered an overarching feudal power structure—which joined church, state, and feudal lords—In the House selectively challenges prevailing cultural and political mores and beliefs; and it counters more directly the dominant forms of artistic production, performance, and consumption. The festival's liberatory character, then, is neither self-conscious nor obvious. Still, it exudes a pervasive, playful subversiveness in private-public spaces that, in a modest way, provides people a "new mode" of experiencing art and relating to each other *through* art.

To appreciate In the House as a *postmodern* form of carnival, Lawrence Grossberg's characterization of the postmodern condition is useful. Grossberg says,

> If people's lives are never merely determined by the dominant position, and if their subordination is always complex and active, understanding culture requires us to look at how cultural practices are actively inserted at particular sites of everyday life and how particular articulations [in other words, modes of interpretation and appropriation] empower and disempower audiences.[70]

In the House inserts itself, with its performers and audience, into a cultural and political context in which there is no singular "dominant position" to upend. The popular cultural or entertainment industries, with their corporate capitalist character, arguably dominate the field of popular cultural and artistic engagement (in music, television, movies, video games, print media, the internet, and others). Moreover, the power dynamics intrinsic to contemporary capitalism are especially extensive in how they structure other power struggles and inequalities, even beyond the field of popular culture. Yet our world is structured by various dominant and subordinate positions—rooted in class, gender, national and regional divisions, sexual, racialized, ethnic/cultural, and religious identities, able-bodiedness/disability, transnational flows of capital, and environmental struggles concerning the human interchange with nonhuman nature—rather than a binary grid of power struggles and inequality. In these ways, as Grossberg says, "people's lives are never merely determined" by a singular dominant position, and their subordination and resistance "is always complex and active."

The In the House Festival, in short, can be seen as a specific, creative articulation of cultural practices at a "particular site of everyday life." In such sites, as Grossberg says, forms of opposition and empowerment

> may be constituted by living, even momentarily, within alternative practices, structures and spaces, even though they take no notice of their relation to existing systems of power. In fact, when one wins some space within the social formation, it has to be filled with something, presumably something that one cares about passionately. . . . And it is here that questions of desire and pleasure must be raised as more than secondary epiphenomena.[71]

Here, as I have already suggested, lies the cultural-political promise of In the House: taken as a whole, it bears witness to possibilities for noncommodified modes of communion via performing art experiences of a sort that have been largely eviscerated in the art that is produced and circulated through the culture industry; and it offers a subversive counterpoint (or set of counterpoints) to how questions of desire and pleasure are answered for people through the entertainment and advertising industries—for instance, with respect to consumption, sexuality, and gendered performance.

In this way, the festival as a whole exhibits in a modest way Adorno's aesthetic aim for "autonomous" works of art—they "point to a practice from which they abstain: the creation of a just life."[72] The varied individual performances that comprise In the House are not all equally compelling as discrete works of art. They sometimes entertain in the way that much popular culture entertains, without offering edification—that is, without offering novel insights into the indignities and injustices of existing human relationships and institutions. Yet in this regard the whole—in its intimacy, generosity, carnivalesque subversiveness, and odd moments of artistic transcendence—is, as I have said, more than the sum of its parts. In its nondidactic way the In the House Festival encourages among its performers and audience members the sort of active, open-minded mutual engagement through art that is vital to a democratic cultural life. Accordingly, it prefigures and supports more broadly an active, inclusive, and thoughtful mode of participation in democratic politics.

Conclusions

Insofar as people's lives and aesthetic experiences are conditioned but "never merely determined" by prevailing relationships of power, the relationship between art and politics is always complexly underdetermined. To focus just on North America, critics now routinely mourn the dearth of challenging cinema, but sometimes suggest that in the "post-network environment" new space has opened up for quality television, or what PBS calls "TV worth watching" (and occasionally provides).[73] Yet, this amounts to a relatively small cultural niche in the terrain of North American popular culture. Much popular culture arguably continues, as Horkheimer and Adorno have said, to "accustom" its audience to existing relationships and practices of domination and subordination—for example, hierarchical work relations; sexism, racism, homophobia, and nationalism; environmentally destructive consumerism.[74] Meanwhile, didactic art often does little more than "preach to the converted."[75] At the same time, some "autonomous" art is still produced, performed, and experienced.

The In the House Festival is notable in this regard because it indicates a creative way that—under favorable conditions—performance art and edifying aesthetic experience can be made accessible to a general population. The festival does this more through its form and carnivalesque spirit than through specific liberatory messages or "great performances." It creatively reimagines the "art festival," blurring the boundary between art and everyday life. In so doing, it offers a promising model for a grassroots democratic cultural politics; it makes space for activist art without relying on activist art as its *raison d'être*.

Part of the promise of In the House is that as a no-frills neighborhood event it could probably be replicated in many cities. That said, particular circumstances in Vancouver make In the House viable, at least for now: a committed artistic director and volunteers along with substantial (but declining) public financial support. The privatization of public life in our neoliberal moment does not bode well for such experiments in cultural democracy.

Notes

1. See Bertolt Brecht, "Against Georg Lukács," in Theodor W. Adorno, Walter Benjamin, Ernst Bloch, Bertolt Brecht, and Georg Lukács, *Aesthetics and Politics* (London: Verso, 2007 [1977]), 68–85.

2. The show had a nine-performance run at the Irondale Center in Brooklyn from June 22–July 9, 2011 (see Felicia R. Lee, "Cut, Baste, Stitch, Sing!" *New York Times*, June 21, 2011).

3. *Pins and Needles* opened on November 27, 1937, at the Labor Stage Theater and moved to the larger Windsor Theater. Its run ended in June 1940, after 1,108 performances (Lee, "Cut, Baste, Stitch, Sing!"). The new *Pins & Needles* was "the final and most elaborate production in a Foundry festival called NYC . . . Just Like I Pictured It, which began in the spring. For each piece, an activist group was matched with theater professionals to come up with a performance that reflected an idealized version of New York" (ibid.).

4. Ibid.

5. Theodor W. Adorno, "Commitment," in Adorno, et al., *Aesthetics and Politics*, 187. In popular music, songs of the iconic sixties U.S. folksinger Phil Ochs exemplified this problem. For instance, his album *I'm Not Marching Anymore* (Elektra Records, 1965) has a humane, progressive spirit with songs that support the civil rights movement and labor activism and oppose the war in Vietnam. Yet the album does not resonate so well beyond its original historical context of particular political struggles for justice.

6. Ibid., 180. A borstal is a type of prison established for youthful offenders for "corrective" purposes.

7. Ibid., 180–81, emphasis added.

8. For the time being, I will leave aside the question of whether form is always more significant than content in committed art. I am not so sure about that.

9. Daniel Maté began the festival in 2003. It did not happen in 2004 but was revived by Myriam Steinberg, the current artistic director, in 2005. See http://www.inthehousefestival.com/index.php?article=more.

10. I went to ten different performances at the 2011 festival (June 3–5) and three or four performances during the festival of 2010.

11. Tickets for a single show were $14. Tickets for four shows were $40, and a weekend pass was $80.

12. Max Horkheimer and Theodor W. Adorno, "The Culture Industry," in *Dialectic of Enlightenment: Philosophical Fragments*, ed. Gunzelin Schmid Noerr, trans. Edmund Jephcott (Stanford, CA: Stanford University Press, 2002 [1947]), 94–136.

13. Daniel Maté, email communication with the author, July 25, 2011.

14. Myriam Steinberg, interview with the author, May 17, 2011.

15. Yvette Narlock, one of the performers who I discuss later, noted the festival's diversity and inclusiveness in an email communication with the author, November 1, 2012.

16. Theodor W. Adorno, *Aesthetic Theory*, trans. C. Lenhardt (New York: Routledge, 1984), 323, quoted in Lorenzo C. Simpson, "Musical Interlude: Adorno on Jazz, or How Not to Fuse Horizons," in *The Unfinished Project: Toward a Postmetaphysical Humanism* (New York: Routledge, 2001), 46.

17. Mikhail Bakhtin, *Rabelais and His World*, trans. Helene Iswolsky (Bloomington: Indiana University Press, 1984), 7.

18. Ibid., 10.

19. Ibid.; Bakhtin, quoted in Krystyna Pomorska, Foreword to Bakhtin, *Rabelais and His World*, x.

20. Gerhard Schweppenhäuser, *Theodor W. Adorno: An Introduction*, trans. James Rolleston (Durham, NC: Duke University Press, 2009), 133–34, 155–57; Simpson, "Musical Interlude," 45–59. See Theodor W. Adorno, "Arnold Schoenberg, 1874–1951," in *Prisms*, trans. Samuel Weber and Shierry Weber (Cambridge, MA: MIT Press, 1983), 147–72; Theodor W. Adorno, "On Jazz" and "On the Current Relationship between Philosophy and Music," in *Night Music: Essays on Music 1928–1962*, ed. Rolf Tiedemann, trans. and introduction by Wieland Hoban (London: Seagall Books, 2009), 118–176, 426–73.

21. Simpson, "Musical Interlude," 46–47, 56–59; Schweppenhäuser, *Theodor W. Adorno*, 133–35, 155–57. Adorno himself provides in passing a basis for such a hermeneutical immanent critique of his specific aesthetic judgments when he cautions listeners against dismissing his essay on Schoenberg's challenging music before they have made a sufficient effort to understand it: "If one does not understand something, it is customary to behave with the sublime understanding of Mahler's jackass, and project one's own inadequacy on to the object, declaring it to be incomprehensible." Adorno, "Arnold Schoenberg," 149. Adorno thought that he understood jazz perfectly well, but as Simpson explains this was not so.

22. See Russell Perkins, "Adorno's Dreams and the Aesthetic of Violence," *Telos* no. 155 (Summer 2011): 33. See also J. M. Bernstein, "'The dead speaking of stones and stars': Adorno's *Aesthetic Theory*," in *The Cambridge Companion to Critical Theory*, ed. Fred Rush (Cambridge: Cambridge University Press, 2004), 139–64.

23. Michael Holquist, Prologue in Bakhtin, *Rabelais and His World*, xxi.

24. Jules Boykoff notes, "In February 2003, Vancouver voters were presented with a plebiscite to gauge public support for hosting the Games. Though pro-Olympics boosters spent $700,000 persuading the public—140 times more than the 'no' side—only 26 per cent of those eligible voted in favour, on the basis of a total turnout of 40 per cent." See Jules Boykoff, "The Anti-Olympics," *New Left Review* no. 67 (January–February 2011): 46.

25. Yasmin P. Karim, "Vancouver 2010: Art Legacy or Art Crash," in *Impact Statements: Crash! Anthology of Critical Texts*, ed. David Garneau (Calgary, AB: EMMEDIA Gallery & Production Society, 2010), 46–47. Wilco performed as part of a series of limited-admission "free" concerts at a downtown public park.

26. Ibid., 45.

27. Ibid., 46.

28. Boykoff notes that leaders "from the Lil'wat, Musqueam, Squamish and Tsleil-Waututh First Nations agreed in 2004 to work together on hosting and assisting the 2010 Games." Meanwhile, despite "financial inducements, 80 of the 203 Indigenous bands in British Columbia flatly refused to participate ("The Anti-Olympics," 48–49).

29. Ibid., 49–50.

30. Ibid., 54.

31. Ibid.

32. Ibid., 56–57.

33. Ibid., 51.

34. Ibid.; Carlito Pablo, "COPE Firebrand Comes Back," *Georgia Straight*, June 16–23, 2011, 13.

35. Ibid., 57.

36. Marsha Lederman, "Money Restored for the *Arts* Not Enough, Groups Say," *The Globe and Mail* (Toronto), March 3, 2010, http://proquest.umi.com. ezproxy.library.ubc.ca/pqdweb?index=6&did=1974588711&SrchMode=1&sid=2 &Fmt=3&VInst=PROD&VType=PQD&RQT=309&VName=PQD&TS=130 9299050&clientId=6993.

37. Andrea Warner, "Buried Alive" (Arts on the Edge), *WE: Vancouver's Urban Weekly*, October 28–November 3, 2010, 22.

38. Steinberg interview. Steinberg notes that the BC Arts Council was never the biggest funder of In the House, but its largest contribution, $4,000 CAN, was significant.

39. Charlie Smith, "Greater Vancouver Housing Prices Go Up and Down," *Georgia Straight*, February 2, 2011, http://www.straight.com/article-371150/vancouver/grater-vancouver-housing-prices-go-and-down. The "benchmark" price is figured for "typical" homes in Greater Vancouver communities as defined by the average home features sold. See http://www.realtylink.org/statistics/buyers_hpi_explained.cfm.

40. "Coldwell Banker Real Estate Issues Home Listing Report Ranking More Than 2,300 of North America's Most Expensive and Most Affordable Housing Markets," http://hlr.coldwellbanker.com/PressRelease.aspx.

41. Boykoff, "The Anti-Olympics," 58; COPE website, http://cope.bc.ca/. There is some division within COPE concerning the coalition's recent decision to align itself with other municipal parties—Vision Vancouver and the center-right Non-Partisan Association—that are more developer friendly. See Pablo, "COPE Firebrand Comes Back," 13.

42. Fredric Jameson, "Reflections in Conclusion," in Adorno et al., *Aesthetics and Politics*, 208.

43. Ibid.

44. Ibid. Jameson mentions the commodification of painting, architecture and other "once scandalous 'perceptual art'" (209).

45. Consider these two recent stories on the state of the North American popular music business. In 2010, the band Cults, made up of Brian Oblivion and Madeline Follin, then two amateur musicians, uploaded their song "Go Outside" onto a popular indie music website, Band Camp. NPR's Laura Sullivan says, "It was a one-in-a-million chance. The song went viral. They became an instant indie success story, but no one knew who they were. . . . Now, they're in the big leagues with a record deal from Columbia and their first album just out" (NPR Staff, "Cults Leave Internet Hype behind for the Big Time," *All Things Considered*, June 19, 2011, http://www.npr.org/templates/transcript/transcript.php?storyId=137245548). A more characteristic music industry story concerns the cost of making and marketing a song ("Man Down") on the singer Rihanna's album *Loud*, from 2010. NPR calculated that the overall cost of making the song and trying (unsuccessfully) to make it a hit was $1,078,000 USD. About one million dollars of this was spent on promotion costs. See Zoe Chace, "How Much Does It Cost to Make a Hit Song?," *All Things Considered*, June 30, 2011, http://www.npr.org/blogs/money/2011/07/01/137530847/how-much-does-it-cost-to-make-a-hit-song.

46. In the run-up to the festival, Steinberg works long hours and pays herself a low wage (Steinberg interview).

47. Steinberg is exploring the development of a sideline, for-profit business that would produce small shows for fees as a way to earn an income and help secure the financial survival of the nonprofit festival (Steinberg interview).

48. Daniel Maté, email communication with the author, July 25, 2011.

49. Ibid.

50. See http://www.inthehousefestival.com/index.php?article=more.

51. There are, of course, already festivals like In the House in other cities. For a helpful discussion of another, more expressly political Vancouver cultural experiment in "doing democracy"—a play called *Practicing Democracy* by Headlines Theatre—see Geraldine Pratt and Caleb Johnston, "Turning Theatre into Law, and Other Spaces of Politics," *Cultural Geographies* 14, no. 1 (2007): 92–113.

52. Other notable examples of this are the two major Vancouver professional sports teams: the BC Lions, of the Canadian Football League, and the Vancouver Canucks of the NHL.

53. There were dinner breaks on Saturday and Sunday (6–7 p.m.), and in the last time slot on Sunday night there was just one performance, the Grand Finale. The festival had the same structure in 2010.

54. Perkins, "Adorno's Dreams and the Aesthetic of Violence," 21–37.

55. See http://www.yvesapple.com/.

56. To my mind, the tradition of artfully political pop rock music is exemplified by Sly and the Family Stone's great antiracist and populist song, "Everyday People" (from Sly and the Family Stone, *Stand!* [Epic, 1969]). Narlock's "One Drop" is on her album *Sweet Bitter* (see www.yvesapple.com). It is also on the two-disc *In the House Festival Compilation Album* (Digital Media Alliance) along with Kate Reid's song "I Go Straight for Ridley Bent." The In the House collection includes twenty-five songs by various musicians who have performed at In the House. Proceeds from CD sales support the festival.

57. See http://www.katereid.net/.

58. See Kate Reid's website: http://www.katereid.net/music-8.html.

59. The performers were Buchman Coe, Chris Murdoch, Alley Oop, Cameron Fraser, Yuki Ueda, and Graham Ellsworth.

60. See http://www.wetspotsmusic.net/. The Wet Spots are in the burlesque tradition of May West.

61. See http://www.wetspotsmusic.net/presskit.html.

62. Bakhtin, *Rabelais and His World*, 7.

63. In conversation, Steinberg gave one example of how she negotiates these questions. A few years back she included in the festival a male comedian who some people might have regarded as not "politically correct" on gender issues. Specifically, in his comedy he called for women to be more forthright in "coming on" to men. In Steinberg's view, this comedian was talented, funny, and not sexist, even if he might have offended a few people (Steinberg, interview with the author).

64. Bakhtin, *Rabelais and His World*, 9–10.

65. Ibid., 88.

66. Holquist, Prologue, xxi.

67. Ibid.

68. Pomorska, Foreword, x.

69. Other examples are perhaps the New Orleans Mardi Gras and various May Day events, like the one in Minneapolis, Minnesota, directed annually by the Heart of the Beast Puppet and Mask Theater.

70. Lawrence Grossberg, "Putting the Pop Back in Postmodernism," in *Universal Abandon? The Politics of Postmodernism*, ed. Andrew Ross (Minneapolis: University of Minnesota Press, 1988), 169–70.

71. Ibid., 170.

72. Adorno, "Commitment," 194. I am not sure that Adorno himself would have considered the In the House Festival to be an example of "autonomous" art, but for reasons I noted at the outset I am not concerned about his particular aesthetic sensibilities.

73. Heather Hendershot, "Losers Take All," *The Nation* 292 (May 30, 2011): 41.

74. "Donald Duck in the cartoons and the unfortunate victim in real life," they write, "received their beatings so that the spectators can accustom themselves to theirs" (Horkheimer and Adorno, *Dialectic of Enlightenment*, 110). Compared to the other topics, North American popular culture recently has better countered homophobia with productions such as NBC TV's *Will and Grace* (1998–2006) and the film *Boys Don't Cry* (IFC Films, 1999).

75. Adorno, "Commitment," 185.

Bibliography

Adorno, Theodor W. "Arnold Schoenberg, 1874–1951." In Adorno, *Prisms*, 147–72. Translated by Samuel Weber and Shierry Weber. Cambridge, MA: MIT Press, 1983.

———. *Aesthetic Theory*. Translated by C. Lenhardt. New York: Routledge, 1984.

———. "Commitment." In Theodor W. Adorno, Walter Benjamin, Ernst Bloch, Bertolt Brecht, and Georg Lukács, *Aesthetics and Politics*. With an afterword by Fredric Jameson. London: Verso, 2007 [1977].

———. "On Jazz." In Adorno, *Night Music: Essays on Music 1928–1962*, edited by Rolf Tiedemann, translated and with an introduction by Wieland Hoban, 118–76. London: Seagall Books, 2009.

———. "On the Current Relationship between Philosophy and Music." In Adorno, *Night Music*, 426–73.

Bakhtin, Mikhail. *Rabelais and His World*. Translated by Helene Iswolsky. Bloomington: Indiana University Press, 1984.

Bernstein, J. M. "'The dead speaking of stones and stars': Adorno's *Aesthetic Theory*." In *The Cambridge Companion to Critical Theory*, edited by Fred Rush, 139–64. Cambridge: Cambridge University Press, 2004.

Boykoff, Jules. "The Anti-Olympics." *New Left Review* 67 (January–February 2011): 41–59.

Brecht, Bertolt. "Against Georg Lukács." In Theodor W. Adorno et al., *Aesthetics and Politics*, 68–85.

Chace, Zoe. "How Much Does It Cost to Make a Hit Song?" *All Things Considered*, June 30, 2011. http://www.npr.org/blogs/money/2011/07/01/137530847/how-much-does-it-cost-to-make-a-hit-song.

COPE website. http://cope.bc.ca/.

Grossberg, Lawrence. "Putting the Pop Back in Postmodernism." In *Universal Abandon? The Politics of Postmodernism*, edited by Andrew Ross, 167–90. Minneapolis: University of Minnesota Press, 1988.

Hendershot, Heather. "Losers Take All." *The Nation* 292 (May 30, 2011): 41.

Holquist, Michael. Prologue. In Bakhtin, *Rabelais and His World*, xiii–xxiii.

Horkheimer, Max, and Theodor W. Adorno. "The Culture Industry." In Horkheimer and Adorno, *Dialectic of Enlightenment: Philosophical Fragments*, edited by Gunzelin Schmid Noerr, translated by Edmund Jephcott, 94–136. Stanford, CA: Stanford University Press, 2002 [1947].

In the House Festival website. http://www.inthehousefestival.com.

Jameson, Fredric. "Reflections in Conclusion." In Theodor W. Adorno, et al., *Aesthetics and Politics*, 196–213.

Karim, Yasmin P. "Vancouver 2010: Art Legacy or Art Crash." In *Impact Statements: Crash! Anthology of Critical Texts*, edited by David Garneau, 46–47. Calgary, AB: EMMEDIA Gallery & Production Society, 2010.

Lederman, Marsha. "Money Restored for the *Arts* Not Enough, Groups Say." *The Globe and Mail* (Toronto), March 3, 2010. http://proquest.umi.com. ezproxy.library.ubc.ca/pqdweb?index=6&did=1974588711&SrchMode=1 &sid=2&Fmt=3&VInst=PROD&VType=PQD&RQT=309&VName=P QD&TS=1309299050&clientId=6993.

Lee, Felicia R. "Cut, Baste, Stitch, Sing!" *New York Times*, June 21, 2011. http://www.nytimes.com/2011/06/22/theater/furee-in-pins-needles-at-irondale-center.html?nl=todaysheadlines&emc=tha28.

NPR Staff. "Cults Leave Internet Hype behind for the Big Time." *All Things Considered*, June 19, 2011. http://www.npr.org/templates/transcript/transcript.php?storyId=137245548.

Pablo, Carlito. "COPE Firebrand Comes Back." *Georgia Straight* (Vancouver), June 16–23, 2011, 13.

Perkins, Russell. "Adorno's Dreams and the Aesthetic of Violence." *Telos* no. 155 (Summer 2011): 21–37.

Pomorska, Krystyna. Foreword. In Bakhtin, *Rabelais and His World*, vii–xii.

Pratt, Geraldine, and Caleb Johnston. "Turning Theatre into Law, and Other Spaces of Politics." *Cultural Geographies* 14, no. 1 (2007): 92–113.

Schweppenhäuser, Gerhard. *Theodor W. Adorno: An Introduction*. Translated by James Rolleston. Durham, NC: Duke University Press, 2009.

Simpson, Lorenzo C. "Musical Interlude: Adorno on Jazz, or How Not to Fuse Horizons." In Lorenzo C. Simpson, *The Unfinished Project: Toward a Postmetaphysical Humanism*, 45–59. New York: Routledge, 2001.

Smith, Charlie. "Greater Vancouver Housing Prices Go Up and Down." *Georgia Straight* (Vancouver), February 2, 2011. http://www.straight. com/article-371150/vancouver/grater-vancouver-housing-prices-go-and-down.

Warner, Andrea. "Buried Alive" (Arts on the Edge), *WE: Vancouver's Urban Weekly*, October 28–November 3, 2010.
Wet Spots website. http://www.wetspotsmusic.net/presskit.html.

Discography

In the House Festival Compilation Album. Digital Media Alliance, CD, n.d.
Narlock, Yvette. "One Drop." From Yvette Narlock, *Sweet Bitter*, CD, n.d. www. yvesapple.com.
Ochs, Phil. *I'm Not Marching Anymore*. Elektra Records, LP, 1965.
Reid, Kate. "Co-op Girlz." From Kate Reid, *Doing It for the Chicks*, CD, 2011. http://www.katereid.net/.
Sly and the Family Stone. "Everyday People." From Sly and the Family Stone, *Stand!* Epic, LP, 1969.

Chapter 13

Democracy despite Government

African American Parading and Democratic Theory

Peter G. Stillman and Adelaide H. Villmoare

Following Michael Jackson's death, New Orleanians staged a parade in his honor. After Katrina in January 2006, the Black Men of Labor (BMOL) sponsored a parade that began on St. Claude Avenue, running through the Ninth Ward and ending on Claiborne Avenue, a main thoroughfare through African American neighborhoods that was destroyed as a commercial heart of Tremé when the I-10 elevated highway was built.[1] And on August 31, 2009, a coalition of groups organized a parade to protest the destruction of Charity Hospital in the face of plans for a new medical center that would require demolition of parts of Mid-City New Orleans rebuilt since the storm. These parades, known as second lines, are part of a long African American tradition in New Orleans (NOLA) using city neighborhoods as public spaces for pleasure, articulations of community, modes of remembrance, and protest.[2] NOLA is a city of parades throughout the year. Many of them wander through city streets and provide opportunities for public claims and challenges to social, economic, and political power.

The authors would like to thank Michael E. Morrell for his comments on an earlier version of this chapter presented at a New England Political Science Association meeting, J. Paul Martin for his insights, Nancy Love and Mark Mattern for shepherding this essay through two lives, and Vassar College for research funds that enabled trips to New Orleans.

African American parading in NOLA raises distinctive questions about "doing democracy." Under conditions of notable inequalities of class and race, residents continue not only to survive but to nurture their own civic and public life and democratic values and encounters.[3] Indeed, those marginalized from formal political and economic power demonstrate a remarkable political resilience and desire to articulate their places in the life of the city. The disempowered actively foster democratic values outside of and sometimes against structures, processes, and outcomes of formal political power—including government. They practice what we call democracy despite government. The concept of democracy despite government takes into consideration ways in which people have sustained themselves, their cultural lives, and their communities in reasonably open and equitable ways in the face of governmental coercion, indifference, failure, and rejection—in this case, in NOLA before, during, and after Hurricane Katrina.

Democracy despite government opens up meanings of democracy to include resistance to and sidestepping of government when it gets in the way of people's lives and their cultural survival and when it is neglectful of the politically and economically marginalized. Democracy despite government does not necessarily generate public policy (although it can ignite governmental backlash) and is often not immediately instrumental in the sense of pursuing particular political interests. It nonetheless expresses lived political values, cultivates inclusive public spaces, and provides cultural sustenance for the marginalized.

The argument here is not that democracy despite government can or should supplant governmental democracy either in practice or in theory. Rather, democracy despite government often exists alongside neoliberal and quasi- or undemocratic processes and policies and provides cultural voice and connections for neighborhoods and people under stress. Democratic practices, evincing values of equality and participation in civil society, may survive or thrive where government is democratic only in the most formal sense of having open elections and a rule of law. And they may survive or thrive where government is far from democratic. This conception of democracy comports with Sheldon S. Wolin's contention that "[d]emocracy is not about where the political is located but about how it is experienced."[4]

For scholars of democracy, democracy despite government cannot and should not replace existing theories of democracy. Rather, the goal is to expand how to think about democracy. For liberal democratic theorists of representative government who see free, unencumbered individuals voting their self-interests or who focus on voting for representatives as central, democracy despite government suggests that there exist other practices, outside of electoral democracy, whereby people can express the values of their community and their sense of freedom and agency. Moreover, for deliberative democratic theorists who wish to encompass as many citizens as possible, including those with little or no political power whose voices have been silenced or ignored, democracy despite government suggests the difficulties some groups face in obtaining equal power, equal respect, and mutual consideration of points of view from those with power, and indeed suggests that some groups may not seek, or may not be in a position to seek, such goals.[5]

We find the concept of democracy despite government compelling for three independent reasons that will become clear through this chapter. First, the phrase is an apt characterization of the political aspects of African American parading in New Orleans. Second, it emphasizes what most theories of democracy downplay: the recurring or systematic exclusion of some groups from effective political voice. These groups act despite government, and they can create democracy for themselves only by claiming their own public spaces and communal practices.[6] Third, democracy despite government fits neatly with Wolin's "fugitive democracy."[7] Wolin is critical of what passes for democracy in contemporary advanced states because such states allow systematic social, economic, and political inequalities; limit political freedom to established channels that dissipate popular political energies; and transform politics into the pursuit of state power and the ability to rule others. Aspirations for equality, self-government, and democratic practices are lost in the modern state and can only be found in "fugitive" groups—transitory, occasional, oppositional groups that create their own community, spaces, and democratic practices; groups that are democratic despite government. Like Wolin, we are concerned with the lived experience and expression of democratic values among the politically marginalized.

Democracy despite government may energize people to undertake politically instrumental actions on their own behalf, ones that do not involve government. NOLA resident Douglas Ahlers, who, in conjunction with the Kennedy School of Harvard University, has been working with the Broadmoor Improvement Association (BIA), shared his observations about the areas devastated by the 2004 Indian Ocean tsunami, where people—absent any government help—rebuilt their homes and reconstituted their communities. They moved ahead rather efficiently and equitably. Drawing parallels between the tsunami and Katrina, he was inclined to believe that government can get in the way of what people need or want and are able to accomplish on their own or with the help of non-governmental organizations (NGOs). Appreciating his insight, we contend that significant democratic politics may exist absent formal government.

In NOLA one vehicle of democracy despite government is parading: residents deploying public streets for cultural, social, and political expression, especially that which finds no or little place in institutions of government.[8] Parades make the streets part of an informal political discourse that is sometimes overtly political and more frequently less so. As Helen A. Regis has shown, second lines are much more than they seem. She notes, for example: "The majority of participants in the second-line tradition are not owners of homes, real estate, or large, public businesses. Yet through the transformative experience of the parade, they become owners of the streets."[9] Second liners fashion a distinctive, egalitarian public square, and they, thus, illustrate Don Mitchell's observation: "What makes a space *public*—a space in which the cry and demand for the right to the city can be seen and heard—is often not its preordained 'publicness.' Rather, it is when, to fulfill a pressing need, some group or other *takes* space and through its actions *makes* it public."[10] In making a space public, second liners make a democratic move.

Scholars of the public sphere have proposed thinking beyond a single public to acknowledge subaltern counter-publics, arising from subordinated groups in response to an exclusionary bourgeois public.[11] These publics provide space for politically excluded discourse, including all forms of cultural expression, not simply explicitly political deliberation. African American second lines, organized by social aid and pleasure clubs and historically banned from white sections of the city, have created their own participatory, subaltern counter-publics over time and place. And parading itself, including Mardi Gras parades, has been a locus of political contestation over democracy in NOLA. Similar to the movements of paraders, democratic values weave in and out of the parades.

Parading: Mardi Gras, Zulu, and Black Indians

While certain parades (for example, Mardi Gras in the main business areas) are now deeply intertwined with the tourism economy of the city, others speak more directly to active community experiences where people from the same neighborhood and across neighborhoods contribute to the music, dance, costumes, and masks of second lines. The history of parades in NOLA (Mardi Gras and social aid and pleasure club second lines) and the krewes (clubs organized to celebrate the season with parading and balls) that constitute them are animated by issues of class, race, and gender.[12]

Mardi Gras may appear to visitors as a once-a-year bacchanalia, an ephemeral pleasure, but its social meanings are embedded in social, economic, and political structures and strains of the city. Old-time krewes celebrated values of white dominance; J. Mark Souther observes: "As had been true before WWII, racialized representations of social hierarchy lay at the heart of the public celebration of New Orleans Carnival in the years following the war."[13] Today krewes are much more diverse in their membership and presentations in Mardi Gras; they include racially integrated, gay, and women's krewes.

In the face of historical exclusion and the subaltern practices of people of color, alternative parading arose. The Zulu Social Aid and Pleasure Club created its own parade in African American neighborhoods in 1909, and second lines proceeded along the streets "back o' town" (back from the river and white areas).[14] Mardi Gras and its exclusions spawned other parades, even as the carnival itself became more inclusive. Today the Zulu are one of the established centerpieces of Mardi Gras. But it was not until 1969 that the club was permitted along the white-controlled main line of parade.

From the beginning Zulu paraded in blackface and grass skirts to mock white images of African Americans. Although the club drew hard criticism from black power and civil rights advocates in the 1960s for what they considered its embracing of racist stereotypes, it has survived and continues to parade in blackface and grass skirts.[15] The Zulu king and queen don elaborately beaded and feathered costumes, and the members of the club leading the parade throw decorated coconuts that are among the favored Mardi Gras souvenirs. The Zulu's tenacious attachment to its origins and its public performances of race in African American neighborhoods and then along the main Mardi Gras parade route illustrate one side of political resilience and racial celebration among African Americans. They are not, however, the only African American–identified group participating in the carnival.

Mardi Gras Black Indians, masking probably since the 1880s, likely appeared in response to the end of Reconstruction.[16] Reid Mitchell maintains that "[m]asking Indian was a form of black protest in a Jim Crow New Orleans . . . that claimed ritual space."[17] The ritual space involved the public performance of cultural voice and traditions, and the physical space was (and is) African American neighborhoods. In its origins, masking Indian may well have been a form of resistance to white domination, a shared political meaning among African Americans to which whites did not have access. Samuel Kinser suggests that historically "although this masked Indian is below, he is also beyond the white man's sanctioned power."[18] Tribes (the groups with whom people in different neighborhoods identified) would claim control of their neighborhoods through masking, parading, and fighting.[19] These tools of the tribes were hardly the implements of formal democracy, and there was an exclusionary character to the tribes that the fighting exhibited. Masking and parading were nonetheless expressions of self-governance and cultural control of traditions and neighborhoods.

Over time, fighting yielded to masking competition. Liza Katzman's 2007, film *Tootie's Last Suit* documents the passion of Tootie Montana, long the big chief of the Yellow Pocahontas tribe, and the competition he and his son, Darryl, had over who was the "prettiest" Indian.[20] Katzman conveys the seriousness of purpose involved in the Indians' creations; fashioning the costumes requires vision, skill, and dedication. Enormous amounts of talent and time go into making the complex plumed and beaded costumes. Behind the fantastic masking and competition are constant preparations. On Mardi Gras and St. Joseph's Day costumes are donned, and members of the tribe dance and sing their way through African American sections of the city. Through frequent practices, children are nurtured in musical and dance traditions. Smith observes that "certainly the most significant aspects of the Black Indian tradition are the tribal organizations and friendships, which continue all year long, and the 'practices' on Sunday evenings, during the fall and winter leading up to Mardi Gras, where the dancing, drumming, and communal traditions are continued."[21]

For the tribes and their neighborhoods, all this activity contributes to community, fosters a distinctive public life for African Americans, and provides constructive responses to crime and violence in the city. In Katzman's documentary, Darryl Montana alludes to troubles he used to have; it is clear that he has left them behind in the affirming activities of African American traditions associated with masking. The 2009, exhibit "One Hundred Years of Zulu" at the Louisiana State Museum discussed the mantra "sew, sew, sew" (on the elaborate costumes) as an explicitly recognized alternative to "fight, fight, fight" on the streets. Kinser explains that Indian masking today "substitutes aesthetic for fighting prowess."[22] There is a clear recognition among the Black Indians about how dedication to and involvement in the tribes and their parades direct people's attentions to constructive and culturally meaningful connections for all in the African American community.

The Zulu and Black Indians both claim public space and have demonstrated political resilience over the years. The style and content of Zulu parading differ from that of the Indians. According to Kinser, "The Zulus' aim diverged from that of the Indians from the beginning. The Mardi Gras Indians developed Carnival freedom toward *ritual* independence of the white society. . . . They developed confrontational rituals. . . . The Zulus on the other hand aimed at satire both of themselves . . . and no less of the whites who lorded it over them."[23] The Zulu forged its way into mainstream Mardi Gras along the traditionally white parade route and in so doing worked for the racial integration of carnival parading.[24] The Black Indians are more connected to particular African American neighborhoods in Central City. Although they differ, both the Zulu and Black Indians resisted white dominance of their traditions and neighborhoods and staked out a public voice for their communities.

Today parading for Zulu and the Black Indians constitutes a form of democracy despite government. While the Social Aid and Pleasure Club and tribes obviously do not act as formal political organizations, they cultivate conditions for people to reject the most harmful aspects of racial and class inequality and government neglect, and to maintain African American cultural and community connections across generations. There is a political self-consciousness about using the streets in rather spectacular and inclusive ways to articulate African American traditions. As Ned Sublette states, "The Indians embody resistance. You can sum it up in four words: 'We won't bow down.'"[25] This political self-consciousness is about resistance, resilience, shared energy, community spirit, and support for a participatory African American public space.

Parading: Second Lines

In response to the history of racial exclusion and the determination to establish streets as their own public spaces, African Americans long ago created second lines. As Breunlin and Regis explain, "The term *second line* refers to a rhythm, a dance step, and a performance tradition said to have originated in 18th century Congo Square on the margins of the colonial city, where enslaved Africans, free people of color, and Native Americans gathered, along with a few onlookers to engage in commerce, music, dance, and religious ceremonies."[26] Early on people of color supported a public square where residents could join in a variety of activities.

Developed as participatory experiences, second lines implicitly invite onlookers to join, to become, if only for a moment, a part of the community. Novelist Andrea Boll captures the spirit, rhythm, and intensity of a second line:

> Sometimes it happens when a man who climbs the roof of a car and dances a one-man riot, other times it's a joint that just enough people hit to remind them of how music pulses in their veins, but this time, it's the tuba who goes deeper, beneath the street, beneath the cobble stones, beneath the roots, and finds a memory as hot and fevered as the swamp. It is a memory without images. It is a memory of a rhythm that returns back to Sundays on Congo Square, through whips and rapes, back across the Atlantic, onto the bright sand, and into the motherland where ancestors whisper back yes yes yes yes, we are here. We are listening. He blows it out of his tuba and everybody recognizes the sound.[27]

Music, movement, and memory meld in second lines.

Second lines invite people into the action.[28] The parade organized by the BMOL in January 2006, was intended to encourage people to return to the city and to maintain "New Orleans black cultural traditions."[29] The second line's route made note of the destruction of African American neighborhoods before and following the flooding and spoke to the hope of rebuilding those neighborhoods. The 2008 tenth anniversary of the Nine Times Social Aid and Pleasure Club, founded to connect people in the Ninth Ward, was a four-hour march across the Ninth Ward with two brass bands and a string of people as far as the eye could see.[30]

Although second lines may appear spontaneous (and certainly there are elements of spontaneity to them), they are in fact planned with care by the social aid and pleasure clubs to affirm community and to memorialize places and events of particular significance to residents and racial boundaries. Breunlin and Regis describe one second liner's perspective: "Raphael Parker, a member of Nine Times, said he believed that parading gives the club a chance to claim a place for the Ninth Ward and the Desire Projects in the social landscape of the city."[31] Desire, a large public housing community, was, again according to Breunlin and Regis, "materially and discursively constructed as a preeminent black space."[32]

And the space often speaks directly from and to strengths within African American communities. According to one of its founders, the Black Men of Labor formed "because we thought that history was writing black men as failures." Fred Johnson continues: "So we put together a crew of men that worked for a living, that didn't sell drugs . . . that was taking care of their responsibilities, and understood the need to also sustain and support their culture."[33] The club's second line affirms a community where people assemble not only to enjoy one another on a Sunday evening but to protect and acclaim African American cultural identities and connections.

Recognizing both contributions to and losses from the neighborhood, stopping places along a parade route include public housing sites, private houses, bars, funeral homes, and spots where individuals have died or been killed.[34] At the Nine Times second line in January 2006, the Hot 8 Brass Band performed "Let My People Go" to a group of Orleans Parish Prison inmates behind a fence.[35] In the notable inclusiveness that marks a second line, the inmates were recognized both as part of and missing from the paraders' lives. At a Father's Day parade, participants wore t-shirts with photos of incarcerated men with the length of their sentences; as Regis remarks, "the photos stand for those very bodies that are missing from the second line."[36] Unlike state governments that often disenfranchise convicted felons, second lines openly embrace them and acknowledge their loss to communities. The parades put forth an alternative, more expansive understanding of citizenship; whether men can vote or even be present, they remain part of a community, its memories, and its future. Even as social occasions, second lines reinforce inclusive, egalitarian community ties.

Through second lines streets become more public and democratic than they might otherwise be. African American parades claim city streets as at least partially theirs and open to all who wish to join them. During the long hours (usually on Sundays) of second lines, neighborhoods are mobbed with participants singing, dancing, walking. Traffic is interrupted or halted as paraders take control of a long, drawn-out line of march. Streets are, for those moments, vibrant public squares defined by subaltern groups who design their own use of them. And those designs are inclusive, participatory, and lively.[37]

While usually not expressly political, second lines can nonetheless make overt political statements. For example, Souther notes that "[t]he Olympia bandsmen also used the jazz funeral idiom as a vehicle for social protest. After several blocks of the Faubourg Tremé (a predominantly

African American neighborhood) were razed for the city government's Cultural Center, part of a locally funded urban renewal scheme designed to rid the inner city of impoverished neighborhoods, the Olympia Brass Band staged a mock jazz funeral to symbolize Tremé's untimely death."[38] Club anniversary parades are, for the most part, social occasions, although historically, according to Michael White, they have demonstrated "a show of strength and unity and a defiant march toward freedom and democracy in a society where such assemblies would normally be discouraged."[39]

These subaltern assemblies have their own rules, distinct from and sometimes at odds with those of government. In gentle ways, second lines challenge city government's control of the streets, when they ignore traffic or traffic lights.[40] The spirit of the parade takes over. Sometimes, in less gentle ways, participants challenge laws through the violence that erupts after a day of second lining (and drinking along the way). The NOLA police department has sought to exercise greater control over these parades through restricting the number of hours during which they can occur, raising the price of permits, and defining the places where people may parade.[41] Parades that used to take all day are now required to be completed in four hours, and the Nine Times club was denied permission to parade through the new Desire housing in 2004.[42]

Sometimes conflicts over second lines arise between residents and the police. In 2007 in Tremé, police broke up a funeral parade, and participants were taken away in handcuffs.[43] In protest against the police action, Tootie Montana, probably the most famous of the Black Indian big chiefs, spoke to the city council (where he collapsed and died). He complained that such policing struck at the heart of the creative character of African American second lining.[44] Writing in the *New Orleans Times-Picayune*, Lolis Elie supports the complaint that the NOLA police department and Mayor Nagin were trampling cultural traditions.[45]

Second lines constitute a form of democracy despite government. For the disempowered and disenfranchised these parades claim a public place to display their cultural and political voices. Second lines provide opportunities for an egalitarian, open, and participatory discourse and, as such, are about inclusion, resilience, connection, and shared pleasures. While they may appear of the moment, they are also about the past and future; they memorialize past events and mark hopes for the future. As spectacle they arise from and foster subaltern, democratic publics. This politics may not be immediately instrumental, although it can overtly recognize exclusion from, and pose a challenge to, dominant political discourse. Sometimes the politics is expressly and instrumentally political, as the second line decrying the planned destruction of Charity Hospital was. Second lines make statements about loss caused by government and its actions and inactions and thus serve, at least in part, as a political critique of dominant policies and processes. And when they are less overtly directed at government and instrumental political actions, they still carve out public space and create discourse about present and past community and neighborhoods.

Democracy despite Government

African American parades in New Orleans, especially second lines, create and express ideas of community, freedom, and agency and reflect and regenerate values held by different subaltern groups. As democratic practices, parades need to be taken into account by democratic theorists. Parades pose a theoretical challenge for those who define democracy primarily as electoral politics because they are democratic practices with no regard for electoral politics. For those who advocate deliberative democracy, parades can push the edges of almost any meaning of "democracy" because parades do not speak the language of formal deliberation at a governmental level. Parades can contribute to debates in contemporary democratic theory and indeed highlight issues of importance for democracy of any vibrant sort.

Since the nineteenth century much democratic theory has traditionally been about the inclusion and representation of citizens in the state. But some have questioned whether representative, constitutional government based on nearly universal suffrage is adequately democratic. For democracy to be limited to voting in competitive elections for candidates chosen by political parties or other political elites seemed, to these critics, a thin and inadequate theory that did not reflect central democratic ideals, like citizen involvement in political life, discussion, and debate, and some degree of citizen influence on or authorship of collective decisions.[46] So some theorists asked: What are the theoretical preconditions for a more robust and deliberative democracy?

Theorists of deliberative democracy sought to discover and to specify the preconditions or prerequisites for successful democratic practice. Citizens should be equally able and free to speak. They should speak sincerely and justify their positions extensively in a rational discourse in which all positions are heard and considered. The state serves as the locus and focus of democratic discussion and debate. And the result of that discourse should be policy decisions by the state firmly grounded in collective consensus.[47] But in specifying and elaborating these preconditions, theorists of deliberative democracy were, some critics argued, not paying adequate attention to remedying existing inequalities and exclusions and not open to varieties of communication other than rational discourse seeking truth and consensus. Whereas deliberative democrats drawing on the Habermasian logic of communicative action look to a rational, deliberative conversation aiming at consensus on state policy, critics seek a more open, heterogeneous, and varied participatory democracy that need not be at the state level, need not focus on policy, and may result in disagreement rather than consensus.[48] Second line parades in NOLA speak directly to the questioning of models of deliberative democracy and the attempts to create democratic alternatives.

NOLA exemplifies the common, real-world situation where the political norm or practice is the exclusion of many from deliberation directly linked to government (from voting to policy-making) and where, even on those occasions where the excluded are invited in, it is very difficult for them to talk effectively in the language of the powerful and even more difficult to have the powerful listen.[49] Recognizing exclusion from the official, governmental sphere, second line parades engage most frequently with civil society and only indirectly with the state.[50]

The politics of parading rarely seeks to join formal, "rational," policy dialogue, although it is nonetheless an element of NOLA's political discourse. The roots of African American parading are deeply embedded in local understandings of power, aspirations of and struggles for freedom, shared cultural voices, and mutually supportive and open public displays of community. African American second lines constitute an informed subaltern, democratic politics connecting people through generations in and across neighborhoods. Residents and organizers of parades understand the varieties of meanings of their parades, which those less familiar with the neighborhoods and communities may find less accessible.

Second liners and Mardi Gras Indians are far from being the politically ignorant citizens portrayed in some critiques of democracy.[51] If one thinks of democracies rather than democracy, what counts as political knowledge needs to be carefully recalibrated to include varieties of knowledge and political experience among different strata and groups in society.[52] These experiences represent one manifestation of democracy as proposed by Wolin: beyond, outside, or different from government. He writes that "[d]emocracy needs to be reconceived as something other than a form of government: as a mode of being that is conditioned by bitter experience, doomed to succeed only temporarily, but is a recurrent possibility as long as the memory of the political survives."[53] Parades revive the common concerns and struggles of the community and animate memory by visiting sites important to the community. The Desire and Florida housing developments have long been demolished, but the Nine Times Social Aid and Pleasure Club preserves their memory by including their locations along the line of march and stopping at McGee's Bar where some of the project's bricks have been saved; and that group signals the need to bridge divisions by always crossing a bridge.

Lying mostly outside government, parades involve various forms of democratic engagement and participation, including those not within the sphere of formal political deliberation.[54] Actors can be democratic without having to live up to the norms of deliberative democracy: they need not be sincere or otherwise pure in motivation; expressions of self-interest or strategic arguments may be allowed; and arrival at consensus need not be assumed or expected.[55] Participation in civil society with political meaning assumes different forms, some of which may at first blush seem neither political nor democratic, but which fit an expanded definition of discourse advocated by some critics of deliberative democracy. Not only rational presentation and discussion but other modes—such as rhetoric or storytelling—are permitted. Indeed, for some theorists deliberation can include any or "all activities that function as communicative influence under conditions of conflict."[56] Second line parades, although regulated by the state, allow individual activities and expressions that are usually prohibited or discouraged, such as taking over streets for parading and music, participating in a community of marchers, dancing on rooftops, and memorializing places of historical importance to the paraders' community. These are activities that reject, even if only for four hours, the rules and expectations of the existing power structure and suggest different ways of living and being outside its discipline. These parades speak to an "agonistic" vision of democracy in which difference and opposition to power are continually expressed and reenforced, not so much by words as by actions that proclaim a "certain mode of being."[57]

Civil society may be the best locus for self-assertion by the social aid and pleasure clubs that organize second line parades, regardless of, despite, or in opposition to government. In other words, democratic politics may exist, as Alan Ryan says, "outside the conventionally defined political sphere."[58] He believes that "democratic realism can only advance social justice and the general well-being of the nation if it rests on a participatory society."[59] NOLA Mardi Gras can appear to be just a party, one essential for the tourism industry. But the old-line, official, white krewes that predominate in the official Mardi Gras parade represent and reassert the traditional powers in the community,[60] and the second lines, masking, and music that make up parading during the year are also part of the politics of class, race, and gender in the city, expressing opposition and an alternative to those traditional powers.

By challenging and changing the character of public spaces and the terms of public discourse, power can be exercised in civil society. Indeed, for the excluded, civil society may be not only the most favorable but the only site for democratic practice.[61] Parades by themselves do not create "deep" or fully emancipatory democracy because they are often disconnected from major governmental and market centers of power.[62] Although the recent second line parade that advocated restoring Charity Hospital stands out as an exception, second line parades usually do not explicitly or directly speak to changing specific public policies, and so they are not part of formal governmental policy determinations. Still, under conditions of substantial inequality and government disregard for the disempowered, parading is communal, political activity that recognizes burdens and lack of access to formal political power, improves the quality of life, spreads pleasures, and speaks to government oppression and neglect.[63]

Parades, therefore, challenge the character of public space and the terms of political discourse. They reject the privatization and instrumentalization of public space and call for its communal and expressive use. They seek to expand political discourse beyond formal rational dialogue aiming at consensus and to extend that discourse into civil society. They open spaces for alternative modes of expression; because civil society is heterogeneous, so too should be what counts as politically relevant dialogue or expression.[64] Wolin writes: "In my understanding, democracy is a project concerned with the political potentialities of ordinary citizens, that is, with their possibilities for becoming political beings through the self-discovery of common concerns and of modes of action for realizing them."[65] Second line parades in New Orleans are part of this democratic project: although planned in outline, each parade is also a spontaneous expression of individual and community, presenting an alternative way of being in opposition to institutionalized power, and reenacting and rediscovering memory as a bridge to the future.

Notes

1. Billy Sothern, "A Second-Line Revival," *The Nation*, February 13, 2006, http://www.thenation.com/article/second-line-revival#.

2. Helen A. Regis describes second lines: "These massive moving street festivals, commonly drawing from 3,000 to 5,000 people, are organized and funded by working-class African Americans to celebrate the anniversaries of their distinctive social clubs and benevolent societies. Second lines are also performed to mark the passing of community members in events more widely known outside New Orleans as 'jazz funerals.'" Regis, "Second Lines, Minstrelsy, and the Contested Landscapes of New Orleans Afro-Creole Festivals," *Cultural Anthropology* 14, no. 4 (1999): 472.

3. Alessandra Lorini offers insights into the concept of public culture: "Unlike in other western countries, public culture in the United States has always been the ground where irreconcilable differences could confront and negotiate their space. Far from being a neutral ground, public culture is a contested space in which collective or subjective identities fight for recognition. Public culture is also broader than political culture as it can include politically conflictual contents. Furthermore, public culture is broader than the notion of public space, a concept take[n] from Jürgen Habermas's *Structural Transformation of the Public Sphere* (Cambridge: Polity Press, 1989), that is more connected to representative democracy." Lorini, *Rituals of Race: American Public Culture and the Search for Racial Democracy* (Charlottesville: University of Virginia Press, 1999), xii. We do not believe that public space is neutral ground or that political culture necessarily does not include serious conflict. But the idea of a public culture as broader than Habermas's understanding aligns with our approach to democracy.

4. Sheldon Wolin, "Fugitive Democracy," in *Democracy and Difference*, ed. Seyla Benhabib (Princeton, NJ: Princeton University Press, 1996), 38.

5. The distinction here between two broad types of democratic theory—liberal representative and deliberative—pervades the literature and is discussed in the final section of this chapter.

6. Many who are concerned with democracy and difference may appear to come close to the idea of democracy despite government, but the remaining contrasts are significant. Those concerned with difference use phrases such as informal democratic practices or "informal deliberative enclaves of resistance," in Jane Mansbridge's words; she goes on to theorize that "democracies need to foster and value" these enclaves "in which those who lose in each coercive move can rework their ideas and their strategies, gathering their forces and deciding in a more protected space in what way or whether to continue the battle." See Mansbridge, "Using Power/Fighting Power: The Polity," in Benhabib, *Democracy and Difference*, 46–47. Democracy despite government, however, does not assume "deliberation" as the only or primary form of political communication, and it does not rely on democratic governments' willingly "fostering" such enclaves.

Rather, it focuses on democratic practices, not on tactical decisions about seeking power, and differs from Mansbridge's views about what "the battle" is.

7. Wolin, "Fugitive Democracy," 31–45.

8. Parades might also be seen as a weapon of the weak, but we believe they serve as more than that in supporting a democratic culture, albeit one that is not institutionally part of government. See James C. Scott, *Weapons of the Weak* (New Haven, CT: Yale University Press, 1985). Of course, not all parading shares in democratic values and actions; indeed, parades can also serve authoritarian regimes or antidemocratic norms in formally democratic countries. Mardi Gras festivities in New Orleans for generations affirmed white supremacy, although African Americans created their own Mardi Gras. For a theoretical discussion about intersections of carnival and politics see Abner Cohen, *Masquerade Politics* (Berkeley: University of California Press, 1993), chaps. 9 and 10.

9. Helen A. Regis, "Blackness and the Politics of Memory in the New Orleans Second Line," *American Ethnologist* 28, no. 4 (2001): 756.

10. Don Mitchell, *The Right to the City: Social Justice and the Fight for Public Space* (New York: Guilford Press, 2003), 32, emphasis in the original.

11. Nancy Fraser, "Rethinking the Public Sphere: A Contribution to the Critique of Actually Existing Democracy," *Social Text* 25/26 (1990): 67. See also Catherine R. Squires, "Rethinking the Black Public Sphere," *Communication Theory* 12, no. 4 (2002): 446–68.

12. See Reid Mitchell, *All on a Mardi Gras Day* (Cambridge, MA: Harvard University Press, 1995); James Gill, *Lords of Misrule* (Jackson: University of Mississippi Press, 1997); J. Mark Souther, *New Orleans on Parade* (Baton Rouge: Louisiana State University Press, 2006); and Rachel Breunlin and Helen A. Regis, "Putting the Ninth Ward on the Map: Race, Place, and Transformation in Desire, New Orleans," *American Anthropologist* 108, no. 4 (2006): 744–64.

13. Souther, *New Orleans on Parade*, 125.

14. Social aid and pleasure clubs were originally established to provide economic assistance and proper burials for those without means, and socializing accompanied the mutual aid functions of the clubs. For a history of the Zulu Social Aid and Pleasure Club see http://www.kreweofzulu.com/Krewe-Of-Zulu/History-Of-the-Zulu-Social-Aid-&-Pleasure-Club.html, and the Louisiana State Museum's exhibit, "From Tramps to Kings: One Hundred Years of Zulu," http://lsm.crt.state.la.us/zulu/html/media.html.

15. In a PBS special Professor Raphael Cassimere Jr. of the University of New Orleans, in response to a question about whether the Zulu's characterizations are racist, answers: "No, it is not about racism, but was considered an alternative to the 'whites only' activities of Carnival. It began as a spoof, but gained popularity with working class and some of middle class as time passed. It was a subtle form of protest against the powers that be without crossing the line of 'expected and accepted' racial behavior." PBS, *The American Experience, New Orleans*, http://www.pbs.org/wgbh/amex/neworleans/sfeature/zulu.html.

16. Dating the appearance of Black Indians (masking as Indian also occurs in Caribbean countries) and explaining the precise reasons for this form of masking are difficult. Michael P. Smith writes: "From the beginning of the 18th Century, throughout the Caribbean and Central and South America, Blacks had been observed parading the public streets on various occasions, elaborately dressed and masked in the style of American Indians. Blacks in Haiti celebrate their freedom from slavery by masking Indian on Mardi Gras. . . . In New Orleans the Mardi Gras or Black Indian tradition seems to have appeared, or perhaps reappeared, shortly after 1872 when the State Legislature made it legal to mask on Mardi Gras from sunrise to sunset." Smith, *Spirit World* (New Orleans, LA: New Orleans Urban Folklife Society, 1984), 85.

17. Mitchell, *All on a Mardi Gras Day*, 116.

18. Samuel Kinser, *Carnival American Style* (Chicago: University of Chicago Press, 1990), 160.

19. Willie J. Clarke, "A Short History of the Mardi Gras Indians," http:// www.mardigrasneworleans.com/mardigrasindians.html.

20. Liza Katzman, *Tootie's Last Suit*, Pomegranate, 2007, DVD.

21. Smith, *Spirit World*, 85. It should be noted that clubs are not necessarily internally egalitarian and that it is men who mask. Women take part through helping create the costumes and joining the parade.

22. Kinser, *Carnival American Style*, 160.

23. Ibid., 232.

24. Contestation over issues of integration in Mardi Gras continued into the 1990s. In 1991, city council member Dorothy Mae Taylor introduced an ordinance requiring krewes to demonstrate that they were desegregated in order to receive a parade permit. Few krewes or clubs met the nondiscriminatory criteria of admitting members, and old-line white krewes decided not to parade in Mardi Gras; see Souther, *New Orleans on Parade*, 213–14. In the end, although a version of the ordinance was passed, the city council, a majority of whom were African American, refused to require Mardi Gras krewes actively to demonstrate nondiscrimination.

25. Ned Sublette, *The World That Made New Orleans* (Chicago: Lawrence Hill Books, 2008), 294.

26. Breunlin and Regis, "Putting the Ninth Ward," 746.

27. Andrea Boll, *The Parade Goes on Without You* (New Orleans, LA: NOLAFugees Press, 2009), 133.

28. Helen A. Regis, "Blackness and the Politics of Memory in the New Orleans Second Line," *American Ethnologist* 28, no. 4 (2001): 757.

29. Sothern, "Second-Line Revival."

30. http://blog.nola.com/notesonneworleans/2008/11/sundays_second_ line_parade_nin.html. According to Breunlin and Regis, Nine Times "not only produces a parade but also effectively produces a new experience of and representation of neighborhood—Nine Times. It also claims a collective ownership

of a landscape that is considered marginal land" in the Ninth Ward. Breunlin and Regis, "Putting the Ninth Ward," 749.

31. Breunlin and Regis, "Putting the Ninth Ward," 749.

32. Ibid., 751. Desire, opened in the Ninth Ward in the 1950s, had fourteen thousand residents at one time. Over the years neglect by government, an increase in violence, and the exodus by residents contributed to the final buildings being torn down in 2003. Plans for redevelopment of mixed-use, mixed-income residences have resulted in limited rebuilding.

33. Sublette, *The World That Made New Orleans*, 124.

34. Breunlin and Regis note that "in the late 1980s, when Helen first began participating in these parades, nearly every social club either started or ended their routes in a project, or they passed through a major housing development during their Sunday afternoon anniversary parades." Breunlin and Regis, "Putting the Ninth Ward," 753.

35. Sothern, "Second-Line Revival."

36. Regis, "Blackness and Politics of Memory," 766.

37. The social aid and pleasure clubs themselves have an exclusive character, as any club does, but the parades are very open affairs.

38. Souther, *New Orleans on Parade*, 127. Lolis Elie's film *Faubourg Tremé* (Serendipity Films and Louisiana Public Broadcasting, 2008) presents a moving story about this section of the city.

39. Michael White, "New Orleans's African American Musical Traditions," in *Seeking Higher Ground*, eds. Manning Marable and Kristen Clarke (New York: Palgrave, 2008), 93.

40. The photograph of the Nine Times second line in 2007 shows streams of people taking over a bridge and street for what looks like a mile or more. http://blog.nola.com/notesonneworleans/2008/11/sundays_second_line_parade_nin.html.

41. In 2006 after the All Star Second Line, a series of shootings prompted the NOPD to raise parade permit fees from approximately $1,600 per club to $3,800. Breunlin and Regis, "Putting the Ninth Ward," 758.

42. Ibid., 754, 757.

43. Lolis Elie, "Ignorance Undermines Culture," *New Orleans Times Picayune*, October 5, 2007, http://pqasb.pqarchiver.com/timespicayune/access/1355257191.html.

44. Katzman, *Tootie's Last Suit*.

45. Elie, "Ignorance Undermines Culture."

46. James Bohman, "Survey Article: The Coming of Age of Deliberative Democracy," *Journal of Political Philosophy* 6, no. 4 (1998): 400–25.

47. André Bächtiger, Simon Niemeyer, Michael Neblo, Marco R. Steenbergen, and Jürg Steiner, "Disentangling Diversity in Deliberative Democracy: Competing Theories, Their Blind Spots and Complementarities," *Journal of Political Philosophy* 17, no. 1 (2009): 1–32.

48. Similar to these criticisms of deliberative democracy is Sheldon Wolin's criticism of Rawls: "Although Rawls posits a citizenry in which all are free and equal" and share equally in political power and influence, "that vision is hopelessly at odds with the central fact of political life," that power is never freely discussed and shared but is only "wrested in conflict." Wolin, "The Liberal/Democratic Divide: On Rawls's *Political Liberalism*," *Political Theory* 24, no. 1 (1996): 108.

49. Emblematic of the difficulty of having the powerful listen are the protests against the destruction of public housing organized by Hands Off Iberville, Survivors Village, and the Coalition to Stop Demolition, and a lawsuit intended to prevent their destruction by the Housing Authority of New Orleans (HANO) in conjunction with Housing and Urban Development (HUD). The 4,500 units of CJ Peete, St. Bernard, Lafitte, and BW Cooper have been torn down with the approval of the NOLA City Council. Only Iberville remains.

50. This argument differs from James Scott's: "Where everyday resistance more strikingly departs from other forms of resistance is in its implicit disavowal of public and symbolic goals. Where institutionalized politics is formal, overt, concerned with systematic, de jure change, everyday resistance is informal, often covert, and concerned largely with immediate, de facto gains." Scott, *Weapons of the Weak*, 33. Parading, for instance, is overt and can involve long-term as well as immediate "gains."

51. See Bruce Gilley, "Doubts on Democracy," *Journal of Democracy* 20, no. 1 (2009): 113–27.

52. See Seyla Benhabib, "Introduction: The Democratic Moment and the Problem of Difference," in Benhabib, *Democracy and Difference*, 3–18; and Wolin, "Fugitive Democracy."

53. Wolin, "Fugitive Democracy," 43.

54. Parades thus have affinities with Carole Pateman's understanding of participatory democracy. She maintains that there is a meaningful distinction between deliberative and participatory democracy: "The tacit acceptance of existing power structures is a major reason why I do not see deliberative and participatory democracy as synonymous or deliberative democracy as the direct successor to participatory democracy. Participatory democracy has a much broader scope. It is about changing the common sense meaning of 'democracy' and the hegemony of the official view; in short it is about democratization. Structural change, refashioning undemocratic institutions, and undermining subordination and domination are the heart of participatory democracy." Pateman, Afterword to *Illusion of Consent*, eds. Daniel I. O'Neill, Mary Lyndon Shanley, and Iris Marion Young (University Park: Pennsylvania State University Press, 2008), 237.

55. Iris Marion Young, *Inclusion and Democracy* (Oxford, UK: Oxford University Press, 2002), 49.

56. Mark E. Warren, "Institutionalizing Deliberative Democracy," in *Deliberation, Participation and Democracy*, ed. Shawn Rosenberg (London: Palgrave Macmillan, 2007), 278.

57. Benhabib, "Introduction: The Democratic Moment," 8.

58. Alan Ryan, "Participation Revisited," in O'Neill, Shanley, and Young, *Illusion of Consent*, 166.

59. Ibid., 183.

60. Even though the mayor greeting the kings of Rex and Zulu signals the commencement of the official Mardi Gras, it is still predominantly white, its krewes and balls segregated, and its economic and symbolic importance to the city apparent.

61. Benjamin R. Barber offers an expansive definition, which can include understandings of democracy beyond the governmental sphere: "Politically, we may define democracy as a regime/culture/civil society/government in which we make (will) common decisions, choose common conduct, and create or express common values in the practical domain of our lives in an ever-changing context of conflict of interests and competition for power—a setting, moreover, where there is no agreement on prior goods or certain knowledge about justice or right and where we must proceed on the premise of the base equality both of interests and of the interested." Barber, "Foundationalism and Democracy," in Benhabib, *Democracy and Difference*, 350. Admittedly his sights are usually set on the formally political; but his construction opens up vistas for understanding democratic practices.

62. See Michael Goodhart, "A Democratic Defense of Universal Basic Income," in O'Neill, Shanley, and Young, *Illusion of Consent*, 139, 142.

63. Parading should not be romanticized as a form of democracy, however. Not all residents agree about issues, and not all join parades. One funeral second line for D-Boy who had been involved with drugs was deliberately avoided by members of his community who felt such recognition was inappropriate and implicitly condoned the life he led. Regis, "Blackness and the Politics of Memory," 762. There is contention within communities about particular parades.

64. See Michael Walzer, *Politics and Passion* (New Haven, CT: Yale University Press, 2004) and John S. Dryzek, *Deliberative Democracy and Beyond* (Oxford, UK: Oxford University Press, 2000).

65. Wolin, "Fugitive Democracy," 31.

Bibliography

Bächtiger, André, Simon Niemeyer, Michael Neblo, Marco R. Steenbergen, and Jürg Steiner. "Disentangling Diversity in Deliberative Democracy: Competing Theories, Their Blind Spots and Complementarities." *Journal of Political Philosophy* 17, no. 1 (2009): 1–32.

Barber, Benjamin R. "Foundationalism and Democracy." In Benhabib, *Democracy and Difference*, 348–59.

Benhabib, Seyla, ed. *Democracy and Difference*. Princeton, NJ: Princeton University Press, 1996.

Benhabib, Seyla. "Introduction: The Democratic Movement and the Problem of Difference." In Benhabib, *Democracy and Difference*, 3–18.

Bohman, James. "Survey Article: The Coming of Age of Deliberative Democracy." *Journal of Political Philosophy* 6, no. 4 (1998): 400–25.

Boll, Andrea. *The Parade Goes on Without You*. New Orleans: NOLAFugees Press, 2009.

Breunlin, Rachel, and Helen A. Regis. "Putting the Ninth Ward on the Map: Race, Place, and Transformation in Desire, New Orleans." *American Anthropologist* 108, no. 4 (2006): 744–64.

Clarke, Willie J. "A Short History of the Mardi Gras Indians." http://www.mardigrasneworleans.com/mardigrasindians.html.

Cohen, Abner. *Masquerade Politics*. Berkeley: University of California Press, 1993.

Dryzek, John S. *Deliberative Democracy and Beyond*. Oxford, UK: Oxford University Press, 2000.

Elie, Lolis Eric. "Ignorance Undermines Culture." *New Orleans Times-Picayune*. October 5, 2007. http://pqasb.pqarchiver.com/timespicayune/access/1355257191.html.

———. *Faubourg Tremé*. New Orleans: Serendipity Films and Louisiana Public Broadcasting, 2008. Film.

Fraser, Nancy. "Rethinking the Public Sphere: A Contribution to the Critique of Actually Existing Democracy." *Social Text* 25/26 (1990): 56–80.

Gilley, Bruce. "Doubts on Democracy." *Journal of Democracy* 20, no. 1 (2009): 113–27.

Gills, James. *Lords of Misrule*. Jackson: University of Mississippi Press, 1997.

Goodhart, Michael. "A Democratic Defense of Universal Basic Income." In O'Neill, Shanley, and Young, *Illusion of Consent*, 139–62.

Katzman, Lisa, dir. *Tootie's Last Suit*. New York: Pomegranate Productions, 2007. DVD.

Kisner, Samuel. *Carnival American Style*. Chicago: Chicago University Press, 1990.

Lorini, Alessandra. *Rituals of Race: American Public Culture and the Search for Radical Democracy*. Charlottesville: University of Virginia Press, 1999.

Louisiana State Museum. "From Tramps to Kings: One Hundred Years of Zulu." http://lsm.crt.state.la.us/zulu/html/media.html.

Mansbridge, Jane. "Using Power/Fighting Power: The Polity." In Benhabib, *Democracy and Difference*, 46–66.

Mitchell, Don. *The Right to the City: Social Justice and the Fight for Public Space*. New York: Guilford Press, 2003.

Mitchell, Reid. *All on a Mardi Gras Day*. Cambridge, MA: Harvard University Press, 1995.

Notes on New Orleans blog. http://blog.nola.com/notesonneworleans/2008/11/sundays_second_line_parade_nin.html.

O'Neill, Daniel I., Mary Lyndon Shanley, and Iris Marion Young, eds. *Illusion of Consent*. University Park: Pennsylvania State University Press, 2008.

Pateman, Carole. Afterword. In O'Neill, Shanley, and Young, *Illusion of Consent*, 231–43.

PBS. "The Zulu Parade of Mardi Gras." *American Experience*. December 1, 2006. http://www.pbs.org/wgbh/amex/neworleans/sfeature/zulu.html.

Regis, Helen A. "Second Lines, Minstrelsy, and the Contested Landscape of New Orleans Afro-Creole Festivals." *Cultural Anthropology* 14, no. 4 (1999): 472–504.

———. "Blackness and the Politics of Memory in the New Orleans Second Line." *American Ethnologist* 28, no. 4 (2001): 752–77.

Ryan, Alan. "Participation Revisited." In O'Neill, Shanley, and Young, *Illusion of Consent*, 165–84.

Scott, James C. *Weapons of the Weak*. New Haven, CT: Yale University Press, 1985.

Smith, Michael P. *Spirit World*. New Orleans, LA: New Orleans Urban Folklife Society, 1984.

Sothern, Billy. "A Second-Line Revival." *The Nation* 282, no. 6 (2006): 213–14. http://www.thenation.com/article/second-line-revival#.

Souther, J. Mark. *New Orleans on Parade*. Baton Rouge: Louisiana State University Press, 2006.

Squires, Catherine R. "Rethinking the Black Public Spheres." *Communication Theory* 12, no. 4 (2002): 446–68.

Sublette, Ned. *The World That Made New Orleans*. Chicago: Lawrence Hill Books, 2008.

Walzer, Michael. *Politics and Passion*. New Haven, CT: Yale University Press, 2004.

Warren, Mark, E. "Institutionalizing Deliberative Democracy." In *Deliberation, Participation and Democracy*, edited by Shawn Rosenberg, 272–88. London: Palgrave Macmillan, 2007.

White, Michael. "New Orleans's African American Musial Traditions." In *Seeking Higher Ground*, edited by Manning Marable and Kristen Clarke, 87–106. New York: Palgrave, 2008.

Wolin, Sheldon. "Fugitive Democracy." In Benhabib, *Democracy and Difference*, 31–45.

———. "The Liberal Democratic Divide: On Rawls's Political Liberalism." *Political Theory* 24, no. 1 (1996): 97–119.

Young, Iris Marion. *Inclusion and Democracy*. Oxford, UK: Oxford University Press, 2002.

Zulu Social Aid and Pleasure Club. "History." http://www.kreweofzulu.com/Krewe-Of-Zulu/History-Of-the-Zulu-Social-Aid-&-Pleasure-Club.html.

Part VIII

Conclusion

Chapter 14

Conclusion

Activist Arts, Community Development, and Democracy

Mark Mattern and Nancy S. Love

> Art cannot be about the people; it cannot be for the people; it must
> be by the people.
>
> —Jan Avgikos, "Group Material Timeline:
> Activism as a Work of Art"

In this concluding chapter we take a closer look at an increasingly important form of activist art: intentional, directed attempts to use art to drive community development. Many neighborhoods, cities, states, and even nations are turning to the arts and culture as a stimulus for community development. These diverse efforts incorporate many different approaches. This chapter addresses two dominant approaches: an elites-driven approach and a community arts approach.[1] These should be seen as polarities, with many arts-related development projects actually falling somewhere in between.[2] Some of the earlier chapters in this volume discuss projects that are located on this continuum. For example, Luke's analysis of the National D-Day Memorial in Bedford, Virginia, might be located near the elites-driven pole. Baum's piece on how the In the House Festival transformed the city neighborhoods and streets in Vancouver, British Columbia, belongs much closer to the community arts pole. Other chapters, such as those on South African resistant theater,

Day of the Dead festivals, and the parades of New Orleans, Louisiana, feature communal uses of the arts for celebration and protest that do not directly engage development-related public or private policies. These examples do not belong on the aforementioned continuum with its emphasis on direct policy interventions in community development. However, by bringing public attention to community needs, these and other uses of the arts and popular culture discussed here may indirectly shape future policy initiatives.

The roots of these two approaches to arts-led community development extend at least to the late nineteenth century,[3] and a lively debate over their relative merits is ongoing. Both approaches are employed today in arts-led community development efforts. After describing the features of elites-driven and community arts approaches, we briefly address two case studies to illustrate the approaches. As illustrated by the Santa Ana, California case study, many cities continue to embrace an elites-driven approach. The second case study, of Music & Performing Arts at Trinity Cathedral in Cleveland, Ohio, is based in a community arts approach and serves as a critical response to some of the shortcomings of an elites-driven approach. We argue that, in its current form, the community arts approach is more intrinsically democratic, and it promises more genuine and lasting community development within urban environments. The elites-driven model can, however, be modified to incorporate more democratic elements.

Community development can mean many different things. Sometimes it is conflated with economic development, where all community development efforts are aimed at increasing a city or region's tax base, commercial activity, or productive capacity.[4] A broader understanding includes this economic component, but adds other considerations such as building social capital, addressing marginalization, preparing a foundation for addressing public problems, and actually addressing those public problems, only some of which are economic.[5] In this chapter, we adopt this broader understanding.

Elites-Driven Public Art

The elites-driven approach to public art is generated by public officials, philanthropists, business leaders, and other elites to raise a city's or region's profile and image; increase tourism, commercial activity, and civic pride; commemorate dominant figures and events drawn from a dominant account of history; and adorn prominent features of a city or region. Characteristic of this approach are big-ticket downtown and other "flagship" projects, cultural centers, and arts districts. This kind of public art is usually linked to "top-down, 'pro-growth' development initiated by or for business elites,"[6] in which community development is understood primarily as economic development. It generally takes as given the already existing "social and artistic conventions."[7]

In this approach, participation in the arts is typically assumed to be synonymous with consumption of the arts, and audience-as-consumer participation at professional arts events is favored over other forms of participation, such as amateur participation in art-making. According to advocates of this approach, audience development is best accomplished by exposing people, especially youth, to so-called high art.[8] This exposure will, in theory, increase understanding and appreciation for (high) art, generating more consumption of it. Related to this, there is an emphasis on the art product apart from the process of making the art. Art is a commodity for consumption rather than an opportunity for widespread participation in a creative endeavor. It is assumed that the creative process itself is the domain of, and should be reserved for, professional artists with acknowledged credentials; others are not invited into this process of creation. The artist in this approach is thus often segregated from the processes in which the public art project is conceived, planned, and implemented by the elites who are driving it. The artist works for the most part in isolation from the social processes that generate and implement the project.[9]

Backers of this approach to public art often argue that its benefits, while direct and immediate for downtowns and other areas near the public art site, will eventually spill outward into surrounding neighborhoods and potentially throughout the city. The benefits they claim include increased visibility, pride, and tourism; the beautification of once-ugly or blighted areas; and overall increases in economic activity as ripple and spillover effects occur. These claims have been backed by relatively few empirical studies; the benefits are often simply assumed.[10]

Many community activists think elites-driven public art contributes to the ongoing disintegration of urban and natural environments. They charge, first of all, that this approach to art is often generated and imposed by elites guilty of "condescension and cultural elitism,"[11] without sufficient community input. Critics refer to it variously as "authoritarian populism,"[12] "plop art,"[13] and "parachuted in" art[14] because of its propensity to "invade public space without any consideration for the people and the environment surrounding them."[15] As a result, critics charge additionally that this form of arts-led development is inevitably exclusive.[16] Typically generated by elites, with elite interests in mind, it excludes most community members from the planning and implementation of the project(s). Not surprisingly, it therefore sometimes generates various forms of reaction and resistance, including graffiti and vandalism, an ongoing problem for many cities' flagship and monumental art installations.[17]

Given its ties to dominant elites and their interests, this kind of public art "reinforces the dominance of the cultural elites"[18] and serves as "propaganda for existing power structures (especially development and banking)."[19] It perpetuates elites' dominance by reinforcing the dominant cultural and political values and narratives that give the art its meaning. Elites-driven public art often offers a narrow and exclusive account of history, memory, and identity. Critics ask: Whose identity and whose culture is represented here? Since elites-driven art is championed and sponsored by powerful elites, it typically presents a dominant account of history and identity consistent with the interests of the elites. Monuments, for example, are "produced within a dominant framework of values, as elements in the construction of a national history. . . . They suppose at least a partial consensus of values, without which their narrative could not be recognized."[20] Henry Lefebvre warns of the ability of monuments to "mask the will to power and the arbitrariness of power beneath signs and surfaces which claim to express collective will and collective thought."[21] The expansive use of monuments during the nineteenth century is inseparable from the history of colonialism, and the growth of European collections plundered from colonies. These public monuments serve to glorify the exploits of colonizers and to present the winners' perspective in a noble light. By perpetuating the dominance of elites, this first kind of public art in effect becomes a form of social control. And as a form of social control, it is "less brutish and costly than armed force."[22]

Elites-driven public art is also charged with legitimizing existing inequality and injustice. It legitimizes existing power structures by beautifying them and giving them the respectability accorded to arts patrons in dominant western culture. It helps justify urban gentrification and the failure to address the interests and concerns of marginalized urban residents. Elites-driven public art may divert attention from pressing problems and issues. It substitutes placing a "shiny veneer" over problems rather than using art for genuine community development.[23] Elites-driven public art thus may perpetuate uneven urban development. This approach tends to increase the likelihood that funds will flow toward downtown and gentrifying areas and away from marginalized communities. Bureaucratic inertia in governments, foundations, and other funding organizations inevitably favors existing organizations, facilities, and city centers already in the funding stream, while slighting new and often marginalized entrants.[24] This leads to inequality of funding and of access to arts and cultural resources, in which the result is a "center-periphery pattern."[25] Some critics conclude that any involvement in elites-driven public art efforts is "inherently linked to collusion with forces that are fundamentally more interested in capital investment or maintaining social order than with improving the lives of residents of a city."[26]

Community Arts

In this section, we look at the source of many of the criticisms of elites-driven public art and also the proposals for reform. Community arts, or "new genre public art," lie at the other pole and first appeared in part as a reaction to elites-driven public art.[27] Their roots are variously attributed to feminist art, sixties activism, the early-twentieth-century settlement house movement, the New Deal's Works Project Administration (WPA), conceptualism, performance art, and more.[28] Considered the cutting edge of public art during the 1990s and into the new millennium, community arts pursue goals that include supporting local artists, building social capital, increasing social cohesion and inclusion, addressing marginality, pursuing justice through collective action, and generating local development. Community arts seek to create a public and address a public issue, not just exist in a public space. If some traditional public art exists to distract viewers from reality, community arts seek to face reality and change it. So community arts are self-consciously activist in orientation.

Community arts build on a foundation of knowledge about a community, its needs and interests, and knowledge that emerges from community members themselves. Many community development attempts have foundered on a failure to take the community on its own terms rather than those imposed by outsiders. Community arts advocates insist that it is crucial to begin by learning about the community. They claim that this approach is more respectful because it presumes that neighborhood residents are experts about their own lives and avoids the all-too-common problem of outsiders imposing their own views on residents of what is good for them. It is also more effective in that it is more likely to address real, as opposed to perceived, needs and interests, and also more likely to succeed if it engages community members in every level of the artistic process. Asking community members about themselves achieves this early engagement.

Increasingly, community arts projects now begin by mapping existing arts and culture resources, and attempting to build on the assets and strengths of a community and its residents. Community arts "focus on people's strengths and interests," rather than externally defined problems and interests.[29] These include the individual skills and talents of residents as well as neighborhood institutions such as community centers, schools, churches, and businesses. Acknowledging and building on existing assets further establishes a model at the outset of equal partners rather than expert-client. It also gives the community development effort a head start by avoiding the necessity of building from nothing.

Community arts are dialogic in that the process of simultaneously creating art and community requires listening and talking among various participants. To avoid the problem of plop art, community arts advocates engage in ongoing dialogue with community members to identify their needs and interests, create the art project(s) that will attempt to address those needs and interests, and evaluate the outcomes of the art project(s). Embracing a dialogic model best ensures that goals and strategies emerge from genuine community needs and interests. Keeping the dialogue going ensures sustained community involvement. Continuous interaction between artists and community members facilitates a communicative infrastructure that serves as the foundation for the art. The work of art is inseparable from this sustained dialogue. According to Suzanne Lacy, the relationship that is developed between the artist and the audience "may *itself* become the artwork."[30]

As the preceding discussion suggests, community arts are collaborative in nature. Collaboration occurs among participating artists, between artists and community members, and among community members representing various constituencies. The artists work within the community rather than bringing art to the community. Members of the community play a central role in identifying the need for a project, in assembling the human and financial resources, in creating art, and in determining the meaning of the art. This ensures that the community retains control of the project and increases the likelihood that community members will invest time and energy into it. Forming multiple partnerships and collaborative relationships with community members multiplies the power and resources held by individual groups and organizations. It eliminates at least some duplication of effort, while creating synergistic opportunities not available to organizations working independently.

Unlike elites-driven arts, community arts emphasize process over the finished product.[31] This process contributes to community development, and the public it produces is more important than the art product. Community arts advocates believe that "the responsibility of public artists is not to create permanent objects for presentation in traditionally accepted public places but, instead, to assist in the construction of a public—to encourage, through actions, ideas, and interventions, a participatory audience where none seemed to exist . . . They implore citizens/viewers to discover the relation between art production and democratic participation."[32] The community artist's "work" is thus a verb, and the community artist's "art" includes the process of community-building as well as any product that may emerge.[33] Public arts projects too often proceed under the assumption that a final arts project must be completed; and that the project must be judged a failure without a final arts product. But if community development is the goal, then the "product" should be just that, community development. The art is the medium through which community members exert their efforts and the community evolves. In other words, community development emerges through, and as, an interactive, communicative process that may span months or years and may begin very indirectly and in unanticipated ways.

Several contributions to this volume illustrate different aspects of this ongoing collaborative process of communication and development. For example, to prevent corruption and increase safety on neighborhood streets, the photo-activists described by Frank Möller are transforming the meaning of surveillance cameras, using them to record the activities of police and drug dealers alike. The dialogues Chou and Bleiker describe between actors and audiences about the meaning of freedom after public performances of George Packer's play, *Betrayed*, are changing participants' views of community and identity. According to Bruce Baum, the community organizing efforts of ordinary citizens that created the In the House Festival in Vancouver, British Columbia, are reshaping public perceptions of underdeveloped city neighborhoods. It may be tempting to shorten the process by taking more efficient shortcuts with more direct policy outcomes. However, for community arts advocates, efficiency is not the paramount value of genuine community development. The development may sometimes occur precisely as a result of an inefficient, but valuable, process of iteration and reiteration of steps. It may result as outcomes of the frustrations and attempts to overcome them dialogically rather than by fiat.

In community arts, the artist catalyzes without imposing. According to community arts advocates, one of the basic reorientations that must occur for successful community art is to stop thinking in terms of bringing art *to* the people and start thinking in terms of making art *with* the people.[34] Community arts can achieve the most by helping community members realize their own capacities. Adopting the role of catalyst rather than the role of expert avoids the pitfalls inherent in provider–client relationships that model a dominant–submissive relationship rather than a partnership and that inevitably exclude community members from power-sharing and control over the project. Viewing the artist as expert rather than catalyst turns community members into passive clients, recipients of others' charity; it does not engage them as agents of their own fate.

Community arts are participatory and inclusive. Community arts are defined by their effort to increase the level and extent of participation in the process of community- and art-building. "Community involvement is the raw material of artistic practice" in a community arts project.[35] Without active participation by community members, the effort inevitably is an imposition. It is art *for* a community—plop art—not art *with* or *by* a community. Because community members are excluded from the process that generates plop art, many may remain indifferent or even hostile to it and ignorant of its meaning. Drawing community members into the entire process, from conception to implementation, increases the meaningfulness of the artwork for them, and increases too the likelihood that the community that develops will include them and address their needs and interests. Community arts self-consciously seek to include participants that "art institutions have barely reached even on those occasions when they have been interested in them."[36] These diverse participants, who are typically marginalized by differences of class, ethnicity, race, age, and gender, lie outside the dominant mainstream of power in the United States. Their inclusion requires exceptional commitment and strategy beyond that invested by mainstream art practices and institutions. The field of community arts is defined in part by that exceptional commitment. Community arts often make good on this promise of inclusion by typically choosing locations that are accessible and familiar: "in places and through organizations that are not primarily concerned with the arts, such as schools, churches, parks, community centers, social service organizations, social clubs and benevolent societies, and sometimes businesses and commercial retail establishments."[37]

Finally, the field of community arts is defined in part by a different aesthetic sensibility than that of elites-driven art. Elites-driven art generally incorporates a commitment to formal aesthetics, marked (as discussed in the introduction to this volume) by commitments to detached observation of art objects and events; formal analysis of art forms viewed as autonomous from a social context; and rejection of popular forms of arts and culture as legitimate art. Community arts embrace a performative aesthetics marked by a more dynamic, inclusive understanding of arts and culture; greater emphasis on the importance of affective engagement with an art form; the artist's and the art form's deep links to, and engagement with, a social context; and an understanding of audiences as direct participants in the process of creation.[38]

We have presented these two approaches to arts-led community development as ideal types. In practice, as noted earlier, there is sometimes considerable overlap between the two approaches. Additionally, disagreement sometimes surfaces within each approach. For example, advocates of a community arts approach sometimes disagree over whether community art should serve primarily as a vehicle for social cohesion or as a means of criticism and social challenge.[39] And community arts practitioners are not immune from the problem of occasionally slipping into "narrow economistic approaches" that betray the community arts emphasis on a broader understanding of community development.[40] We turn now to two case studies, the first of an elites-driven approach and the second of a community arts approach.

The City of Santa Ana, California

The city of Santa Ana is an important case study in elites-driven community development.[41] With an official population of approximately 325,000, it is Orange County's largest city and, with a per capita income of approximately $13,000, also its poorest. Complicating matters, a deep chasm separates the city's young, economically marginal, majority Hispanic population from its older, affluent, minority white population. Santa Ana has the largest percentage of Hispanics in Orange County and among the highest nationwide, listed officially at 78.2 percent of the city's population but likely higher, depending on variable estimates of undocumented residents. The need for community development in Santa Ana is both evident and pressing.[42]

To drive community development, in 1994, Santa Ana initiated an Artists Village in an approximately nine square block area in downtown. The village would eventually include several older buildings converted to artists' space and new construction oriented toward artists' and art consumers' needs. The early centerpiece of the Artists Village was the privately owned Santora Arts Building, housing approximately thirty studios and galleries. The Artists Village today also includes the Grand Central Art Center (which hosts a California State University, Fullerton branch campus for the arts), the Orange County Center for Contemporary Art, the Empire Arts Building, and several smaller galleries and design studios.[43] Live-work loft buildings that include their own galleries and showrooms have also been added to the mix. Direct city investment has been relatively modest. The city modified the zoning so that artists could live and work in the Artists Village, spent approximately $7.2 million on acquiring and rehabbing Grand Central (which they subsequently leased to Cal State, Fullerton for $1.00 per year), and invested approximately $1 million in acquiring and renovating Parkers Garage for the Orange County Center for Contemporary Art. Finally, the city spent modest sums on infrastructure improvements and banners.[44]

In addition to living and working there, the most apparent avenues for direct participation in the Artists Village are shopping and attending the monthly open houses (art walks). Typically, hundreds of people attend these events. Others patronize the growing number of restaurants and bars in or around the Artists Village. The impact of the Artists Village on downtown development has at least partly met the expectations of its backers. It has attracted new businesses into downtown, increased property values in the area as well as interest in Santa Ana among arts and culture patrons throughout southern California, and helped turn Santa Ana into a destination for many affluent arts patrons and consumers in the region.

Whatever positive effects have occurred must be measured against the negative effects, understood most clearly in terms of the impact of the Artists Village on the majority Hispanic population of Santa Ana. The level of Hispanic participation has always been, and remains, very low. This low level of participation by Hispanics is especially ironic given that Fourth Street, known informally as "Little Mexico" because of its predominately Hispanic character, lies only one short block to the north. This urban strip is lined with Hispanic businesses that primarily serve Hispanic customers. It is frequently crowded with pedestrians, most of them Hispanic, and is a central destination for the region's Hispanic population, where people shop, eat, and simply hang out to converse and watch others. The contrast between Fourth Street and the Artists Village one block away is stark. Hundreds and even thousands of Hispanics, but few whites, pass through or linger on Fourth Street on any given day. Mostly white people, and very few Hispanics, visit or occupy the Artists Village. In short, though physically the two communities exist within a few steps of each other, they are culturally and socially worlds apart.

Several reasons for Hispanic nonparticipation can be identified. The Artists Village is primarily a "high art" and commercial art venue that appeals to relatively affluent consumers, and the restaurants and bars similarly appeal to a relatively affluent crowd. Most Hispanics in Santa Ana do not fit this target profile. Little of the art that is showcased at the Artists Village is recognizably Hispanic or Latino influenced, and relatively few of the artists living and working in the Artists Village have Spanish surnames.[45] This is unsurprising since the Artists Village has been driven from the beginning primarily by Anglo political and commercial elites whose deliberations often appear "shrouded in secrecy."[46] These elites have made relatively little effort to incorporate either significant community input in general or Hispanic participation in particular. This inevitably leaves many Hispanics concluding that they are being both "ignored and pushed out of the city."[47]

The inevitable gentrification pressures accompanying the Artists Village development have driven some artists and small businesses out of downtown.[48] As downtown develops, nonartists move in to live and work in an increasingly desirable urban environment. New businesses hoping to relocate into downtown further bid up real estate values. Small Hispanic-owned businesses have been among the first to yield to these pressures, since they rarely enjoy significant capital backing.[49] El Centro Cultural de Mexico, a Santa Ana nonprofit offering arts and cultural classes and events on the edge of the Artists Village, issued a news release in June 2011, saying it was "being forced out of its space for reasons that members suspect have to do with the city's continuing gentrification aims."[50]

Some of this gentrification is due to straightforward market pressures, but some of it is deliberate. This is evident in plans for development of Fourth Street. Recently, evidence has emerged of plans to deliberately purge Fourth Street of its "Little Mexico" feel in favor of a heavily gentrified, Anglicized character more in line with the adjacent Artists Village. For example, Santa Ana's Renaissance Specific Plan of 2008, included a provision outlawing sidewalk vendors, a fixture along

Fourth Street contributing to the "Little Mexico" sensibility of the area.[51] More recently, plans to dramatically rework Fourth Street to conform to Artists Village styles and sensibilities surfaced as artist renditions of a "new" Fourth Street. The plans matched photos of existing landmarks with artists' renditions after a significant facelift; for the most part, the facelift entailed transforming the existing Hispanic-themed buildings into something resembling the latest trends in shopping mall development.[52] Finally, Anglo property owners along Fourth Street increasingly pressure their tenants to gentrify by refusing to renew their leases unless they "upgrade" their inventory to appeal to affluent shoppers.[53] These represent clear plans to make over Fourth Street, transforming it from "Little Mexico" into a shopping and entertainment destination for the affluent visitors attracted by the Artists Village. Inevitably, it entails purging Fourth Street of its defining Hispanic character.

Undoubtedly, the Artists Village has brought affluent arts patrons, shoppers, and diners into downtown Santa Ana, raised Santa Ana's profile and improved its image in Orange County among white, affluent residents, and at least marginally increased the flow of dollars into the city. As proponents of an elites-driven approach would claim, it may have a positive ripple effect on all of Santa Ana as the city's image improves and the tax base at least partly stabilizes. However, the most notable result of Santa Ana's attempt to use art to drive community development is a divided community, starkly exposed by Hispanic exclusion from development efforts and the immediate benefits of those efforts. The city's arts-led community development strategy thus divides people within Santa Ana along class and ethnic lines by segregating experience and offering inequitable opportunities for participation in the public and civic life of Santa Ana. Art is thus being used by the city, inadvertently or not, as a social wedge for dividing the two groups rather than as a social bridge.

The Santa Ana case study illustrates many of the problems identified with an elites-driven model of community development: a failure to engage or include diverse communities living in Santa Ana; the consequent exclusion of the majority Hispanic population; the reinforcement and perpetuation of existing Anglo domination; and the legitimation of existing inequalities. These problems could have been avoided, and a historic opportunity seized to generate genuine, inclusive community development that benefits all of Santa Ana residents, by incorporating at least some of the lessons drawn from a community arts approach. The Santa Ana experience prefigures a world in which art is used by elites, whether intentionally or inadvertently, to perpetuate deep class and racial fissures that reinforce their own privilege and the marginality of diverse populations.

Music & Performing Arts (M&PA) at Trinity Cathedral, Inc.

We turn now to a case study of a relatively elite institution that has adopted a community arts approach. Trinity Cathedral, the seat of the Northeast Ohio Episcopal Diocese, sits in the Quadrangle neighborhood of downtown Cleveland. The Quadrangle is not a typical neighborhood with single-family residences, tree-lined streets, parks, and public areas to shop and congregate. Such a neighborhood offers stable roots, ample public spaces, and multiple opportunities for interaction and communication. The Quadrangle, by contrast, is a fractured neighborhood, divided by freeways, commercial corridors, and architectural features that discourage or prohibit access, interaction, and communication. Parts of the neighborhood are run down, cluttered, and dirty. Other parts have benefited from redevelopment. Its boundaries were arbitrarily drawn to encompass parts of several different neighborhoods.

Trinity Cathedral created Music & Performing Arts in 1977, as a community outreach program. Until the late 1990s, M&PA concentrated primarily on providing free musical events to the community on a regular basis, especially through its noontime concert series. In the late 1990s and early 2000s, however, cathedral and M&PA staff decided to work more proactively at drawing connections between the cathedral and various parts of the neighborhood. Though long rooted in the neighborhood, cathedral staff nevertheless knew relatively little about its diverse residents and had cultivated few direct ties to them (most members of the Trinity congregation commute into the neighborhood from surrounding areas). M&PA staff decided to use an arts project to "burrow" into the community to learn more about it as a preliminary step in community development efforts. Supported by funds provided by the Ohio Arts Council, M&PA initiated an Urban Artist in Residence (UAIR) project for this purpose of "burrowing in."[54]

The goals of UAIR included identifying subcommunities and learning more about them; identifying community leaders; identifying already existing relationships and lines of communication; creating new relationships and lines of communication; and identifying common interests. These goals inform a concrete attempt to use the arts to foster a cross-cultural spirit of generosity and understanding. As we discussed in the introduction, political theorists from John Dewey to Stephen White have argued that the arts and popular culture can open up new possibilities for cross-cultural understanding and democratic community.[55] In doing so, they can counter the anger and resentment that unfortunately shapes much of our public discourse, as Love's portrait of the white power music scene reveals. To pursue UAIR's goals, the artist Anjelica Pozo conducted map-making sessions within various groups and organizations. Participants drew maps expressing their histories, their present lives, and their plans for the future. Participants were asked, "Where have you been and where would you like to go?" and were instructed to position themselves on a geographical, historical, and emotional map. Pozo conducted over three hundred mapping sessions with more than forty different nonprofit, social service, and commercial organizations. Since very few of the participants brought notable drawing skills to the task, the maps were almost entirely amateurish in quality; this is of little significance given that their primary purpose was to serve as windows into the identity and interests of Quadrangle residents and workers and to act as catalysts for forging new relationships among M&PA and Quadrangle individuals and organizations.

UAIR offered different groups in the Quadrangle a venue for participation in a community development project encompassing much of the Quadrangle. It increased ties and developed relationships among Trinity Cathedral and other organizations. UAIR helped identify some of the needs and interests of participating organizations and their members, clients, and employees. In addition to setting a foundation for future programming, this increased the overall level of knowledge and awareness about the identity of groups and individuals within the Quadrangle.

Having learned more about the Quadrangle and its diverse groups, organizations, and populations, M&PA staff began approaching some of these about possible collaborations. Given space limitations, only one will be described here. The DePaul Young Parent Program[56] is an alternative high school that enrolls approximately fifty young women, all of them either pregnant or recent mothers. DePaul and M&PA held mutual, overlapping interests and aims. M&PA wished to expand its efforts to use art to drive community development, and DePaul needed an arts component in its curriculum.

Over the course of several years, three programs of note emerged from this collaboration. First, the collaboration began by building on M&PA's existing noontime concert series. The series offered an opportunity to develop projects tying the music to DePaul's curriculum in literature, history, and science by using the music of the week to study the history of the country from which the music originated, as well as the poetry or literature from the period in which the music was written. Subsequently, approximately twenty-five to thirty of the students attended the Wednesday noontime concerts. In the second year, concert attendance was augmented when possible by bringing the noontime concert artists into DePaul to talk about the art form they were going to present. Via these "artist chats," the students could get a deeper understanding of the art form and talk to the artists informally and personally.

The second project grew out of one of the artist chats. Performer RaSheryl McCreary visited DePaul to talk about her one-woman show on the life of Sojourner Truth. This "chat" led to the establishment of a ten-week arts residency, subsequently repeated over several years, based on her Living Legacy Project, "an arts-based oral history project for teenagers, which encourages them to think about the legacy they want to leave behind by examining the choices they are currently making."[57] By 2003, the Living Legacy Project had been produced three times at the DePaul School—under the titles "Stumbling Blocks and Stepping Stones," "I Rise," and "His Eye Is on the Sparrow"—and performed as a noontime "concert" at Trinity Cathedral and other venues. For each Living Legacy Project, the process began with each participant writing their own eulogy. The point of the eulogy was to force the students to begin thinking about what they wanted to accomplish in their lives. The process continued with participants interviewing elder female family members to learn about the important decisions they made en route to their current position in life. These were used as the basis for short stories, poems, and monologues that were gradually fashioned into a coherent story line by the participants. The participants created a script from this story line, assumed roles, and added music and movement. Each project was completed when the students performed the piece for the public.

During the 2002–2003 academic year a third component was launched. Discussions led to the hiring of textile artist Mary Anne Breisch to engage the students in a quilting project. The Quilting Project ran from November 2002 through May 2003. It included a Mother's Day presentation by the participants, with DePaul staff and some of the participants' mothers and grandmothers in attendance. It also included a gallery show at Trinity Cathedral, opening in September 2003, that documented and highlighted the project. The students who participated created a collage representing something personal about themselves. These collages were ultimately integrated into the quilt's pattern.

The defining features of M&PA's approach to community development included targeting marginalized populations for inclusion in development efforts; initial listening and learning about the community; the development of collaborative relationships; ongoing dialogue between M&PA and participating organizations, and among artists and other participants; participation of community members in the definition and creation of art; and a heavy emphasis throughout on process rather than creation of professional art products. Results included building relationships and commonalities that define community, building social capital, and setting the stage for problem-solving within a marginalized neighborhood.

Closing

With its emphasis on equality, participation, inclusion, local and popular sovereignty, and accountability, a community arts approach is deeply democratic in comparison to an elites-driven approach, which typically emphasizes hierarchy, centralized control, an expert-client relationship between artists and community residents, and exclusion of marginalized populations. Despite frequent differences in size and scale between elites-driven and community arts projects, there is no reason in principle why an elites-driven approach cannot be modified to incorporate more of the democratic elements of community arts. Of course, this assumes that the elites have a genuine interest in genuine community development and not simply increasing and reinforcing their privilege.

Many of the criticisms against an elites-driven approach have been acknowledged by city planners and other backers of elites-driven public art, and at least some of them have motivated reform of existing practices. Some advocates of this approach have begun adapting it to take account of the criticisms. For example, at least some advocates of an elites-driven approach recognize that audience development can be improved by encouraging perspectives and participation from multiple, diverse communities and using these as catalysts for broadening inclusion and programming.[58] Further democratic reform of an elites driven approach is possible and necessary.

First, building flagship projects with the expectation that their benefits will eventually reach into marginalized neighborhoods and populations—essentially a "trickle out" strategy—is no substitute for community development efforts that benefit marginalized people directly. And as Santa Ana vividly illustrates, flagship projects may exacerbate already existing chasms between rich and poor, white and nonwhite, included and excluded. While cities such as Santa Ana can be commended for their efforts to develop their downtown via the arts, they also need to commit significant resources to development efforts in surrounding, outlying, and marginalized neighborhoods. Related to this, in order to build an inclusive community through the arts and culture, policy-makers, planners, and community leaders must commit fully to serving all residents, not just those with exceptional power and resources. Barriers to participation by all community members must be identified and eliminated. The primary barriers to participation by marginalized populations are, unsurprisingly, stubborn inequities of class, race, and ethnicity. The economic strain the National D-Day Memorial placed on the residents of Bedford, Virginia, that Luke describes, and the contrast Baum highlights between the financial backing for the 2010 Winter Olympic Games and In the House Festival in Vancouver, British Columbia, provide additional illustrations of this first point.

Second, art must be understood broadly to include the types of popular art that most people actually produce and consume if it is to serve as the basis for inclusive community development. Related to this, the commitment to art as product must, at a minimum, be counterbalanced by a healthy focus on the process of community development. Some earlier chapters in this volume even suggest that process may matter more than content. Mattern's discussion of how performative poetry builds community and Stillman and Villmoare's presentation of how New Orleans parades do "democracy despite government" are best seen in these terms. If genuine community development is to emerge, it must occur through an extended process of community engagement. Any other route to community development may achieve, at best, the "authoritarian populism" identified earlier.

Finally, if the arts are to integrate diverse audiences into extensive participation in an ongoing dialogue aimed at creation of community and a public, artists must adopt a role radically different from the stereotypical role assigned them in the mainstream art of nonconformist rebels. They must become citizens rather than lone renegades. In short, artists must become community organizers who "immerse themselves in the most unglamorous media—community meetings, zoning boards, redevelopment reports, school-board task forces, planning groups and the occasional tree-planting party."[59] Rather than a solitary, misunderstood genius, the artist must act "as a catalyst for other people's creativity, political imagination being perhaps as valued as drawing skill."[60] Chatterjee's discussion of the interplay between democracy and injury in political cartoons, Njoya's invocation of "the blues people" as carriers of a renewal of democratic spirit, and more directly, Street and Inthorn's research on how musical artists shape the political identity of young voters provide instructive examples here. Of course, the role of artist as solitary and nonconformist rebel is a relatively recent invention and one peculiar to western culture. Historically, in most cultures, artists have played roles that are more integral to the everyday lives of their communities, helping celebrate, commemorate, and mark important events and processes.[61] Today these events and processes increasingly prefigure a democracy that links global with local communities. Successful community development requires a greater emphasis on this role of artists in "doing democracy."

In this chapter we have concentrated on intentional, directed attempts to achieve the goal of community development. However, as the chapters in this volume repeatedly show, community development also may occur routinely in the daily practices of arts and culture, apart from the efforts of city planners and community organizers. Before residents of a neighborhood or city can act collectively to address their common problems, they must recognize their shared interests and imagine themselves as part of a collective body—a "we"—with those shared interests. Achieving that sense of "we" requires that members communicate shared interests and concerns with each other, forge common bonds, and translate shared interests into shared goals. This communication occurs extensively through arts and culture, as well as in communicative venues emphasizing traditional political speech. Festivals, theater, cartoons, music, monuments, poetry, photography, literature, and parades: each of these is a communicative arena in which residents can become engaged citizens and political action is made possible. All of these allow and encourage widespread participation, drawing upon many individuals whose active participation is constitutive of the community and without whom doing democracy would be impossible. Of course, there is no guarantee of successful translation of community into effective political action, and there is no inherent connection between community and democracy; indeed, community can also be used to undo democracy. Nevertheless, the contributors to this volume all demonstrate decisively that arts and culture can represent a rich resource for "doing democracy."

Notes

1. On this distinction, see for example Carl Grodach, "The Local Arts Planning System: Current and Alternative Directions," *New Village Press*, 2008, http://commons.newvillagepress.net/commons/new-village-online/the-local-arts-planning-system-current-and-alternative-directions/; and Martin Zebracki, Rob Van Der Vaart, and Irina Van Aalst, "Deconstructing *Public Artopia*: Situating Public-Art Claims within Practice," *Geoforum* 41 (2010): 786–95.

2. Malcolm Miles, *Art, Space and the City: Public Art and Urban Futures* (London: Routledge, 1997), 84.

3. For a brief history, see Karen Chapple and Shannon Jackson, "Commentary: Arts, Neighborhoods, and Social Practices: Towards an Integrated Epistemology of Community Arts," *Journal of Planning Education and Research* 29, no. 4 (2010): 478–90, especially 478–84.

4. See especially Chapple and Jackson, "Arts, Neighborhoods, and Social Practices."

5. See for example, Mark Stern and Susan Seifert, *"Natural" Cultural Districts: Arts Agglomerations in Metropolitan Philadelphia and Implications for Cultural District Planning* (Philadelphia: University of Pennsylvania, Social Impact of the Arts Project, 2005); and Ann Markusen, Sam Gilmore, Amanda Johnson, Titus Levi, and Andrea Martinez, *Crossover: How Artists Build Careers Across Commercial, Nonprofit and Community Work* (Minneapolis: Project on Regional and Industrial Economics, University of Minnesota, 2006).

6. Tom Finkelpearl, *Dialogues in Public Art* (Cambridge, MA: MIT Press, 2000), 5.

7. Miles, *Art, Space and the City*, 84.

8. Chapple and Jackson, "Arts, Neighborhoods, and Social Practices," 482.

9. Maria Rosario Jackson, "Art and Cultural Participation at the Heart of Community Life," in *Understanding the Arts and Creative Sector in the United States*, eds. Joni Cherbo, Ruth Stewart, and Margaret Wyszomirski (New Brunswick, NJ: Rutgers University Press, 2008), 94; Carl Grodach, "Art Spaces in Community and Economic Development: Connections to Neighborhoods, Artists, and the Cultural Economy," *Journal of Planning Education and Research* 31, no. 1 (2011): 76.

10. See especially Sara Selwood, *The Benefits of Public Art* (London: Policy Studies Institute, 1995); Tim Hall and Iain Robertson, "Public Art and Urban Regeneration: Advocacy, Claims and Critical Debates," *Landscape Research* 26, no. 1 (2001): 5–26; and Arthur H. Sterngold, "Do Economic Impact Studies Misrepresent the Benefits of Arts and Cultural Organizations?," *The Journal of Arts Management, Law and Society* 34, no. 3 (2004): 166–87.

11. Chapple and Jackson, "Arts, Neighborhoods, and Social Practices," 479.

12. Joanne Sharp, Venda Pollock, and Ronan Paddison, "Just Art for a Just City: Public Art and Social Inclusion in Urban Regeneration," *Urban Studies* 42, nos. 5/6 (2005): 1014.

13. Linda Frye Burnham, "The Artist as Citizen," in *The Citizen Artist: 20 Years of Art in the Public Arena*, eds. Linda Frye Burnham and Steven Durland (Gardiner, NY: Critical Press, 1998), 183.

14. Sharp, Pollock, and Paddison, "Just Art for a Just City," 1017.

15. Burnham, "The Artist as Citizen," 183.

16. Zebracki et al., "Deconstructing *Public Artopia*," 788.

17. See especially Sharp, Pollock, and Paddison, "Just Art for a Just City."

18. Finkelpearl, *Dialogues in Public Art*, 44.

19. Lucy Lippard, "Looking Around: Where We Are, Where We Could Be," in *Mapping the Terrain: New Genre Public Art*, ed. Suzanne Lacy (Seattle, WA: Bay Press, 1995), 119; see also Judy Baca, "Whose Monument Where? Public Art in a Many-Cultured Society," in Lacy, *Mapping the Terrain*, 131–38.

20. Miles, *Art, Space and the City*, 58.

21. Henry Lefebvre, *The Production of Space* (Oxford, UK: Basil Blackwell, 1991), 143. See also Sharp, Pollock, and Paddison, "Just Art for a Just City," 1002.

22. Miles, *Art, Space and the City*, 58, 63. One notable exception to the tendency to glorify colonizers, Maya Lin's Vietnam Veterans Memorial, provoked opposition precisely because it steadfastly refused to glorify the war. Opponents of her design succeeded in their efforts to commission a more traditional monument—more heroic in tone—that now stands near the Vietnam Veterans Memorial. See Charles L. Griswold, "The Vietnam Veterans Memorial and the Washington Mall: Philosophical Thoughts on Political Iconography," in *Art and the Public Sphere*, ed. W. J. T. Mitchell (Chicago: University of Chicago Press, 1990), 79–112.

23. Mark Stern and Susan Seifert, "Cultural Clusters: The Implications of Cultural Assets Agglomeration for Neighborhood Revitalization," *Journal of Planning Education and Research* 29, no. 3 (2010): 262. See also Grodach, "Art Spaces," 76; Richard Florida, *The Rise of the Creative Class: And How It's Transforming Work, Leisure and Everyday Life* (New York: Basic Books, 2002); and Patricia Phillips, "Public Constructions," in Lacy, *Mapping the Terrain*, 60–71.

24. Graeme Evans and Jo Foord, "Cultural Mapping and Sustainable Communities: Planning for the Arts Revisited," *Cultural Trends* 17, no. 2 (2008): 65.

25. Grodach, "Local Arts Planning System," 4, 2. See also Hall and Robertson, "Public Art and Urban Regeneration," 20; and Phillips, "Public Constructions," 63–64.

26. Sharp, Pollock, and Paddison, "Just Art for a Just City," 1014.

27. On community arts, see for example Michael Brenson, "Where Do We Go from Here? Securing a Place for the Artist in Society," in *The Artist in Society: Rights, Roles, and Responsibilities*, eds. Carol Becker and Ann Wiens (Chicago: New Art Examiner Press, 1995), 66–76; Mary Jane Jacob, "An Unfashionable Audience," in Lacy, *Mapping the Terrain*, 50–59; Felshin, "*But Is It Art?*"; Cheri Gaulke, "Acting Like Women: Performance Art of the Woman's Building," in Burnham and Durland, *The Citizen Artist*; Burnham and Durland, *The Citizen Artist*; Maryo Gard Ewell, "The Arts and Community Strengthening," script of a talk given at a conference of the Michigan Association of Community Arts

Agencies, November 8, 2000; Thomas Borrup, *The Creative Community Builder's Handbook* (St. Paul, MN: Fieldstone Alliance, 2006); Jackson, "Art and Cultural Participation"; Maria Rosario Jackson, Florence Kabwasa-Green, and Joaquin Herranz, *Cultural Vitality in Communities: Interpretation and Indicators* (Washington, DC: Urban Institute, 2006); François Matarasso, "Common Ground: Cultural Action as a Route to Community Development," *Community Development Journal* 42, no. 4 (2007): 449–58; Grodach, "The Local Arts Planning System"; and Zebracki et al., "Deconstructing *Public Artopia*," 791.

28. See, for example, Chapple and Jackson, "Arts, Neighborhoods, and Social Practices," 478–90.

29. Matarasso, "Common Ground," 449.

30. Lacy, *Mapping the Terrain*, 20.

31. See especially Sharp, Pollock, and Paddison, "Just Art for a Just City."

32. Phillips, "Public Constructions," 67.

33. See especially Jeff Kelley, "Common Work," in Lacy, *Mapping the Terrain*, 139–48. Paolo Freire, the Brazilian educator, makes the same point about the process of consciousness-raising through education. According to Freire, "the process is the product" (interviewed in Finkelpearl, *Dialogues in Public Art*, 280).

34. See for example Lippard, "Looking Around," 126; and Andrea Wolper, "Making Art, Reclaiming Lives: The Artist and Homeless Collaborative," in Felshin, *But Is It Art?*, 252.

35. Phillips, "Public Constructions," 67.

36. Brenson, "Where Do We Go from Here?," 74–75.

37. Jackson, "Art and Cultural Participation," 92.

38. Suzi Gablik posed this distinction as one between "modernist" and "connective" aesthetics. Modernist aesthetics, according to Gablik, are nonrelational, noninteractive, and nonparticipatory, while connective aesthetics entail listening, engagement, dialogue, collaboration, and interdependence, and "the audience becomes an active component of the work and is part of the process." Suzi Gablik, "Connective Aesthetics: Art after Individualism," in Lacy, *Mapping the Terrain*, 82–83.

39. See for example Claire Bishop, "Antagonism and Relational Aesthetics," *October Magazine* 110 (Fall 2004): 51–79; Tom McDonough, ed., *Guy Debord and the Situationist International* (Cambridge, MA: MIT Press, 2004); Nato Thompson, ed., *The Interventionists* (North Adams: Massachusetts Museum of Contemporary Art, 2004); Tom McDonough, *"The beautiful language of my century": Reinventing the Language of Contestation in Post-War France* (Cambridge, MA: MIT Press, 2007); and Shannon Jackson, "What Is the 'Social' in Social Practice? Comparing Experiments in Performance," in *Cambridge Handbook to Performance Studies*, ed. Tracy Davis (Cambridge: Cambridge University Press, 2008), 136–50.

40. Chapple and Jackson, "Arts, Neighborhoods, and Social Practices," 478.

41. Parts of this case study are adapted from Mark Mattern, "Art and Community Development in Santa Ana, California: The Promise and the Reality," *The Journal of Arts Management, Law and Society* 30, no. 4 (2001): 301–15.

42. Data found at https://fwww.census.gov%2fprod%2fcen2010%2fbriefs %2fc2010br-04.pdf and http://www.city-data.com/income/income-Santa-Ana-California.html.

43. See Sarah Rose Attman, "Art beyond Laguna," *Coast Magazine*, November 18, 2010, http://www.coastmagazine.com/entertainment/arthubs-1461--. html. See also Art Pedroza, "The City of Santa Ana Spent Millions on the Artists Village, 10 Years Later—Was It Worth It?," Orange Juice: "Orange County's Top Political Blog," March 8, 2009, http://www.orangejuiceblog.com/2009/03/ the-city-of-santa-ana-spent-millions-on-the-artists-village-10-years-later-was-it-worth-it/.

44. Sources describing the early development of the Artists Village include Howard Fine, "Plan Under Way to Expand Santa Ana's Artists Village," *O.C. Business Journal Weekly*, June 30, 1997; Zan Dubin, "Santa Ana Artists Village Edging Closer to Reality," *Los Angeles Times*, Orange County Edition, October 31, 1997; Laura Bleiberg, "The Art of Revitalization," *Orange County Register*, August 20, 1998; Zan Dubin, "Grand Design," *Los Angeles Times*, Orange County Edition, February 27, 1999; Valeria Godines and Laura Bleiberg, "Builders Quit Artists Village Project," *Orange County Register*, May 21, 1999. For a map of the Artists Village, see http://www.santaanaartwalk.com/general_info.html.

45. See Art Pedroza, "Santa Ana Spent Millions."

46. Gustavo Arellano, "Santa Ana Refuses to Answer Pertinent Questions about Downtown Issues Posed by Artists," *OC Weekly*, Tuesday, December 28, 2010, http://blogs.ocweekly.com/navelgazing/2010/12/santa_ana_refuses_to_answer_pe.php. See also Gustavo Arellano, "The Renaissance Reconquista Will Be Televised," *OC Weekly*, Tuesday, August 26, 2008, http://blogs.ocweekly.com/navelgazing/2008/08/the_renaissance_reconquista_wi.php, and the ensuing exchange.

47. Gabriel San Roman, March 9, 2009, comment on Pedroza blog, "The City of Santa Ana Spent Millions on the Artists Village," March 8, 2009. For more concerns about the process, see Adam Elmahrek, "Debating Santa Ana's Downtown Facelift," *Voice of OC: Orange County's Nonprofit Investigative News Agency*, March 29, 2011, http://www.voiceofoc.org/oc_central/article_66e73eb8-5a7e-11e0-a3f1-001cc4c002e0.html; and Adam Elmahrek, "Something's Happening in Santa Ana's Downtown," *Voice of OC: Orange County's Nonprofit Investigative News Agency*, May 31, 2011, http://www.voiceofoc.org/oc_central/article_7d782164-8b30-11e0-8480-001cc4c03286.html. For more concerns about attempting to drive out Hispanics, see Gustavo Arellano, "Brown, Out!" *OC Weekly*, Thursday, June 23, 2005, http://www.ocweekly.com/2005-06-23/news/brown-out/; and Arellano, "The Renaissance Reconquista Will Be Televised."

48. Lofts were originally supposed to be affordable to artists, at $200,000 each. But they actually sold for $350,000–$500,000. See Nick Schou, "Lofty Ambition," *OC Weekly*, Thursday, March 6, 2003, http://www.ocweekly.com/2003-03-13/news/lofty-ambition/.

49. See the story by Agustin Gurza, "In with the Art, Out with the Old," *Los Angeles Times*, Orange County Edition, March 6, 1999.

50. Andrew Galvin, "What's behind the Ouster of El Centro Cultural?," *Orange County Register*, June 23, 2011, http://santaana.ocregister.com/2011/06/23/whats-behind-the-ouster-of-el-centro-cultural/.

51. See Gustavo Arellano, "The Renaissance Blob," *OC Weekly*, Thursday, January 10, 2008, http://www.ocweekly.com/2008-01-10/news/the-renaissance-blob/.

52. See Gustavo Arellano, "Artist Renditions of the 'New' Fourth Street for Santa Ana: Bye-Bye, Virgin of Guadalupe!" *OC Weekly*, Thursday, February 3, 2011, http://blogs.ocweekly.com/navelgazing/2011/02/artist_renditions_of_the_new_f.php. See also Arellano, "The Renaissance Reconquista Will Be Televised."

53. See the story by Adam Elmahrek, "Fourth Street Property Owner Puts Heat on Merchants," *Voice of OC: Orange County's Nonprofit Investigative News Agency*, April 14, 2011, http://www.voiceofoc.org/oc_central/santa_ana/article_243fcdf6-66d5-11e0-91e2-001cc4c002e0.html.

54. Mark Mattern and Mike Telin, "Burrowing into Community: Art and Social Science as Partners in Community Research and Development" (paper presented at the annual meeting of the Midwest Political Science Association, Chicago, Illinois, April 24–28, 2002).

55. John Dewey, *Art as Experience*, in *John Dewey: The Later Works, 1925–1953*, volume 10: 1934, ed. Jo Ann Boydston (Carbondale: Southern Illinois University Press, 1989 [1934]); and Stephen K. White, *The Ethos of a Late-Modern Citizen* (Cambridge, MA: Harvard University Press, 2009).

56. For an extended discussion of the arts collaboration between M&PA and the DePaul Young Parent Program, see Mark Mattern, Mike Telin, and Terri Thomas, "Art, Self-Creation, and Community Development: The DePaul Young Parent Program" (paper presented at the annual meeting of the Social Theory and Politics of the Arts Annual Meeting, Columbus, Ohio, October 16–18, 2003).

57. The Living Legacy Project, "Stumbling Blocks and Stepping Stones," videotape of performance at Trinity Cathedral, Cleveland, Ohio, November 7, 2001.

58. See for example Shannon Jackson, *Lines of Activity: Performance, Historiography, Hull-House Domesticity* (Ann Arbor: University of Michigan Press, 2000); Jan Cohen-Cruz, *Local Acts: Community-Based Performance in the United States* (New Brunswick, NJ: Rutgers University Press, 2005); Sonja Kuftinec, *Staging America: Cornerstone and Community-Based Performance* (Carbondale: Southern Illinois University Press, 2005); Petra Kuppers and Gwen Robertson, eds., *The Community Performance Reader* (London: Routledge, 2007); and Alan Read, *Theatre, Intimacy, and Engagement: The Last Human Venue* (London: Palgrave, 2007).

59. Aida Mancillas, "The Citizen Artist," in Burnham and Durland, *The Citizen Artist*, 339.

60. Miles, *Art, Space and the City*, 8. For a criticism of the stereotypical role of artists as nonconformist rebels, see for example B. Ruby Rich, "Dissed and Disconnected: Notes on Present Ills and Future Dreams," in *The Subversive Imagination: Artists, Society and Responsibility*, ed. Carol Becker (New York: Routledge, 1994), 223–48. According to Rich (224), "there persists an image of the artist as rebel, renegade, or nonconformist—identities which mitigate against any role being created for the artist as citizen, or even neighbor, of any specific city, nation, or global moment." On the artist as citizen, see, for example, Steven Durland, Introduction, in Burnham and Durland, *The Citizen Artist*.

61. See Durland, Introduction, in Burnham and Durland, *The Citizen Artist*.

Bibliography

Arellano, Gustavo. "Brown, Out!" *OC Weekly*, Thursday, June 23, 2005, http://www.ocweekly.com/2005-06-23/news/brown-out/.

———. "The Renaissance Blob." *OC Weekly*, Thursday, January 10, 2008, http://www.ocweekly.com/2008-01-10/news/the-renaissance-blob/.

———. "The Renaissance Reconquista Will Be Televised." *OC Weekly*, Tuesday, August 26, 2008, http://blogs.ocweekly.com/navelgazing/2008/08/the_renaissance_reconquista_wi.php.

———. "Santa Ana Refuses to Answer Pertinent Questions about Downtown Issues Posed by Artists." *OC Weekly*, Tuesday, December 28, 2010, http://blogs.ocweekly.com/navelgazing/2010/12/santa_ana_refuses_to_answer_pe.php.

———. "Artist Renditions of the 'New' Fourth Street for Santa Ana: Bye-Bye, Virgin of Guadalupe!" *OC Weekly*, Thursday, February 3, 2011, http://blogs.ocweekly.com/navelgazing/2011/02/artist_renditions_of_the_new_f.php.

Attman, Sarah Rose. "Art beyond Laguna." *Coast Magazine*, November 18, 2010, http://www.coastmagazine.com/entertainment/arthubs-1461--.html.

Avgikos, Jan. "Group Material Timeline: Activism as a Work of Art." In Felshin, *But Is It Art?*, 85–116.

Baca, Judy. "Whose Monument Where? Public Art in a Many-Cultured Society." In Lacy, *Mapping the Terrain*, 131–38.

Becker, Carol, ed. *The Subversive Imagination: Artists, Society and Responsibility*. New York: Routledge, 1994.

Bishop, Claire. "Antagonism and Relational Aesthetics." *October Magazine* 110 (Fall 2004): 51–79.

Bleiberg, Laura. "The Art of Revitalization." *Orange County Register*, August 20, 1998.

Borrup, Thomas. *The Creative Community Builder's Handbook*. St. Paul, MN: Fieldstone Alliance, 2006.

Brenson, Michael. "Where Do We Go from Here? Securing a Place for the Artist in Society." In *The Artist in Society: Rights, Roles, and Responsibilities*, edited by Carol Becker and Ann Wiens, 66–76. Chicago: New Art Examiner Press, 1995.

Burnham, Linda Frye. "The Artist as Citizen." In Burnham and Durland, *The Citizen Artist*, 179–84.

Burnham, Linda Frye, and Steven Durland, eds. *The Citizen Artist: 20 Years of Art in the Public Arena*. Gardiner, NY: Critical Press, 1998.

Chapple, Karen, and Shannon Jackson. "Commentary: Arts, Neighborhoods, and Social Practices: Towards an Integrated Epistemology of Community Arts." *Journal of Planning Education and Research* 29, no. 4 (2010): 478–90.

Cohen-Cruz, Jan. *Local Acts: Community-Based Performance in the United States.* New Brunswick, NJ: Rutgers University Press, 2005.

Dewey, John. *Art as Experience.* In *John Dewey: The Later Works, 1925–1953*, volume 10: 1934, edited by Jo Ann Boydston. Carbondale: Southern Illinois University Press, 1989 [1934].

Dubin, Zan. "Santa Ana Artists Village Edging Closer to Reality." *Los Angeles Times*, Orange County Edition, October 31, 1997.

———. "Grand Design." *Los Angeles Times*, Orange County Edition, February 27, 1999.

Durland, Steven. Introduction. In Burnham and Durland, *The Citizen Artist*, xv–xxiv.

Elmahrek, Adam. "Debating Santa Ana's Downtown Facelift." *Voice of OC: Orange County's Nonprofit Investigative News Agency*, March 29, 2011, http://www.voiceofoc.org/oc_central/article_66e73eb8-5a7e-11e0-a3f1-001cc4c002e0.html.

———. "Fourth Street Property Owner Puts Heat on Merchants." *Voice of OC: Orange County's Nonprofit Investigative News Agency*, April 14, 2011, http://www.voiceofoc.org/oc_central/santa_ana/article_243fcdf6-66d5-11e0-91e2-001cc4c002e0.html.

———. "Something's Happening in Santa Ana's Downtown." *Voice of OC: Orange County's Nonprofit Investigative News Agency*, May 31, 2011, http://www.voiceofoc.org/oc_central/article_7d782164-8b30-11e0-8480-001cc4c03286.html.

Evans, Graeme, and Jo Foord. "Cultural Mapping and Sustainable Communities: Planning for the Arts Revisited." *Cultural Trends* 17, no. 2 (2008): 65–96.

Ewell, Maryo Gard. "The Arts and Community Strengthening." Script of a talk given at a conference of the Michigan Association of Community Arts Agencies, November 8, 2000.

Felshin, Nina, ed. *But Is It Art? The Spirit of Art as Activism.* Seattle, WA: Bay Press, 1995.

Fine, Howard. "Plan Under Way to Expand Santa Ana's Artists Village." *O.C. Business Journal Weekly*, June 30, 1997.

Finkelpearl, Tom. *Dialogues in Public Art*. Cambridge, MA: MIT Press, 2000.

Florida, Richard. *The Rise of the Creative Class: And How It's Transforming Work, Leisure and Everyday Life*. New York: Basic Books, 2002.

Freire, Paolo. Interview by Tom Finkelpearl. In Finkelpearl, *Dialogues in Public Art*, 276–93.

Gablik, Suzi. "Connective Aesthetics: Art after Individualism." In Lacy, *Mapping the Terrain*, 74–87.

Galvin, Andrew. "What's behind the Ouster of El Centro Cultural?" *Orange County Register*, June 23, 2011, http://santaana.ocregister.com/2011/06/23/whats-behind-the-ouster-of-el-centro-cultural/.

Gaulke, Cheri. "Acting Like Women: Performance Art of the Woman's Building." In Burnham and Durland, *The Citizen Artist*, 13–21.

Godines, Valeria, and Laura Bleiberg, "Builders Quit Artists Village Project." *Orange County Register*, May 21, 1999.

Griswold, Charles L. "The Vietnam Veterans Memorial and the Washington Mall: Philosophical Thoughts on Political Iconography." In *Art and the Public Sphere*, edited by W. J. T. Mitchell, 79–112. Chicago: University of Chicago Press, 1990.

Grodach, Carl. "The Local Arts Planning System: Current and Alternative Directions." *New Village Press*, 2008, http://commons.newvillagepress.net/commons/new-village-online/the-local-arts-planning-system-current-and-alternative-directions/.

———. "Art Spaces in Community and Economic Development: Connections to Neighborhoods, Artists, and the Cultural Economy." *Journal of Planning Education and Research* 31, no. 1 (2011): 74–85.

Gurza, Agustin. "In with the Art, Out with the Old." *Los Angeles Times*, Orange County Edition, March 6, 1999.

Hall, Tim, and Iain Robertson. "Public Art and Urban Regeneration: Advocacy, Claims and Critical Debates." *Landscape Research* 26, no. 1 (2001): 5–26.

Jackson, Maria Rosario. "Art and Cultural Participation at the Heart of Community Life." In *Understanding the Arts and Creative Sector in the United States*, edited by Joni Cherbo, Ruth Stewart, and Margaret Wyszomirski, 92–104. New Brunswick, NJ: Rutgers University Press, 2008.

Jackson, Maria Rosario, Florence Kabwasa-Green, and Joaquin Herranz. *Cultural Vitality in Communities: Interpretation and Indicators*. Washington, DC: Urban Institute, 2006.

Jackson, Shannon. *Lines of Activity: Performance, Historiography, Hull-House Domesticity*. Ann Arbor: University of Michigan Press, 2000.

———. "What Is the 'Social' in Social Practice? Comparing Experiments in Performance." In *Cambridge Handbook to Performance Studies*, edited by Tracy Davis, 136–50. Cambridge: Cambridge University Press, 2008.

Jacob, Mary Jane. "An Unfashionable Audience." In Lacy, *Mapping the Terrain*, 50–59.

Kelley, Jeff. "Common Work." In Lacy, *Mapping the Terrain*, 139–48.

Kuftinec, Sonja. *Staging America: Cornerstone and Community-Based Performance*. Carbondale: Southern Illinois University Press, 2005.

Kuppers, Petra, and Gwen Robertson, eds. *The Community Performance Reader*. London: Routledge, 2007.

Lacy, Suzanne, ed. *Mapping the Terrain: New Genre Public Art*. Seattle, WA: Bay Press, 1995.

Lefebvre, Henry. *The Production of Space*. Oxford, UK: Basil Blackwell, 1991.

Lippard, Lucy. "Looking Around: Where We Are, Where We Could Be." In Lacy, *Mapping the Terrain*, 114–30.

The Living Legacy Project. "Stumbling Blocks and Stepping Stones." Videotape of performance at Trinity Cathedral, Cleveland, Ohio, November 7, 2001.

Mancillas, Aida. "The Citizen Artist." In Burnham and Durland, *The Citizen Artist*, 335–40.

Markusen, Ann, Sam Gilmore, Amanda Johnson, Titus Levi, and Andrea Martinez. *Crossover: How Artists Build Careers across Commercial, Nonprofit and Community Work*. Minneapolis: Project on Regional and Industrial Economics, University of Minnesota, 2006.

Matarasso, François. "Common Ground: Cultural Action as a Route to Community Development." *Community Development Journal* 42, no. 4 (2007): 449–58.

Mattern, Mark. "Art and Community Development in Santa Ana, California: The Promise and the Reality." *The Journal of Arts Management, Law and Society* 30, no. 4 (2001): 301–15.

Mattern, Mark, and Mike Telin. "Burrowing into Community: Art and Social Science as Partners in Community Research and Development." Paper presented at the annual meeting of the Midwest Political Science Association, Chicago, Illinois, April 24–28, 2002.

Mattern, Mark, Mike Telin, and Terri Thomas. "Art, Self-Creation, and Community Development: The DePaul Young Parent Program." Paper presented at the annual meeting of the Social Theory and Politics of the Arts Annual Meeting, Columbus, Ohio, October 16–18, 2003.

McDonough, Tom, ed. *Guy Debord and the Situationist International*. Cambridge, MA: MIT Press, 2004.

———. *"The beautiful language of my century": Reinventing the Language of Contestation in Post-War France*. Cambridge, MA: MIT Press, 2007.

Miles, Malcolm. *Art, Space and the City: Public Art and Urban Futures*. London: Routledge, 1997.

Pedroza, Art. "The City of Santa Ana Spent Millions on the Artists Village, 10 Years Later—Was It Worth It?" Orange Juice (blog), March 8, 2009. http://

www.orangejuiceblog.com/2009/03/the-city-of-santa-ana-spent-millions-on-the-artists-village-10-years-later-was-it-worth-it/.

Phillips, Patricia. "Public Constructions." In Lacy, *Mapping the Terrain*, 60–71.

Read, Alan. *Theatre, Intimacy, and Engagement: The Last Human Venue*. London: Palgrave, 2007.

Rich, B. Ruby. "Dissed and Disconnected: Notes on Present Ills and Future Dreams." In Becker, *The Subversive Imagination*, 223–48.

San Roman, Gabriel. "The City of Santa Ana Spent Millions on the Artists Village." Orange Juice (blog), March 9, 2009. http://www.orangejuiceblog.com/2009/03/the-city-of-santa-ana-spent-millions-on-the-artists-village-10-years-later-was-it-worth-it/.

Schou, Nick. "Lofty Ambition," *OC Weekly*, Thursday, March 6, 2003, http://www.ocweekly.com/2003-03-13/news/lofty-ambition/.

Selwood, Sara. *The Benefits of Public Art*. London: Policy Studies Institute, 1995.

Sharp, Joanne, Venda Pollock, and Ronan Paddison. "Just Art for a Just City: Public Art and Social Inclusion in Urban Regeneration." *Urban Studies* 42, nos. 5/6 (2005): 1001–23.

Stern, Mark, and Susan Seifert. *"Natural" Cultural Districts: Arts Agglomerations in Metropolitan Philadelphia and Implications for Cultural District Planning*. Philadelphia: University of Pennsylvania, Social Impact of the Arts Project, 2005.

————. "Cultural Clusters: The Implications of Cultural Assets Agglomeration for Neighborhood Revitalization." *Journal of Planning Education and Research* 29, no. 3 (2010): 262–79.

Sterngold, Arthur H. "Do Economic Impact Studies Misrepresent the Benefits of Arts and Cultural Organizations?" *The Journal of Arts Management, Law and Society* 34, no. 3 (2004): 166–87.

Thompson, Nato, ed. *The Interventionists*. North Adams: Massachusetts Museum of Contemporary Art, 2004.

White, Stephen K. *The Ethos of a Late-Modern Citizen*. Cambridge, MA: Harvard University Press, 2009.

Wolper, Andrea. "Making Art, Reclaiming Lives: The Artist and Homeless Collaborative." In Felshin, *But Is It Art?*, 251–82.

Zebracki, Martin, Rob Van Der Vaart, and Irina Van Aalst. "Deconstructing *Public Artopia*: Situating Public-Art Claims within Practice." *Geoforum* 41 (2010): 786–95.

Contributors

Bruce Baum is Associate Professor of Political Science at the University of British Columbia. He is author of *Rereading Power and Freedom in J. S. Mill* (University of Toronto, 2000) and *The Rise and Fall of the Caucasian Race: A Political History of Racial Identity* (New York University Press, 2006, 2008). He is also coeditor (with Duchess Harris) of *Racially Writing the Republic: Racists, Race Rebels, and Transformations of American Identity* (Duke University Press, 2009) and (with Robert Nichols) of *Isaiah Berlin and the Politics of Freedom: Berlin's "Two Concepts of Liberty" 50 Years Later* (Routledge, 2012).

Emily Beausoleil is Lecturer in Politics at Massey University, New Zealand. Her doctoral research at the University of British Columbia examined the potential and practice of the performing arts as forms of democratic engagement, with a particular interest in how such modes impact communication of marginalized positions in comparison with conventional political processes. Her current research investigates the affective and embodied dimensions of receptivity, as well as how embodied practices might be harnessed to facilitate listening and accountability in politics. Connecting affect, critical democratic, postcolonial, neuroscience, and performance scholarship, Beausoleil's work responds to compelling calls to find new models for coalition, community, and post-home politics by asking how we realize these ideals in concrete terms.

Roland Bleiker is Professor of International Relations at the University of Queensland, Australia. His books include *Popular Dissent, Human Agency and Global Politics* (Cambridge University Press, 2000), *Divided Korea: Toward a Culture of Reconciliation* (University of Minnesota Press,

2005) and *Aesthetics and World Politics* (Palgrave, 2009). His most recent coedited volumes are *Security and the War on Terror* (Routledge, 2007) and *Mediating Across Difference: Pacific and Asian Approaches to Security and Conflict* (University of Hawaii Press, 2010). Bleiker's current research on linkages between aesthetics and politics includes projects on how images shape responses to humanitarian crises and on how political theater can contribute to democratic debates.

Sushmita Chatterjee received a dual-degree PhD from the Departments of Political Science and Women's Studies at the Pennsylvania State University and is currently Assistant Professor of Women's Studies and Government & Justice Studies at Appalachian State University. Sushmita enjoys teaching, learning, and writing about democratic theory, visual politics, feminist-queer theory, and postcolonial, transnational politics. She is currently working on a book manuscript that studies post-9/11 identity politics through an examination of Art Spiegelman's visual politics.

Mark Chou is Lecturer in Politics in the School of Arts and Sciences at Australian Catholic University. He is the author of *Greek Tragedy and Contemporary Democracy* (Bloomsbury, 2012) and *Theorising Democide: Why and How Democracies Fail* (Palgrave, 2013).

Sanna Inthorn is a Senior Lecturer in Society, Media, and Culture at the University of East Anglia, United Kingdom. She is coauthor (with Justin Lewis and Karin Wahl-Jorgensen) of *Citizens or Consumers? What the Media Tell Us about Political Participation* (Open University Press, 2005) and (with John Street and Martin Scott) of *From Entertainment to Citizenship: Politics and Popular Culture* (Manchester University Press, 2013), and the author of *German Media and National Identity* (Cambria Press, 2007).

Nancy S. Love is Professor of Government and Justice Studies and affiliated faculty with the Interdisciplinary Studies Program at Appalachian State University. She is the author of *Musical Democracy* (State University of New York Press, 2006), *Understanding Dogmas and Dreams: A Text*, 2nd ed. (CQ Press, 2006), and *Marx, Nietzsche, and Modernity* (Columbia University Press, 1986), and the editor of *Dogmas and Dreams: A Reader in Modern Political Ideologies*, 4th ed. (CQ Press, 2010). She also coedits (with Mark Mattern) *New Political Science: A Journal of Politics and Culture*. Her current research focuses on the music and politics of the radical right.

Timothy W. Luke is University Distinguished Professor and Chair of the Department of Political Science at Virginia Polytechnic Institute and State University in Blacksburg, Virginia. He also serves as Chair for the Government and International Affairs Program in the School of Public and International Affairs, and as the Director of the Center for Digital Discourse and Culture (CDDC) in the College of Liberal Arts and Human Sciences. His main research interests are political and social theory, global conflict, environmental politics, and cultural analysis.

Regina Marchi holds a PhD in Communication from the University of California at San Diego and is Associate Professor in the School of Communication and Information at Rutgers University. She teaches and conducts research about media, culture, and politics.

Mark Mattern is Professor of Political Science at Baldwin Wallace University in Berea, Ohio, where he teaches political theory and political economy. He is the author of *Acting in Concert: Music, Community, and Political Action* (Rutgers University Press, 1998) and *Putting Ideas to Work: A Practical Introduction to Political Thought* (Rowman & Littlefield, 2006). He coedits (with Nancy Love) *New Political Science: A Journal of Politics and Culture*. His current research focuses on anarchism and art.

Frank Möller is a Senior Research Fellow at the Tampere Peace Research Institute, School of Social Sciences and Humanities, University of Tampere, Finland. A former coeditor of *Cooperation and Conflict*, Möller is a member of the European Consortium for Political Research (ECPR) Standing Group on Politics and the Arts. From 2005 to 2011, he was a member of the Finnish Centre of Excellence in Political Thought and Conceptual Change, Research Team Politics and the Arts. His research interests include theory and practice of peaceful change and visual peace research. Möller's recent work has been published in such journals as *Alternatives*, *Review of International Studies*, *Security Dialogue*, *New Political Science*, and *Peace Review* as well as in several edited volumes.

Wairimu Njoya is Visiting Assistant Professor of Political Science at Williams College. Her research covers cultural politics, the Enlightenment, and political thought of the African diaspora.

Peter G. Stillman is Professor of Political Science at Vassar College, where his primary teaching interests lie in modern political thought from the Renaissance through the present. In addition to his ongoing work on post-Katrina New Orleans with Adelaide Villmoare, his research interests include Hegel's political philosophy, Marx's thought, environmental issues, and utopian political theory; he has published more than forty articles and book chapters on these topics. He has also edited *Hegel's Philosophy of Spirit* (State University of New York Press, 1987), coedited special issues of journals on "revolutions in advanced industrial societies" and on Henry Neville's *Isle of Pines*, coedited and cotranslated a new edition of Rousseau's *Confessions* (University Presses of New England, 1995), and most recently edited a collection of essays with Laurence Davis entitled *The New Utopian Politics of Ursula K. Le Guin's The Dispossessed* (Lexington Books, 2005).

John Street is Professor of Politics at the University of East Anglia, United Kingdom. He is the author of several books on the politics of media and culture, including the second edition of *Mass Media, Politics and Democracy* (Palgrave Macmillan, 2011) and *Music and Politics* (Polity, 2012), and coauthor (with Sanna Inthorn and Martin Scott) of *From Entertainment to Citizenship: Politics and Popular Culture* (Manchester University Press, 2013).

Adelaide H. Villmoare is Professor of Political Science at Vassar College, where her primary teaching interests in U.S. politics are law and society, politics of public and private, and media and democracy. She has published articles on policing in post-Katrina New Orleans, teaching the death penalty, and women and the politics of rights. With Peter G. Stillman she has published articles on issues of rebuilding and return and social justice in post-Katrina New Orleans.

Index

Abu Ghraib, 56, 68n8

Adorno, Theodor: aesthetics of, 292–93, 300, 308n21; on autonomous art, 19, 292, 305; on the culture industry, 296; on didactic art, 290; failure to understand popular culture, 292–93; on form versus content in art, 289, 290; on intransigent artists, 11

aesthetics: definition of, 5; fascist, 205–6, 209–16; formal versus performative, 6–7, 210, 347; Indigenous, in anti-apartheid theater, 263, 265; of inverted totalitarianism, 203–6; liberal privatizing of, 7–8; modernist versus connective, 359n38; performative, 210, 42, 43; subversive potential of, 266

affect: in anti-apartheid theater, 267–69; in Day of the Dead, 86; and the National D-Day Memorial, 104; in slam poetry, 134; in white power music, 202, 213–16

Ahlers, Douglas, 317

All Saints' Day. *See* Day of the Dead

All Souls' Day. *See* Day of the Dead

Altieri, Charles, 267

Ambrose, Stephen, 101, 104

American Indian Movement, 75

anarchism, 4, 11

Anderson, Benedict, 16, 183, 222n39. *See also* imagined communities

Anti-Vietnam War movement, 75

Arendt, Hannah, 14, 31–32

art: affective dimensions of, 6–7, 267–69; as agitational weapon, 259; as alternative media, 76–78; autonomous, 5, 7, 292, 306; central role in contemporary life, 12; and character, 9–10; committed, 290; as communication, 356; and community development, 339–66; and creativity, 10–11; as cultural commodity, 296; definition of, 4–8; as downplayed by democratic theorists, 205; as engaging whole person, 5–6, 10; form versus content of, 289, 290; as globalizing force, 13; high versus low, 4–8, 20, 122, 181; and imagination, 219; mobilized for (un)democratic ends, 145; as nation-building tool, 114n2; plop, 98, 341–42, 344, 346; popular, 355; and progressive social movements, 8; and public policy, 20, 339–66; as resource for political engagement, 8–9, 41, 98, 275, 356; role in defending ideals, 165–66; as site for political action, 9; as site for public memory, 114n2; as social